HOW AMERICA
GOT ITS GUNS

HOW
AMERICA
GOT ITS
GUNS

A History of the
Gun Violence Crisis

William Briggs

University of New Mexico Press | Albuquerque

Library of Congress Cataloging-in-Publication Data
Names: Briggs, William, 1949–, author.
Title: How America got its guns : a history of the gun violence crisis / William Briggs.
Description: First Edition. | Albuquerque : University of New Mexico Press, 2017.
Identifiers: LCCN 2016033852 (print) | LCCN 2016051539 (ebook) | ISBN
    9780826358134 (pbk) | ISBN 9780826358141 (electronic)
Subjects: LCSH: Gun control—United States—History. | Firearms ownership—
    United States—History. | Violent crimes—United States—History. | United States.
    Constitution. 2nd Amendment. | Firearms—Law and legislation—United States. |
    BISAC: LAW / Constitutional. | HISTORY / Military / Weapons.
Classification: LCC HV7436 .B75 2017 (print) | LCC HV7436 (ebook) |
    DDC 363.330973—dc23
LC record available at https://lccn.loc.gov/2016033852

Cover illustration courtesy of Lisa Tremaine and Felicia Cedillos
Designed by Felicia Cedillos
Composed in Minion 10.25/14.5

Thanks, JK

Contents

Acknowledgments

Work on this book has been in progress—at least intermittently—for a decade. So it is not surprising that during those years many people contributed in different ways to the book's eventual completion. To protect the identity of my accomplices, let me thank them namelessly.

First, there were friends, relatives, and strangers, on all sides of the gun debate, who read (many) drafts of the manuscript. They did their best to steer me away from tedium toward accuracy, clarity, and balance. Equally important, they encouraged me with their enthusiasm when a final manuscript seemed a faraway goal.

Next there were the experts, who helped me navigate the many technical precincts of the firearm landscape, from conflicting interpretations of the Fourteenth Amendment to the links between mental illness and violence to the tactics of practical shooting competitions to the intricacies of homicide data. Their knowledge and patient tutoring helped me make sense of my rambling research.

I am also indebted to those people who consented to either live or telephone interviews. Their thoughts and pastimes, which they were willing to share with readers, became valuable profiles in the book.

Finally, I am grateful to Clark Whitehorn and the staff at the University of New Mexico Press for their willingness to publish this book and for their guidance in reaching that end. Perhaps they share my hope that this book might contribute in some small way to the goal of eliminating gun violence in this country.

1 | GUNS IN AMERICA

Certainly one of the chief guarantees of freedom under any government, no matter
how popular and respected, is the right of citizens to keep and bear arms.

—HUBERT HUMPHREY, Democratic vice president (1965–1969)

For too long, we've been blind to the unique mayhem
that gun violence inflicts upon this nation.

—BARACK OBAMA, Democratic president (2009–2017)

IT HAPPENED AGAIN, like demonic clockwork. Shortly after midnight on
July 20, 2012, a twenty-four-year-old former neuroscience graduate student,
dressed in black, wearing a gas mask and body armor, slipped into a movie
theater in Aurora, Colorado. He detonated a tear gas canister and began
spraying the audience, first with a shotgun and then with an AR-15 semiautomatic rifle—both legally obtained. By the time he calmly surrendered
to police, twelve people were dead and fifty-eight people had been wounded.
Later that day, police discovered six thousand rounds of ammunition in the
man's booby-trapped apartment. As with other mass shootings in this country, the incongruous reaction was shock but not surprise.

Just as predictable as a recurrence of such tragedies were the reactions
from all directions. Within hours of the shooting, CNN's Piers Morgan—a
British citizen accustomed to strict gun laws and negligible gun homicide
rates—unleashed a Twitter torrent. One tweet was prescient: "More Americans will buy guns after this to defend themselves, and so the dangerous spiral
descends. When/how does it stop?"[1] Indeed, the state of Colorado approved
43 percent more background checks in the weekend after the Aurora shootings than in the previous weekend.[2]

Gun rights advocates wasted no time firing back. Erich Pratt of Gun

Owners of America, a no-compromise gun rights organization, claimed that the Aurora shootings provided further evidence of the failure of gun control laws. He observed that the Aurora theater was a gun-free zone and that "the victims were disarmed by law or regulation. . . . They were made mandatory victims by restrictions which never stop the bad guys from getting or using guns."[3] If just one person in the theater had been armed, so he implied, the carnage could have been stopped.

Gun regulation supporters piled on. New York Mayor Michael Bloomberg, cofounder of Mayors Against Illegal Guns, suggested that police officers across the country should take a stand and say, "We're going to go on strike. We're not going to protect you unless you, the public, through your legislature, do what's required to keep us safe."[4] Never mind that a police strike might only exacerbate gun violence.

Three days after the shootings, the National Rifle Association (NRA) sent a fund-raising letter, not mentioning the Aurora tragedy, to its 4.3 million members, claiming that the re-election of President Obama would result in the "confiscation of our firearms."[5] Obama, in the heat of an election campaign, used the Aurora tragedy to affirm his support for Americans' Second Amendment rights. He then cautiously added that "the majority of gun owners would agree that we should do everything possible to prevent criminals and fugitives from purchasing weapons. . . . These steps shouldn't be controversial. They should be common sense."[6]

Conservative blogger Stacy Washington weighed in during an NRA interview, saying that "the key is not to limit lawful ownership and carrying of firearms. And please don't even talk to me about assault weapons, because I've heard it all; it's ridiculous. If the military has assault weapons, private citizens should be able to own them."[7]

PBS's Bill Moyers excoriated the NRA, calling it "the enabler of death—paranoid, delusional and as venomous as a scorpion. With the weak-kneed acquiescence of our politicians, the National Rifle Association has turned the Second Amendment of the Constitution into a cruel hoax, a cruel and deadly hoax."[8]

Reciting a familiar theme that one madman does not represent all gun owners, Dave Workman, senior editor at TheGunMag.com, reminded readers that "what this incident . . . proves undeniably is that laws cracking down on law-abiding gun owners will not prevent such crimes. To suggest otherwise is both dishonest and delusional."[9]

A few tireless and outnumbered lawmakers proposed new laws. Senator Frank Lautenberg (D-NJ) and Representative Carolyn McCarthy (D-NY) (a widow of the Long Island Rail Road shooting in 1993) introduced legislation to ban the sale of large quantities of ammunition through the mail or Internet. "It's time to close the loophole that's allowing killers—deranged, insane—and even terrorists to buy ammunition online. . . . You don't have to be a scientist to understand how wrong this is."[10] Their bills never became law.

Supreme Court justices are rare sightings on Sunday-morning talk shows. However, Justice Antonin Scalia, aligned with the majority in two landmark cases that overturned handgun bans in Washington, DC, and Chicago, reminded listeners on Fox News that "like most rights, the Second Amendment right is not unlimited. It is not a right to keep and carry any weapon whatsoever in any manner whatsoever and for whatever purpose."[11]

The Aurora tragedy and the consequent outrage have become a part of life in an armed America. Whether or not you own a gun, you likely live within range of someone's gun. In the next year, one in thirty people will be a victim of gun violence or know one. Over thirty-two thousand people die each year because of gun violence—in 2014, about 11,400 homicides and 21,300 suicides.[12] Astoundingly, each year between 2011 and 2014, thirty children less than four years of age and eighty children less than fourteen years of age were killed accidentally by guns.[13] In 2014, an additional eighty-one thousand nonfatal injuries were attributed to firearms, bringing the annual toll of gun violence victims to well over one hundred thousand.[14] One study in 2000 estimated the annual cost of gun violence to be $80 million.[15] However, guns are also used defensively to escape injury, assault, or death somewhere between 80,000 and 2.5 million times per year.[16] Among the many social issues that torment Americans—as contentious as abortion, the death penalty, immigration, or same-sex marriage—gun rights is certainly among the most combustible and divisive. There are several reasons why.

A Few Gun Numbers

Data on gun ownership are obtained primarily from surveys, so they should be digested with care. Nevertheless, polls lead to the inescapable conclusion that gun owners make up a significant and diverse cross-section of American society. In a 2014 Gallup poll, 42 percent of adult American respondents (48 percent of male respondents and 38 percent of female respondents) reported a gun in their household or on their property, a decrease from about 51 percent in 1993, but now part of a rising trend. According to the same poll, 30 percent of adult respondents reported personally owning a gun in 2011.[17]

Questions about stricter gun laws appear regularly in public opinion surveys. Despite shocking mass killings during the last twenty years—events that might have caused a public rethinking of gun ownership—support for stricter gun laws has not increased in the past decade. One typical poll taken in 2014 showed that 54 percent of respondents (26 percent of Republican respondents and 83 percent of Democratic respondents) favored stricter laws regulating the sale of guns, with 42 percent opposed to stricter gun laws.[18] In another 2014 poll, 26 percent of adults favored a ban on handguns, down from 38 percent in 1999.[19] And 63 percent of adults polled in 2014 believed that a gun in the home makes the home safer, up from 35 percent in 2000.[20] Generally, acceptance of current gun laws or assent to more lenient gun laws has increased in all categories (gender, politics, geography). As part of that trend, Americans tend to believe that existing laws should be better enforced before new laws are passed.[21]

Other measures also suggest a thriving gun culture. Gun sales, applications for permits, new federally approved firearm dealers are all on the rise. In the run-up to the 2012 presidential election and in the aftermath of Obama's victory, gun sales took a sharp turn upward.[22] Retailers reported that guns, ammunition, and accessories were flying out the doors. In the month prior to the election, FBI criminal background checks, which are required for the legal purchase of guns from licensed dealers, increased 10 percent over the previous month and 20 percent over the same month of the previous year.[23]

A 2016 poll showed that 58 percent of those surveyed had a (very or mostly) favorable opinion of the NRA (up slightly since 1993, although there have been ups and downs along the way).[24] In a 2013 poll, 48 percent of responding gun owners said that protection was the first reason for owning a gun, up from 26 percent in 1999.[25] Another 2013 poll found that 60 percent of gun owners cited protection as one reason for owning a gun.[26] Neither of these two polls detected another reason for gun ownership: fear of government tyranny. That reason was expressed in a 2013 poll, in which 29 percent of responding gun

owners (44 percent of Republicans, 27 percent of Independents, and 18 percent of Democrats) said that an armed revolution might be necessary in the
next few years in order to protect our liberties.[27]

The total number of guns in America continues to rise and stands somewhere between 270 and 310 million—approaching one gun per person or, on
average, six guns per gun-owning adult.[28] A recent study revealed that 3 percent
of adult Americans own roughly 50 percent of the guns.[29] The total gun figure is slippery for several reasons: there is no national gun registration system;
sales data are difficult to find and proxies, such as background checks, may be
unreliable; and guns are bought, sold, traded, and destroyed in many legal and
illegal ways. However, it would require enormous sophistry to deny the obvious
conclusion: the United States leads the world in personal gun ownership.[30]

The Gun Tapestry

To understand the complexity of the gun debate in America, it is essential to
appreciate the diversity of gun owners. Gun ownership varies significantly by
state: Wyoming leads the list with roughly 60 percent of adults owning guns
and Hawaii is at the other end at about 7 percent. Ownership is almost twice
as high among whites as nonwhites, and it is nearly twice as high among
Republicans as Democrats. The gun ownership rate among men is higher
than for women, and the total guns owned by men appreciably outnumber
the total guns owned by women.[31]

When you think of gun owners, imagine a California housewife who participates in trapshooting events and carries a handgun for protection. Picture legions of antique gun enthusiasts who belong to their state collector
associations. There are athletes training for international marksmanship
competitions, some of which have Olympic status. Consider the men and
women who participate in highly competitive practical shooting events. And
then there are the weekend plinkers and the buddies who get together for an
annual shoot on the farm. The image of gun owners as—pick your stereo-
type—stockpiling survivalists or raging ranchers is simply wrong. Of course,
stereotyping goes both directions: former NRA president Charlton Heston
once summoned all those who "prefer the America where you can pray without feeling naïve, love without being kinky, sing without profanity, be white
without feeling guilty, own a gun without shame" to join the culture war.[32]

In terms of politics, race, education, and economics, gun owners do not cut a clean, homogeneous swath through our society. They form threads woven throughout the American tapestry. To understand guns in America, one must appreciate the number and diversity of gun owners and the extent to which guns have seeped—deeply and broadly—into the culture. This state of affairs only makes the gun debate more complex.

History

Guns have always been a part of American history. From the arming of patriots and the mustering of militia during the Revolutionary War, to the disarming of slaves and freedmen in the nineteenth century, to the street wars of Prohibition, to the assassination of four presidents (and the attempted assassination of thirteen other presidents), to the current drumbeat of mass shootings, to recent gang wars in Chicago, guns were there. Those nearly four centuries of history complicate the gun debate, because both sides use it, selectively and often erroneously, to support their positions.

Guns were an essential part of colonial life, particularly near the frontiers. Several New England colonies had laws requiring all households to be armed and colonial marksmen distinguished themselves in battles before, during, and after the Revolutionary War.[33] However, the lore of gun-toting sheriffs battling armed outlaws in order to civilize America's Wild West frontier may be a bit exaggerated. According to gun-book author and constitutional scholar Adam Winkler,[34] towns such as Dodge City, Tombstone, and Deadwood had gun control in the form of "blanket ordinances against the carrying of arms by anyone."[35] In fact, crime and homicide rates in these towns were remarkably low.

Author Erik Larson attributes the lore of guns on the frontier to calculated myth-making over the last century by "Hollywood directors, TV producers, nineteenth-century reporters, dime novelists, and the frontier heroes themselves." These creative opportunists, driven more by profits than historical accuracy, were simply rising to a challenge: "how to rationalize the sheer excitement of the westward expansion, with its attendant gold and land fevers, and the mundane, harsh reality of ordinary frontier life."[36]

The temptation to oversimplify history afflicts both sides of the gun debate. For example, fluctuations in the homicide rate over the last two hundred years cannot be explained simply by the availability of guns or the strength of gun control laws or the political climate of the time—despite correlations in the data. There are too many interlocking variables, and the relationships among them are convoluted. Randolph Roth summarizes the difficulties clearly:

> Except for a brief period in the 1950s, America's homicide rate has been stuck between 6 and 9 per 100,000 per year for a century. In the late 1990s the United States had full employment, a war on drugs, a million people employed in law enforcement, 1.8 million people incarcerated, a ban on assault weapons, gun-registration laws, conceal-carry laws, . . . and the highest rate of church membership in the Western world. If liberal or conservative hypotheses about homicide were right or if both were right, the annual homicide rate should have been close to 1 per 100,000 persons by the year 2000; but it wasn't, and it has risen since.[37]

History and data are certainly important parts of the gun debate. However, cause and effect relations are often difficult to establish. Specious arguments often cite a pattern in two variables (such as gun sales and crime rate) and mistakenly conclude that one causes the other. It is rarely that simple. This book traces the history of gun laws and court cases and the tortured compromises that led to major legislation and court decisions. On nearly every page of that history, outcomes were never as conclusive as we would like to believe today. Nevertheless, both sides in the modern gun debate—perhaps unknowingly or perhaps to sow confusion—use their own versions of history to support their arguments.

The Constitution

Since the day the ink dried on the Bill of Rights in 1791, scholars and jurists have debated legal questions associated with guns, and those questions have divided a nation that just wants simple answers. Most of these questions originate with the enigmatic Second Amendment, surely the most parsed, conjugated, and explicated twenty-seven words in the legal canon:

> A well regulated Militia, being necessary to the security of a free State, the right of the people to keep and bear arms, shall not be infringed.[38]

What did the founders mean by these words? Does "bearing arms" mean carrying weapons openly in public? Or does it mean using them only for sanctioned military activities? How do we interpret "*the* right"? Does it imply that the right to keep and bear arms already existed and the Second Amendment only affirms it? Or does the amendment actually establish the right? And how should we interpret "the people"? Does it mean each individual (white male) person? Or, preceded by the militia clause, does it mean a collection of people, such as those who served in a militia—whatever that means today?

And what about those commas? In an earlier draft of the amendment, the first and third commas were missing, which makes the militia clause an explanation for the rights clause. However, the final version, with three commas, leaves the reader wondering whether it is the *Militia* or the *right* that *shall not be infringed*. More to the point, does it even matter today what the founders meant over two hundred years ago, at a time when arms meant muskets and today's only remnant of the militia is the National Guard? How should the amendment be interpreted today?

Many years of scholarly acrobatics have led to three general interpretations of the Second Amendment (to be elaborated in coming chapters). The individual rights interpretation claims that the Second Amendment guarantees the right of every individual to own arms for personal use. The collective rights interpretation asserts that owning and using firearms is restricted to the functions of a militia organization. Carefully splitting the difference between these two views is the civic rights interpretation. This interpretation asserts that all rights carry responsibilities and that individuals have a right to bear arms in order to fulfill their civic responsibility to ensure public safety and defense.[39]

Regardless of the founders' original intent in framing the Second Amendment, here is an important observation. The Bill of Rights was an afterthought of the Constitution, forged in a passionate debate and ratified by the states two years after the Constitution was ratified. The founders intended the Bill of Rights to protect its enumerated rights (such as speech, assembly, religion, press, bearing arms, life, liberty, property) only from laws passed by Congress; it was not intended to protect those rights from state actions. (This fact is seen most clearly in the First Amendment, which begins, "Congress shall make no law . . .") At the time the Bill of Rights was ratified, there were no constitutional measures to prevent states from restricting possession of guns. As we will see, various states passed their own gun control laws during the nineteenth century.

The Fourteenth Amendment, ratified in 1868, suggested for the first time that the rights enumerated in the Bill of Rights are also protected from violation by state and local laws. However, it has taken the Supreme Court 150 years to determine exactly which constitutional rights are protected under the Fourteenth Amendment from state and local action—a process called incorporation. In fact, the Supreme Court did not incorporate the Second Amendment until 2010, finally protecting the individual right to keep and bear arms at the state and local levels. And despite that Supreme Court decision, debate about the meaning of the Second Amendment, and the extent to which it can be limited, still persists.

Passion and Logic

The language we use to discuss volatile social issues is often a source of disagreement—and the gun debate is no different. As a matter of convenience, I frequently use *gun control* and *gun rights* to label two opposing viewpoints on firearms. These labels streamline the discussion, but they also vastly oversimplify the real picture. Even if we somehow divide the map between gun control and gun rights, there are many perspectives on each side and many paths to those perspectives.

A gun rights advocate may passionately oppose strict gun laws because she sees them as a government intrusion into the lives of citizens. A gun control supporter may read the news and conclude that stricter gun laws make sense because they reduce crime. A parent may put safety for himself and his family above all other considerations and choose to own a gun. A history scholar may decide that America has a tradition of strict gun control that should be upheld. Based on two centuries of court decisions, a legal scholar may decide that America's gun rights tradition should serve as a precedent. A statistician may do a data-intensive cost-benefit analysis and conclude that the cost of enforcing stricter gun laws cannot be justified. And an emergency room nurse in a Chicago hospital does his own cost-benefit analysis every night he sees the street slaughter caused by gun violence.

Discourse about guns is complicated because opinions are the product of every faculty from passion to logic: moral arguments, religious principles, emotional reactions, political biases, statistical analyses, legal investigations, and every combination thereof. And when opinions are formed quickly with no willingness for reconsideration, positions become zealously galvanized. At that point, listening becomes a lost art and conversations turn to verbal warfare. A wide and deep chasm in the gun debate certainly occurs on personal levels. However, that standoff—inflamed by the media—also typifies the dialogue among gun advocacy organizations. No resolution in the gun debate will be achieved and no reduction in gun violence will be seen until each side starts listening and learning more about the other.

Life Goes On

Back in Aurora, Colorado, the cinema tragedy unfolded in a somewhat predictable way. Within ten days of the shootings, James Holmes was charged on 141 counts, including first-degree murder, attempted murder, and possession of explosive devices. University of Colorado records indicate that a month prior to the shootings, a faculty psychiatrist alerted a campus assessment team about Holmes's alarming mental-health condition. Because Holmes had withdrawn from the university about the same time, no one followed up on the psychiatric report. The university could be named in suits for negligence or indifference. Families of victims will undoubtedly file civil suits, and the legal machinery will turn at glacial speeds for several years.[40]

Two weeks after the Aurora shootings, that tragedy was no longer a headline story. Other mass public shootings had already taken its place. In a three-week period around the Aurora tragedy, two people were killed and nineteen injured at an outdoor party in Toronto; seventeen were shot and injured by a disgruntled FedEx employee in a Tuscaloosa bar; seven were killed in a Sikh temple near Milwaukee; and four people were killed and ten were wounded in a single, sadly typical weekend in Chicago. And in the background of those "newsworthy" events was the refrain of some eighty-five gun deaths each day. Despite the horror of the Aurora shooting, it was not an unusually lethal month in the life of the country.

These tragedies forever transform the lives of the victims' families. Added to prolonged legal proceedings, media scrutiny, and medical costs is an enormous and incurable emotional toll. Such tragedies elicit many different reactions. Some people contribute to a victim-assistance fund as a gesture of support and sympathy. Others buy a gun out of fear. Tom Mauser, whose son was killed in the 1999 Columbine shootings, became a gun control advocate and organized Colorado Ceasefire. Dan Gross, whose brother was shot on the observation deck of the Empire State Building in 1997, and Colin Goddard, who survived four gunshot wounds in the Virginia Tech shootings, joined the Brady Campaign to Prevent Gun Violence (Gross is now its president). Guided by lessons from the Holocaust, Aaron Zelman founded the Wisconsin-based Jews for the Preservation of Firearms Ownership, one of whose goals is to destroy gun control. Gun rights organizations turn to their mailing lists and solicit funds to fight the threat of new gun laws.

For the rest of us, life resumes, and the latest tragedy is added to a long list that we file under convenient names: University of Texas, Luby's, Columbine, Virginia Tech, Fort Hood, Gabby Giffords, Aurora, Sandy Hook, San Bernardino, and Pulse Nightclub. Life resumes not because we are indifferent or unsympathetic. Rather, many on both sides of the gun divide feel numb and helpless in changing the violence that seems an inescapable part of American life. Hopefully, this book offers a path forward.

About This Book

High above America's fractious gun dispute—above the legislative skirmishes, the vagaries of court decisions, and the million-dollar lobbying campaigns—there is one goal around which both sides, "gun nuts" and "gun grabbers" alike, can surely unite. That goal is to overcome America's epidemic of gun violence in its many forms: suicides, accidents, crime, domestic and gang violence, personal defense, and mass shootings. This book aims to propose realistic solutions to this seemingly intractable crisis. However, before solutions can be presented and made plausible, two themes must be elaborated.

The first theme is the history of the Second Amendment and the legislation and court decisions that it spawned, from colonial days to the present. Without knowing some of that history, with its scalding legislative debates and its contentious, often contradictory, court decisions, it is impossible to see today's gun debate in the proper perspective. For example, an understanding of that history exposes the founders fallacy—the belief that a particular position in the gun debate is justified by *the* intent of the founding fathers. Knowing the history makes it clear that there was no single, unified, exclusive intent of the founding fathers with respect to the Second Amendment. And even if there were, it is hard to imagine that it would have somehow survived for over two centuries to be read transparently by today's judges and legislators. In other words, appeals to the intent of the founders—by either side—should be viewed skeptically.

The second essential theme that runs through the book is the complex landscape of today's gun culture; it begins with the diversity of Americans whose lives involve guns. Using profiles of protagonists in the gun debate—gay people, women, competitive trapshooters, participants in cowboy action events, people in the gun rights and gun control trenches, among others—the book portrays the many ways in which guns have become a part of Americans' lives. Equally important in understanding that landscape is the challenge of enforcing gun laws. That subject requires a look at the system of federal background checks, the web of state and federal gun laws, recent Supreme Court decisions, and the roles of law enforcement agencies. And finally, that complex landscape involves the sad and vexing reality of mental illness and its treatment. The book offers a balanced investigation of all these crucial topics. It is difficult to propose a realistic path to reducing gun violence without understanding these topics and appreciating the extent to which guns have defined our character as a nation.

These two themes—history and landscape—are thoroughly interwoven in the gun debate. This fact is captured in the structure of the book by the following scheme: the even chapters of the book tell the history of the Second Amendment and key court cases; the odd chapters explore the landscape of today's gun culture.

Readers who prefer continuity may want to read the even chapters first, followed by the odd chapters. Those who want a sense of how the past is never forgotten and how it shapes our lives today should read the chapters sequentially.

This book should make it clear—if you did not already believe it—that guns are here to stay. To some, that is good news because guns make life safer and more enjoyable. To others, it is bad news because the availability of guns is anywhere from unsettling to morally abhorrent. Regardless of one's opinion, it makes sense to learn more about guns—perhaps to be a better campaigner in gun control battles, but certainly to be better educated about an issue of urgent national importance. Hopefully, this book provides the objective background needed to follow American gun politics, to analyze legislation, to understand court decisions, and to make informed decisions.

The tide of gun violence will be diverted only when the breach between opposing sides in the gun debate is narrowed. Progress in that direction requires neither the total disarmament of America nor giving Americans unconstrained Second Amendment rights; in fact, those options are neither practical nor constitutional. However, progress can be made if individuals and organizations, on both sides of the breach, decide to live, work, negotiate, lobby, and campaign with a better understanding of the issues, a greater tolerance of other perspectives, and a fresh willingness to compromise—all principles this book aims to promote.

2 | THE ADVANTAGE OF BEING ARMED

The advantage of being armed, which the Americans possess
over the people of almost every other nation, . . . forms a barrier against
the enterprises of ambition, more insurmountable than any which
a simple government of any form can admit of.

—JAMES MADISON, Federalist No. 46

PAUL REVERE'S ENGRAVING depicts a bright afternoon with a tower clock showing 3:50.[1] Other accounts refer to a snowy evening and "a few minutes after nine o'clock."[2] According to some, the dispute arose over an unpaid bill to a wigmaker, and others attribute it to baiting and taunting between Boston youths and British officers. Despite the many variations on the story, a relatively minor street skirmish escalated into an event that twisted the arc of American history.

In the decade preceding the Revolutionary War, King George III and his appointed governors subjected American colonists to increasingly oppressive measures, among them restrictions on trade, unjust taxation, limitations on trial by jury, and the dissolution of the Massachusetts legislature. The colonists resisted these measures in many ways, each of which only tightened the British grip. As the spring of 1770 neared, four thousand British soldiers—one for every four residents—occupied Boston, living in barracks and public houses, as stipulated by the Quartering Acts.[3] One mission of the troops was to enforce the new and repressive Townshend Acts, a collection of laws variously designed to raise revenue for the Crown at the expense of colonists. To add to the tension and enmity created by these laws, the poorly paid British soldiers often sought additional work in Boston, which took jobs from the colonists. It all became a recipe for combustion.

The various accounts of the afternoon of March 5 agree that a young wigmaker's apprentice named Edward Garrick encountered a British soldier named Hugh White in the vicinity of the Customs House on Boston's King Street. Did Garrick taunt White and claim that "there were no gentlemen left in the regiment," as one report alleges? Or was White, like many redcoats, acting with insolence and provoking another street fight with the town boys, as another report claims? Either way, a crowd soon gathered on King Street. An altercation also broke out in nearby Dock Square, drawing another crowd. When someone rang a fire bell, the two crowds merged and swelled to some four hundred people. White was overwhelmed and he retreated to the Customs House, where he called for assistance. He was soon joined by a group of soldiers led by Captain Thomas Preston. As the soldiers confronted the crowd with muskets and bayonets, the townspeople filled the air with snowballs, lumps of coal, sticks, and oyster shells. The ensuing mayhem guaranteed that no two eyewitness accounts would agree.

The British soldiers may have first attempted to disband the crowd with unloaded muskets. Captain Preston may have been struck by a club, after which he ordered his soldiers to load and fire into the crowd. Or a British soldier may have fired without orders after being struck by a projectile, and Captain Preston may have attempted to stop the gunfire. What is known with certainty is that the British soldiers fired into the crowd, killing five men and injuring six. One of the fatalities was "a mullato man named Crispus Attucks, who was . . . killed instantly, two balls entering his breast, one of them in special goring the right lobe of the lungs and a great part of the liver most horribly."[4] Samuel Gray was "killed on the spot, the ball entering his head and beating off a large portion of his skull." James Caldwell died "in like manner killed by two balls entering his back." Seventeen-year-old Samuel Maverick died of his wounds the next morning and Irish immigrant Patrick Carr died two weeks later. After the shooting, the crowd dispersed and the soldiers retreated to their barracks. Later the same night, Captain Preston was arrested and jailed. One week later, a grand jury issued indictments against Preston and eight of his soldiers.

The Boston Massacre (as it was named many years later) instantly became provender for newspapers, pamphlets, and other anti-British writings. It was memorialized in paintings and engravings, and the resulting trial was the most closely watched legal spectacle of the day.[5] In hopes of giving Preston and his soldiers a fair trial, acting governor Thomas Hutchinson postponed the trial for several months to let passions cool. Impartial jurors were hard to find, as was a committed defense team for the accused men. Finally, a prominent thirty-four-year-old Boston attorney named John Adams accepted the job of representing the defendants. Adams was an aspiring politician with a successful legal practice, so he understood the risks of defending royalists accused of murdering colonists. He also understood the necessity of giving the defendants a fair trial.

Preston's week-long trial began seven months later on October 24, 1770, at the Queen Street Courthouse. The verdict rested on whether Preston had given orders for his soldiers to fire into the crowd on March 5. The witnesses called by the defense and the prosecution gave conflicting accounts of Preston's role. In the end, Adams planted sufficient doubt in the jurors' minds that Preston was acquitted after a few hours of deliberation.

The trial of the eight soldiers, who were also represented by John Adams, began on November 27. Adams argued that the soldiers acted in self-defense, claiming, "if an assault was made to endanger their lives, the law is clear, they had a right to kill in their own defence."[6] The defense case also featured a legal curiosity. On his deathbed, one Boston Massacre casualty, Patrick Carr, told his surgeon that "he forgave the man whoever he was that shot him, he was satisfied he had no malice, but fired to defend himself."[7] This testimony, normally regarded as hearsay, was accepted under an unusual "dying declaration" exception. In the end, six of the soldiers were acquitted of all charges.

The jury determined that the two remaining soldiers knowingly fired into the crowd and found them guilty of manslaughter. In another legal twist, their sentence of imprisonment was reduced by a "benefit of the clergy" appeal, which was once used in English law for clergymen and for first-time offenders. The two guilty soldiers were sentenced to a public branding of their thumbs with the letter *M* (for murder).

The verdicts in the Boston Massacre trials were an outrage to many colonists. However, even those who opposed the verdicts recognized the trials as a victory for the young colonial judicial system. The verdicts also upheld the legitimacy of using firearms for self-defense. Representing unpopular defendants apparently did not alter John Adams's path to the presidency. Writing in his journal three years after the event, he confided:

> The Part I took in Defence of Cptn. Preston and the Soldiers, procured me Anxiety, and Obloquy enough. It was, however, one of the most gallant, generous, manly and disinterested Actions of my whole Life, and one of the best Pieces of Service I ever rendered my Country.[8]

In the same entry, Adams also observed prophetically:

> This however is no Reason why the Town should not call the Action of that Night a Massacre, nor is it any Argument in favour of the Governor or Minister, who caused them to be sent here. But it is the strongest Proofs of the Danger of Standing Armies.[9]

The Boston Massacre had significant consequences. First, it likely hastened the onset of the Revolutionary War. Second, as John Adams noted, it only elevated the colonists' dread of a standing army—a state of mind that would shade the thinking that shaped the US Constitution. And finally, the incident was recognized as an attack on unarmed colonists who could not defend themselves. It was a lesson in the necessity of keeping and bearing arms for self-defense.

The American Revolutionary War

Understanding the Second Amendment of the US Constitution requires a familiarity with its origins and with its interpretation in two hundred years of court cases. And it is impossible to understand the genesis of the Second Amendment without appreciating the convulsions of the American Revolution, the contentious debates of the Constitutional Convention, and other decisive events in colonial America. It was in this crucible, which nearly brought the young nation to ruins, that the Second Amendment was forged.

At the time of the Boston Massacre, the thirteen British colonies in North America were growing quickly and had a total population of two million people. Half of the population lived in Massachusetts, Pennsylvania, and Virginia, and roughly 20 percent of it consisted of enslaved black people. With a population over thirty thousand, Philadelphia was the largest colonial city and the third largest port in the British Empire, with a flourishing trade in sugar, tobacco, grain, and tea.

Less than four years after the Boston Massacre, in December 1773, a band of patriots defiantly dumped forty tons of tea into Boston's harbor in protest of excessive taxes; the incident was later called the Boston Tea Party. The response from the British was a set of new laws known as the Intolerable Acts that closed the Boston port, placed the Massachusetts government under the control of the English Parliament, and allowed the quartering of even more British troops throughout the colonies. Virginian Richard Henry Lee described the laws as "a most wicked system for destroying liberty in America."[10]

Relevant to the history of the Second Amendment were the colonists' efforts to stockpile weapons, manufacture ammunition, and organize militias to resist British tyranny. These efforts were countered by an intensified campaign on the part of the British to confiscate arms. The colonists saw the threat of disarmament as a violation of the English Bill of Rights of 1689, which guaranteed "that the subjects which are Protestants may have arms for their defense suitable to their conditions and as allowed by law." Furthermore, the right to self-defense was taken as a "natural right" under English common law that applied equally to the colonists. Reacting to these attempts at disarmament, Boston patriot Samuel Adams cited the renowned English jurist Sir William Blackstone:

> Having arms for their defence [Blackstone] tells us is "a public allowance, under due restrictions, of the natural right of resistance and self preservation, when the sanctions of society and laws are found insufficient to restrain the violence of oppression."[11]

In other words, possessing and using firearms for self-defense, in the face of oppression when no other form of resistance is effective, is within the law.

In response to British oppression, the First Continental Congress met for the first time in Philadelphia on October 14, 1774. Among the fifty-six delegates were George Washington, John Adams, Patrick Henry, and Samuel Adams. The result of that convention was the Declaration and Resolves of the First Continental Congress, which was a litany of grievances and rights. Among the rights were:

> that these, his majesty's colonies, are likewise entitled to all the immunities and privileges granted and confirmed to them by royal charters, or secured

by their several codes of provincial laws; and that the keeping of a standing army in these colonies, in times of peace, without the consent of the legislature of that colony, in which such army is kept, is against law.[12]

The reference to royal charters and provincial laws was an appeal to rights assured under English law. And the illegality of standing armies would be a recurring theme in the eventual formulation of the US Constitution.

Ironically, the distinguished British statesman Edmund Burke was an ardent minority supporter of the colonial cause. He argued for a repeal of the tea tax and reconciliation with the colonists. Burke captured the spirit of the American colonists poignantly in a speech to the House of Commons in March 1774, observing:

In this character of the Americans, a love of freedom is the predominating feature which marks and distinguishes the whole. . . . Your colonies become suspicious, restive, and untractable, whenever they see the least attempt to wrest from them by force . . . what they think the only advantage worth living for. This fierce spirit of liberty is stronger in the English colonies probably than in any other people of the earth.[13]

Burke's character analysis of Americans explains a temperament that would evolve in the next two hundred years and lead to the American predilection for guns.

The "shot heard 'round the world"[14] that marked the start of the American Revolutionary War was fired in Concord, Massachusetts, on April 19, 1775. The conflict began when British redcoats marched on Concord to seize arms and ammunition reportedly stored in nearby houses. Warned of the British advance by Paul Revere and his companions, the militias of Concord and Lexington were ready for the attack.[15] The militiamen, generally white males aged sixteen to sixty, were self-armed with muskets and hunting rifles, and they proved to be unexpectedly good marksmen. Fighting unconventionally, firing from behind trees and walls, the patriots eventually forced the redcoats to retreat. After one day of fighting, 50 patriots were killed and 39 were wounded, compared to 65 redcoats killed and 157 wounded. The patriot victory is generally attributed to the fact that the colonial militias were well-armed and trained in the use of firearms. Not surprisingly, the British responded to the defeat with renewed efforts to search homes, seize munitions, and disarm militias throughout the colonies.

The Revolutionary War did not end formally until the Treaty of Paris was signed on September 3, 1783. However, between the signing of the Declaration of Independence on July 4, 1776, and the Treaty of Paris, the colonies moved ahead as if genuine independence were inevitable: The states set about the business of holding conventions and drafting constitutions and bills of rights. These documents reflected the impact of an oppressive British occupation, the fear of standing armies, and the necessity of maintaining armed militias for common defense. They also formed the roots of the US Bill of Rights—still fifteen years in the future.

Virginia was the second state to ratify a state constitution and the first to include a bill of rights. On June 12, 1776, three weeks before the signing of the Declaration of Independence, delegates at a state convention adopted the Virginia Declaration of Rights. Among the sixteen rights of the declaration, drafted by George Mason, were:

> that a well-regulated Militia, composed of the body of the people, trained to arms, is the proper, natural, and safe defence of a free State; that Standing Armies, in time of peace, should be avoided as dangerous to liberty; and that, in all cases, the military should be under strict subordination to, and governed by, the civil power.[16]

This list of rights also included provisions assuring freedoms of press, religion, and speech; the right to free elections; the right to confront accusers in court; protection from warrantless searches; and the "enjoyment of life and liberty."

Late in the summer of 1776, Benjamin Franklin presided over the Pennsylvania convention. Its Declaration of Rights included the provision "that the people have a right to bear arms for the defence of themselves, and the state," the first state declaration of the right to use arms specifically for personal protection. A long and tumultuous process led to the adoption of the Massachusetts Constitution on March 2, 1780. Its language regarding firearms was also significant:

The people have a right to keep and to bear arms for the common defence. And as in time of peace armies are dangerous to liberty, they ought not to be maintained without the consent of the legislature; and the military power shall always be held in an exact subordination to the civil authority, and be governed by it.[17]

For the first time the phrase "right to keep and bear arms" appeared in a declaration of rights and it would find its way into the Second Amendment ten years later.

One by one, the colonies met in conventions and approved their constitutions in various forms. By 1784, eleven colonies had adopted constitutions. (Connecticut and Rhode Island chose to use existing colonial charters until they approved new constitutions in the nineteenth century.) Seven of those eleven constitutions included language about firearms in their declarations of rights. (New York, New Jersey, South Carolina, and Georgia did not write bills of rights.) Of the seven constitutions with declarations of rights, six specified that the right to bear arms was for the defense of the state or for common defense. Only Pennsylvania's constitution specifically asserted the right to bear arms for personal defense. In 1791, Vermont became the fourteenth state to join the Union; it adopted a declaration of rights with the Pennsylvania language on bearing arms.

Militia

Much of the discussion about the Second Amendment hinges on the meaning of *militia*. In colonial times, a militia was a group of armed volunteer citizens, trained to oppose British tyranny and ensure public safety. Boston judge and mayor Josiah Quincy Jr. referred to "a well regulated militia composed of freeholders, citizens, and husbandmen, who take up arms to preserve their property as individuals, and their rights as freemen." He concluded "the supreme power is ever possessed by those who have arms in their hands, and are disciplined in the use of them."[18] Similarly, Maryland lawyer and politician Daniel Dulany claimed that "the power is in the hands of the people and there is not the least difficulty . . . about putting arms into the hands of every man in the country," conjecturing that there were "several hundred thousand or perhaps near a million men capable of bearing arms in their own defence."[19]

The modern historian Saul Cornell has a broader perspective on militias:

It would be impossible to overstate the militia's centrality to the lives
of American colonists. For Americans living on the edge of the British
Empire, in an age without police forces, the militia was essential for the
preservation of public order and also protected Americans against exter-
nal threats.[20]

In addition to their martial purpose, militias had another important function. Members of militias and their families regularly gathered in musters
that served not only as training sessions but as social events in the life of the
community. It is evident that during this period, militias were an important
civic institution in colonial America.

The several forms that a militia might take ranged from universal militias to standing armies. A universal militia consisted of men meeting some
general qualifications, such as "able-bodied men between the ages of eighteen and sixty." In this sense, militia duty was viewed as a responsibility to be
fulfilled by all capable citizens. The idea of a select militia—a militia chosen
using conscription or special admission requirements—was often resisted as
being on the path to a standing army. A universal citizens' militia "embodied
virtue and liberty" and "a standing army symbolized tyranny."[21] At the time of
the Revolutionary War, a universal militia was seen as the best defense against
foreign forces and against a standing army.

Before the Revolutionary War, the term *well-regulated* described clocks
and courts that were in reliable working order. Applied to militias, the term
suggests organized meetings and coordinated training sessions. Furthermore,
the nascent colonial firearm industry consisted of a handful of gunsmiths
making guns with less than assembly-line precision. The colonists also had
access to European-made rifles and muskets. Therefore, with such a mixed
supply of weapons and ammunition, *well-regulated* also implied some com-
patibility in the arms and ammunition used by militiamen. Perhaps the real
intent of the term *well-regulated* was to ensure that militias were effective
functioning units and not random vigilante mobs inciting rebellion.

Today, as we look back and try to divine the founders' intent in writing the
Second Amendment, the meaning of *militia* is important. Was the right to

bear arms a collective right, limited to militia duty and defense of the state? Or was the right an individual right that extended to the personal use of firearms for self-defense? Judging by their constitutions, the states seemed divided on this question. As noted earlier, only the state constitutions of Pennsylvania and Vermont specifically mention the use of arms for personal defense—which is not to say that other states prohibited such uses.

Another understanding of the right to bear arms falls somewhere between the collective and individual interpretations. According to this civic interpretation, there are two sides to every right: a privilege and a duty. As a proponent of this view, historian Saul Cornell claims the right to bear arms is a "civic right that guaranteed that citizens would be able to keep and bear those arms needed to meet their legal obligations to participate" in a militia.[22] In other words, the right to bear arms was an individual privilege intended to fulfill a civic duty.

The civic interpretation provides a realistic perspective on the role of the militia and the right to bear arms in the late 1700s. Emerging from a brutal war against a tyrannical government, the founders had a widely shared fear of a nation with a standing army. Creating a militia system that was distributed throughout the states and consisted of citizens who provided their own arms helped abate that fear. At the same time, there was universal acceptance of a right to self-defense, inherited from British common law. Combining the need for citizens to maintain personal arms for defense of country and the belief in the right of self-defense leads to a plausible conclusion: citizens (eligible white males) were expected to use their arms to fulfill a civic duty to defend their country and were entitled to use their arms for personal purposes, such as self-defense and hunting.

The First Constitution

While the states were creating their own constitutions, some leaders felt the need for a national constitution to formalize the structure of a federal government. In June 1776, the Second Continental Congress began work on the Articles of Confederation and Perpetual Union and released them to the states for ratification in November 1777. The Articles of Confederation, as they are known, remained a provisional agreement for four years until the document was fully ratified and became official on March 1, 1781.

By the time the Revolutionary War ended with the Treaty of Paris in 1783, leaders and lawmakers had already realized the deficiencies in the Articles of Confederation. The document provided for no executive or judicial branch of the federal government, and the Congress did not have the authority to collect taxes, recruit troops, or conduct foreign affairs. Among the sad consequences of the Articles of Confederation, the federal government had no way to pay back war debts or honor pensions for war veterans.

Between 1781 and 1788, ten different men served as "President of Congress," although at that time, the position carried limited executive powers. Future president George Washington argued for a stronger federal government, writing in a letter to John Jay in August 1786:

> I do not conceive we can exist long as a nation without having lodged somewhere a power, which will pervade the whole Union in as energetic a manner, as the authority of the State Governments extends over the several States. To be fearful of investing Congress, constituted as that body is, with ample authorities for national purposes, appears to me the very climax of popular absurdity and madness.[23]

The six-year test run of the new government ended when the Constitutional Convention met in the summer of 1787 to rethink the Articles of Confederation. The purpose of the convention was unclear; for some, its goal was to fine-tune the Articles of Confederation, and for others the goal was nothing short of inventing a new government. The period during which the new constitution was written and ratified proved to be one of the most suspenseful and critical periods in American history. The issue of federal vs. state power, the role of the militia, and the meaning of the right to keep and bear arms all figured decisively in the final outcome.

3 | NUMBER GAMES

Perhaps the greatest obstacle to acquiring an understanding of . . . the gun control
debate is the firm conviction of many on both sides that most of the critical facts
are self-evident. . . . The debaters begin with premises that are so thoroughly taken
for granted that they never consider evaluating them.

—GARY KLECK, *Targeting Guns*

REGARDLESS OF THE topic, we tend to grasp at numbers because they have
a reassuring certainty—as if assigning a number to a measurement makes it
a fact. Numbers fill headlines, fortify political campaigns, bolster arguments
in court cases, and are glorified in glitzy graphics. Numbers seem like a good
way to understand the issues quickly and to get oriented. However, they often
have the opposite effect: numbers are easily misreported, manipulated, care-
lessly gathered, lifted from context, and otherwise misused. When this sort
of abuse occurs, the numbers become all but meaningless. Making this number addiction even more irresistible are powerful search engines that provide
instant data displays and numerical factoids that can be used as ammunition
on any side of an argument. As a result, many critical public debates become a
firestorm of numbers, with both sides believing that numbers will ultimately
settle the score.

If there is one realm in which number madness runs wild, it is the gun
debate. Indeed, following gun statistics can feel like a five-hour tennis match,
as opponents fire conflicting number volleys back and forth at each other.
Before long, the experience is neither entertaining nor informative. One
social scientist surmised that "individuals adopt one position or another
because of what guns mean rather than what guns do." Therefore, "empirical
data are unlikely to have much effect on the gun debate."[1] As I show in this
chapter, one should approach firearm data with thoughtful skepticism.

Studies and surveys about guns are used in different ways. Politicians cite them to justify their positions on gun issues. Public-policy wonks use them to write laws and craft new programs. Law-enforcement agencies rely on them to improve crime-intervention programs. And for ordinary citizens, they may inform personal decisions about guns. In order to produce credible results in such studies, researchers must perform experiments, conduct surveys, and collect and analyze data—all of which are challenging when it comes to guns.

The following pairs of statements about a variety of gun issues capture the bewilderment one might feel trying to make sense of gun numbers. Despite the apparent discrepancy in each pair, every statement appears virtually verbatim somewhere in print. Explanations follow.

1 A: In 2012, there were about 1.2 million violent crimes (primarily murder, rape, robbery, aggravated assault) in the United States, down from 1.4 million in 2001.[2]
1 B: There has been a decrease in violent crimes in the United States, but the number stood at 2.1 million in 2012.[3]

2 A: In 2013, there were 16,121 homicides in the United States.[4]
2 B: In 2013, there were 13,716 homicides in the United States.[5]

3 A: There are 270 million guns in the United States.[6]
3 B: Right now, there are as many guns in this country as there are people—over 310 million.[7]

4 A: Each year 2.5 million people use guns for defensive purposes. That is almost three hundred defensive uses per hour! In 15 percent of those cases, someone's life was probably saved.[8]
4 B: Each year, there are at most one hundred thousand incidents of guns used for self-defense.[9]

5 A: There are 2.39 accidental or criminal deaths by firearms in the home for every justifiable fatal shooting in the home.[10]
5 B: A person with a gun in the home is forty-three times as likely to shoot someone in the family as to shoot a criminal.[11]

6 A: In 2014, guns killed about 2,500 children, or about seven kids every day.[12]

6 B: In fact, 350 children die each year from gun shots—still too many but closer to zero.[13]

7 A: It is illegal to possess automatic weapons in this country.[14]

7 B: Sale and possession of automatic weapons are highly regulated, but it is legal to own automatic weapons in this country.[15]

Gun and Crime Data

The above statements illustrate the difficulties that arise in interpreting crime and gun data. The first pair of claims cites significantly different figures for the violent crime rate in the United States—even though both figures originate with the Department of Justice. The smaller crime count (1.2 million violent crimes in 2012) comes from the Uniform Crime Reporting program (UCR) of the Federal Bureau of Investigation (FBI). These numbers reflect "offenses known to law enforcement" (not actual arrests); they are collected for many different crimes and reported by roughly eighteen thousand local law-enforcement agencies. Because these law-enforcement agencies file reports voluntarily, the collected data represent only approximately 90 percent of the US population. To correct for this underreporting, the reported crime figures are then adjusted upward to make final estimated crime figures.[16] The UCR system defines violent crime as murder and nonnegligent manslaughter, rape, robbery, and aggravated assault.

The larger crime figure (2.1 million violent crimes in 2012) comes from the Bureau of Justice Statistics (BJS), which administers the National Crime Victimization Survey (NCVS). Using a sample of approximately ninety thousand households (160,000 people), the Census Bureau collects nonfatal crime data for the BJS through interviews with victims. The national violent crime rate is then estimated from the sample data. The data represent crime incidents in many different categories—whether or not the crimes are reported to law enforcement. Serious violent crimes in the NCVS system include rape, robbery, and aggravated and simple assault. However, it does not include homicides because homicides leave no victims to interview. The net effect is that the NCVS violent crime rates are greater than the UCR rates.

The second pair of claims involves homicide numbers. According to the FBI's Uniform Crime Report, the United States saw 14,610 homicides in 2013. However, another equally reputable source, the National Center for Health Statistics—within the Centers for Disease Control and Prevention (CDC), itself within the Department of Health and Human Services (HHS)—collects homicide data from state coroners' offices. This reporting path is not only mandatory but also the oldest system for reporting homicides. It reported about 1,500 more homicides than the UCR in 2013. The difference is in the agencies' definitions of homicide.

The FBI reports only murder and nonnegligent manslaughter, which together it calls criminal homicide. However, the CDC additionally reports negligent (or accidental) homicide and justifiable homicide, which includes the killing of a felon by a law-enforcement officer and some cases of self-defense. Because the CDC reports a larger class of homicides, its estimates are higher than the FBI estimates. (Negligent homicides and justifiable homicides together amount to approximately 1,200 per year, which accounts for most of the difference.)

Homicide data may seem confusing, but when it comes to the gun debate, homicide data may be the most reliable data available. Imagine stalking far more elusive variables, such as the number of guns or gun owners in America at any given time. Because most states do not have gun registration laws, there is no systematic reporting system to keep track of gun owners. While it is possible to find data on gun sales at licensed retail stores, guns are also obtained from many other legal and illegal sources. The problem is further complicated by the fact that during its long lifetime, a gun may change hands, become inoperative, become part of a collection, or be destroyed. For these reasons, estimating the number of gun owners is no easier than doing a national bird census; not surprisingly, estimates are prone to errors.

One way to estimate gun ownership is with surveys. And if you are in the market for survey data in the social sciences, the first stop should be the General Social Survey (GSS). Launched in 1972 by the National Opinion Research Center at the University of Chicago, GSS data can be found at a cavernous website that is surely one of the architectural wonders of the Internet.[17] The GSS site is the repository of forty years of data that can be accessed through powerful search and analysis tools. Its 5,500 cataloged variables provide an intriguing window into American attitudes ("Generally speaking, would you say that people can be trusted or that you can't be too careful in dealing with people?"), demographics ("Within the past 12 months, how many people have you known personally who were victims of homicide?"), and behaviors ("How often have you seen events that happened at a great distance as they were happening?").

The GSS has asked questions about gun ownership almost from the start. For example, over the years from 1973 to 2008, when asked "Do you happen to have in your home any guns or revolvers?" an average of 44 percent of respondents answered yes, 55 percent answered no, and 1 percent did not answer. Of those who answered yes, 61 percent answered that they personally own a gun and 38 percent said they did not own a gun. These GSS results on ownership are fairly consistent with the results of a 2014 Gallup poll cited in chapter 1 (42 percent of respondents reported a gun in their household or on their property and 30 percent of respondents reported owning a gun). Using these survey results and 2010 census data, we could estimate that approximately 52 million American households have guns and approximately 70 million adult Americans are gun owners. The NRA gives an unattributed estimate of 70–80 million American gun owners. Accounting for multiple-gun ownership, estimates of total guns between 270 and 310 million, as indicated in the third pair of claims above, are reasonable.

Estimates of gun ownership from surveys differ for several reasons. First, a relatively small sample (often around one thousand people) is used to infer characteristics of a much larger population of 230 million adults. Statisticians know how to estimate these sampling errors—provided the sample is representative and respondents are honest. However, surveys that deal with sensitive matters, such as gun ownership, are prone to response errors (lying, exaggerating, and dissembling). And without correction, these errors tend to skew gun-ownership data downward. Furthermore, nonresponse rates in gun surveys are unusually high. Without knowing the gun ownership habits of the nonrespondents, it is difficult to extract meaningful results. For these reasons, survey data provide a rather impressionist picture of gun ownership.

Defensive Gun Uses

Perhaps the most prized, elusive, and disputed number in the entire gun debate goes by the name defensive gun uses (DGUs): the number of times a gun is used in an attempt to prevent a crime. Opposing sides in the debate argue over this single number as if it were the last electoral vote in a toss-up presidential election. And the argument is heated for good reason: If the number of DGUs is large, as gun rights people claim, it justifies self-defense as a fundamental reason to carry a firearm. If the number of DGUs is small, or if DGUs have tragic consequences, as gun control people claim, then it is one more reason to restrict firearms.

It is a whopping understatement to say that counting and classifying DGUs is difficult. Consider the case of a seventy-two-year-old grandmother who shot at (and missed) a man attempting to break into her home shortly after midnight in June 2013. The assailant fled and was arrested a short while later. If there is an ideal DGU, this is it—crime averted and no casualties.[18]

Or consider a student party in College Park, Georgia, that was invaded by two masked gunmen in May 2009. The gunmen separated the men and women into two rooms and were intent on murdering the men and raping the women. When the gunmen started counting their bullets to see if they had enough, one of the students grabbed his own gun. One gunman was killed on the spot and the other gunman fled.[19] This time multiple violent crimes were likely prevented at the cost of a life.

Or there is the September 2012 case of Jeffrey Giuliano, whose phone rang at one in the morning. It was his sister, who lived next door, calling to say she saw an intruder in the yard between their houses. A popular fifth-grade teacher in New Fairfield, Connecticut, Giuliano grabbed a handgun and stepped outside. When a masked man with a knife lunged at him, Giuliano fired several shots. Only when paramedics removed the body several hours later did Giuliano learn that he had shot and killed his fifteen-year-old son. While this incident started out as a possible DGU, it turned into an unthinkable tragedy, and there was likely no crime to be averted.[20]

The castle doctrine (more in chapter 13) refers to the right to defend one's home if there is a suspicion of a deadly threat. The castle doctrine and a DGU met in Kalispell, Montana, in October 2012. Angry, but unarmed, Dan Fredenberg visited the home of Brice Harper, who was known to be having an affair with Fredenberg's wife. When Fredenberg walked into Harper's open garage, he was fatally shot three times. Under Montana's castle doctrine—which was opposed by state law-enforcement officials and supported by the

NRA—Harper was not prosecuted. The county attorney explained, "Given his reasonable belief that he was about to be assaulted, Brice's use of deadly force against Dan was justified."[21]

Then there are many "what-if" DGUs; they occur after every mass shooting in this country. Suzanna Hupp was with her parents in a Luby's Cafeteria in Killeen, Texas, on October 16, 1991. Their lunch came to a crashing end when a truck plowed into the restaurant and a man opened fire on the patrons. Twenty-three people, including Hupp's parents, were killed in the massacre. Had her handgun been in her purse and not in her car, Hupp might have intervened and stopped the carnage. Instead, she was abiding by a Texas law at that time that prohibited carrying a concealed weapon. Hupp went on to serve in the Texas House of Representatives for ten years, as a champion of citizens' right to carry concealed weapons.[22]

Research on DGUs has a long history that gained attention in the 1970s. Using a variety of survey methods, the early studies produced estimates between about 100,000 and 3 million DGUs per year. This wide range of estimates indicates the well-known errors that plague survey methods. First, there are false negatives that skew the numbers downward. For example, respondents may be understandably reluctant to report the use of a gun even for self-defense, particularly outside of the home. Then there are false positives that inflate the numbers: Because of an effect called telescoping, respondents may claim that a significant event occurred during the last year when it actually occurred several years ago. Or some respondents may report a DGU out of bravado or social desirability, when in fact such heroism never occurred. Further complicating the count is the fact that, in some incidents, guns may be brandished but never fired. And in some cases, when both parties have guns, it may be difficult to determine who is actually on the defense. Finally, most surveys do not include criminals, who may have DGU incidents to report.

In 1995, Florida State University criminologist Gary Kleck set out to eliminate the flaws of previous studies and produce a better DGU estimate. Using refined methods, carefully designed survey questions, and a sample size of nearly five thousand respondents, Kleck's estimate of DGUs was between 2.1 and 2.5 million per year. He also teased out of the data the conclusion that as many as four hundred thousand of those DGUs were cases in which a life was saved.[23] At about the same time, two other national surveys arrived at DGU estimates of 108,000 and 1.5 million.[24] Kleck's study has been acclaimed and widely cited, and it has been criticized and roundly repudiated. However, more recent studies have neither narrowed the range of DGU estimates nor produced numbers with more consensus. It all begins to sound like numerology.

The DGU skirmish was taken to another level just a few years after Kleck's study with the release of a book provocatively titled *More Guns, Less Crime*.[25] Its author was John Lott, a smart, UCLA-trained, PhD economist armed with a toolkit full of quantitative methods that he focused on gun and crime data. The message in his research, stated succinctly in the book's title, is that crime rates actually decrease when gun ownership rises. While that theory sounds counterintuitive to some, it is persuasive to others. Lott proposed two mechanisms that explain his proposed effect. First, armed citizens can confront assailants with authority during a confrontation, thus averting a possible crime. More important, the fact that some citizens are armed is a deterrent to criminals (and, conversely, the fact that many citizens are disarmed is an incentive to criminals). In fact, the percentage of armed citizens may be small, but because of their halo effect, they inoculate the entire community against crime—or so the theory goes.

With help from the media, Lott's research leaped out of the pages of arcane scholarly journals into the bright light of day. Gun rights advocates immediately seized the work as the scientific proof needed to justify less gun control. Lott went to the top of the charts as a celebrity at conferences, as a key witness for Congressional subcommittees, and as a high-profile public commentator. However, the research also attracted its share of censure, not only from gun control proponents but from academic types, who had little stake in the gun debate but doubted Lott's data and methodology. In one instance, Lott was accused of fraud when he could not produce the data behind the claim that in 98 percent of confrontations simply brandishing a weapon was enough to deter an attacker.[26]

Even Lott's critics had to admire him for the difficulty of his undertaking and the wave of new quantitative gun research that it spawned. Lott's strategy was to examine fine-grained crime data (at the county level) and focus on states in which new, less restrictive gun laws had been recently passed (usually concealed-carry laws where none had existed before). The goal was to chart the crime rates in several different categories before and after the new laws went into effect. It was important to analyze the problem using both a time-series approach (looking at one location over many years) and a cross-sectional approach (looking at several different areas at the same time). This sort of analysis was right in Lott's strike zone.

The first caveat that goes with any study of this sort is that correlation does not imply causality. Even if Lott were to show that in all the test states, crime rates decreased significantly in the wake of new, more lenient gun laws, it does not follow that the new laws caused the decrease in crime rates. Lott understood that many other variables could contribute to the changes he observed in the crime rate. For that reason, his analysis controlled for other variables, such as population, population density, national trends in crime rates, income levels, underlying crime rates, and racial composition. Even subtler in a study like this is the so-called endogeneity effect. Suppose more lenient gun laws are put into effect at the time that crime rates are already decreasing. Do the new laws account for the decrease in the crime rate or were the more lenient laws a result of a decreasing crime rate?

As critics noted, "Lott recognizes the potential problems with his crime-trend analysis."[27] Lott understood these difficulties and believed he accounted for them. His results showed significant decreases in many crime categories in the wake of more lenient gun laws. For example, according to his analysis, over all states in the study, the adoption of a more lenient gun law resulted in decreases of 10.1 percent in violent crime, 8.6 percent in murder, 6.0 percent in rape, and 10.9 percent in aggravated assault.[28] Similar results were found within individual states. Montana showed a 10 percent decrease in violent crime and rape after adopting a more lenient gun law.[29] Lott's thesis seemed to get additional support when he compared counties with a new lenient gun law to neighboring counties with a stricter law. In these cases, he saw the crime rate decrease in the county with the lenient law and increase in the neighboring counties. This displacement effect was allegedly due to criminals avoiding the more heavily armed county in favor of the less-armed county.

One of the more concerted attacks on Lott's work came from two law professors, Ian Ayres at Yale and John Donohue at Stanford. Their comprehensive response to Lott's work came in the paper "Shooting Down the 'More

Guns Less Crime' Hypothesis."[30] They began on a conciliatory note, saying that Lott's "remarkable paper . . . amassing a powerful statistical argument . . . has triggered an unusually large set of academic responses, with talented scholars lining up on both sides of the debate."[31] Ayres and Donohue used more extensive data sets, different statistical models, and various sets of control variables but were unable to reproduce Lott's results. In some cases, they observed the opposite of Lott's results: their models showed crime rates increasing after the passage of more lenient gun laws. They claimed that Lott's results "should be thought of as statistical artifacts"—occurrences that could be explained by chance.[32] In the end, Ayres and Donohue summarized their "extended odyssey" down the crime-guns tunnel:

> There remains no robust, credible statistical evidence that the adoption of [more lenient] shall-issue laws will generally lower crime, and indeed the best, albeit admittedly imperfect, statistical evidence presented thus far points in the opposite direction: that the adoption of shall-issue laws will generally increase crime.[33]

And then, more equivocally:

> While the best evidence suggests that shall-issue laws generally tend to increase crime, there is still too much uncertainty to make strong claims about their effects.[34]

Ayres and Donohue's analysis elicited counterpunches from Lott's supporters. To this day, the debate continues in various venues with no decisive consensus. In 2014, Donohue and two colleagues extended previous analyses by including thirty years of data and using more refined statistical methods.[35] Donohue noted that different statistical protocols can yield different results; nevertheless, "the totality of the evidence based on educated judgments about the best statistical models suggests that right-to-carry laws are associated with substantially higher rates"[36] of violent crimes. That is likely not the final word.

A refreshingly different approach to DGUs was offered in a recent report called *Tough Targets*.[37] In this study, gun historian Clayton Cramer and gun rights advocate David Burnett avoid the temptation to estimate DGUs; rather, they focus on the details of individual DGUs. Using a sample of nearly five thousand DGU incidents culled from news stories between 2003 and 2011, they compiled an anthology of true-crime stories. Then they created a taxonomy of DGUs with a long list of categories. Among the many revealing observations were that 488 DGUs in the sample involved home burglaries and 1227 involved home invasions (incidents in which an intruder entered a house knowing that it might be occupied, possibly for reasons other than burglary). In the study, 34 DGUs involved pizza deliveries, 25 involved rape, and 65 involved carjackings. In 154 incidents, the defender was a woman; in 21 incidents, the defender was a minor; and in 201 incidents, someone over sixty-five years of age was behind the gun.

One fear in arming citizens for self-defense is that a defender who is inexperienced with guns may be easily disarmed. The Cramer-Burnett study shows that in 11 incidents, the attacker disarmed the defender, while in 227 incidents—20 times more often—the defender disarmed the attacker. And are DGUs always successful in averting a crime? The study shows that in 36 cases, the defender was killed and in 210 cases the defender was wounded. Ironically, for all the analysis the authors did, the report has no estimate of the number of successful DGUs. That is, in what percentage of the incidents was the intended crime prevented because of the presence of a gun? The incidents cited in the report suggest that a majority of the DGUs were successful in this sense.

International Comparisons

It is evident that gathering accurate data on US crime rates, gun ownership, and defensive gun use is formidable. It follows that comparing US crime or gun data with analogous data from other countries—as scholars often do—is even more perilous. International studies unavoidably require apples-to-oranges comparisons, and we know how difficult it is to count the apples in America alone.

Difficulties begin because the definitions of crime categories—such as violent crime, murder, and homicide—vary from one country to another. Furthermore, the agencies responsible for collecting crime and gun data vary across countries; perhaps it is law enforcement in one country and public-heath agencies in another. Crime-reporting protocols vary and different countries have different gun laws, judicial systems, and arrest and conviction rates. And then there are outright improprieties. A 2014 report by Her Majesty's Inspectorate of Constabulary documented a 19-percent national rate of underreporting of crimes (often violent and sexual offenses) in England and Wales.[38] Such "no-criming" effects certainly skew international comparisons.

Meaningful international comparisons must somehow account for immense differences in culture, economic development, politics, and legal systems. Travel the world and you can find just about any combination of homicide and suicide rates, with and without guns. For example, roughly two-thirds of the gun deaths in the United States are suicides, whereas in Brazil and Mexico, where the overall gun death rate is even higher than in the United States, gun suicides are negligible. However, Japan and Germany have relatively few gun deaths of any kind, but they have high non–gun suicide rates. The explanations for such differences are deeply rooted and defy simple numerical comparisons. Therefore, using policies that work in other countries to justify a position in the American gun debate is problematic at best.

Finally, there is another fact that might explain why America looks like an outlier when it comes to guns and crime, particularly among developed countries: with a few exceptions (Mexico, Haiti, Guatemala), no other country has a Second Amendment. Public-policy scholars Philip Cook and Kristin Goss sum up the situation concisely:

> The U.S. system starts with the premise that citizens should be allowed to own guns unless there is a compelling reason to bar them from doing so, while other nations begin with the opposite premise—severely restrict or ban ownership unless there is a good reason to allow it.[39]

A recent development in the campaign to collect more complete and accurate gun violence data is the online Gun Violence Archive.[40] Created in 2013 as a nonprofit, nonadvocacy group, GVA monitors 1,200 "media sources, aggregates, police blotters, and police media outlets" daily to gather data on incidents of gun violence, gun crime, DGUs, and illegal or stolen weapons. The site keeps a real-time, continually updated tally of gun violence incidents (about 50,000 in 2015), gun fatalities (about 12,800), gun injuries (about 26,000), mass shootings (about 320), and DGUs (surprisingly, only 1,200 incidents reported and verified in 2015). The stated intent of the site, to provide "information [that] will inform and assist those engaged in discussions and activities concerning gun violence, including analysis of proposed regulations or legislation relating to gun safety usage," is virtuous and nonpartisan. It can only elevate our understanding of gun violence.

|

We need data to make personal decisions, to formulate public policies, and to pass laws. If those decisions are to be sound, if those policies are to be realistic, and if those laws are to be effective, then the data must be reliable. This chapter is a cautionary tale about overreliance on data and the methods used to analyze them. In the spirit of any scientific endeavor, we can hope that in the future, better data and more refined methods will lead to more conclusive results. However, for the moment, when all the data collection and analysis are said and done, few of us are any wiser about the relationships among crime, gun laws, and gun ownership.

In 2005 the Committee to Improve Research Information and Data on Firearms released its report *Firearms and Violence* through the prestigious National Academies Press. The committee consisted of eminent and unbiased scholars in criminology, law, and gun policy. Let's leave the number wars with the following admonitions from that report:

> The major scientific obstacle for advancing the body of research and further developing credible empirical research to inform policy on firearms is the lack of reliable and valid data.[41]

And even more telling:

> No authoritative source of information exists to provide representative, accurate, complete, timely, and detailed data on the incidence and characteristics of firearm-related violence in the United States.[42]

4 | TWENTY-SEVEN WORDS

[Rights] not mentioned are surrendered.

—*Federal Farmer* XVI

AMONG THE THINGS that have not changed in two hundred years are unpaid war debts and neglected veterans' benefits. The Revolutionary War left the new nation with a crushing debt and a devastated economy.[1] Because the national government under the Articles of Confederation had no taxing authority, the states were forced to raise taxes or impose new taxes. The irony did not escape some Americans: less than a decade after escaping the ruinous taxation of the British, their own state governments were now using the same tactics. To make matters worse, many of the farmers and laborers hit hardest by the taxes were war veterans who were struggling because their impoverished government could not pay promised benefits. Plough Jogger, a western Massachusetts farmer, summarized his plight and those of others:

> I have been greatly abused, have been obliged to do more than my part in the war; been loaded with class rates, town rates, province rates, Continental rates and all rates . . . been pulled and hauled by sheriffs, constables and collectors, and had my cattle sold for less than they were worth. . . . The great men are going to get all we have and I think it is time for us to rise and put a stop to it.[2]

The situation worsened in Massachusetts in the summer of 1786 when the government seized farmers' property, crops, and livestock. Farmers were hauled into debtor court and threatened with imprisonment. In response, they converged on local courthouses to demand that foreclosures cease until the Massachusetts legislature could hear their grievances. In one such demonstration, a former captain in the Continental army named Luke Day, who had also spent time in debtor prison, appeared at the Springfield court-house with a fife-and-drum corps backed by fifteen hundred armed farmers. When the sheriff called the militia to suppress the crowd, he soon realized that most of the militia was in the protesting crowd.

Similar scenes took place that summer in other states as well. The pro-testors were called Regulators and their goal was to regulate government excesses in their own state capitols. They were simply fighting for the same rights and representation that compelled the patriots to rise against British rule only a few years earlier. The Regulators were self-armed and organized much like a militia. In fact, many Regulators also belonged to the local mili-tia, which led to conflicting allegiances. This paradoxical situation raised the question: Who controls the militia?

Daniel Shays was a Revolutionary War veteran who had fought in the Battles of Lexington, Bunker Hill, and Saratoga. After being wounded, he resigned from the militia in 1780 with no pay or benefits and returned to a life of poverty in western Massachusetts. As one of many farmers ordered to court for unpaid debts, Shays joined the growing campaign to block court bankruptcy proceedings. On September 26, 1786, he organized eight hundred men for a march on the Springfield courthouse. The march was successful in that the court temporarily suspended hearings; but the reprieve was short-lived. Governor James Bowdoin, who had little sympathy for the embattled farmers, called on the legislature to pass a new law, called the Riot Act, allow-ing authorities to ban gatherings of more than twelve people.[3] As local sheriffs enforced the Riot Act, skirmishes and demonstrations continued throughout the fall of 1786 and into the winter.

The breaking point came in January 1787 when the government sent a large militia, financed by wealthy Boston businessmen, to Springfield to shackle Shays's rebels. In anticipation of the assault by government troops, Shays organized a daring raid on the Springfield Armory.[4] When a second rebel battalion failed to arrive to assist Shays's troops, the government forces dispersed the rebels and killed four Regulators. Shays fled to Vermont where he stayed until he was pardoned and allowed to return to Massachusetts. Many other arrested Regulators received pardons in exchange for a new oath of allegiance. In the end, two rebels were convicted of treason and hanged.[5]

The farmers' protests and demonstrations, which came to be known as Shays' Rebellion, effectively ended after the armory conflict.

While Shays' Rebellion appeared to be a defeat for the protesting farmers, it received national attention and the fallout was significant. Combined with similar demonstrations in other states, it led to questions about the stability of the nation under the Articles of Confederation. Perhaps most important, the unrest once again cast light on the role of the militia. Was the militia a local organization designed as a check on strong central governments or was it a tool of the government to be used to prevent insurrections? This question would confound the nation's leaders later the same year.

The Constitutional Convention

When modern gun control advocates and gun rights activists promote their causes, both sides often use similar historical arguments. They claim that their position is aligned with either the intent of the founding fathers or the original public meaning of the Constitution (often called originalism). It is difficult to lean heavily on these interpretations without understanding the turbulent process that led to the ratification of the US Constitution. Just as important is the equally tumultuous ordeal—two years later—that produced the Bill of Rights and the Second Amendment.

The fifty-five delegates who attended the Constitutional Convention in Philadelphia in the summer of 1787 comprised a pantheon of political and intellectual luminaries. Among them were Alexander Hamilton representing New York, Benjamin Franklin and Governor Morris from Pennsylvania, Elbridge Gerry of Massachusetts, two Pinckneys brothers (Thomas and Charles) from South Carolina, and James Madison, George Mason, and George Washington from Virginia. Patrick Henry of Virginia did not attend because he "smelt a rat in Philadelphia, tending toward the monarchy," and Rhode Island boycotted the convention fearing it had nothing to gain from a new constitution.[6] Thomas Jefferson corresponded with the delegates from Paris, where he was serving as Ambassador to France. The convention began with unanimity when George Washington was elected president of the convention, but that harmony did not last.

Although the convention took place in closed sessions in Independence Hall, the notes of thirty-six-year-old James Madison provide a remarkably detailed account of the proceedings.[7] A modern scholar describes Madison's role in the convention unequivocally:

> James Madison outdistanced all the other delegates by his initial preparation and by his sustained and ubiquitous efforts in the Convention. He came to the Convention after an intensive scholarly preparation.[8]

A quorum of delegates from seven states gathered on May 25 in the smothering Philadelphia heat. After proposing and amending various governance plans for three weeks, the delegates coalesced around two general proposals. Drafted by James Madison and favored by the large states, the Virginia Plan recognized the deficiencies of the Articles of Confederation, particularly the weak central government it mandated. The plan proposed radical changes to the articles, including a national government with two legislative houses, an executive branch, and a judicial branch. Furthermore, it proposed drastic limitations on the states' power to make laws and elect representatives. (Believing that the Virginia Plan did not go far enough in empowering the central government, Alexander Hamilton even proposed a president elected for life—an idea that was rejected.)

Some delegates, primarily from the smaller states, sought a less radical overhaul: a revision of the Articles of Confederation but not a new Constitution. They proposed the New Jersey Plan, which gave greater power to state governments and sought ways for the smaller states to have equal representation in the national government.

The stalemate between the Virginia and New Jersey Plans was broken near the end of June. Noting that the nation needed aspects of both plans, Connecticut delegate Oliver Ellsworth brokered the Connecticut Compromise, a plan in which one legislative house would have equal representation and the other house would have proportional representation. The delegates approved the Connecticut Compromise (over Madison's opposition) and appointed a committee under Massachusetts delegate Elbridge Gerry to write the first draft of the Constitution.

On August 6, the writing committee finished its work and released the first draft of the Constitution to the convention. The delegates debated and amended the draft for the next six weeks, negotiating compromises on thorny issues such as slave trade and the election of the president. Quite remarkably, throughout the entire convention, there was virtually no discussion of a declaration of individual rights, a feature of many of the state constitutions. On September 12, with the end in sight and the delegates packing to leave town, delegates George Mason and Elbridge Gerry moved that a bill of rights be included in the Constitution.

Delegates argued furiously for several days over the wisdom of including a bill of rights. Roger Sherman of Connecticut (who, according to Thomas Jefferson, "never said a foolish thing in his life")[9] claimed that the states' declarations of rights protected individual rights and that a national version was unnecessary: "Congress could be trusted."[10] Mason countered that without a declaration of rights, the federal government could "constitute new crimes, and inflict unusual and severe punishment, . . . so that the state legislatures have no security for the powers now presumed to remain to them; or the people for their rights."[11] Mason also promised that a bill of rights could be prepared "in a few hours."

Like exhausted marathon runners asked to run an extra five miles beyond the finish line, the delegates dutifully worked for several more days before defeating the motion for a bill of rights. On September 17, thirty-nine of the forty-two delegates still in town signed the Constitution.[12] In closing remarks, the elder statesman of the convention, Benjamin Franklin, wisely observed:

> I confess that there are several parts of this constitution which I do not at present approve, but I am not sure I shall never approve them: For having lived long, I have experienced many instances of being obliged by better information, or fuller consideration, to change opinions even on important subjects, which I once thought right, but found to be otherwise. It is therefore that the older I grow, the more apt I am to doubt my own judgment, and to pay more respect to the judgment of others.[13]

The Constitutional Convention featured enormous personalities, grandiloquent speeches, feisty debates, suspense, intrigue, and decisive moments in American history. But how did it influence the future Second Amendment? Woven throughout the convention were deliberations about the role of the militia, with proposals and arguments on all sides. The Revolutionary War had exposed the limitations of the militias in defending against a foreign power, which led some delegates to argue for stronger central control of the militias. Recent uprisings, such as Shays' Rebellion, had also displayed the contradictions of using local militia to control domestic insurrections. The uncertainty about militias was further elevated by fears of government tyranny, which pervaded the convention and led some delegates to propose a constitutional ban on standing armies. The resolution of these various perspectives was, not surprisingly, a carefully balanced compromise that divided the control of the militia between the states and the national government.

The draft of the Constitution written by Gerry's committee "made the militia a creature of both the states and the new national government."[14] The committee gave Congress the following powers (as article I, section 8 reads today):

> To raise and support Armies . . .
> To provide for calling forth the Militia to execute the Laws of the Union, suppress Insurrections and repel Invasions . . .
> To provide for organizing, arming, and disciplining, the Militia, and for governing such Part of them as may be employed in the Service of the United States, *reserving to the States respectively, the Appointment of the Officers, and the authority of training the Militia according to the discipline prescribed by Congress.* (Emphasis added.)[15]

In other words, without spelling out many critical details, the Constitution gave the national government the authority to summon, organize, arm, and discipline the militia, while the states would handle appointing officers and training the militia. Clearly, under this arrangement, control over militias was shifted heavily to the federal government and away from the states.

The new Constitution, approved without a bill of rights, contained no language about the right to keep and bear arms. And yet the issue was never far beneath the surface. Delegates such as George Mason expressed the common fear that without a declaration of rights, the federal or state governments could disarm individuals and usurp their rights. The opposing argument claimed that a declaration of rights was unnecessary; as long as the populace was armed, individual rights were secure. Noah Webster wrote in support of the Constitution:

Before a standing army can rule, the people must be disarmed; as they are in almost every kingdom of Europe. The supreme power in America cannot enforce unjust laws by the sword; because the whole body of the people are armed, and constitute a force superior to any band of regular troops.[16]

The action now moved to the states, where committees in each state scrutinized the new Constitution and voted on ratification. Those committees revisited many of the same issues that tormented the delegates in Philadelphia—chief among them, the absence of a declaration of rights, specifically the right to keep and bear arms.

Ratification

The yearlong, thirteen-act ratification drama played out differently in each state. Reactions to the new Constitution quickly fell into two camps. The name *Federalist* was attached to those people who supported the new Constitution with its strong national government and without a bill of rights—the vestiges of the Virginia Plan. The (unfortunate) name *Antifederalist* described those who distrusted a strong central government, favored greater states' rights, and opposed the draft Constitution—reflecting the New Jersey Plan. The most common Antifederalist criticism was the missing bill of rights.

The ratification debate was amplified in a long-lasting storm of newspaper opinions, pamphlets, and published letters. By far the most widely distributed and powerful writings in the debate were the *Federalist Papers*. Written by Alexander Hamilton, James Madison, and John Jay, this series of eighty-five essays appeared in newspapers between October 1787 and August 1788.[17] The essays eloquently spelled out the strengths of the new Constitution and refuted Antifederalist arguments against ratification.

One of the most persuasive Antifederalist responses to the *Federalist Papers* was a set of eighteen articles called the *Federal Farmer*. The articles, by unknown author(s), appeared in newspapers and pamphlets in 1787 and 1788.[18] The *Federal Farmer* carefully explored the interplay between federal powers and individual rights, noting that while the Constitution specified the powers of the federal government, "individual rights are numerous, and not easy to be enumerated in a bill of rights." However, the articles argued that it is important to attempt an enumeration of rights; otherwise, rights "not mentioned are surrendered."[19] The *Federal Farmer* elaborated many of the rights that ultimately appeared in the future Bill of Rights, observing that "to preserve liberty, it is essential that the whole body of the people always possess arms, and be taught alike, especially when young, how to use them."[20]

James Madison opposed enumerating rights with the claim that the powers delegated to the federal government were limited and could not threaten the "lives, liberties, and properties of the people."[21] Madison famously deflected fears of a standing army trampling the rights of citizens:

> [To a standing army] would be opposed a militia amounting to near half a million of citizens with arms in their hands, officered by men chosen from among themselves, fighting for their common liberties, and united and conducted by governments possessing their affections and confidence. It may well be doubted, whether a militia thus circumstanced could ever be conquered by such a proportion of regular troops.[22]

Eventually, each state reached a decision in its own unique and often unexpected way.[23] On December 7, 1787, Delaware became the first state to ratify the Constitution, and it did so with little dispute. Pennsylvania was next, but only after protracted deliberations among prominent spokesmen on both sides. In the end, the Federalists prevailed, and the Constitution was ratified by Pennsylvania on December 11. However, within a week, the Antifederalists in Pennsylvania published their *Dissent of the Minority*, which amounted to a draft of a bill of rights. Among the fourteen enumerated rights was the provision:

> The people have a right to bear arms for the defence of themselves and their own state, or the United States, or for the purpose of killing game; and no law shall be passed for disarming the people or any of them, unless for crimes committed, or real danger of public injury from individuals; and as standing armies in the time of peace are dangerous to liberty, they ought not to be kept up: and that the military shall be kept under strict subordination to and be governed by the civil powers.

Coming so early in the overall ratification game, the *Dissent of the Minority* was widely read, and it undoubtedly influenced the deliberations in the other states.

New Jersey had no bill of rights in its own constitution and ratified the Constitution with no bill of rights. Similarly, Georgia and Connecticut voted for ratification in early January 1788 without demanding a bill of rights. Next was Massachusetts, where the need for a bill of rights was disputed vigorously for five months. Antifederalists John Hancock and Sam Adams proposed a specific declaration of individual rights for the Constitution, which included the right to keep arms. Nevertheless, the Federalists prevailed and Massachusetts voted for ratification on February 6.

In Maryland, the Federalists, knowing they had a majority, refused to debate the opposition. Ratification without a bill of rights followed on April 26. The Antifederalists were well-represented in South Carolina but failed to make their case, leading to another vote for ratification.

With eight of nine required states voting for ratification, the fate of the Constitution was still uncertain. None of the remaining states was an assured vote for ratification. On June 21, New Hampshire became the ninth state to vote for ratification, apparently making the Constitution official. However, the vote came with a condition: the new Constitution would not be effective in New Hampshire without a bill of rights. In fact, the New Hampshire convention, with a majority of Antifederalists, proposed a set of amendments, one of which was that "Congress shall never disarm any citizen."

The high-stakes debates in the remaining four states were momentous—particularly in Virginia. The 168 delegates to the Virginia ratifying convention were heavyweights on both sides the bill of rights question. James Madison led the Federalist cause, making the familiar argument that a bill of rights could list only *some* rights and the rights not enumerated would be lost. Prominent among the Antifederalists were George Mason, who had refused to sign the Constitution, and the scintillating rhetorician Patrick Henry, who spoke passionately about the need for a bill of rights and the fear of "people losing their liberty by their own carelessness and the ambition of a few."[24] George Mason observed that with the new Constitution:

Under various pretences, Congress may neglect to provide for arming and disciplining the militia; and the state governments cannot do it, for Congress has an exclusive right to arm them.[25]

Patrick Henry dramatically expressed his lack of trust in Congress, claiming:

The great object is, that every man be armed. . . . But we have learned, by experience, that, necessary as it is to have arms, and though our Assembly has, by a succession of laws for many years, endeavored to have the militia completely armed, it is still far from being the case. When this power is given up to Congress without limitation or bounds, how will your militia be armed? You trust to chance; for sure I am that that nation which shall trust its liberties in other hands cannot long exist.[26]

According to one modern scholar, the matter of slavery also entered the debate in Virginia and other southern states. At that time, local white militias were used to suppress slave insurrections. A strong federal government with the power to disarm local militias—so the theory went—could undermine the entire system of slave control. For this reason, the southern states were willing to support a bill of rights that protected private gun ownership.[27]

The Virginia convention met for all but three days between June 2 and June 27 in 1788. The records reflect an intense, prolonged, painstakingly detailed debate that was cordial except when it was combative. Delegate George Nicholas opened the penultimate session of June 25 declaring, perhaps in exhaustion, "I do not mean to enter into any further debate. The friends of the Constitution wish to take up no more time, the matter being now fully discussed."[28] By the end of the day, the delegates voted eighty-nine to seventy-nine to ratify the Constitution, but only with the condition that the new Congress approve certain amendments. Within two days, a committee of the delegates drafted a declaration of twenty rights to be included as amendments to the Constitution. Among the rights, taken largely from the 1776 Virginia Declaration of Rights, was:

17th. That the people have a right to keep and bear arms; that a well-regulated militia, composed of the body of the people trained to arms, is the proper, natural, and safe defence of a free state; that standing armies, in time of peace, are dangerous to liberty, and therefore ought to be avoided, as far as the circumstances and protection of the community will admit; and that, in all cases, the military should be under strict subordination to, and governed by, the civil power.[29]

Virginia's conditional endorsement of the Constitution, with its demand that Congress approve a bill of rights, was a turning point in the ratification process. With that vote, the Constitution became operative and support for a bill of rights gathered strength. On July 26, 1788, New York also ratified the Constitution with the condition that a bill of rights be included. North Carolina and Rhode Island did not ratify the Constitution until the following year.

A Bill of Rights

The First United States Congress met from March 4, 1789, to March 3, 1791, in New York (first session) and then in Philadelphia (second session). By the end of the first session, the twenty-six Senate seats had been filled with a Federalist majority.[30] The House of Representatives had sixty-four seats, also with a Federalist majority. The inauguration of President George Washington took place at Federal Hall in New York City on April 30, 1789. He gave the first State of the Union address on January 8, 1790.

Crafting a bill of rights was among the first tasks of the young Congress. During the ratification process, James Madison had been a vocal Federalist and opposed a bill of rights. In a remarkable and calculated reversal, he became an advocate of a bill of rights, realizing that the authority of the new Constitution depended in part on a declaration of individual rights. In the months leading up to the First Congress, the states submitted an estimated four hundred draft amendments to the Constitution. As a newly elected representative and the author of Virginia's proposed amendments, Madison took on the job of consolidating the amendments and shepherding them through Congress. He presented his proposed bill of rights to the House of Representatives on June 8, 1789.

It is worth following the transformations of the arms amendment as it worked its way through the Congress. Madison's original text of that amendment read:

> The right of the people to keep and bear arms shall not be infringed; a well armed and well regulated militia being the best security of a free country: but no person religiously scrupulous of bearing arms shall be compelled to render military service in person.[31]

Today, much is made of this draft of the amendment in which the rights clause not only appears first but is clearly separated from the militia clause. Modern gun rights advocates claim that this ordering places primacy on the individual possession of guns and secondary emphasis on their use in a militia. Gun control advocates reason that this draft never survived and the next draft, in which the clauses are reversed, gives priority to the militias.

Once in the crucible of the House, the amendments were debated, some more furiously than others. Some Federalists viewed the exercise of forging a bill of rights with disdain; those who followed Madison's conciliatory lead understood the necessity of reaching agreement with the Antifederalists. A commentary on the proposed amendments by Pennsylvania Federalist Tench Coxe was widely read. About the arms amendment he observed:

> As civil rulers, not having their duty to the people duly before them, may attempt to tyrannize, and as the military forces which must be occasionally raised to defend our country, might pervert their power to the injury of their fellow-citizens, the people are confirmed by the next article in their right to keep and bear their private arms.[32]

Such a statement is irresistible grist for modern commentators. Author Michael Waldman, sympathetic to a collective interpretation, noted that Madison scarcely responded to Coxe's commentary and concluded that the passage merely "sought to deflect oppression."[33] Historian Stephen Halbrook, an individual-rights champion, concluded that the proposed amendment, via Coxe's commentary, "was designed to guarantee the right of the people to have 'their private arms' in order to prevent tyranny and to overpower an abusive standing army."[34]

Madison's draft bill of rights went to a House select committee in July 1790, where it spent one week. The changes in the future Second Amendment were significant; the next revision read:

> A well regulated militia, composed of the body of the people, being the best security of a free state, the right of the people to keep and bear arms shall not be infringed; but no person religiously scrupulous shall be compelled to bear arms.[35]

In this version, the so-called declaratory clause, stating that a well-regulated militia is the best security for a free state, introduces the amendment as in today's version. Placing this clause at the beginning of the amendment gave the militia more prominence but arguably created confusion for future generations of constitutional exegetists.

The draft bill of rights then returned to the full House for another week of debate in August. The records of this debate are not complete because the House stenographer was "incompetent, often inebriated."[36] Several issues emerged in the full House debate. First, Madison's plan to scatter the amendments throughout the Constitution, placing them in the most relevant sections, was overruled. The motion to put the amendments at the end of the Constitution, where they appear today, passed.

Another question contested in the House was whether the Bill of Rights protected its enumerated rights only from action by Congress or whether it also limited the powers of the states. The consensus that emerged during these discussions was that the enumerated rights gave protection only from laws passed by Congress but provided no protection from state actions. This vital question would persist and affect constitutional law for another two centuries.

The House approved the draft bill of rights and in the process reduced the number of rights to seventeen. From the House, the draft went to the Senate, where the secret deliberations were not recorded. The Senate reduced the number of rights to twelve and it made or considered three changes to the fourth amendment on the list, which would eventually become the Second Amendment. First, because of fears that the "religiously scrupulous" exemption might be used dishonestly to avoid military service, the Senate removed the provision. Second, the House version of the amendment suggested that a militia "being the best security to a free state" could imply that a standing army was the second best security to a free state. Therefore, the words "necessary to the security" replaced "the best security." Finally, and significantly for today's gun debates, the Senate considered inserting the words "for the common defence" or "for their common good" after "bear arms." These phrases were eventually rejected. Had either one of them survived, it would have resulted—subject to interpretation—in a more restrictive Second Amendment.

With these changes, the Senate approved the amendment in essentially its present-day form:

> A well regulated militia being necessary to the security of a free state, the right of the people to keep and bear arms, shall not be infringed.[37]

The House debated and approved the Senate's version of the amendments, and on September 25, 1789, the twelve amendments were given final approval by both houses and released to the states for ratification. The last change to the future Second Amendment was the addition of a comma after the word "militia." The result was the modern Second Amendment:

> A well regulated militia, being necessary to the security of a free state, the right of the people to keep and bear arms, shall not be infringed.[38]

The state debates of the proposed amendments lasted more than two years but produced no change in the language of the arms amendment. The states continued to haggle over the balance between state power and federal power. In their quest for greater power and autonomy in the states, the Antifederalists believed the amendments were insufficient and did not provide adequate protection from an overreaching federal government. Nevertheless, in November 1789, New Jersey became the first state to ratify the amendments. Shortly after, North Carolina became the twelfth state to ratify the Constitution and the third state to ratify the amendments. By June 1790, Rhode Island became the thirteenth state to ratify the Constitution and the ninth state to ratify the amendments.

According to the Constitution, three-quarters of the states must ratify amendments in order to make them "valid." So the arithmetic changed when, in early 1791, Vermont ratified the Constitution and became the fourteenth state of the Union, meaning that the amendments required ratification by at least eleven (rather than ten) states. That threshold was reached on December 15, 1791, when Virginia became the eleventh state to ratify the amendments.[39] During the state ratification process, the first two of the twelve amendments (dealing with apportionment and compensation of members of Congress) were rejected. The effect was that the remaining ten amendments moved up two positions on the list and became the Bill of Rights (with capital letters). The amendment ensuring the right to keep and bear arms became the Second Amendment.

By the end of 1791, the Bill of Rights was complete, burnished by debate, negotiation, and compromise. The language was settled and has not changed to the present day. The next two centuries would be spent—particularly for the Second Amendment—trying to understand exactly what the language meant.

5 | GUNS IN AMERICAN LIVES

I own a weapon because I really enjoy going to the range and shooting.
I'm a Buddhist: I don't believe in violence and I don't believe in using
a weapon for violence.

—SEAN, Florida[1]

GUNS BECOME ENMESHED in lives and they divert lives, occasionally in unbidden ways. For some, they are a means for recreation and competition. They call others to unexpected paths of politics or advocacy. Some people buy and sell guns legally as a profession. And some make a career of teaching their firearm skills and experience to others. The portraits in this chapter illustrate the remarkable extent to which guns have become a part of ordinary American lives.

|

You are not likely to see the names Nora Martin, Harlan Campbell, or Stu Welton in the headlines of any sports page, and they will not be featured on ESPN's *SportsCenter*. But the millions of Americans who play their game recognize them as champions and Hall of Famers. That game is perhaps the oldest organized sport in the country, officially founded in 1831 at the Sportsmen's Club in Cincinnati. The sport has been an Olympic event since 1900. Its national championship—a two-week event that attracts over six thousand competitors from around the world—is called the Grand American and has been held every year since 1900.

The "trap" in trapshooting once referred to the cage that held live pigeons before they were released as targets for sportsmen wielding 12-gauge shotguns. In the 1860s, glass balls stuffed with feathers mercifully replaced live pigeons as targets. Two decades later, the targets—still called traps—became clay discs, about four inches in diameter, launched skyward by a spring-loaded catapult. In the early 1900s, there were eight thousand trap clubs in America. Ever since Annie Oakley set numerous trapshooting records in the early 1900s, women have distinguished themselves in the sport. From its inception, the sport has welcomed shooters of all ages, from all corners of society.[2]

While the trap machines, the weapons, and the rules have been refined over the years, the sport is essentially unchanged after a century. Marksmen stand between eighteen and twenty-seven yards behind the traphouse (the launchpad) and have fractions of a second to aim and fire at a target that is released at various angles at roughly fifty miles per hour. One variation of the basic event is the double trap, in which two clay pigeons are launched simultaneously, the goal being to shatter both targets before they hit the ground.

Trapshooting may not make headlines today, but in 1883 it had the country in its thrall, like a pre-TV forerunner of *Sunday Night Football*. For several weeks of that year, the two greatest shooters in the world dueled each other on the trap field. William Frank "Doc" Carver moved west from Illinois as a young man, where he sharpened his skills as a ferocious buffalo hunter and a dazzling marksman. At six feet four and 265 pounds, he could "put a bullet through a silver quarter while the coin is flying through the air."[3] Photographs of Carver, in a fringed jacket with long hair flowing from a wide-brimmed hat, show a resemblance to Buffalo Bill Cody. In fact, later in life, Carver would join Cody's Wild West show. Carver wanted the title of best marksman in the world, which meant toppling the champion trapshooter of the day, General Adam Henry Bogardus. (Carver was never a doctor and Bogardus was never a general.) Bogardus had no reason to risk his reputation on a challenge from an unknown sharpshooter, so for six years, he evaded Carver's challenges—while Carver toured Europe earning fame and prize money. Eventually, Bogardus could no longer ignore the challenges, and he agreed to a live-pigeon shoot in Louisville, Kentucky, on February 22, 1883. The suspense leading up to the long-overdue showdown swept the country. The *New York Times* wrote:

> Both of the contestants are now in [Louisville]. The expressed jealousy between the two men, amounting to open dislike, will make the match very spirited, as each is determined to win. Sporting men from all over the country are arriving tonight and a large attendance is insured.[4]

At stake was $500, the gate money, and, most important of all, the title. One thousand people watched in person as Carver and Bogardus each shot at one hundred live pigeons. Carver won the match 83–82, but so close was the victory that Bogardus challenged Carver to additional matches. In two shoots in Chicago, one with live pigeons and one with clay pigeons, Carver prevailed again. Now it was Bogardus issuing the challenges and Carver eagerly accepting them.

At that time, George Ligowsky was a leading maker of clay pigeons and had a lot to gain if the entire shooting world decided to use clay, rather than live, pigeons. To promote his product, he put up $7,500 in prize money—$300 for each of twenty-five matches between Carver and Bogardus—plus a $100 bonus every time either shooter scored at least 0.82 (82 hits out of 100). Both men quickly accepted the offer and agreed to make it winner-take-all. For the next two months, Carver and Bogardus crisscrossed the country with large crowds in their wake, from St. Louis and Kansas City to Pittsburgh and Providence. In the end, Carver won nineteen of twenty-five matches, with three ties, had an overall average of 0.93, and won $9,800 (over $200,000 in modern dollars). Bogardus allegedly never performed up to his usual standards, finished with an overall average of 0.87, and conceded his title.

Never again, after 1883, did trapshooting have such an electrifying grip on the country. But for those who follow the sport, it has had its share of thrilling shoot offs and stunning records. In the 1987 Eastern Zone Singles Championship in Maryland, four shooters were tied after hitting two hundred straight targets. The competition went into sudden death and the next five twenty-five-shot rounds resulted in perfection from all four shooters. The competition resumed the next day when, after another 150 shots, Charles Doll was eliminated when he missed a single target. Then Darrell Dowler missed a single target during the next twenty-five-shot round. Two men, Frank Little and Kay Ohye, were still standing. Neither man missed the next two hundred targets, and the competition continued into territory no one had witnessed before. It was 10:30 at night on the second day of the competition when Ohye missed one of the next twenty-five targets, while Little hit them all. Counting all shots over the entire championship, Little had finally won by a score of 725–724.

The Little-Ohye marathon broke all records until the 2008 Clay Target

Championships, in which Foster Bartholow and Leo Harrison battled in the longest shoot off in history. After nine hundred shots, they both had perfect scores and they were declared co-champions.

A high distinction in trapshooting is a 100 straight: hitting one hundred consecutive targets—something like bowling a perfect game. Al Bandle got the first 100 straight in 1887 with live birds (in a match against Bogardus). Today, the feat is accomplished many times each year, not only in single shot but in doubles and from the outermost 27-yard line. A higher distinction is the Grand Slam: in a single match, the shooter must have two hundred straight hits in a singles event, one hundred straight hits in a doubles event, and— like hitting three-pointers in basketball—one hundred straight hits from the 27-yard line. On the order of twenty Grand Slams occur in any given year.

For the nearly thirty thousand people who participate in Amateur Trap-shooting Association events, using a gun is far removed from Supreme Court decisions and gun rights demonstrations. It is a way to join a long and venerable sporting tradition, much as a polo player might feel the ancient roots of his sport. And in its ordinariness, the sport would hardly seem a part—and certainly not a cause—of the social rending associated with the use of guns.[5] Admittedly, trapshooting accounts for a small fraction of gun ownership. Nevertheless, it is one of hundreds of reasons that Americans own and use guns, that they are passionate about guns, find careers involving guns, devote their recreational lives to guns, or otherwise find meaning in guns.

Advocacy

"Tuesday, April 20, 1999, started out no differently than any other day."[6] Looking back many years later, that is how Tom Mauser recalled the day that changed many lives unpredictably and irreversibly. Until then, gun violence received relatively little attention and mass shootings were infrequent. However, the shootings at Columbine High School, in the suburbs of Denver, which took the life of Tom's son, attracted massive media attention and penetrated the American psyche. Columbine became a lasting image of gun violence in America and Tom was swept up in the vortex.

Ten days after the Columbine shootings, Tom was invited to speak at a rally on the steps of the Colorado state capitol to protest the NRA's annual meeting a few blocks away. While the organization had scaled back its long-planned meeting, anything more than a total cancellation appeared—to many—profoundly heartless. With little experience in activism or public speaking, Tom accepted the invitation and made an impassioned speech to the crowd of twelve thousand, saying, "I am here today because my son Daniel would expect me to be here today. If my son Daniel had not been one of the victims, he would be with me here today."[7]

After Tom's Denver speech, an unimagined path opened before him: an appearance on the *Today Show*, a visit with First Lady Hillary Clinton at the White House, and a balcony seat at the State of the Union address, where President Clinton said:

> Like all parents who lose their children, . . . Tom has borne unimaginable grief. Somehow Tom has found the strength to honor his son by transforming his grief into action. Earlier this month, he took a leave of absence from his job to fight for tougher gun safety laws. I pray that his courage and wisdom will move this Congress to make common-sense gun safety legislation the very next order of business.[8]

For someone who "never hunted or had an opportunity to handle a gun" in his youth, Tom's sudden plunge into the gun debate was unexpected. Nevertheless, he has become a trailblazer for many other people who turned to advocacy after their lives were dreadfully altered by guns: Gabby Giffords, who, with her husband, founded Americans for Responsible Solutions; Mark Barden, Nicole Hockley, Tim Makris, and James Belden of Sandy Hook Promise; and Shannon Watts of Moms Demand Action for Gun Sense in America, to name just a few.

Almost seventeen years had passed since Columbine when I met with Tom to talk, not about the past but about gun control—now and in the future. The picture he sketched of the gun control movement was of a meandering pilgrimage, consisting of individuals and organizations, all moving toward a few common goals, such as gun safety and reduction of gun violence. But like many pilgrimages, the participants are diverse, they are fired by different motivations, and they travel different paths with varying degrees of coordination. Tom's own group, Colorado Ceasefire, started out as a lobbying group; it now has an educational arm and a political action committee (PAC). The organization interacts with other local gun control groups, such as Colorado Coalition against Gun Violence and Colorado Faith Communities United to End Gun Violence. Occasionally, there is commerce with national groups such as Everytown for Gun Safety and the Brady Campaign. In practice, when goals, issues, and tactics align, there is cooperation among these groups; otherwise they go their own ways. Presumably, a similar situation exists in every state.

Tom's picture of the gun control movement is quite a contrast to the monolithic presence of the NRA and its ability to instantly mobilize some four million members. I asked if the apparently uncoordinated work of so many groups compromises the overall effectiveness of the gun control movement. Is there a central command center that unifies gun control groups and coordinates their efforts? Tom's answer was a quick, terse, "It doesn't exist." He continued, "You must have that organization and that database of members. We don't have it. The NRA does."[9]

I asked Tom to elaborate on the potency of the NRA. He observed that, at least in comparison to gun control supporters, NRA members tend to be one-issue people.

> In the case of the [gun rights] side, it's always a little bit easier to rally people when they feel like they are losing something. You're going to lose your guns, you're going to lose your rights, and they get fired up. You'd think telling people they were going to lose your life or your child's life would be enough to rally them. But unfortunately, it's not. It gets people to you for a while. But the more they see, they think I'm not sure I'm in imminent danger so I'm going to deal with this other issue. I'm going to raise my family. I'm going to go to church. I've got other things on my agenda, whereas the one-issue guys, I'm sorry, but a lot of them are very much in love with their weapons and it's a very personal issue, not just the weapon itself, but the whole idea of freedom. That's what they are selling. They are selling freedom and they are selling fear.

Gun control supporters can be passionate, but because they are often multi-issue people, that passion can be intermittent. For example, in 2000, Colorado successfully passed Amendment 22 to close the gun show loophole (with 70 percent support). Tom lamented:

One of the *greatest* things that happened in 2000 was passing Amendment 22. One of the *worst* things that happened in 2000 was passing Amendment 22. Because once we passed that, a lot of people said, yeah! Look what we did. What a great thing. Thank you very much. Let's move on to the next issue.

For this reason, Tom has always felt that the gun rights side has an advantage. The gun control side has a harder job: "My side really has to work a lot more on convincing people in the middle."

I imagined that when Tom began his gun control advocacy, he had an idealistic zeal that energized him for public appearance, debates, and organizing. However, his many years in the gun trenches have replaced some of that idealism with a tempered realism. He knows that with every shift of political winds comes the possibility that new laws will be passed or old laws will be repealed. The year 2013 was a high-water mark for gun control in Colorado: the legislature passed laws for universal background checks and magazine limits, thanks in part to the efforts of people like Tom. However, he is circumspect:

> Let's face it. The 2013 laws were passed when you had the Democrats in control of all three branches. And likewise, if you see Republicans take over, you'll see a wiping out of those laws. Otherwise there's going to be a stalemate because that's what we've had ever since 2013. . . . It's become so partisan; it's hard to imagine going beyond that.

He is also realistic about his hopes. If he could pass one gun law in the state, what would it be? With little hesitation, he said:

> Licensing. As much as we talk about these other issues, I am now more convinced of the need for licensing. That raises the blood pressure of a number of people. It has worked in states that have done it. And in states like Missouri that had it and dropped it, they saw an increase in deaths.

Realistically, is a licensing law likely to pass in Colorado? "No. We are still largely a pro-gun state."

Finally, I asked what it might take to move the center of gravity of the gun debate one way or the other. What might end the standoff that exists now?

I'm sorry, it's going to take a tragedy of tremendous proportions that would make it change. If twenty first-graders' deaths don't change anything, I don't see things changing. All the action is at the state level. And it's going to be that same split again. Blue states say yes and red states say no. It's coming down to ideological lines. It's sad.

Pink Pistols

Many Americans reeled in revulsion and disbelief when twenty-one-year-old Matthew Shepard was heartlessly tortured and murdered outside of Laramie, Wyoming, in October 1998—the victim of an unspeakable anti-gay hate crime. A year later, the Matthew Shepard attack and other brutal homophobic assaults were on the mind of Jonathan Rauch as he wrote an article for Salon.com called "Pink Pistols." Currently a contributing editor to the *Atlantic* and *National Journal*, Rauch has earned his reputation as a prolific journalist and an everywhere-at-once activist. His Salon article remains one of the most influential pieces of his large portfolio. Lamenting the increase in hate crimes in the 1990s and the glacial progress of hate-crime legislation, Rauch issued a call to arms among gay people.

It is remarkable that the gay movement in America has never seriously considered a strategy that ought to be glaringly obvious. In those states [that issue concealed carry permits], homosexuals . . . should set up Pink Pistol task forces, sponsor shooting courses, and help homosexuals get licensed to carry.[10]

He presaged a now-common argument for carrying guns for self-defense: if it became widely known that gay people carry guns and know how to use them, it would likely lead to a decrease in homophobic attacks. In fact, not that many gay people would need to carry guns, as long as gay-bashers could not tell which ones did.

Rauch predicted that arming the gay community would not only save lives but change lives. Noting that "no other minority has been so consistently identified with contemptible weakness," he claimed that Pink Pistols "would do far more for the self-esteem of the next generation of gay men and women than any number of hate-crime laws."[11]

One person who heard Rauch's alarm was a Boston gay libertarian named Douglas Krick. He and three friends began meeting at a local firing range and soon formed a club, which became the Massachusetts chapter of—with Rauch's blessings—the Pink Pistols. The chapter had the mottos "Pick on someone your own caliber" and "Armed gays don't get bashed." It produced a website, landed a short article in *Newsweek* in September 2001, and that was enough to get the "snowball rolling downhill."[12] Within a year, ten local chapters had sprouted around the country.

Among the people who caught wind of the Pink Pistols was Krick's long-time friend Gwen Patton, who lived in Philadelphia. Krick's suggestion that she form a new chapter received a resonant and energetic response. Together with her partner, Patton launched the Delaware Valley chapter of the Pink Pistols in the spring of 2001. With the new chapter came a new gun and a Pennsylvania concealed-carry permit.

When I spoke to Patton, she was still a member of the Delaware Valley chapter, but she had also risen to the position of first speaker of the entire organization. She recounted the early days of the Pink Pistols and the organization's ups and downs. It is evident why Patton found Pink Pistols a good match. She grew up in a gun house and her father taught her to shoot his army-issued, World War I–vintage, Remington .45 pistol when she was eleven years old. She also had a predilection for self-defense that was expressed in her lifelong training in various martial arts.

Patton is a pragmatic, no-nonsense, earthbound soul, who is rightfully proud of where the organization stands today. It lists nearly sixty chapters in the United States and Canada, although only half of them are deemed active. One of the larger chapters is Valley of the Sun Pink Pistols, based in Phoenix. While the chapters have considerable autonomy, Patton keeps the national organization focused on its only cause, which is training members to use firearms for self-defense. "The purpose of the Pink Pistols is to teach queers to shoot and to teach the world that we've done it," she laughs; that's the "poetic" version of the mission statement.[13] Everything else—annual meetings, elections, newsletters, boards of directors—is a distraction. A simple website serves as town crier, and volunteers, like herself, handle all of the work. So fund-raising and membership dues are also unnecessary distractions. She advises members, "Don't give us money; spend it on training. Spend it on a weapon. Spend it on your licensing fee. . . . Keep your money, spend it on getting better at using your firearm." The organization is most effective when it avoids excessive overhead—what she calls "imperial entanglements."

I asked Patton how Pink Pistols survives at the stormy intersection of two powerful political currents: gay and lesbian rights is traditionally a liberal cause, while gun rights tends to be a conservative cause. She resolves that dilemma by looking at her members.

> We don't have just right-wingers, we don't have just left-wingers, we don't have just libertarians, we don't have just statists or just authoritarians. . . . Every possible aspect of the political spectrum exists somewhere in our organization. But they have all accepted this one premise: Owning a firearm in lawful self-defense is important.

Where many people might see insurmountable barriers, Patton somehow sees unity: "We're proud of who we are, but because of our similarities. We try to build bridges . . . along lines of similarity rather than across lines of difference."

Over the years, Patton has worked with hundreds of new members, many of whom come to Pink Pistols reluctantly because of their fears about guns. She begins by telling prospective members that "choosing a firearm is a deep, personal, and very convoluted process, which starts with the willingness to use it." A new gun owner must know "that in your heart of hearts, if someone is trying to kill or grievously harm you or a loved one, you *will* use this device to defend them. . . . If you can't say yes to it or you don't know yet, go away, think about it, because every day that you strap on this gun you will have to make the same decision again."

But even those who accept their identity as gun owners within a sexual minority must deal with its public side. Patton estimates that for every Pink Pistol who shows up at a public range, there are twenty-five to fifty invisible members. As someone who has been there personally and has been a shepherd for others, she summarizes the conflict:

There's as much of a difficulty to come out of the gun closet as it is to come out of the gay closet. And it's even worse when you are coming out of both. Because then you've got one community that's reviling you for one thing and another community that's reviling you for the other.

Patton's belief in Pink Pistols was sealed early on by an incident involving one of the charter members of her chapter. As he left a gay bar in Philadelphia, a group of young men followed him to his car, shouting epithets and circling him with steel pipes in their hands. The gay man reached into his coat and drew a .38 revolver. As Patton tells it, "the next thing he hears is 'Holy shit, he's got a gun!' and the clang of metal pipes falling to the ground as the thugs beat feet." Her friend averted a severe beating or his own death because he carried a gun and was willing to use it. "He's our poster boy and he's the sweetest guy you'd ever want to know."

The decision to carry a gun for self-defense is rarely easy. Patton explained it with a paean to self-reliance.

You are choosing a path where instead of requiring that someone else save you, you are choosing to be responsible for your own safety by your own actions. That is an incredibly difficult divide for some people to cross because they're used to being told, don't take the law into your own hands, call the police.

She spiked that observation with the old saying that when seconds count, the police are minutes away. Then she begged to differ with Martin Luther King Jr., who said that opposing violence with violence only leads to a destructive spiral. Patton has a different view:

The idea that all force is violent, that there is no form of force you can use on another human being without it being violent is the most pernicious obstacle to someone defending their life . . . that I have ever heard.

And then she walked the knife-edge on which every argument for armed self-defense rests.

> The other person who is attacking you is seeking to violate you. That is
> what makes it violent. You're not trying to murder [the attacker]; you're
> not trying to shoot them down in cold blood or anything like that. They
> are bringing the attack to you, they are intent on doing you harm, so you
> are going to use the exact amount of force required to stop them. This is
> not violence. This is the antithesis of violence because it stops violence.

She noted that thousands of self-defense incidents have proved that the difference between an assault averted and a crime committed depends on "finding the exact amount of force" in the swirling seconds of an unfamiliar encounter. And that is never easy.

Gwen Patton found a reason to carry a gun for self-defense when she was "the spry thing that used to study aikido." Since then, an accident left her with a broken neck and she now fights a daily battle with pain. If she is not hurting too much, she still takes her regular day at the shooting range. She travels less and has relinquished most of the chapter duties. Ironically, now that she might need it more than before, she does not carry her gun as regularly as she once did. Instead, she walks everywhere with a stout oak cane and practices Cane-Fu for exercise and self-defense.[14]

Practical Shooting

> It's called Stargazer. Start position is standing in box A, B, or C, hands
> relaxed at sides, handgun is loaded, and holstered per 8.1.1 and 8.1.2. The
> stage procedure is upon start signal, engage targets as they become visible
> from within A, B, or C. The only requirement here is USA popper 1 and
> USA popper 2 must be shot from box A. Other than that you shoot 'em
> from wherever you can see 'em. Any questions?[15]

Those were the instructions given to shooters at a recent match of the United States Practical Shooting Association (USPSA). A friend assured me that as a spectator, I would get a good feel for a sport that is wildly popular among participants and nearly invisible to everyone else. He was right; as soon as I stepped into a long, windowless Quonset hut, I was down a rabbit hole into another world. Half an hour before the match began, the place was humming with activity, as competitors donned ammunition belts, loaded magazines, and holstered pistols. And there was plenty of friendly ribbing and shop talk—"I just scored three hundred rounds of mini-mags at Walmart" and "Comstock, twenty-six rounds, 130 points, thirteen metric targets" and "These young guys don't know what it's like to lose your eyesight and your memory at the same time." No one wore a competitive game face. Instead, camaraderie prevailed—even giddy exuberance on a warm winter day.

The fifty registered shooters—many seniors, one ten-year-old, and only two women—gathered to hear a recitation of match rules and walk through the five stages of the event. In addition to the Stargazer stage, there were two other outdoor stages called One Port or Two (with no-shoot obstacles simulating hostages partially concealing twenty-five different targets) and Ambush in the Bathroom (with shooting starting in a sitting position). There were also two indoor stages called Sight Covers Brown (the shooter starts by opening a door, which triggers a target that rocks back and forth between obstructions) and Mini-Mart (simulating the plight of a clerk during a hold-up in a convenience store). By the end of the walk-through, the shooters were eager to shoot.

The ultimate governing body of practical shooting events is the International Practical Shooting Confederation (IPSC). Its motto is "Diligentia, Vis, Celeritas" (accuracy, power, speed), and the competitions require all of those skills. The organizational chart for the IPSC, surely rivaling that of the Defense Department, is an immense pyramid with eighty-seven national organizations lined up beneath the Canada-based headquarters. The United States Practical Shooting Association (USPSA) was incorporated in 1984 and is supported by over four hundred local clubs. The local clubs organize hundreds of competitions each year and offer gun classes and training sessions. And USPSA's glossy magazine, *Front Sight*, is packed with local club news, match schedules, profiles of stars, training tips, opinions, and advertisements for guns, ammunition, and paraphernalia.

While safety and inclusive family fun are essential features of practical shooting, the sport is also highly regimented and competitive, particularly at the upper levels. The National Range Officers Institute trains and certifies match officials. Detailed rules—nearly one hundred pages of weapon specifications, target dimensions, scoring minutiae—govern all matches. Shooters compete in one of several weapon categories, each with its own national championship. One tangible benefit of practical shooting is that its competitions are a popular form of training for military and law-enforcement personnel.

Once the match began, I put on noise-canceling headphones and safety glasses and wandered between stages. The challenge and intrigue of the sport were soon evident. On any given stage, the official timer gives the start signal and the shooter begins the course of fire, shooting two-handed, through windows and around obstacles, at all the targets that are visible and strategically sensible at a particular shooting station. Then there is a run or shuffle to the next station, a possible reload, and more shooting. The action is often called run and gun. Paper targets are roughly shaped like a human torso with A, B, C, and D regions to measure accuracy. Metal targets (plates and poppers) fall over when hit squarely.

When the shooter fires the last shot—usually in less than a minute—the clock stops. The range official inspects the targets and tallies the score, assessing penalties for missed targets and errant shots on no-hit zones. At the same time, other competitors tape the bullet holes on the targets and courteously comb the area for spent shells, returning them to the shooter (many shooters reload their own ammunition to save the cost of new ammunition). The range official's handheld computer combines the accuracy score and the time elapsed to give an overall stage score for that shooter. Within the scoring formula is the complicating matter of counts. Neglecting a few technical details, some stages are designated Comstock count, which means the shooter is allowed unlimited shots; extra shots just take additional time. On Virginia count stages, shooters can take only a fixed number of shots at each target and missed targets carry penalties.

That is the physical side of the sport—what a spectator sees. But as several shooters told me, the precarious trade-off between time and accuracy means that at least half of the game is mental. My friend summed it up saying, "Just like in life, the best way to be fast is to be smooth and perfect." As shooters quickly realize, that is easy to say and difficult to do. One shooter, upset at his performance, told me simply, "I was just going too fast."

I approached a hale and sociable septuagenarian, whom I had been following. "I've been watching you and it looks like your strategy is to take a little bit of extra time so as not to miss."

GUNS IN AMERICAN LIVES | 71

"Yeah," he said, "it's usually because my eyes are bad enough with iron sights, it makes me slow down to try and make sure I get 'em lined up. . . . It's kind of like shoot fast until you miss and then you go damn it, was it really worth missing? So you slow down a little bit." He continued, "It's addictive. Every time you do something like this, you think damn, I coulda done this, I coulda that. You want to go back and try again."

Also hidden from the spectator is the strategizing that shooters do before each course of fire. Of the many targets on a single course, some are visible only from certain shooting stations. The shooter needs to decide which targets to engage from each station and then remember the plan while the clock is running. Complicating matters, most courses require at least one reload—quickly exchanging a spent magazine for a full magazine. Greater accuracy means fewer reloads and less time on the course. Ideally, to save time, a shooter would like to reload on the run between shooting stations. In the end, the best-laid strategy often does not work out as planned. Once a stage is finished, a shooter often replays it in his mind (or on his GoPro) and imagines what could have been done differently—another good metaphor for many life endeavors.

As I left the match, I could still hear gunshots echoing off the shale berms behind the range. A competitor stopped me and asked, "Did you shoot today?"

"No, I was just a spectator."

"Well, next time be sure to bring a gun."

And so the sport grows.

Cowboy Action Shooting

The idea of dressing up in costumes and re-enacting cowboy westerns was probably inspired many decades ago by the films of Tom Mix or John Wayne. According to legend, the idea of making a formal event out of these antics came to Harper Creigh in 1981. The Sam Peckinpah film *The Wild Bunch* certainly had something to do with it. After watching it, Creigh corralled two gun buddies, Gordon Davis and Bill Hahn, and they formed the Wild Bunch, which eventually became the steering committee for the Single Action Shooting Society (SASS). Under the guidance of SASS, Cowboy Action Shooting burgeoned into the youngest of the shooting sports. The organization now has seventy-five thousand members and five hundred local clubs in all fifty states and twenty foreign countries. It oversees hundreds of local matches, several regional competitions, and a world championship, and it publishes a fleet of magazines and bulletins.

What is the excitement about? Cowboy Action Shooting is an amiably competitive sport that combines shooting skills with a nostalgic resurrection of the late-nineteenth-century Old West. A typical match often lasts several days and takes place in a re-created Old West venue, complete with storefronts, banks, saloons, corrals, and barns, as well as human-shaped targets. Many matches have a theme, often expressed in names such as Show-Me Shootout and Smoking Guns at Rabbit Ridge. The matches attract anywhere from a handful to hundreds of men and women, who compete in a variety of staged events that require marksmanship, speed, agility, and occasionally precision horseback riding. Each event is scored and winners are declared in many different categories.

Three mandatory features of any match are costumes, period weapons, and aliases. Competitors dress in authentic costumes—hoop dresses, petticoats, frilly blouses, and ornate hats for women, and chaps, suspenders, vests, and ten-gallon hats for men. Weapons used in the matches must be of late-nineteenth or early-twentieth-century vintage, which means single action revolvers, single- and double-barreled shotguns, and pump action and lever action rifles; replicas are generally allowed. Finally, competitors use a unique alias created at the time a person joins SASS. Of course, aliases must have an Old West flavor and be approved by the organization. For example, everyone knows SASS founder Harper Creigh as Judge Roy Bean. The SASS website allows members to check on available aliases. You can be sure that Annie Oakley and Doc Holliday are already taken.

Several years ago, anthropologist and gun enthusiast Abigail Kohn embedded herself in the West Coast gun scene in order to do an ethnographic study of the gun culture. Her experiences in gun clubs, gun classes, and shooting events are illuminating. Her reporting on Cowboy Action Shooters stresses that the experience of a match goes far beyond the competition and the shooting. For most participants, a match is a rich social experience that involves campfires, singing cowboy songs, flag-waving, and valorizing a bygone era. Kohn's studies offer insight on the motivations of cowboy action shooters.

She observes that cowboy action shooting events are a way to preserve and re-enact the creation myths of the country. Cowboy action shooters "are literally performing their status as native sons and daughters, claiming their identity as authentic American citizens."[16]

Matches are also an opportunity to renew and make friendships, although, ironically, participants often know little about each other, except for their alias and assumed identity. It does not really matter that gunslinger Wild Bill Hickok might be a proctologist or that Calamity Jane is really a corporate attorney and mother of three kids. For a weekend, participants live alter-lives in a century-old world. If nothing else, that experience must offer a fresh perspective when shooters return to their regular lives on Monday morning.

Most gun owners do not participate in Cowboy Action Shooting; however, many gun owners share the sentiments that animate that sport. They believe that owning a gun is an affirmation of a tradition of freedom and independence that flows from the nation's wellsprings, that it is the exercise of the right of citizenship, and that it is a proudly worn emblem of patriotism. As elaborated in chapter 15, these values of tradition, freedom, and patriotism appear to rouse many gun owners and validate their use of guns.

For the people who choose guns for recreation or a pastime, there is nothing extraordinary—let along sinister or threatening—about owning and using guns. Their pursuit depends on their right to own guns, but most believe that right is secure and does not need to be preserved through activism. For this reason, most recreational gun owners avoid the acrid politics and big-budget lobbying that make the news. In fact, only a small fraction of American gun owners are dues-paying members of national firearm advocacy groups. In talking to gun enthusiasts, one is repeatedly reminded of how ordinary they find their lives with guns.

6 | INTERPRETING THE SECOND AMENDMENT

What country can preserve its liberties, if their rulers are not warned
from time to time, that their people preserve the spirit of resistance?
Let them take arms. . . . The tree of liberty must be refreshed
from time to time, with the blood of patriots and tyrants.

—THOMAS JEFFERSON, letter from Paris, November 13, 1787

THE PRESIDENTIAL ELECTION of 1800 was rambunctious from the start, as
the candidates campaigned energetically and were certainly not above personal
attacks on each other. One modern scholar noted a "similarity between politics and politicians then and now. Politicians then . . . were driven by personal ambition."[1] A lot was at stake in 1800. After two terms under George
Washington and one term under John Adams, the Federalist domination of the
presidency was vulnerable. The Federalist candidates in 1800 were the incum-
bent John Adams and his running mate, Charles Pinckney of South Carolina.
Opposing the Federalists were the Democratic-Republicans Thomas Jefferson
(who had served as vice president under Adams) and his running mate, Aaron
Burr. A critical factor in the race was the fractured condition of the Federalist
Party, due to a public feud between Adams and Alexander Hamilton. Although
he was a Federalist and Washington's treasury secretary, Hamilton had worked
to defeat Adams in 1796 and was doing so again in 1800.

The election itself had the script of a political thriller. As spelled out in the
Constitution at that time, the election process called for each member of the
Electoral College to cast two votes. The two candidates with the greatest number of electoral votes were declared president and vice president regardless of
their party. This method had the possible outcome (as in 1796) of producing
a president and vice president of different parties. In 1800, the process led to
yet a different outcome and made the election among the most significant in
American history.

When the electoral ballots were counted on February 11, 1801, Jefferson and Burr were tied with seventy-three votes apiece. (A plan for one of the Democratic-Republican electors to cast only one vote, thereby giving Jefferson the presidency, backfired.) The Federalists Adams and Pinckney trailed with sixty-five and sixty-four votes, respectively. The tied election went to the House of Representatives, where the Federalist majority was given the choice of two Democratic-Republican candidates. Because Jefferson had been an outspoken Federalist opponent, many representatives favored Burr. One exception was Hamilton, whose long-standing hatred of Burr led him to support Jefferson. (Hamilton's feud with Burr would cost Hamilton his life in a gun duel three years later.)

Electoral history was made in the House. In 1800, there were sixteen states in the Union, and a candidate needed to carry nine states in order to win the presidency. In thirty-five successive, suspenseful ballots between February 11 and February 17, Jefferson carried eight states, Burr carried six states, and the representatives in Maryland and Vermont were evenly divided, so their votes did not count. According to some sources, the behind-the-scenes deal-making by Hamilton eventually persuaded some of the representatives of Maryland and Vermont to change their votes. On the thirty-sixth ballot, Thomas Jefferson carried ten states and became the next president; as runner-up, Aaron Burr became his vice president.

The election of 1800 was convoluted and potentially life-threatening for the new nation. However, it brought a new political party to power peacefully not only in the White House but in Congress. It was also the beginning of the eventual demise (in 1816) of the Federalist Party, which had dominated American politics for over a decade. The outcome of the election, combined with old political rivalries, produced animosities that eventually escalated. A case in point—and another decisive chapter in America's history of guns— occurred in Boston in the summer of 1806.

Benjamin Austin was a prominent Jeffersonian who published one of Boston's leading newspapers, the *Independent Chronicle*. He was also head of a political committee that organized a Fourth of July celebration for the city's Democratic-Republican faithful. Held in a tavern on Copp's Hill, the event was intended to surpass other political celebrations of the day in extravagance. It attracted more people than planned, and the bill for the food and drink was much more than expected. A few weeks after the celebration, having received no payment from the committee, the tavern owner took legal action with the help of Thomas Selfridge, one of Boston's eminent attorneys. As destiny would have it, Selfridge was a zealous Federalist.

At this point, the story is a series of who-said-what-to-whom allegations (according to trial records written several months later).[2] What is known is that the tavern owner filed suit against Austin's committee to recover lost expenses. The tavern attorney, Selfridge, heard a rumor that he had actually instigated the suit as a way to even the score with the Republicans. Furthermore, Selfridge became convinced that Austin had started the rumor. Through a courier, Selfridge sent a letter to Austin, dated July 29, denying the allegation that he had instigated the suit and asking Austin "to make voluntary reparation." When Selfridge did not receive a satisfactory apology from Austin, Selfridge sent another letter to Austin dated July 30, asking for a retraction and claiming that whoever started the rumor was "in grain a liar and a scoundrel."[3] According to a witness:

> Mr. Selfridge said his only motive in moving in the affair was to [rescue] his professional conduct from the foul imputation which Mr. Austin had so unjustifiably thrown upon it, and that he would not relinquish the pursuit till the object was accomplished.[4]

When Austin did not reply to the second letter, Selfridge considered a "triple alternative, a prosecution, chastisement, or posting."[5] He ruled out the first two options and chose to publish the following "post" in the *Boston Gazette* on August 4 in order to clear his name publicly:

> AUSTIN POSTED
> Benjamin Austin, loan officer, having acknowledged that he has circulated an infamous falsehood concerning my professional conduct . . . and having refused to give the satisfaction due to a gentleman in similar cases—I hereby publish said Austin as a COWARD, a LIAR, and a SCOUNDREL.[6]

Not wanting to aggravate the situation any further, Austin responded with the following note the same morning in his own newspaper, the *Independent Chronicle*:

Considering it derogatory to enter into a newspaper controversy with one T. O. Selfridge, in reply to his insolent and false publication in the Gazette of this day; if any gentleman is desirous to know the facts, on which his impertinence is founded, any information will be given by me on the subject.[7]

However, the situation *did* escalate on that same morning after the posts appeared. Austin's son Charles, an eighteen-year-old Harvard student, was offended by the public humiliation of his father caused by Selfridge's post. At midday, he was with friends in Boston, carrying a large cane; "it was a good piece of hickory—heavy for hickory."[8] Young Austin was apparently looking for Selfridge to avenge his father's honor. Quite independently, Selfridge had "some intimation that he should be attacked," not by "old Mr. Austin, . . . but some bully employed by him."[9] Therefore, when Selfridge left his office at one o'clock "on business," he decided to carry a loaded pistol under his coat. Young Austin and Selfridge met on State Street amid a large lunchtime crowd. As Austin raised his stick to attack Selfridge, a shot resounded from point-blank range. Young Austin managed to deliver four or five blows to Selfridge and then collapsed on the street. Bystanders carried Austin into a nearby shop where he died in minutes. Selfridge was taken into custody and readily admitted, "I am the man."[10]

The public, daylight, downtown murder of young Austin set legal wheels in motion. On December 2, a grand jury returned an indictment charging Selfridge with manslaughter, having "feloniously, willfully, and of the fury of his mind" killed Charles Austin.[11] Selfridge pleaded not guilty and three weeks later jury selection began. With the help of partisan newspapers eager to turn headlines into sales, the trial was an instant spectacle that captivated Americans far beyond Boston.

In their prolix remarks to the jury, the presiding justice, Isaac Parker, the lead prosecutor and attorney general, James Sullivan, and the defense team scarcely questioned Selfridge's right to carry a pistol; that much was taken for granted. Instead, the decision turned on the meaning of self-defense. The prosecution argued that Selfridge could have found less violent means of self-defense on a crowded street in broad daylight. By carrying a concealed pistol and by firing immediately when threatened, he clearly had motives other than self-defense.

The defense reminded the jury that manslaughter "consists in the unlawful and willful killing of a reasonable being, without malice express or implied, and without any justification or excuse."[12] It followed that self-defense is one possible "justification or excuse" that could acquit a person of manslaughter. The defense argued that Selfridge, "a weak and feeble man," had "a right to attempt the destruction of the assailant, that he himself might not be destroyed."[13] The defense further declared that "the law says, that if there be reasonable ground to suspect that life is in danger, a man shall be excused."[14]

This remarkable claim—that self-defense requires only a "reasonable ground" to fear for one's life rather than an actual threat or assault—gave much more latitude in the interpretation of justifiable homicide. The claim may have also been the deciding argument for the jury: it found Thomas Selfridge not guilty of manslaughter.

The decision in the Selfridge case reverberated in the press for weeks and in legal annals for decades. It fueled Republican outrage and led to hangings in effigy of Selfridge and Justice Parker in several cities. In the end, the Selfridge case did not involve the Second Amendment. Because the decision ultimately rested on the meaning of self-defense, the case was "one of common law, not constitutional law."[15] Nevertheless, the case foreshadowed present-day gun confrontations and court cases, particularly because of its expansive interpretation of self-defense.

State Arms Amendments

As the United States entered the nineteenth century, conditions were changing rapidly on many fronts. The population was exploding, doubling nearly every twenty years between the Revolutionary War and the Civil War. The nation was also expanding geographically: By 1820, the thirteen colonies had become a union of twenty-three states, the westernmost being Illinois. By 1845, there were twenty-eight states, including Texas. In 1800, President John Adams became the first resident of the White House, and the Congress, the Supreme Court, and the Library of Congress all moved into the Capitol Building. The federal government was solidly entrenched in Washington, DC, and going about its business of making laws and ruling on legal issues. At the same time, as each state joined the Union, it drafted its own constitution, began making laws, and established its own courts. Because legislative and judicial systems developed in parallel on the state and federal levels, the tension between federal authority and states' rights soon bubbled to the surface. Those countercurrents cut a deep course through the legislation and jurisprudence of the nineteenth century. And matters related to the militia, the right to bear arms, and the Second Amendment were swept into the resulting turbulence.

Sixteen states joined the Union in the eighteenth century, twenty-nine states joined in the nineteenth century, and five states joined in the twentieth century. In so doing, each state ratified its constitution along with a declaration of rights. These documents have generally undergone multiple revisions over the years, in addition to the ongoing addition of amendments. One way to gauge the wide range of perspectives on the Second Amendment is to survey these state constitutions with a focus on right-to-bear-arms language.

The arms language in state constitutions as it appears today could be categorized as follows. Five states have no provision about bearing arms in their constitutions. Fourteen states have language similar to that used in Pennsylvania (approved in 1790): "The right of the citizens to bear arms in defense of themselves and the State shall not be questioned."[16] This language specifically cites defense of self and state as the purpose for having arms.

The language of the Delaware constitution, ratified in 1897, enumerates additional purposes for bearing arms and was used by nine states:

A person has the right to keep and bear arms for the defense of self, family, home and State, and for hunting and recreational use.[17]

Ten other states use a less specific paraphrasing of the US Second Amendment. For example, the Georgia declaration of rights (in an 1877 revision) states that "the right of the people to keep and bear arms shall not be infringed."[18]

Eight states use the words *defense and security*, which first appeared in the Ohio constitution (as revised in 1851): "The people have the right to bear arms for their defense and security."[19] And three states use the words *common defense*, which first appeared in the Massachusetts declaration of rights (as approved 1780): "The people have a right to keep and to bear arms for the common defence."[20]

For those keeping score, that amounts to forty-nine states; Maryland is the unusual case. The only provision in the Maryland declaration of rights concerning weapons is "that a well regulated Militia is the proper and natural defence of a free Government."[21] This provision seems to say nothing about the individual right to keep and bear arms.

One further step of constitutional taxonomy is revealing. In addition to the various arms provisions mentioned above, seven state constitutions have language that allows the state legislature to regulate the use of arms. For example, the Tennessee declaration of rights (as revised in 1870) declares:

> The citizens of this State have a right to keep and to bear arms for their common defense; but the Legislature shall have power, by law, to regulate the wearing of arms with a view to prevent crime.[22]

Of some relevance today, nine states have constitutions that give the legislature the power to regulate or prohibit the carrying of concealed weapons. A typical example is the Mississippi bill of rights, as revised in 1890:

> The right of every citizen to keep and bear arms in defense of his home, person, or property, or in aid of the civil power when thereto legally summoned, shall not be called in question, but the legislature may regulate or forbid carrying concealed weapons.[23]

This litany of arms provisions demonstrates a widespread agreement among the states over the past two hundred years that a right to bear arms *exists*. At the same time, it reveals the broad variety of viewpoints on the precise boundaries of that right.

Commentaries and Courts

There are other ways to organize the interpretations of the Second Amendment in the decades after it was approved. The early 1800s marked the beginning of a long stream of legal commentary that has continued to this day. The source of that stream is usually recognized as the renowned legal scholar St. George Tucker, the patriarch of a dynasty of Virginia politicians, judges, and writers, whose legacy exists today.

In 1766, the English legal scholar and jurist Sir William Blackstone wrote

Commentaries on the Laws of England, an influential four-volume work on English common law. Tucker wrote the first text on American law, which was an annotated version of Blackstone's *Commentaries*, plus an entire volume of appendices relevant to American law and legal issues. Released in 1803, Tucker's prodigious work was known as the *American Blackstone*. It was required reading for generations of American lawyers and has been cited in numerous Supreme Court decisions. Tucker's fame was built on more than erudite writings. He is credited with building the first bathroom in Williamsburg, Virginia, complete with a copper bathtub fed with hot water. St. George Tucker was not a saint; his first name is the last name of a great-great-grandfather.

Of particular interest here is Tucker's commentary on the right to bear arms, which is addressed in several place in the *Commentaries*. Tucker had Antifederalist sympathies and he affirmed states' rights positions during the writing of the Constitution. Not surprisingly, he condemned the Federalists' use of select militias and believed the Second Amendment authorized the use of state-controlled militias as a check on federal power. Referring to the Second Amendment, Tucker wrote memorably:

> This may be considered the true palladium of liberty. . . . The right of self defense is the first law of nature: in most governments it has been the study of rulers to confine this right within the narrowest limits possible. Wherever standing armies are kept up, and the right of the people to keep and bear arms is . . . prohibited, liberty, if not already annihilated, is on the brink of destruction.[24]

Tucker was an early and strong advocate of judicial review, trusting the courts to intervene when Congress threatened individual rights. With respect to the right to bear arms, Tucker wrote:

> If, for example, [C]ongress were to pass a law prohibiting any person from bearing arms, as a means of preventing insurrections, the judicial courts . . . would be able to pronounce decidedly upon the constitutionality of these means.[25]

Tucker's overall commentary on the Second Amendment finds favor with modern gun rights advocates, and his writing is cited frequently today to support the individual rights position.

The first decade of the 1800s brought increased strain between the United States and the British Empire (which included present-day Canada). Among various economic and political aggravations, the British resisted American expansion into the Northwest Territory (present-day Ohio, Indiana, Illinois, Michigan, and Wisconsin) by providing arms to Native American tribes in that region. With Republican-Democrat James Madison in the White House, Congress's decision to declare war in 1812 was met with widespread opposition, particularly in New England, where the states considered secession from the Union. The War of 1812 divided the country and intensified the ongoing uncertainty about the role and control of the militia. In states opposed to the war, individuals resisted mustering with their state militias and governors were reluctant to commit their state militias to the war effort. Madison went so far as to propose national conscription to fill the ranks of the military. The idea of conscription met firm Federalist opposition and put the Federalists in the ironic position of supporting state controls of the militia.[26] Questions about control of the militia were the focus of a Supreme Court case that confounded the roles of the state and federal governments with respect to the militia. The case is also the first to mention (briefly) the Second Amendment.

In 1814, Pennsylvania passed a law requiring eligible state militia members to report for duty when called into service by the president, a power he had under the federal Uniform Militia Act of 1795. When a Pennsylvania militia private named Houston failed to report for militia duty to support the war effort, he was arrested, appeared before a state court martial, and was convicted and fined. The appeal of the verdict eventually reached the US Supreme Court, where the case *Houston v. Moore* pitted state authority against federal power. Houston's side argued that the Pennsylvania law was unconstitutional because the Constitution (article I, section 8, clauses 15 and 16) grants Congress—not the state—authority over the militia. The state argued that federal power was concurrent with, but not exclusive of, state power in the matter. Furthermore, Houston would receive similar penalties even if he were prosecuted under the federal law.[27]

The Supreme Court returned a split decision with Justice Bushrod Washington (George Washington's nephew) writing the majority opinion. The conclusion of that opinion was that Pennsylvania was within its powers to enforce its law, which was consistent with the federal law. As a result of that decision, Houston's conviction at the state level was upheld. In his opinion, Washington prophetically wrote that the division of authority over militia between the states and the federal government had not been "formed with as much wisdom as, in the opinion of some, it might have been, or as time and experience may hereafter suggest."[28]

Another justice in the *Houston v. Moore* decision was Joseph Story, the youngest justice ever appointed to the Supreme Court (at age thirty-two), who served on the court for thirty-four years. Story was a titan in American legal history, a pioneer of Harvard Law School, and the author of the seminal work *Commentaries on the Constitution of the United States*. His *Commentaries* and its many later editions are still among the most thorough and scholarly historical treatments of the Constitution. Justice Story wrote a long dissent in the *Houston v. Moore* case that demonstrated the profound uncertainty about the militia, not only within the courts but undoubtedly for the public at large.[29] Story claimed that the authority of the federal government to prosecute militia resistors was exclusive and could not be shared with the states, essentially stating that the Pennsylvania law was unconstitutional.

In his dissent and in later writings, Story affirmed the importance of the right to bear arms to guard against federal repression. Echoing language first used by St. George Tucker, in 1840 Story wrote:

> The right of the citizens to keep and bear arms has justly been considered, as the palladium of the liberties of a republic; since it offers a strong moral check against the usurpation and arbitrary powers of rulers; and it will generally, even if these are successful in the first instance, enable the people to resist and triumph over them.[30]

While *Houston v. Moore* exposed disparate opinions about the militia, it really was not a Second Amendment case. However, genuine individual gun rights cases would soon make their way to the courts. The first half of the nineteenth century saw a marked increase in the possession of personal firearms. This rise is consistent with the rise in individualism often associated with the first Democratic president, Andrew Jackson, who served from 1829 to 1837. It also coincides with Samuel Colt's American patent of the revolver in 1836 and the subsequent founding of Colt's Manufacturing Company in Hartford, Connecticut. The revolver quickly became popular for both personal and military use.[31] And the availability of smaller guns led to the practice of carrying concealed weapons. Recent research by historian Randolph Roth provides evidence that for three decades following the War of 1812, homicide rates were as low as they would ever be but then rose for the remainder of the century.[32] This violence was often directed at marginal groups such as African Americans, abolitionists, Mormons, and Catholics.[33]

States responded to the increase in gun use with constitutional amendments and new laws. Kentucky passed the first state law dealing with concealed weapons in 1817, and it was given a thorough test a few years later. A man named Bliss was arrested for carrying a sword concealed in a cane, in violation of the state law prohibiting "the wearing of concealed arms." A lower court found Bliss guilty and fined him one hundred dollars, which resulted in an appeal that reached the state supreme court. Citing the state constitution (at that time), that the right of the citizens to bear arms in defense of themselves and the state shall not be questioned, the defense argued that the state law was unconstitutional. The state responded, writing that "a distinction was taken between a law prohibiting the exercise of the right, and a law merely regulating the manner of exercising that right."[34]

In other words, according to the state, a state law could prohibit a specific act of carrying a concealed weapon (in this case, a sword in a cane) without violating the state constitution. Therefore, the state argued, Bliss was guilty.

In the *Bliss v. Commonwealth* decision, the high court of the state resoundingly supported the defense:

It is the right to bear arms in defence of the citizens and the state, that is secured by the constitution, and whatever restrains the full and complete exercise of that right, though not an entire destruction of it, is forbidden by the explicit language of the constitution.[35]

The lower court decision was reversed and Bliss was acquitted in a clear affirmation of the individual right to bear arms. (In 1850, the Kentucky constitution was revised to allow prohibition of concealed weapons.)

Kentucky was not the only state that passed laws dealing with the possession of arms, and the court cases that followed had various outcomes. In 1837,
the Tennessee legislature passed a law prohibiting any person from carrying a
concealed "bowie knife, Arkansas tooth-pick (a heavy dagger), or other knife
or weapon" of a similar shape.[36] When William Aymette was arrested in June
1839 in Pulaski, Tennessee, with "a bowie knife concealed under his vest and
suspended to the waistband of his breeches," he was subsequently found guilty
of violating the state law.[37] On appeal, the case went to the state supreme court
on the grounds that the state law violated the state constitution.

While the case has similarities to *Bliss v. Commonwealth*, the decision in
Aymette v. State was notably different. The Tennessee high court ruled:

> The legislature, therefore, have a right to prohibit the wearing, or keeping
> weapons dangerous to the peace and safety of the citizens, and which are
> not usual in civilized warfare, or would not contribute to the common
> defence. The right to keep and bear arms for the common defence is a
> great political right. . . . And although this right must be inviolably pre-
> served, yet, it does not follow that the legislature is prohibited altogether
> from passing laws regulating the manner in which these arms may be
> employed.[38]

The Tennessee court cited *Bliss v. Commonwealth* but respectfully claimed
"we cannot concur in their reasoning." Instead, the Aymette decision recognized the need to regulate the right to bear arms and to limit it to militia-class
arms. The language of this decision—that there is a right but not an unrestricted
right—would be echoed in twenty-first-century Supreme Court decisions.

Similar variances in opinion can be found in other state cases. In 1844,
the Arkansas Supreme Court ruled in *State v. Buzzard* to uphold a state law
banning concealed weapons. It ruled that the right to bear arms was subject
to regulation, claiming that the right was intended to "enable each member
of the community to protect and defend by individual force his private rights
against every illegal invasion."[39]

Because of its narrow interpretation of the Second Amendment and its
emphasis on regulation, modern scholar David Kopel calls *State v. Buzzard*
"the birth of the anti-individual version of the Second Amendment."[40]

Two More Matters

Two other developments influenced Second Amendment interpretation in the years leading up to the Civil War—one with a relatively short-term effect and one whose impact lasted 150 years. During the antebellum years, slaves had no arms-bearing rights, which enabled well-armed slave owners to prevent slave insurrections. This disparity fueled abolitionists and led to a radical interpretation of the right to bear arms. In effect, the Second Amendment became an argument to arm slaves and topple slavery. At least among the more extreme abolitionists, the Second Amendment guaranteed a right to bear arms in a militia or for self-defense and "provided the foundation for a collective right of revolution."[41] While this interpretation was used to justify the uprisings of populist militant groups, the right to collective resistance took on new meaning with respect to slavery. Specifically, it meant that the right to bear arms also applied to slaves.

Lysander Spooner was surely one of the most creative thinkers and writers of the nineteenth century. Born in Massachusetts, his iconoclastic life spanned most of that century and was devoted to many causes including libertarian principles, labor laws, postal-service reform, and, most passionately, the abolition of slavery. He was a legal autodidact, a prolific writer, and a tireless activist. His most influential work, the 1845 book *The Unconstitutionality of Slavery*, became the first testament of abolitionists; it gave long intricate arguments refuting the notion that the Constitution justified slavery.[42] Spooner's famous argument that the Second Amendment implies the abolition of slavery can be given in a syllogistic nutshell:

All men have a right to keep and bear arms.
Slaves do not have the right to keep and bear arms.
Therefore, no men are slaves.

While Spooner's argument may have been too abstract for slavery advocates, his writing certainly further entangled the Second Amendment with the explosive issue of slavery.

The second development affecting Second Amendment interpretation is more complex and far-reaching. The Bill of Rights was ratified in 1791 in response to fears that, if not checked, the newly empowered federal government might overwhelm the states and violate the civil liberties of individuals. Yet, with all the eloquence and brevity of the first ten amendments, one obvious question was not answered: to which governments did the Bill of Rights apply?

The opening words of the First Amendment, "Congress shall make no law respecting an establishment of religion, or prohibiting the free exercise thereof," make it clear that this amendment restricts the powers of the federal government. The passive voice of the remaining amendments is not as explicit. Specifically, did those amendments restrict the powers of only the federal government? Or did they also limit the reach of state and local governments? For example, could a state pass a law restricting freedom of religion without violating the Bill of Rights? Did antebellum state laws in the South that banned abolitionist speech and literature violate the Bill of Rights?

The dominant opinion on this question in the early nineteenth century was that the Bill of Rights restricted only the federal government. That position was emphatically staked out in the 1833 Supreme Court case, *Barron v. Baltimore*. When street repairs in Baltimore made the waters around John Barron's wharf too shallow to be navigated, Barron sued the city for damages. The trial court ruled in Barron's favor and awarded him damages. However, the ruling was reversed on appeal and the case went to the US Supreme Court. Chief Justice John Marshall was a leading Federalist, a former congressman and secretary of state, and one of the longest-serving Supreme Court justices (1801–1835). In his opinion, written on behalf of a unanimous court, Marshall famously wrote that the Bill of Rights "contains no expression indicating an intention to apply them to the state governments. This court cannot so apply them."[43] The Court's state's-rights position was clear:

> The constitution was ordained and established by the people of the
> United States for themselves, for their own government, and not for the
> government of the individual states; that is, the states have their own con-
> stitutions and have the authority to make and enforce their own laws.[44]

The decision in *Barron v. Baltimore* hardly settled the matter of the reach of the Bill of Rights, nor did it defeat those who believed that the Bill of Rights imposed restrictions on the states. However, the immediate implication of the decision was that (hypothetically) a state could pass laws prohibiting public speeches on Sundays or allowing warrantless searches or banning the individual possession of all weapons without violating the US Constitution. Such a possibility surely struck some in the legal community as unintended. And indeed, *Barron v. Baltimore* notwithstanding, court decisions in several states asserted that the Bill of Rights, and the Second Amendment in particular, also limited the authority of the states.[45]

As the nation approached the cauldron of the Civil War, which began in April 1861, the status of the right to bear arms was unclear. Given the variety of language in state constitutions and the range of court opinions during the first half of the nineteenth century, it would be difficult to find a prevailing legal or public position on the right to bear arms. In addition, several court cases exposed the uncertainty about the very scope of the Bill of Rights and the extent to which to it applied to the states. The question raised—and not settled—by *Barron v. Baltimore* would persist throughout the twentieth century, and its bearing on the Second Amendment was settled only in the present century.

7 | MAGIC NEVER MADE A GUN

I'm proud of my invention, but I'm sad that it is used by terrorists. . . .
I would prefer to have invented a machine that people could use and
that would help farmers with their work—for example a lawnmower.

—MIKHAIL KALASHNIKOV

IT WAS THE fall of 1833 when Jonathan Browning, a blacksmith and gunmaker from Sumner County, Tennessee, packed up his wagon and took his
wife and five children to Quincy, Illinois. The move to the banks of the Mississippi River was bold, but it also promised new opportunities. Browning
established his gun shop in Quincy and began applying his skills to improving the single-shot rifles of the day. The result of his ingenuity was one of the
first, and by far the simplest, repeating rifles in America—a rifle that loaded
the next round after each shot. While in Quincy, Browning gained fame and
prosperity, served as a local judge, and made the acquaintance of a young
lawyer named Abraham Lincoln.[1]

At that same time, just forty miles upstream, a community of Mormons
led by the prophet Joseph Smith was turning a swamp into a thriving community called Nauvoo. So it was not surprising that one day an enthusiastic
Mormon came to Browning's gun shop with a repair job. And it was not long
before Browning had a copy of the Book of Mormon, which resonated with
his spiritual leanings. In 1842, now with eight children, Browning moved to
Nauvoo to join one of the fastest-growing communities in the country. His
new gun business thrived, he helped build the new Mormon temple, and he
supplied parishioners with guns. He also armed the bodyguards of Joseph
Smith, whose life was often threatened by local Mormon antagonists.

Once in Nauvoo, the life of Jonathan Browning became part of familiar
Mormon history. On June 27, 1844, Joseph Smith and his brother were killed
by a mob while in jail in nearby Carthage. The future of the fledgling faith

fell into the hands of the less visionary, but more practical, Brigham Young, who began organizing an exodus to the West, to a land called Zion. As a skilled blacksmith, Browning was indispensable in the preparations for the long journey, providing guns, wheels, axes, knives, and farm implements for the convoy. In the winter of 1846, Browning and his family joined the saints as they set out over the ice-bound Mississippi River, on foot and in wagons, leaving most of their possessions behind. Four arduous months later, the winter-battered convoy reached the Missouri River near present-day Council Bluffs. At Brigham Young's insistence, Browning remained at this site, set up his business, and provided the tools needed to establish winter quarters for the thousands of pilgrims who would pass through in the coming years. Most of the caravan followed Brigham Young westward.

A year later, in July 1847, a party of 150 souls emerged from a canyon overlooking the basin of the Great Salt Lake. Meanwhile, Jonathan Browning spent five more years at the winter quarters on the Missouri River before making the journey west. In 1852, he and his family—now flush with eleven children—arrived in the Promised Land and once again began a new life. There probably could not have been a more ideal pilgrim to settle in the young community of Ogden. Browning was industrious, tenacious, and devout. He became a master of all trades, making and repairing the tools needed to scratch out an existence in the harsh surroundings. And abiding by the teachings of the church, he took up polygamy.

In 1855, Browning's second wife, Elizabeth, gave birth to John Moses, who was followed four years later by Matthew Sandifer. Browning then married his third wife, Sarah Ann, who gave birth to seven children, including the sons Ed, Sam, Will, and George. The six brothers had adventurous childhoods, but they also lived under their father's unforgiving hand. He exacted his religious principles on his sons (no cursing, smoking, or drinking) and gave his sons sparse praise. The eldest son, John, spent hours in the shop that adjoined their large house, developing "mechanical talents far beyond his years."[2] He learned how to braze and weld, to sew and cobble, and he quickly learned about guns. At the age of ten, John built a crude shotgun from scrap parts; it was good enough to take down three birds and provide a meal for the family. When John was caught stealing gunpowder for his shotgun from his father's secret stash, his father overlooked the obvious sin; however, he was upset that his son did not build a better gun.

John's chance came when he was thirteen and a stranger came into the shop with a badly damaged single-barrel percussion-lock shotgun. After buying a reconditioned gun, the stranger tossed the damaged gun in John's direction, saying, "Sonny, it's yours if you want it." John saw an opportunity, grabbed the gun, and quickly disassembled it down to the last screw. Once the gun parts were spread out on his bench, he realized that he had the skill to make all the parts that needed to be replaced. The job would require nothing more than patience and persistence. He later recalled the task saying, "Magic never made a gun that would work."[3] Within a few weeks, John finished rebuilding the gun and his father grudgingly acknowledged the rite of passage he had witnessed. His approval was registered only by giving John a prized piece of walnut for the gunstock. John soon had the finest shotgun in Ogden.

With the confidence gained by rebuilding the broken shotgun, John's skills, inventiveness, and knowledge of guns grew effortlessly. He absorbed gun mechanics and gun lore with a precocious thirst. At age fifteen, he finished school, and as Jonathan devoted more time to civic duties, John and eventually his brothers assumed more responsibilities in the gun shop. The completion of the transcontinental railroad in 1869 and a spur to Ogden in 1870 brought more business to the Browning shop. It was soon rebuilt and expanded. More than once, a shop patron would ask John to see the owner of the shop, only to be amazed that the youngster behind the counter had all the skills needed to solve any problem that came through the door.

John eventually tired of repairing muzzle-loaders and grew exasperated with the inefficient gun designs he saw every day. As he recalled later in life, he was repairing a complicated "freak" of a gun when he exclaimed to his father, "I could build a better gun than that myself." His father replied, "I know you could and I wish you'd get at it. I'd like to live to see you do it."[4] The result of that exchange was a creative flourish that would recur throughout John's life. Beginning in early 1878, he made design sketches, created templates, forged parts, and built models for a simple, ingenious, breech-loading single-shot rifle. A successful prototype was completed in less than a year. He then navigated the unfamiliar process of applying for a patent, which he did on May 12, 1879, at the age of twenty-three. Five weeks after applying for the patent, John's father "died of weariness," knowing that John had succeeded in building a better gun.

John and his brothers now confronted the challenges of maintaining the gun repair business while building an arms factory to start production of John's new rifle. At the same time, they opened a supply store for ammunition, gun accessories, and other sporting goods for a growing hunting and target-shooting market. There was enough work to keep all six brothers plus a newly hired shop manager busy, but finances were tight. The first run of twenty-five rifles put the brothers in debt, but the guns sold out in one week at a price of twenty-five dollars. John was able to pay each of his crew a bonus of a five-dollar gold piece.

As the brothers found their roles in the growing business, John struggled to balance running the business with his true ambition, which was inventing guns. The conflict was resolved in early 1883. T. G. Bennett, vice president and general manager of the Winchester Repeating Arms Company, was in his office in New Haven, Connecticut, when an employee showed him a Browning single-shot rifle. Bennett was impressed with the design of the rifle, saw a place for it in his inventory, and within a week he was on a train to some frontier outpost called Ogden, Utah. The swarthy aristocratic easterner wandered into the rustic Browning gun factory, where he found a crew young enough to be apprentices hard at work. Once Bennett believed that the young men were really the owners, he and John settled into negotiations. Within a few hours the two no-nonsense businessmen had scribbled their names on a scrap of paper, giving Winchester the rights to the single-shot rifle for $10,000. Browning got more than he hoped and Bennett paid less than he expected. Later the same day, Bennett was on a train headed back east.

The signing of the deal between Winchester and Browning Brothers was a watershed moment for both companies. Winchester took over production of the rifle and spun off many versions. For decades, Winchester ruled the market for single-shot rifles. The deal also gave Browning Brothers the financial injection it needed. More important, it gave John the chance to unleash his creative energies. He went to work immediately on a repeating rifle[5] and within months had produced a rifle whose "action is probably the smoothest job ever developed in a lever action gun."[6] The gun had the virtue that it could be easily adapted to larger caliber cartridges and to the higher pressures produced by the new smokeless gunpowder.

John applied for a patent in May 1884 and, in October of that year, he and his brother Matt—now the chief financial officer of the company—set out for the East Coast to show the new rifle to Bennett at Winchester. The trip to New Haven passed through New York City, where the brothers got their first view of life east of Utah. "Unsophisticated even by Ogden standards," the wide-eyed twenty-somethings were shown the tourist sights, taken to high-end restaurants, and even had their first sip of alcohol.

John Browning wanted to give Winchester first rights to the new rifle, but he also knew that other companies would deal with him if Winchester hesitated. Once again, the negotiations with Bennett were brief, and a deal was signed. Winchester paid an estimated $50,000—"more money than there is in Ogden"—for the rifle, which became the Winchester Model 86.[7] And John left New Haven with a commission for a new lever-action repeating shotgun.

With characteristic determination, John produced the repeating shotgun in a matter of months. It was patented in June 1885, bought by Winchester, and became the Winchester Model 87. It was the first successful repeating shotgun and it "showed Browning's versatility by inventing such an action."[8] Browning's ingenuity and Winchester's eagerness to buy his designs now soared. During a two-year period before he reached the age of thirty, Winchester bought eleven Browning gun designs.

Throughout his life, John was an observant Mormon; he participated in community activities and exhibited Mormon virtues, one of which was an aversion to idleness. So at the age of thirty-two, he fulfilled his duties as a missionary, leaving behind a wife, a family, and a thriving business. The two years he spent proselytizing in Georgia were uneventful, but they gave him time to fill his head with ideas for new gun designs. Indeed, in the three years following his travels, as if making up for lost time, he applied for twenty patents—an astonishing rate of invention, far exceeding that of any other gun designer. Once again the business moved to larger quarters in Ogden, the sporting-goods arm expanded to include mail orders, and the name Browning Brothers was known throughout the west. Browning-designed Winchester guns accounted for 75 percent of the sporting-gun market by the mid-1890s. Despite his fame and growing wealth, John had only the simplest of personal needs. He was generous to others, but never wanted much for himself.

During the seventeen years from 1883 to 1900, the Browning-Winchester relationship thrived: Winchester purchased forty-four significantly different Browning guns, while making no guns designed by its own engineers. Of those forty-four designs, only eleven were actually produced; the others were bought by Winchester to keep them out of the hands of competitors.

During a casual shoot-around with friends near Ogden in late 1889, John had an epiphany that accelerated firearms history. Watching a friend shoot a (Browning) rifle, John noticed the force of the muzzle blast on the weeds in front of the rifle. The thought of the wasted energy in every gunshot sparked an idea for a long-sought automatic rifle. John fled the shooting session and spent the afternoon in the shop testing his idea. At the end of the day, he told his brothers, "We may not be more than ten years away from a pretty good automatic machine gun."[9] John's prophecy was a bit conservative. By four o'clock the next afternoon, he had built a prototype that gave proof of concept. A few months later, he filed a patent for a gas-operating principle on which a machine gun or automatic rifle could be built. Again, the flood-gates opened. During the next several years, he filed patents for increasingly sophisticated automatic-gun designs. In 1891, he patented an automatic machine gun; 1895 saw a patent for a semi-automatic pistol; and in 1896 he obtained patents for three different and original mechanisms, all of which would be used for automatic firearms.

In late 1890, only one year after John made his ten-year prophecy, the Brownings approached Colt's Patent Fire Arms Manufacturing Company—a contractor for military artillery—about its interest in an automatic machine gun. Although Colt already made a hand-cranked Gatling gun, improvements in its performance were needed. Within a few months, John and Matt were in New Haven, Connecticut, meeting with Colt's president and putting their prototype machine gun through its paces. The gun, at half the weight of a Gatling gun, performed superbly, and Colt was ready to make a deal. A few months later, John and Matt returned to Colt with a refined machine gun and several long hand-stitched ammunition belts. On this visit, naval ordnance people were on hand to observe the tests. The gun met the navy's requirements, firing six hundred rounds per minute for three minutes without jamming.

At the celebration dinner that night with the Colt president, John had his first glass of champagne. The company began production of the Colt Model 1895 Automatic Machine Gun—the first of many Browning guns that Colt manufactured over the next seventy-five years. Throughout the Boxer

Rebellion, the Spanish-American War, World Wars I and II, and the Korean War, US forces used Browning-designed machine guns.

At the same time that Browning was producing automatic weapons for military use, he designed a line of automatic pistols for Colt.[10] His .38-caliber automatic pistol that appeared in 1900 was the first automatic pistol manufactured in the United States. The millions of pistols produced by Colt since 1900 have all been Browning-designed guns.

Two other automatic weapons designed by Browning around 1910—by themselves—would have guaranteed him immortality among gun designers. Modifying his machine-gun designs, he met the military's need for "walking fire" with the Browning Automatic Rifle or BAR. First manufactured by Colt, this fully automatic rifle was fired from the shoulder at a rate of 480 rounds per minute and its design was so simple that it could be disassembled and reassembled in less than a minute. Also appearing at this time was the Colt .45-caliber Automatic Pistol, which became the standard-issue US military sidearm.

As America's involvement in the World War I became inevitable, Browning's output only increased. As the American armament effort accelerated, many of his military weapons were produced not only by Winchester and Colt but by Remington, Westinghouse, and Marlin-Rockwell. After the war ended, the Associated Press revealed that Browning had received $750,000 for his military designs. Combined with royalties on every gun sold, his earnings amounted to $13 million (upward of $100 million in today's dollars).

Browning's prolific output from the turn of the century through World War I is remarkable, and yet it all took place alongside another significant phase of his life. In 1897, he opened discussions with Fabrique Nationale d'Armes de Guerre (FN), in Herstal, Belgium. FN was initially interested in Browning's design for an automatic shotgun, a gun rejected by Winchester several years earlier. The FN automatic shotgun, released in 1902, was an immediate success in Europe. At the same time, FN manufactured a Browning semiautomatic .32-caliber pistol; that gun made *Browning* synonymous with "pistol" in Europe. Browning provided FN with designs for handguns and military weapons for the rest of his life. All told, he made sixty-one trans-Atlantic voyages and spent several years living in Belgium. He was recognized on the streets of Europe and greeted as "Le Maître" (The Master).

John's last trip to Europe was in the fall of 1926. He and his wife, Rachel, spent Thanksgiving with their son, Val, and his family in Belgium. The next day, John and Val went to the FN factory for another day of work. After climbing the stairs to Val's office, John collapsed with chest pains and within minutes he was dead. As recognition for his prodigious contribution to the US war effort, Browning's flag-draped casket returned to America with a military escort, and he was eulogized by the secretary of war.

John Browning worked until his last breath. Talking with his family in the last year of his life, John explained his extraordinary forty-seven years of invention with typical humility: "The time and place for a gunmaker just got together on this corner. And I happened along."[11] During Browning's lifetime, he was granted 128 patents for over eighty complete and distinct firearm models. Those designs included everything from .22-caliber handguns to a 37mm cannon. One historian claimed he was "the greatest figure in the history of firearms."[12] Another authority, comparing Browning to Edison, Steinmetz, Westinghouse, and Marconi, said that Browning "stood alone, and there never was in this time or before, one whose genius . . . could remotely compare with his."[13]

Before Browning

Dominant as he was, John Browning did not invent firearms. His contributions were part of a much longer history that began centuries earlier in places far from Ogden, Utah. Historians, who have excavated the medieval origins of firearms and gunpowder, generally agree that in the ninth century, Chinese alchemists discovered the extraordinary explosive properties of saltpeter (potassium nitrate), charcoal, and sulfur.[14] If similar independent discoveries were not made in India and the Middle East at the same time, the Chinese technology soon spread to these areas. Gun historians Harold Peterson and Robert Elman claim that the "first provable reference to gunpowder" can be traced to England when Roger Bacon recorded a formula for gunpowder in about 1250.[15] By the thirteenth century, intrepid inventors in China, the Middle East, and Europe had begun designing primitive weapons.

What followed during the next several centuries is an extraordinary example of technological evolution. Ideas diffused between neighboring villages and across continents. Without patent systems, innovations were shamelessly copied. Gunmakers and blacksmiths invented continuously and prolifically, usually in small steps, adjusting the position of a lever or the location of a spring. Occasionally, game-changing leaps in innovation propelled the process forward. A kind of natural selection steered the development of new firearms. Those designs that were accepted for reasons of safety, simplicity, efficiency, elegance, ease of use, or cost survived and were further refined. Those that did not meet those standards ended up in museums and scrap piles.

The early days of this inventive spree produced a bewildering variety of relatively primitive devices—hand cannons, harquebuses, calivers, petronels, and tanegashimas. It did not take long for people to appreciate both the utility and the dangers of these strange new devices. The fifteenth-century "journalist" Wilhelm Rem tells the story of an Augsburg man "who invited a handsome whore. And when she was with him in a little room, he took up a loaded gun in his hand. . . . Accordingly he played around with the gun and pressed the trigger and shot the whore through the chin, so that the bullet passed out through the back of her neck."[16] The woman survived with compensation of forty florins per year for the rest of her life.

At about the same time, the rulers of Ferrara, Italy, enacted gun control:

> Since an especially dangerous kind of firearms have come to be used . . . with which a homicide can easily be committed; in knowledge of this, His Excellency, knowing that there are devilish arms, prohibits . . . their being carried . . . without explicit authorization, under penalty of having a hand publicly cut off.[17]

Other Italian cities followed with similar ordinances.

Starting in about 1500, we see a progression of designs for the ignition systems of firearms in roughly one-century intervals. The matchlock used a long fuse (the match) dangling from the gun. The fuse was attached to a spring-loaded hook (the serpentine) that lowered the lit end of the fuse into the priming pan. The resulting explosion ignited the main charge and propelled a lead ball or load of shot down the barrel. These matchlocks were muzzleloaders—the ammunition was loaded through the open end of the barrel. Gunmakers tinkered with the design of matchlocks to overcome its many deficiencies: wet weather extinguished the fuse; the firing time was slow and unpredictable; when used at night in combat, the lit fuse was a marker for the enemy; and the loading procedure required some eighteen steps for a single shot.

The wheel lock represented a clear break from the matchlock, although no single person is credited with the invention. Some attribute an early design to Leonardo da Vinci. The ingenious firing mechanism, with up to fifty moving parts, used a grooved, spring-loaded, metal wheel that rotated against a piece of pyrite to produce sparks. The sparks fell into the priming pan, igniting the main charge. Despite its complexity, the wheel lock offered significant advantages over previous designs. To fire the gun, the wheel lock was cocked into a safe position, powder was added to the pan, and the trigger activated the firing mechanism. The wheel lock, used on either a pistol or a long gun, fired quickly and was less prone to accidental discharges. The disadvantage was the cost. Often highly embellished with carved and inlaid stocks, wheel locks were favored by hunters and target shooters but saw little action on battlefields.

Another critical invention took place at the time of the wheel lock. The "bullets" of the day were steel or lead balls that varied randomly in size. As a result, the balls often bounced along the barrel as they were fired and then wobbled or veered off course once in flight. Many years of observation and tinkering (again, no single inventor can be identified) led to the idea of rifling. Spiral grooves etched on the inside of the barrel gave the projectile a spin that stabilized its trajectory. Long guns with rifling in their barrels became rifles. Smooth barrels still had a place, primarily for guns that fired shot, which eventually became shotguns.

With its complexity and high cost, the wheel lock was an evolutionary dead end; it was over-engineered. A simpler and more effective design evolved in the form of the flintlock. As the name suggests, the flintlock uses a piece of flint (easily found in most parts of Europe) attached to a spring-loaded cocking mechanism. With the gun half-cocked, the gun was loaded (still from the muzzle), powder was put in the priming pan, and the gun was fully cocked. Pulling the trigger released the flint, which struck a steel plate in the priming pan, which in turn ignited the main charge. Flintlocks appeared throughout Europe more or less simultaneously in the early eighteenth century, making it impossible to pinpoint a single origin of the idea. The mechanism had clear advantages in terms of simplicity, mass production, and ease of loading and firing. With and without rifling, it appeared on pistols (often for dueling), carbines (short rifles), muskets (military rifles), blunderbusses (wide barrel guns), and shot guns (one and two barrels). In England, it resulted in the Brown Bess and in France it led to the Charleville, both military rifles that would see action in European and North American wars for over a century.

At this point, the firearm story begins to merge with American history. Immigrant gunmakers, particularly from England and Germany, brought their craft to the colonies in the early 1700s. The first American rifles were most likely made in Lancaster County, Pennsylvania, but soon the gun craft spread to New England and the Carolinas. One distinctly American product of this first wave of gun making came to be called the Kentucky rifle— although it likely originated in Pennsylvania. Once perfected, it was a handsome gun, with a long, sleek, small-bore barrel and a decorated curly maple stock. It was slow to load but supremely accurate, so it was preferred for hunting on the frontier rather than for military use. Captain John Dillin's 1924 panegyric captures the mystique of this remarkable invention:

> From a flat bar of soft iron, hand forged into a gun barrel; laboriously
> bored and rifled with crude tools; fitted with a stock hewn from a maple
> tree in the neighboring forest; and supplied with a lock hammered
> to shape on the anvil; an unknown smith, in a shop long since silent,
> fashioned a rifle which changed the whole course of world history; made
> possible the settlement of a continent; and ultimately freed our country
> of foreign domination. Light in weight; graceful in line; economical in
> consumption of powder and lead; fatally precise; distinctly American; it
> sprang into immediate popularity; and for a hundred years was a model
> often slightly varied but never radically changed.[18]

Another flurry of invention in the early 1800s led to a momentous advance in gun design. Once again, concurrent inventions across Europe—some independent and some using borrowed ideas—leave historians uncertain about the exact course of events. What is known is that in about 1807, Alexander John Forsyth, a Scottish clergyman and hunter with a penchant for chemistry, discovered compounds called fulminates that ignite when struck. With this discovery, and after many harrowing experiments, Forsyth produced the first percussion-lock firing system. His idea was to keep all the virtues of flintlocks but replace the flint-on-metal mechanism by a hammer that struck a fulminate primer. At nearly the same time, gunmakers in France and Germany were taking the percussion lock idea one large step further.

In 1812, Jean Samuel Pauly, a Swiss gunmaker working in Paris, received a "patent" for a gun that was loaded not through the muzzle but through the closed end of the barrel, or the breech. The idea of a breech-loading gun required the invention of a cartridge. Pauly's first cartridge was a self-contained package with a copper base that held the primer, the charge, and the bullet in a paper casing. With a cartridge loaded in the breech, a pull of the trigger released a hammer, which ignited the primer, lit the charge, and fired the bullet. The result was a quick-loading gun that could fire ten rounds in a minute.

Combining breech-loading guns with cartridges, gunmakers throughout Europe, notably Johann Nikolaus von Dreyse of Germany, revolutionized the firearms industry. In the United States, John Hall and William Thornton produced a breech-loading rifle that was adopted by the military in 1817. Breech-loading was soon built into all sorts of rifles, shotguns, and pistols. Cartridges were quickly improved and the first all-metal cartridges appeared in 1845. These inventions opened the door to modern firearms, all of which are built on these nineteenth-century inventions.

America's first major manufacturer of firearms was the Springfield Armory in Springfield, Massachusetts. George Washington approved its location on an impregnable bluff overlooking the Connecticut River in 1777. During the Revolutionary War, the armory produced ammunition and stored muskets, cannons, and other artillery. Daniel Shays and his rebels tried to storm the armory to seize guns in 1787. In 1794, the Springfield Armory began manufacturing muskets and produced a long line of Springfield rifles up until its closing during the Vietnam War in 1968. (The private gun manufacturer Springfield Armory inherited the name of the federal facility in 1974 but is otherwise unrelated.)

More flamboyant and widely recognized during his lifetime than John Browning was Samuel Colt. He was not a gunsmith, but he was a prolific inventor, an irrepressible entrepreneur, an aggressive lobbyist, and one of the country's most successful industrialists. He received patents—first in England, then in America—for his design of a "revolving gun" in 1836. He claimed that the idea for a revolver was not his but originated with Elisha Collier, who invented a flintlock revolver in 1814. Colt's first two attempts at business failed, in part due to mismanagement and his own extravagance. However, when the Texas Rangers ordered one thousand revolvers for the Mexican-American War in 1847, the Colt Patent Fire Arms Manufacturing Company in Hartford, Connecticut, quickly prospered. Samuel Colt died in 1862 at the age of forty-seven as one of the wealthiest men in America, and he left a company that endured. The unquestionable key to Colt's success was the manufacturing of interchangeable gun parts, which enabled the use of assembly lines; both developments coincided with the rise of the Industrial Revolution.

During the Civil War, Colt Manufacturing employed 1,500 people and produced over 150,000 muskets and pistols per year. According to a slogan of the day, "Abe Lincoln may have freed all men, but Sam Colt made them equal."[19] In 1873, the company introduced the Single Action Army revolver. Crowned "the gun that won the West," Colt Manufacturing sold over 350,000 of these guns during the next seventy years. The company flourished during America's wars, with large government contracts for Browning M1911 pistols during World War I, pistols and machine guns during World War II, and M16 rifles during the Vietnam War. Despite increasing competition, mergers, changes in ownership, and one bankruptcy filing, Colt prospers to this day.

It has been said that Samuel Colt's worst professional mistake involved a gunsmith named Rollin White. By about 1850, most revolvers were loaded by pouring black powder, a bullet, and a percussion cap into each cylinder of the gun—a slow process to be sure. Also at that time, the design of cartridges with a metal casing was being perfected. The challenge was modifying existing revolvers to accept the new cartridges. White showed Colt his invention of a revolver that used metal cartridges, but Colt was unimpressed with the idea and parted ways with White. Believing in the worth of his invention, White took it to a new company owned by Horace Smith and Daniel Wesson, who knew a good idea when they saw it. For a decade, Smith, Wesson, and White fought off patent infringements by other companies and manufactured the Smith & Wesson Model 1 with great success. The future of the company was ensured with the arrival of the Civil War, followed by a foreign marketing campaign that opened new markets in Europe and Russia. Today, Smith & Wesson Holding Corporation is a leader in the firearms industry.

The distinction of longest continuously operating American gunmaker goes to Remington Arms. Founded in 1816 in Ilion, New York, by Eliphalet Remington, the company has made rifles, shotguns, and ammunition for the military, law enforcement, and recreational uses. (The company also launched a typewriter business that was spun off as Remington Rand in 1886.) After mergers and changes in ownership over the years, Remington thrives today as a subsidiary of the Freedom Group (along with ten other firearm companies).

Another American company surviving since the nineteenth century is Savage Arms. Organized in 1894 in Utica, New York, by the adventurous Arthur Savage, the company made innovations in rifle design, produced machine guns during World War I, and donated millions of firearms to the World War II campaign. The company survived buyouts, bankruptcy, and reorganization in the 1980s to remain a leading innovator and producer of firearms.

After Browning

The global landscape of today's firearms industry is complex. A few old legacy companies have survived for centuries. For example, Beretta, an Italian company founded in 1526, is still owned by the same family. Today, it manufactures the semiautomatic M9 pistol, the official US military sidearm. In other cases, large conglomerates have absorbed, merged with, and otherwise transformed existing companies. For example, FN Herstal (itself a subsidiary of the Belgian Herstal Group) owns Browning Arms Company and the US Repeating Arms Company (originally Winchester).

Crossbreeding has occurred in a bewildering variety of ways. The venerable German company Walther was founded in 1886 and is now owned by Umarex, maker of everything from knives and crossbows to paintball accessories. The brothers Wilhelm and Paul Mauser began making rifles in Germany in 1872. Respected for its precision military arms, pistols, and hunting rifles, the company was bought by the Rheinmetall Group in 1995. Founded in 1853, the Swiss Industrial Company (SIG) originally made wagons, until it landed a contract to provide rifles for the Swiss Army. By 1980, it had engulfed several other European firearm companies and opened business in America as SIGARMS; it became SIG SAUER in 2007 and is now just one piece of a global arms-manufacturing empire.

In addition to mergers, splittings, takeovers, and rebrandings, hundreds of new companies are born to battle in the highly competitive firearms market. Founded in 1949 in Southport, Connecticut, the eponymous company of William Ruger and Alexander Sturm is now a thriving publicly traded maker of .22 rifles and semiautomatic handguns, rifles, and shotguns. An even more recent giant on the field is Glock. Responding to a request for bids by the Austrian military in 1980, Gaston Glock—not a gun designer, but a material scientist—won the job with a design for a handgun with a polymer frame. Glock's "plastic guns," among them the Glock 17, currently dominate the law-enforcement handgun market.

From its primitive origins in the Middle Ages, through eight centuries of innovation and entrepreneurial evolution, the firearms industry has emerged as a global, inbred, multibillion-dollar enterprise. And yet it is astounding that in many respects, the firearms industry is a mystery—concealed and protected from public scrutiny. How big *is* the industry? Who are the leaders? Are firearms sales increasing or decreasing? Which are the best-selling models?

Revenue figures for US casinos, sales data for motorcycles, and wages for CEOs of nonprofits can be found in trade publications or from required government filings or by curious journalists. But finding answers to questions about firearms sales is harder than figuring out how much the music industry loses each year in illegal downloads.

Cameron Hopkins, who writes the Industry Insider column for the NRA's *American Rifleman* magazine, observed:

Unlike other industries that can be analyzed, quantified, objectified and measured, the metrics of the gun business are largely unknown. It's amazing how mysterious the industry is when you think about it. Even an industry analyst like the Insider cannot get hold of basic data that other industries take for granted.[20]

More conspiratorially, Josh Horwitz of the Coalition to Stop Gun Violence claims that the "gun lobby," which consists largely of the National Shooting

Sports Foundation (NSSF) and the NRA, "doesn't actually provide any gun sales data to the media. The NSSF and the NRA have this data because gun manufacturers have to understand what their dealers are selling in order to produce the proper amount of product and maximize profits. But the gun lobby has blocked public access to this information for decades."[21] Horwitz's suspicion is that the media are fed inflated sales figures to make the gun industry look more prosperous than it really is.

A few isolated facts can be found in the mandatory reports of the few publicly traded gun manufacturers. Smith & Wesson Holding Corporation reported net sales of $552 million for the year ending April 2015, a decrease over the previous two years but a healthy 62 percent increase over the year ending April 2011. Gross profits for the year ending April 2015 were $195 million compared with $105 million for the year ending April 2011.[22] Publicly traded Sturm, Ruger & Co. also enjoyed strong sales numbers during the "Newtown boom," when sales of guns and accessories soared. In a one-year period ending August 2012, Ruger produced over one million guns.[23] However, the boom then subsided: Ruger's profits dropped to $15.5 million during the first quarter of 2015, down from $24.3 million during the first quarter of 2014.[24]

The fact remains that nearly all international and domestic firearm companies are privately held and not required to file financial reports. So we are left to read shadows on the wall and use proxy data to infer sales data. One possible indicator of overall sales data is the annual *Firearms Commerce in the United States* report released by the Bureau of Alcohol, Tobacco, Firearms, and Explosives (ATF).[25] Compiled with data submitted by licensed gun dealers (Federal Firearms Licensees or FFLs), the report gives an annual snapshot of firearm manufacturing, exports, and imports. According to the 2016 report, over nine million firearms were manufactured in the United States in 2014, an increase of 6 percent over 2012 but a small decrease over 2013. Over 3.9 million firearms were imported into the United States in 2015. Imports of firearms have actually decreased since a high in 2013; handguns imported from Brazil, Austria, Croatia, and Germany account for roughly 50 percent of all US imports. Unfortunately, guns produced are not guns sold. As extremely durable items, firearms could be piling up in warehouses far from retail dealers. As one skeptical analyst notes, "the domestic automobile industry overproduced itself into bankruptcy."[26] One study, accounting for the 25 percent of all sales in used guns, estimated that total guns sold in America in 2011 amounted to 12.7 million.[27]

Another often cited source for firearm sales is the FBI's National Instant Criminal Background Check System (NICS) (see chapter 9). However, positive background checks do not always result in a sale; for example, a buyer may change his mind during a waiting period. Background checks are also required for applications for a concealed-carry permit, which may not be accompanied by a sale. And in some states, concealed-carry permit holders are not required to have a background check. If that is not enough, one background check suffices for a purchase of multiple firearms. Given all these factors, it is not even clear whether NICS data underestimate or overestimate actual sales data. The warning is that NICS data should not be mistaken for sales data.

The history of firearms spans the Earth and covers nearly one millennium of civilization. From the smoke-choked forges of fourteenth-century gunsmiths to the frontier design studios of John Browning to the high-volume assembly lines of modern gun factories, it is a story of wondrous innovation and entrepreneurial intrigue. Guns provide a textbook example of technological crossbreeding and evolution. All of that history has given us a world in which firearms are manufactured, sold, imported, exported, traded, smuggled, and destroyed every day—and remarkably, there are no reliable figures that capture all of this activity. The Small Arms Survey, an ambitious international organization that tracks the sale, distribution, and uses of weapons, estimates that there are 875 million small arms (handguns through light machine guns) in circulation worldwide, produced by more than one thousand companies.[28] We know that production rates are increasing and that firearms have long lifetimes. It follows that between military armories, manufacturers' warehouses, retailers' stock rooms, and the closets and garages of gun owners, the number of firearms on the planet is immense and immeasurable—and continues to rise every year.

8 | THE OTHER AMENDMENT

In all except the actual results of the physical struggle,
I consider the South to have been the real victors in the [Civil] war. . . .
The way in which they have neutralized the results of the war and
reversed the verdict of Appomattox is the grandest thing in American politics.

—ALBION W. TOURGÉE, civil rights activist, *New York Tribune*, 1879[1]

IMAGINE A SIX-INCH-LONG, eight-ounce firearm that could be easily concealed in a coat pocket or purse. It may sound like a typical semi-automatic
handgun that could be bought today from an online catalog. But in 1860,
a gun like this Deringer pocket pistol was a ballistic wonder; it was also an
assassin's dream.

The son of a German gunsmith, Henry Deringer grew up in Pennsylvania
watching his father make Kentucky rifles. He began his own career making
rifles for the military and then moved to small guns. His famous Philadelphia
Deringer was a single-round percussion pistol and, from 1852 to 1868, he manufactured some fifteen thousand of these guns. Deringer never patented the
pistol, so it was widely imitated and other companies such as Remington Arms
produced similar small guns that came to be called derringers (double *r*). While
the Deringer's single-shot capacity was a limitation, the guns were often sold
in pairs for twenty dollars to double the firepower. Soon companies such as
Colt and Smith & Wesson were making revolvers that carried multiple rounds.
Deringer's pocket pistol would be the instrument of enduring change in American history.

By early 1865, the conflagration of the Civil War was in its fourth year.
During those years, the handsome John Wilkes Booth was not in the killing
fields but performing in cities along the East Coast and building a reputation
as an accomplished stage actor. What many of his theater fans may not have
known was that Booth was also a rabid anti-abolitionist with a long-brewing

hatred for Abraham Lincoln. His odium only intensified with Lincoln's re-election in 1864 and the imminent Confederate defeat. Two days after General Lee's surrender on April 9, 1865, Booth heard Lincoln give a speech proposing that former slaves be granted rights of citizenship. The speech sent Booth over the edge as he allegedly vowed, "Now, by God, I'll put him through. That is the last speech he will ever give."[2] And with Deringer's help, he had the perfect weapon to make good on his word.

Booth and a group of conspirators planned to assassinate not only Lincoln but Vice President Andrew Johnson and Secretary of State William Seward. On Good Friday, April 14, Booth learned that Lincoln, General Grant, and their wives would be attending a performance of *My American Cousin* in the capitol's Ford's Theatre that same night. With the bonus of including Grant in his plan, Booth prepared for his "decisive" deed.

Booth was a familiar figure at Ford's Theatre, so when he slipped inside the theater at ten o'clock that night, no one questioned his presence or suspected that he was armed. Furthermore, Lincoln's bodyguard had left the theater during intermission to visit a nearby tavern. After the intermission, Booth crept into the presidential box and with 1,700 people in the house, shot Lincoln in the head at point-blank range with his Philadelphia Deringer. Booth leaped to the stage, injuring his left foot, and then fled. Lincoln was wounded mortally and died at 7:22 the next morning across the street in the Petersen House.

The rest of Booth's plot failed. Grant and his wife had decided to spend the evening elsewhere (the men's wives were not friendly). Johnson's appointed killer had a change of heart and Seward survived a knife attack at his home. Booth was captured and killed twelve days after the assassination at a farm in rural Virginia. A military tribunal convicted Booth's conspirators, and four of them were hanged at the Old Arsenal Penitentiary on July 7.

Lincoln was the first American president to be assassinated, although Andrew Jackson survived an assassination attempt in 1833. Lincoln's slaying is the first in a long list of murders of prominent Americans. That list includes the assassinations of President James Garfield (1881, .44 Webley British Bulldog revolver), President William McKinley (1901, .32 Iver Johnson revolver), Robert Kennedy (1968, .22-caliber revolver),[3] and John Lennon (1980, five hollow-point bullets from a Charter Arms .38 Special revolver). It also includes attempts on the lives of Theodore Roosevelt (1912, .38-caliber revolver), Franklin Roosevelt (1933, .38-caliber revolver), Gerald Ford (1975, .45 Colt revolver and 1975, .38-caliber revolver), Ronald Reagan (1981, .22 Rohm RG-14), and US Representative Gabrielle Giffords (2011, 9mm Glock-19).

In all of these cases, history was changed or would have been changed if not for chance. And in all of these cases, when a knife, a bomb, a shotgun, or a rifle might have done the job, the weapon of choice was an easy-to-conceal, easy-to-obtain handgun. The notable exceptions in this tragic record of political violence were the assassinations of John F. Kennedy and Martin Luther King Jr., whose assassins used rifles.

Reconstruction Amendments and Laws

Counting combat deaths and disease, the Civil War took the lives of 360,000 Union soldiers and 260,000 Confederate soldiers. The financial cost of the war on the Union side alone has been estimated at $2.6 billion (in 1860 dollars); forty years later, veterans' benefits had added another $3.3 billion to this cost. The Civil War wrought unimaginable destruction on the South. It reduced Atlanta, Charleston, Columbia, and Mobile—and hundreds of smaller cities—to smoldering piles of timber and stone. Farms and plantations were destroyed. Roads, bridges, and railways were decimated. Confederate currency was worthless and the Confederate debt was overwhelming.

Illinois journalist Sidney Andrews, traveling through the South in the fall of 1865, wrote about the absence of schools, books, and newspapers outside the cities. Referring to the impoverished "mass of whites," he observed that "there were two kinds of slavery, and negro slavery was only more wicked and debasing than white slavery."[4] Forty years later, the historian W. E. B. DuBois wrote that "guerrilla raiding, the ever-present flickering after-flame of the war, was spending its force on Negroes, and all the Southern land was awakening as from some wild dream to poverty and social revolution."[5]

Lincoln is remembered as the first Republican president (the party of Lincoln). His assassination left the formidable job of guiding the nation through Reconstruction to his Democratic vice president, a dirt-to-distinction Tennessee tailor named Andrew Johnson. One could be excused for doubting Johnson's fitness for the job. At his inaugural address, one observer reported that Johnson "was too drunk to perform his duties and disgraced himself and the Senate by making a drunken foolish speech."[6] Shortly after becoming president, he told a Missouri newspaper, "This is a country for white men, and by God, as long as I am President, it shall be a government for white men."[7]

If the meaning of the Second Amendment was unclear before the Civil War, the next tumultuous fifteen years only further obscured the picture. Familiar debates, such as state vs. federal power and collective vs. individual rights to bear arms, persisted and became more contentious. Healing the Union meant ensuring that four million newly freed slaves had the same civil rights enjoyed by white citizens—and that included the right to bear arms. As a result, the new laws and constitutional amendments of the Reconstruction period affected the Second Amendment and the right to bear arms in unexpected ways. It is worth following a few of the significant legal and political events during these critical years.

In 1865, a Republican-controlled Congress adopted the Thirteenth Amendment, declaring that "Neither slavery nor involuntary servitude . . . shall exist within the United States or any place subject to their jurisdiction."[8]

The amendment abolished slavery and gave Congress enforcement power with "appropriate legislation." However, it did little to grant specific rights to black people or change their legal status (and women of any color would not be part of the discussion for another fifty years). Southern states continued to enforce Black Codes that deprived black people of basic civil rights. Even new laws purporting to grant civil rights to black people sounded strangely contorted. For example, an 1866 Texas law sounds egalitarian:

All persons heretofore known as slaves, and free persons of color, shall have the right to make and enforce contracts, to sue and be sued, to inherit, purchase, lease, hold, sell, and convey real, personal and mixed estate; to make wills and testaments, and to have and enjoy the rights of personal security, liberty, and private property.[9]

However, the same act also states:

Nothing herein shall be so construed as to repeal any law prohibiting the inter-marriage of the white and black races, nor to permit any other than white men to serve on juries, hold office, vote at any election.[10]

A South Carolina law of the same period asserted:

> Although [persons of color] are not entitled to social or political equality
> with white persons, they shall have the right to acquire, own, and dispose
> of property; to make contracts; to enjoy the fruits of their labor; to sue
> and be sued; and to receive protection under the law in their persons and
> property.[11]

Significantly, the Black Codes often outlawed the ownership and use of
firearms by black people. The Mississippi militia confiscated "every gun and
pistol found in the hands of (so-called) freedmen," claiming that the "laws of
Mississippi do not recognize the negro as having any right to carry arms."[12]
The Black Codes led to a new gun rights debate, now overlaid with race: discriminatory gun control measures, favored by traditional Southern whites,
clashed with demands for equality of gun rights, favored by abolitionists.

Congress responded to the Black Codes with the Civil Rights Act of 1866.
New York Times founder and Republican Congressman Henry Raymond
called it "one of the most important bills ever presented to this House for its
action."[13] Its purpose was to clarify and fortify the Thirteenth Amendment
in statute. The law claimed that "all persons born in the United States and
not subject to any foreign power, excluding Indians not taxed, are hereby
declared to be citizens of the United States," independent of "race and color,
without regard to any previous condition of slavery."[14]

It entitled citizens to "full and equal benefit of all laws and proceedings for
the security of person and property, as is enjoyed by white citizens."[15] Arguing
for passage of the law, its sponsor, Republican Senator Lyman Trumbull of
Illinois, cited the discriminatory practice of prohibiting black people from
owning firearms.

The Civil Rights Act was significant in another way. For the first time in
American history, a major law was passed over a president's veto. Some legislators opposed the law because it was an intrusion of the federal government in the affairs of the states. However, President Johnson vetoed the act
by persuading himself that it would "operate in favor of colored and against
the white race" and lead to reverse discrimination.[16] The veto was yet another
confrontation with the Republican Congress that ultimately led to Johnson's
impeachment in 1868.

Even before the Civil Rights Act was finalized, Congress began work on the Fourteenth Amendment, designed to give constitutional authority to racial equality and civil rights. The dramatic ratification of this amendment is a critical chapter in American history. Its cast featured some of the greatest nineteenth-century legislators, notably Ohio Representative John Bingham, who is recognized as the architect of the amendment's first section; Massachusetts Senator Charles Sumner, who ten years earlier was brutally attacked on the floor of the Senate by an irate southern legislator; a former attorney general and future ambassador to the United Kingdom, Democratic Maryland Senator Reverdy Johnson; and the flamboyant Republican congressman from Pennsylvania Thaddeus Stevens, who was the amendment's shepherd as it twisted its way to final passage.

For six months, legislators engaged in roof-raising oratory, political acrobatics, cultural sword-crossing, and dueling theories of governance as they drafted, rejected, and revised over seventy versions of the amendment. At the defeat of one of those versions, Stevens wailed that the amendment had been "slaughtered by a puerile and pedantic criticism."[17] The debate in Congress exposed deep political and cultural chasms among legislators, and the result was a miracle of compromise. When the oratorical dust settled, the amendment received final approval by the House on June 13, 1866; every Republican voted for it and every Democrat voted against it. In his closing speech, Thaddeus Stevens acknowledged the compromises and imperfections of the amendment, famously saying, "I live among men, not among angels."[18] Two years later, on July 9, 1868, the Fourteenth Amendment was ratified by the required twenty-eight (of thirty-seven) states.

Often called the "second Constitution," the Fourteenth Amendment is the longest amendment in today's Constitution. Of its five sections, the first section contains the language that has been the fulcrum in hundreds of Supreme Court decisions; it would also bear significantly on future interpretations of the Second Amendment. The first section begins by reaffirming the citizenship terms of the Civil Rights Act:

> All persons born or naturalized in the United States, and subject to the jurisdiction thereof, are citizens of the United States and of the State wherein they reside.[19]

Then comes the privileges and immunities clause:

> No State shall make or enforce any law which shall abridge the privileges or immunities of citizens of the United States.[20]

Followed by the due-process clause:

> Nor shall any State deprive any person of life, liberty, or property, without due process of law.[21]

It concludes with the equal-protection clause:

> Nor deny to any person within its jurisdiction the equal protection of the laws.[22]

Never before were so many fundamental democratic principles expressed so compactly, yet so ambiguously. Civil War scholar Eric Foner observes that "for more than a century, politicians, judges, lawyers, and scholars have debated the meaning of this elusive language." But at its heart, the amendment is "a national guarantee of equality before the law."[23] Among the rights not included in the amendment was the right to vote. Nevertheless, passing the Fourteenth Amendment was a historic achievement. Yet to come was an interpretation of what exactly it meant. That was left to the courts and it has occupied them until this day.

Even within the Republican ranks, different understandings of the amendment emerged. The weak interpretation claimed it was simply an extension of language already in the Constitution ensuring equality for all citizens.[24] According to this interpretation, the amendment did not compromise states' rights or assert national citizenship over state citizenship. As Representative John Bingham put it at the time:

> It is a simple, strong, plain declaration that equal laws and equal and exact justice shall hereafter be secured within every State of this Union. . . . It takes from no State any right which hitherto pertained to the several States of the United States.[25]

The strong interpretation of the amendment, as expressed by Republican Senator Jacob Howard of Michigan among others, claimed much more. Until now, the Bill of Rights was assumed to constrain only the federal government. According to Howard, the Fourteenth Amendment protected the rights in the Bill of Rights from state and local action as well. When applied specifically to the Second Amendment, Republican Kansas Senator Samuel Pomeroy claimed that the Fourteenth Amendment ensures that the right to "bear arms for the defense of himself, his family, and his homestead" cannot be violated by the states.[26]

These different interpretations of the Fourteenth Amendment presaged one of the great legal debates of the last 150 years—the question of incorporation. Exactly which of the rights in the Bill of Rights are protected from abridgement by state and local—as well as federal—laws? For example, even if a particular state constitution does not include a particular provision in its bill of rights, does the Fourteenth Amendment compel the state to respect that right and not pass laws that violate it?

Soon, an even subtler question emerged. The Fourteenth Amendment may limit state action in violating basic rights, but does it say anything about actions by individuals or organizations? For example, if an organization, such as the Ku Klux Klan, violates another person's civil rights, can that organization be prosecuted under federal laws, by virtue of the Fourteenth Amendment? The questions were profound, and decades would be needed to formulate answers.

It is worth mentioning section 2 of the Fourteenth Amendment, which dealt with an unintended consequence of emancipation. According to the original Constitution, slaves counted as three-fifths of a person for purposes of apportionment (determining the number of seats in the House of Representatives and the Electoral College). With the abolition of slavery, the three-fifths provision was nullified, and each black citizen was counted as one whole citizen. However, this change gave the southern states additional representation—an estimated twenty-five additional "slave seats" in the House (even though freedmen still had no voting power). The resulting shift of power was not lost on northern lawmakers and they sought a remedy.

Debate on this representation paradox was feverish. Several proposals received little support because they were politically impractical or had unexpected consequences. For example, one simple solution was to grant voting rights to black people. However, even in the North, there was widespread doubt about black suffrage. The black writer and statesman Frederick Douglass reacted contemptuously, saying that "to tell me that I am an equal American citizen, and, in the same breath, tell me that my right to vote may be constitutionally taken from me by some other equal citizens, is to tell me that my citizenship is but an empty name."[27] The Fifteenth Amendment, extending the right to vote to black males, would not pass until 1870.

Another solution to the representation dilemma was to base representation on the number of actual voters in a state. However, states with a large proportion of women or unnaturalized immigrants (both nonvoting classes) realized the disadvantages of this plan. Seeing an opportunity, feminists Elizabeth Cady Stanton and Susan B. Anthony justifiably demanded "an amendment to the Constitution that shall prohibit the several States from disfranchising any of their citizens on the ground of sex."[28] This plan was also rejected. The Nineteenth Amendment, extending voting rights to women, was not ratified until 1920.

In the end, representation of a state remained based on its population. However, section 2 of the Fourteenth Amendment imposed a penalty (a reduction in representatives) for those states that denied voting rights to males at least twenty-one years of age. While not a satisfactory solution to many, this halfway step to black suffrage hastened the passage of the Fifteenth Amendment, giving black males the right to vote.

While Washington, DC, built the legislative and constitutional framework for Reconstruction, much of the South remained in another world. The backlash to the coming changes was relentless, defiant, and violent. The Ku Klux Klan was founded in Pulaski, Tennessee, in 1865 and was soon joined by other white terrorist groups dedicated to the "better preservation of the white race and to see that the white blood was handed down unmixed."[29] In May of 1866, a case of racial road rage led to riots in Memphis that took the lives of forty-six black and two white people. Later that summer, white onlookers disrupted a parade of black Republicans in New Orleans. When the white police force intervened, the skirmish became a massacre; 38 people, all but 4 black, died, and 184 people were injured. The violence only escalated; according to one report, nearly 1,100 political murders occurred during a six-month period in 1868 in Louisiana alone.[30]

In response to the violence in the South, Congress passed the Enforcement Acts in 1870 and 1871 to put claws into the Fourteenth and Fifteenth Amendments. The third Enforcement Act, known as the Ku Klux Klan Act, made it a federal crime to deprive citizens of the "rights, privileges, or immunities secured by the Constitution."[31] The debates in Congress prior to passage of the Enforcement Acts foreshadowed the same divisions that would emerge in upcoming court cases. The Republicans argued that the acts justifiably gave the federal government authority to take action—including military intervention—when states failed to protect the civil rights of citizens. Furthermore, those protections included violations by individuals. The Democrats saw the Enforcement Acts as more unwarranted intrusions by the federal government that threatened the sovereignty and authority of the states. Emphasizing a deep rift of opinion, one Democratic senator claimed, "The Radical laws to enforce the 15th or 14th Amendment are unconstitutional clearly so far as they deal with *individuals*, not with the *states*."[32]

With the passage of the Enforcement Acts, the nascent Justice Department, under Attorney General Amos Akerman, put the Klan in its sights. Hundreds of Klansmen were arrested and brought to justice in the ensuing KKK trials. By 1872, the Klan had been significantly weakened—only to be replaced by other supremacist paramilitary groups, such as the Knights of the White Camellia and the White League. (The Ku Klux Klan was resurrected in 1915 and again in the 1950s.) The KKK trials gave the new federal laws and amendments their first legal tests. Anyone who thought that the intent of these acts was obvious or that their language was clear soon learned otherwise. American courts were sailing into unmapped waters.

Entrails and the Courts

Once the Fourteenth Amendment was on the books, it did not take long for the courts to test and interpret it. The difficulties that arose are illustrated by two lower court cases and a history-bending Supreme Court decision.

A Ku Klux Klan raid on a Republican campaign meeting in Alabama in October 1870 left four black people dead and over fifty wounded. In the resulting federal court case, *United States v. Hall*, the Justice Department prosecuted the Klansmen for violating the federal Enforcement Acts. The defense claimed that the Constitution did not empower Congress to pass laws prohibiting the criminal actions of individuals in Alabama and that such matters remained strictly under the purview of the state. The prosecution argued that fundamental rights, notably the First Amendment rights of speech and assembly, were now protected from state infringement by the Fourteenth Amendment. The prosecution also pointed to section 5 of the Fourteenth Amendment, which empowers Congress to pass legislation, such as the Enforcement Acts, protecting those rights.

Federal court judge William Woods, after consultation with Supreme Court justice Joseph Bradley (both of whom would play prominent roles in upcoming court cases), ruled for the prosecution. Woods wrote, "by the *original* Constitution, citizenship in the United States was a consequence of citizenship in the state." By virtue of the Fourteenth Amendment, "this order of things is [now] reversed."[33] By his opinion, the rights guaranteed by the Bill of Rights were now pre-eminent and could not be breached by state laws.

Clear as the Hall decision may have seemed in affirming the Fourteenth Amendment, other cases clouded the waters. In a raid on a South Carolina home, Klansmen inflicted unimaginable violence on freedman Amzi Rainey, his wife, and daughters. The resulting federal case, *United States v. Crosby*, featured two celebrated defense attorneys of the day. Reverdy Johnson, one of the combatants in the 1866 Civil Rights Act debate, and Henry Stanbery, attorney general under Andrew Johnson, brought their formidable skills and reputations to the defense of the Klansmen. They argued forcefully that the Fourteenth Amendment did not protect rights expressed in the Bill of Rights from state action and that in this case, the federal government did not have the authority to prosecute the actions of individuals.

In their decision, federal judges Hugh Bond and George Bryan gave something to both sides. They accepted the state's claim that the Fourth Amendment, providing protection from unreasonable search and seizure, applies to the federal government but not to the states; that is, at least in some circumstances, states could violate Fourth Amendment rights with impunity. Score one for the defense. However, they upheld two counts of the indictment, recognizing that Rainey's right to vote, guaranteed by the Fifteenth Amendment, had been violated. In this curious split decision, the judges appeared to recognize the authority of the Fifteenth Amendment but not that of the Fourteenth Amendment.

The most significant court case of this period had little to do with racial violence and everything to do with incorporation of fundamental rights. It is worth looking at the *Slaughterhouse Cases* in some detail. The resulting Supreme Court decision set off a chain reaction that echoed for over a century, coloring the meaning of the Bill of Rights and the Second Amendment.

For many years, the white butchers of New Orleans had slaughtered livestock on the banks of the Mississippi River; an estimated one thousand butchers dispatched some three hundred thousand animals per year. The resulting offal (entrails, blood, and feces) was dumped into the river, upstream from the intake for the city's water supply. In 1869, the state legislature passed a Republican-sponsored cleanup law to move the slaughterhouses downstream from the city and replace them by a state-regulated facility operated by a private contractor. The new law required all butchers to use the new facility.

What appeared to be a sensible public health act quickly turned into a high-profile legal battle. The Butchers' Benevolent Association sued to overturn the law, claiming:

> [It] deprives a large and meritorious class of citizens—the whole of the butchers of the city—of the right to exercise their trade, the business to which they have been trained and on which they depend for the support of themselves and their families.[34]

Democratic lawmakers backed the butchers for at least two reasons: they feared racial integration of the new facility and they opposed any Republican law on principle.

The lower courts ruled in favor of the state (supporting improved sanitation and the new facility), triggering appeals that eventually reached the Supreme Court. In the high court, the Reconstruction obstructionist and former Supreme Court justice John Campbell represented the butchers. A political and legal chameleon, Campbell had supported the Black Codes and opposed the Thirteenth and Fourteenth Amendments. Now that it was expedient, he used those same amendments, claiming that they "secure to all protection from state legislation that involves the rights of property, the most valuable of which is to labor freely."[35] In other words, according to the defense, by requiring the butchers to use the new state-operated facility, the state was depriving the butchers of their fundamental right to pursue a lawful trade.

On April 14, 1873, the Supreme Court, in what became known as the *Slaughterhouse Cases*, upheld the Louisiana state law in a 5–4 vote. Justice Samuel Miller, ironically a physician who had studied cholera and water-borne diseases, wrote the majority opinion. Miller began by shredding Campbell's claim that the new law subjected the white butchers to "involuntary servitude," thus violating the Thirteenth Amendment. Then the *Slaughterhouse* decision became quite intricate. In ruling for the eminently reasonable state law requiring a cleanup of the water supply, Miller also had to either oppose the Fourteenth Amendment or give it a narrow interpretation. He chose a narrow interpretation, but it required a high-wire act that would be debated for years to come.

In Miller's opinion, the Fourteenth Amendment makes it clear that "there is a citizenship of the United States, and a citizenship of a state, which are distinct from each other, and which depend upon different characteristics or circumstances in the individual."[36] The challenge is to determine which rights are guaranteed and protected by the federal government and which should be left to the states. Miller declared that the Louisiana law was entirely within the bounds of state power and was not a violation of the Fourteenth Amendment. He then argued that the privileges and immunities protected by the Fourteenth Amendment were not civil rights, as many had assumed, but rather "those rights which depended on the Federal government for their existence or protection."[37] The rights Miller had in mind were very narrow in scope—the right to pursue a lawful trade, the right to habeas corpus, the right to travel freely between states, and the right to make financial claims on the federal government—and not the rights enumerated in the Bill of Rights.

As a sympathizer of civil rights and racial equality (and better public health), Miller may have thought his decision would be a victory for Republicans and a warning to Southern whites. However, the decision had a disastrous and opposite effect. As one modern observer writes, "Miller went too far. In destroying Campbell's extreme and self-serving view, Miller substituted a definition of privileges and immunities so cramped that it emptied the clause of practical meaning."[38] One of the dissenting justices in the *Slaughterhouse Cases* wrote that Miller's opinion could make the Fourteenth Amendment "a vain and idle enactment, which accomplished nothing."[39]

Rather than clarifying the Fourteenth Amendment for future courts, the *Slaughterhouse Cases* only obscured and enervated it. More technically, the decision "read all meaning out" of the privileges and immunity clause of the amendment. As a result, future debates over incorporation would focus on its due-process clause. The decision also served as a prelude for an even more decisive Supreme Court case within the decade. But between those two cases was one of the most tragic and overlooked episodes in American history.

9 | PLAYING BY THE RULES

> I love my country but fear my government.
>
> —Bumper sticker

AMERICANS LIVE IN a federalist system in which lawmaking powers are divided—often precariously—between the federal government and the states. The Federalist Alexander Hamilton claimed that "the general government will at all times stand ready to check the usurpations of the state governments; and [the states] will have the same disposition towards the General Government."[1] The Democratic-Republican Thomas Jefferson recognized the same polarity, saying, "It is not by the consolidation, or concentration of powers, but by their distribution, that good government is effected."[2] The tension was baked into the system from the start.

The federalist structure means that firearm laws are made and enforced on several different levels. At the federal level, firearm laws must fall within the legislative powers assigned to Congress by the Constitution (article I, section 8). Of the several legislative powers granted to Congress by the Constitution, only two realistically cover firearms: the powers to tax and to regulate commerce. Partly for this reason, major federal firearm laws are passed infrequently, and when they are passed, they generally set minimum standards that must be met by all states.

The US Code is the current and cumulative codification of all the laws ever passed by Congress.[3] If you burrow deep into its two hundred thousand pages, locate Title 26—Internal Revenue Code, burrow even deeper to Subtitle E—Alcohol, Tobacco, and Certain Other Excise Taxes, Chapter 53—Machine Guns, Destructive Devices, and Certain Other Firearms, and then settle on Subchapter B—General Provisions and Exemptions, Part I—General Provisions, Section 5841—Registration of Firearms, you will find the following provision:

The Secretary [of the Treasury] shall maintain a central registry of all firearms in the United States which are not in the possession or under the control of the United States. This registry shall be known as the National Firearms Registration and Transfer Record. The registry shall include (1) identification of the firearm; (2) date of registration; and (3) identification and address of person entitled to possession of the firearm.[4]

The law goes on to spell out taxes paid by dealers and manufacturers, taxes paid on firearm transfers, and record-keeping requirements. It appears to be a gun owner's worst nightmare: a national gun registry. Only several paragraphs later do we find that, for the purposes of this law, *firearm* is defined very narrowly to include automatic weapons such as machine guns, short-barreled rifles and shotguns, destructive devices, and other relatively uncommon weapons.

US Code, title 26, section 5841 has the longest history of any federal firearm legislation. It originated in the 1934 National Firearms Act (NFA), which was passed at the height of the crime wars to get "gangster weapons" off the streets. Because an outright ban on machine guns was not within Congress's authority, the law took the form of a tax measure. However, the law was an effective ban because its $200 tax on transfers of such weapons was prohibitive for most people at the time; the amount of the tax has never changed.

Three decades later, Congress was already debating new firearms laws when, in the spring of 1968, the assassinations of Robert Kennedy and Martin Luther King Jr. stunned the nation; those killings only amplified the call for tighter federal restrictions on firearms. At the same time, a cottage industry of illegal gun sellers was on the rise. By importing surplus military rifles at virtually no cost and reselling them cheaply, mail-order houses were cutting into the sales of established firearm companies. These companies, five of which were located in Connecticut, found a champion in the conservative Senator Thomas Dodd, who introduced legislation restricting imports and interstate sale of firearms.[5] (Dodd allegedly kept a pistol in his Senate desk.) On the other side, gun rights groups, still in their infancy, opposed the gun manufacturers and resisted any tightening of gun laws. Finally, the Supreme Court had just ruled that part of the NFA was unconstitutional: in certain cases, the registration required by the NFA could lead to Fifth Amendment violations (self-incrimination)—a flaw that required immediate remedy.[6]

Taken together, these events led to the Gun Control Act (GCA) of 1968. The sweeping law ultimately revised much of the 1934 NFA and added new provisions.[7] The act opens on a conciliatory note:

> It is not the purpose of this title to place any undue or unnecessary Federal restrictions or burdens on law-abiding citizens with respect to the acquisition, possession, or use of firearms appropriate to the purpose of hunting, trapshooting, target shooting, personal protection, or any other lawful activity, and that this title is not intended to discourage or eliminate the private ownership or use of firearms by law-abiding citizens for lawful purposes.[8]

This placating overture belied the law's new restrictions that many gun rights advocates found onerous and detestable.

Most notably, the GCA established the Federal Firearms License (FFL) system, which requires the licensing of firearm dealers. The FFL system remains the backbone of federal gun regulation today. The law also expanded the list of prohibited purchasers to nine categories, including felons, fugitives, addicts, aliens, and "mental defectives." It lists types of illegal transactions, requires that new firearms be imprinted with a serial number, and bans the import of firearms that do not have a "sporting purpose." It also expanded the original list of machine guns and automatic firearms subject to NFA taxation and registration.

After the contentious passage of the Gun Control Act of 1968, it took Congress eleven years to find the appetite for another major piece of firearms legislation. And when it did, the process was just as tumultuous. One impetus for a new law was the claim by the NRA that the ATF needed to be muzzled: it was harassing licensed firearm dealers and generally abusing its power in enforcing the Gun Control Act. One government report alleged that 75 percent of ATF prosecutions were violations of Second Amendment rights.[9]

As the proposed new law took shape, it was condemned as an "almost monstrous idea" and a "national disgrace," and it was also praised as "necessary to restore fundamental fairness to our nation's firearms laws."[10] It took seven years of tactical floor fights; furious lobbying; negotiations among the Treasury Department (overseer of the ATF), the NRA, and Congress; riders;

amendments; and rule changes to finally pass the Firearms Owners' Protection Act (FOPA).

The FOPA that was signed by Ronald Reagan in 1986 ended up relaxing many of the provisions of the Gun Control Act. The law allowed licensed dealers to sell firearms away from their place of business—for example, at gun shows. It limited ATF warrantless inspections of licensed dealers to one per year, loosened requirements for dealer record-keeping on gun and ammunition sales, and forbade the federal government from keeping a central database of most sales. It generally relaxed regulations on interstate sales and allowed transport of firearms, if securely stored, through states with strict laws. It exempted pawnbrokers from licensing for ammunition sales. As a consolation prize for gun safety advocates, the FOPA stiffened restrictions on sales and transfers of machine guns—already the most tightly regulated class of firearms. The passage of FOPA confirmed that passing firearms legislation would never be easy. The next legislative saga only emphasized that fact.

The Brady Handgun Prevention Act

It was about 2:30 p.m. on March 30, 1981—less than seventy-five days into Ronald Reagan's first term of office. The president had to walk only thirty feet from an exit of the Washington Hilton Hotel to his waiting limousine. But in that short distance, an obsessed twenty-five-year-old named John Hinckley Jr. penetrated a security line and stood a few body-lengths from Reagan. In less than two seconds, Hinckley fired six shots from an illegally purchased blue steel revolver; none of the shots found its target directly. A Secret Service agent and a Washington, DC, police officer were wounded shielding the president. One bullet ricocheted off the limousine into Reagan's lung, narrowly missing his heart. Most seriously injured was Press Secretary James Brady, who was hit in the head with an exploding bullet. Reagan and the two officers recovered from their wounds. James Brady would spend the rest of his life partially paralyzed and a near martyr for the cause of gun control.[11] Hinckley was found not guilty by reason of insanity and has spent most of his life in a psychiatric hospital in Washington, DC.[12]

The killing of John Lennon in New York City, followed four months later by the assassination attempt on President Reagan, reawakened the nation to gun violence and opened a fresh national debate on gun control. In 1987,

Congress introduced a new gun control bill requiring waiting periods and background checks. It was greeted with predictable opposition and failed on a House floor vote. A revised bill failed in the Senate in 1991. Finally, in February 1993, then-Representative Charles Schumer (D-NY) introduced a bill that passed both houses of Congress and was signed by President Bill Clinton on November 30. The new law was named after James Brady.

The Brady Handgun Violence Prevention Act called for a mandatory five-day waiting period and a state background check on firearm purchases. NRA opposition to the bill had been relentless and resulted in one important provision: within five years, the five-day waiting period would be replaced by a system of computerized instant background checks. According to plan, in 1998 the National Instant Criminal Background Check System (NICS) was launched, allowing licensed dealers to detect—usually immediately—prohibited buyers before making a firearm sale.

In its first full year of use (1999), NICS carried out 9.1 million background checks. The number of checks has increased steadily since then, reaching 21 million in 2014 (the most recent year for data). As of the end of 2014, NICS had processed over 200 million background checks. Approximately two million of those checks resulted in an initial rejection, and about 57 percent of those rejections were attempted purchases by felons. (See chapter 11 for more on federal background checks.)

Assault Weapons Ban

Bill Clinton's 1992 campaign platform included the plank:

> It is time to shut down the weapons bazaars in our cities. We support a reasonable waiting period to permit background checks for purchases of handguns, as well as assault weapons controls to ban the possession, sale, importation and manufacture of the most deadly assault weapons.[13]

With the passage of the Brady Act, Clinton could tick off background checks from his platform to-do list. And that victory gave him the momentum needed to tackle the next item—assault weapons. Debates on an assault weapons ban first occurred in 1989, so the subject was familiar when, in the fall of 1993, the Clinton initiative began. Within a year—the speed of light for gun legislation—the Violent Crime Control and Law Enforcement Act of 1994 became law. Title XI of that sprawling legislation became known as the Federal Assault Weapons Ban (AWB). Clinton got his law, but it was one of the most reviled and controversial pieces of gun legislation ever passed.

The AWB prohibited the "manufacture, transfer, and possession" of certain semiautomatic weapons and large-capacity magazines.[14] The first of several practical flaws in the law was that it did not effectively define *assault weapon*—in fact, the law made *assault weapon* the most regrettable term in the gun lexicon. The assault weapons of the AWB were not fully automatic weapons such as machine guns; the 1934 National Firearms Act already effectively banned that class of weapons. According to the law, an assault weapon is one of nineteen named semiautomatic weapons (including the AK-47, AR-15, and Uzi) or any semiautomatic rifle, pistol, or shotgun with at least two of a list of several specific features. For example, an otherwise legal semiautomatic rifle became a banned assault weapon if it accepted a detachable magazine and had at least two of a collapsing stock, a pistol grip, a bayonet mount, a flash suppressor, or a grenade-launcher mount. Critics of the law screamed that these defining features were purely cosmetic: they made an otherwise legal rifle look more lethal, but they did not actually make it more lethal.

To make matters worse, with a list of what makes a banned assault weapon, gunmakers quickly designed functionally identical weapons without the key features. The pro-gun control Violence Policy Center declared, "The gun industry made a mockery of the federal assault weapons ban, manufacturing 'post-ban' assault weapons with only slight, cosmetic differences from their banned counterparts."[15] Further compromising the AWB was a gaping grandfather clause insisted on by the gun rights lobby: the law did not ban weapons and magazines bought before its passage. An estimated 1.5 million "pre-ban" assault weapons and 25 million magazines were already in circulation and not affected by the law. Needless to say, these newly banned items suddenly became more valuable on the secondary market. Finally, the AWB contained a ticking bomb also bearing the fingerprints of the gun rights lobby: a ten-year sunset provision.

Observers attributed Democratic losses in Congress in 1994 and 1996 to the passage of the AWB. And some blamed Al Gore's losses in Arkansas, West Virginia, and his home state of Tennessee in the 2000 presidential race on his support of the AWB. So when the AWB came up for renewal in 2004, few politicians had any interest in touching the poison pill. Ten years to the day after the AWB was enacted, it died by a large majority vote in the Senate and without a vote in the House.

Was the AWB an effective gun law during its short lifetime? Because pre-ban weapons freely circulated after the ban was enacted and because only about 6 percent of all gun crimes before the ban were committed with assault weapons, detecting an AWB effect on the crime rate is difficult. A balanced and comprehensive 2004 study concluded that the AWB had "mixed" success in reducing crime, that definitive assessments were "premature," and that "greater impacts might have resulted had the ban been in effect longer."[16] A balanced analysis by FactCheck.org threw penalty flags on both sides of the debate for abundant cherry-picking of the studies.[17] It is fair to say that the AWB had less of an impact on crime rates than its proponents hoped.

Other Federal Laws and Attempts

After the 1934 NFA, the 1968 GCA, the 1986 FOPA, the 1993 Brady Act, and the 1994 AWB, the list of new federal firearm laws fits on a large postage stamp. One provision of the sprawling 1990 Crime Control Act is the Gun-Free School Zone Act, which prohibits possession of a firearm within one thousand feet of any public or private elementary or secondary school.[18] In 1995, a 5–4 Supreme Court majority struck down the law, on grounds that it did not fall within Congress's commerce-regulating authority.[19] The law was quickly amended to include references to interstate commerce and was signed by President Clinton later the same year.

Passed in 2005, the Protection of Lawful Commerce in Arms Act (PLCAA)[20] was a gun rights victory, acclaimed by the NRA as the "the most significant piece of pro-gun legislation in twenty years."[21] Prior to passage of the law, victims of firearm crimes had some success in suing firearm dealers and manufacturers for criminal uses of their products. The new law protected dealers and manufacturers from damages in such cases (although it did not shield them from liability for defective products). The law passed resoundingly by a 2–1 margin in both houses of Congress.

One consolation in the PLCAA for gun control advocates was a provision known as the Child Safety Lock Act.[22] It required all handguns to be sold with either a safety lock on the gun or a secure storage box for the gun. There was a good reason for including the restrictive Child Safety Lock Act in the otherwise permissive PLCAA: provided their guns had the required safety features, handguns owners had protection from damages resulting from criminal use of their guns by third parties.

A curious Trojan horse firearm law was the Credit Card Accountability Responsibility and Disclosure Act.[23] Signed by Barack Obama in 2009, the bill provided an overdue comprehensive reform of credit-card practices. Buried in the bill was an amendment permitting possession of firearms in national parks (subject to the laws of the surrounding state). Gun rights groups lobbied for the bill and it passed easily, in part because of the merits of credit-card reform.

The Future

The 1980s saw the invention and widespread use of handguns (like the Glock 17) made primarily of plastic. Fearing that guns of the future might eventually evade metal detectors and x-ray machines altogether, Congress passed the Undetectable Firearms Act in 1988 and renewed it in 2003.[24] The law prohibited the manufacture of guns that either have less than 3.7 ounces of metal or are unrecognizable as guns.

However, in May 2013, the future arrived. That is when the website Defense Distributed released blueprints for the all-plastic, single-shot Liberator handgun. With a 3-D printer and a fast Internet connection, it is possible to make a functional handgun at home. The spark behind Defense Distributed was a twenty-five-year-old self-described crypto-anarchist named Cody Wilson, who released a video of himself firing .38-caliber bullets from the Liberator. Wilson admits that 3-D printing technology may not be practical for guns. According to one source, Wilson "has been very honest in saying that the point of promoting 3-D printed guns is to essentially foment insurrectionism, to send a message to our government and other governments around the world that you cannot regulate firearms because we can print our own if necessary, and if you go too far, we can use them."[25] In the two days the US State Department needed to remove Wilson's website, users downloaded (and undoubtedly forwarded) an estimated one hundred thousand blueprints.

The Undetectable Firearms Act bans all-plastic guns unless they have a metal strip that can be detected by x-ray machines. Noting that a metal strip is easily removed to make the gun undetectable, legislators debated tightening the law. In the end, the law was hurriedly reauthorized for another ten years, without tighter restrictions. The renewal of the Undetectable Firearms Act was the only firearm legislation passed by Congress in 2013.

Given two centuries worth of opportunities, the dearth of federal firearm laws may seem surprising. It can be attributed, in part, to the delicate separation of state and federal powers that comes with a federalist system of government. That separation combined with a historical reluctance to pass federal laws at cross-purposes with the Second Amendment explains much of that dearth. Federal gun laws are a nearly blank canvas on which the states paint their own complex collages of laws. And when the states get involved, the picture gets more interesting.

10 | COLFAX AND CRUIKSHANK

> I would rather go to the bar of God with the chances of the souls of the . . .
> human beings so inhumanly butchered than carry to God a soul
> so debased as to defend such a crime.
>
> —US ATTORNEY J. R. BECKWITH, 1874

IN 1869, THE seat of Louisiana's Grant Parish was Colfax, a plantation community and riverboat stop on the Red River.[1] Its majority of impoverished black residents lived in shacks nestled between forested hills and the fields of cane and cotton on the fertile river bottom. Colfax was originally named Calhoun's Landing after a wealthy slave-owning family that had lived on fourteen thousand acres of plantation land in the Red River Valley since the 1830s. William (Willie) Calhoun was the iconoclastic heir to this vast wealth and real estate. Raised in Paris and permanently injured in a childhood accident, he was a pugnacious abolitionist who lived with a "mulatto teenager."[2] After the Civil War, he released the slaves from his plantation, gave them their own land, and built schools for their children. To the dismay of his white neighbors, who wanted nothing to do with Reconstruction, Calhoun fought tirelessly for black civil rights.[3]

The Grant Parish sheriff was a white Republican (abolitionist) and former Union officer named Delos White; he originally came to Colfax to work in the schools established by Willie Calhoun. The parish judge, William Phillips, was another white Republican who shared Calhoun's passion for lifting the lives of local black people. The efforts of White and Phillips to promote Reconstruction and foster racial harmony in the parish enraged the rampant white-supremacist groups such as the Knights of the White Camellia.

The tragic events in Colfax can be traced to the murder of Sheriff Delos White. Here is how it all happened. The 1870 election replaced Sheriff White with a "hard-drinking, illiterate . . . farmer from Tennessee," Alfred Shelby, who flaunted his contempt for White and Phillips.[4] Sheriff Shelby's side-kick was an ex-Confederate officer, Union prisoner, and Colfax storekeeper, Christopher Columbus Nash. On a September night in 1871, Shelby, Nash, and a heavily armed mob of vigilantes descended on the house where White and Phillips lived and set it on fire. When White fled the house, Nash was waiting and put three bullets in his head. As gunfire riddled the burning house, Phillips escaped into the woods through the back door and avoided a similar fate by playing dead in the darkness.

Judge Phillips fled to New Orleans where he sought warrants for the arrest of Shelby and Nash, for violations of the recently passed federal Enforcement Acts. Two federal marshals, backed by the state militia under the command of Captain William Ward, were sent to Colfax to serve the warrants. Ward was born a slave, fought for the Union, and arrived in Colfax just a year before the murder of Delos White. With a large scar on his forehead left from a barroom brawl, Ward had a powerful, daunting personality that incited the hatred of local white people; he also had the will to resist their threats. Ward's posse quickly arrested Shelby, Nash, and four conspirators in Colfax and returned them to New Orleans.

The prosecutor in White's murder trial was J. R. Beckwith, a capable New York–born attorney who moved to New Orleans with his wife in 1860. President Grant appointed him US attorney for Louisiana in 1870, and he stayed in Louisiana for the rest of his life. The trial was a tortuous display of Louisiana justice in which Democratic (pro-slavery) defense attorneys tried to overturn the arrest warrants, white witnesses openly perjured themselves, and the US attorney general advised Beckwith not to make the case a cause of further violence. The contentious case resulted in acquittals of the four conspirators, and four months after the death of Delos White, his murderers walked free. Within days, Captain Ward was dismissed from the militia for his overzealous pursuit of white criminals, the militia company assigned to Grant Parish was disbanded, Phillips resigned as judge, and white Democrats controlled the parish with a reign of terror.

Even by Louisiana standards, the 1872 governor's race was a free-for-all. The anti-slavery Republican Party was divided and its conservative wing joined the Democratic Party to form a hybrid party dedicated to thwarting Reconstruction. The Democratic candidate for governor was John McEnery, "one of Louisiana's fiercest Negro-baiters."[5] The Republican candidate for governor was Vermont-born William Pitt Kellogg, one of Louisiana's US senators. Each parish drafted its own slate of candidates for local offices, and in Grant Parish, the candidates were familiar combatants. Acclaimed white supremacist and Democrat Jim Hadnot ran against the irrepressible William Ward for state representative. Not six months out of jail, Democrat Christopher Columbus Nash opposed white Ohioan Daniel Shaw for sheriff.

Elections throughout Louisiana were fraudulent mockeries of justice—rife with voter intimidation, ballot stuffing, and obstruction of black registration. In Grant Parish, the white Democratic candidates claimed victory, despite the fact that registered black voters easily outnumbered registered white voters. At the state level, both parties claimed victory in the governor's race, both candidates held inaugurations, and both candidates began making state and parish appointments. In February 1873, a federal judge settled the governor's race by declaring Republican Kellogg the next governor; the decision was enforced by US Army troops sent to New Orleans by President Grant. The decision ignited Democrats, who on March 5 attempted a coup in downtown New Orleans that was eventually suppressed by federal troops.

The disputed elections took an ominous turn in Grant Parish. Despite the ruling for Republicans in the governor's race, the Democratic candidates summarily took office in Grant Parish and self-proclaimed Sheriff Nash grabbed the keys to the courthouse. The certified Republican office holders attempted unsuccessfully to negotiate a transfer of power. In the dead of the night of March 25, sheriff-designate Daniel Shaw and another Republican, aided by a small black boy, crawled through a window and took control of the courthouse. The move only inflamed white Democrats. State-legislator candidate Jim Hadnot assembled his white thugs to retake the courthouse and vowed to hang his opponent William Ward. In response to the imminent white onslaught, Republican Sheriff Shaw formed a posse led by William Ward to protect black people in and around Colfax. With matters careening wildly toward a deadly conflict, there was a last-ditch effort by leaders on both sides to negotiate a compromise. That effort ended when supremacist vigilantes murdered long-time Colfax resident and former slave Jesse McKinney in broad daylight in front of his family.

After McKinney's murder, terror swept through the black community. Black folks flocked from the surrounding woods and gathered in the relative security of the Colfax courthouse. Ward and his posse sealed the town and the white population retreated to neighboring villages, not just for safety but to regroup and gather forces. Two desperate letters from William Ward describing the escalating tension in Colfax reached Governor Kellogg in New Orleans. However, the request to send troops to forestall the impending conflict was denied by Kellogg, who had already proved to be a duplicitous and indecisive leader. Instead, Kellogg sent two US marshals to Colfax with arrest warrants for fifty white insurgents. It was April 12 when the marshals began the two-day journey from New Orleans to Colfax.

April 13, 1873, was Easter Sunday and 165 white warriors gathered near Colfax in the dawn light under the leadership of Nash and Hadnot. Ku Klux Klan grand wizard Dave Paul was also present and rallied his troops from neighboring parishes crying, "Boys, this is a struggle for white supremacy!"[6] The cavalcade headed toward Colfax armed with rifles, shotguns, handguns, and a small, two-foot cannon.

Anticipating the assault of the white force, the black population defending the courthouse spent the night attempting to fortify it with a two-foot-deep defensive trench. In terms of weapons and ammunition, the occupants of the courthouse were lightly armed and at an enormous disadvantage. As the sun rose Easter morning, they waited, helpless and cornered.

The white cavalcade slowly approached the courthouse throughout the morning. Nash sent a final ultimatum to everyone in the courthouse, offering one last opportunity for surrender under conditions that no black man could possibly trust. In the only civilized act of the day, the remaining women, children, and white people were allowed to leave unharmed. Only black men remained to defend the courthouse.

At noon, Nash's forces moved to within two hundred yards of the courthouse and began the assault. The artillery fire sent most of the defenders into the courthouse; those that fled into the nearby woods were captured or shot. At three o'clock, Nash decided against a long siege and forced a captive black man to set fire to the courthouse roof. The defenders waved a white flag of surrender, laid down their arms, and fled the blazing courthouse. Then the slaughter began. The white attackers opened fire, picking off fleeing black men like targets in a shooting gallery. The defenders who chose to stay in the courthouse were burned to death in the conflagration. Those who escaped were taken prisoner. In the exuberant mayhem, Jim Hadnot and two other white attackers were fatally shot—most likely by friendly fire.

An hour after the shooting began, the massacre was over. Whiskey flowed, celebrations began, and the victors entertained themselves by hanging black people from a large pecan tree that stood near the courthouse. As darkness fell, the surviving prisoners were marched out of Colfax to be mutilated and executed. Luke Hadnot, son of the slain Jim Hadnot, lined up five black men and proudly killed them with two bullets. A black shoemaker, Clement Penn, begged for his life, before being shot in front of his wife. Benjamin Brim was shot in the head but played dead and crawled through the woods for two days, surviving to become a witness. To his credit, Nash attempted to halt the bloodshed. But he was overruled, and when his neighbor Bill Cruikshank took command, the atrocities continued into the night.

Around eight o'clock that evening, a riverboat headed downstream eased into the Colfax landing. Curious passengers stepped ashore and approached the ghastly abattoir. In the distance, the courthouse was still smoldering and the air was filled with a powerful stench. Bodies could be seen in dim lantern light, scattered in the grass, "most facedown and shot almost to pieces."[7] A day and half later, the riverboat arrived in New Orleans, and the first reports of the carnage in Colfax reached the outside world.

Two days after the massacre, on April 15, the two US marshals commissioned by Governor Kellogg rode into the Colfax killing field on horseback. With the help of widows and survivors, they personally buried nearly sixty bodies in the defensive trench around the courthouse. Corpses dumped in the river during the slaughter were never recovered or counted. It is known that 150 black men were in the courthouse when the attack began, and 45 of those men survived to testify in upcoming trials; this reckoning puts the death count above 100.

A historical marker that stands in Colfax today reads:

On this site occurred the Colfax Riot in which three white men and 150 negroes were slain. This event on April 13, 1873 marked the end of carpetbag misrule in the South.

Regardless of the exact toll, the Colfax Massacre was likely the worst single-day

loss of civilian (nonwartime) lives in America until the Oklahoma City bombing in 1995. For that reason alone, it should be remembered in the pages of
American history. However, the Colfax Massacre also played a decisive part in
the history of guns and US jurisprudence that begs for much more recognition.

The Trials

US Attorney J. R. Beckwith, who prosecuted the 1871 murder trial of Delos
White, lost no time in gathering evidence and writing indictments in the Colfax Massacre. He wired US Attorney General George Williams that he had
never prosecuted "a crime so revolting and horrible in the details of its perpe-
tration and so burdened with atrocity and barbarity."[8] The case named only
two victims: Levi Nelson was captured during the massacre, miraculously
survived a gunshot wound to the neck, and testified in the trials, and Alexander Tillman was killed at the courthouse.

Beckwith's 150 pages of indictments listed thirty-two counts and named
ninety-eight defendants. He carefully formulated the counts to take advantage of the Enforcement Acts and the legal precedents, as he understood
them. Among the counts were charges that the defendants "banded together"
to "injure, oppress, threaten, intimidate" the victims, and as a result, deprived
them of various rights guaranteed by the Constitution. Among these rights
were the right to peaceably assemble, the right to "keep and bear arms for a
lawful purpose," as well as other civil and voting rights.[9] Using language of the
Fourteenth Amendment, one count specifically charged violations of "rights,
privileges, immunities and protection as citizens of the state of Louisiana and
the United States . . . on account of [the victims'] race and color and for the
reason that they, being such citizens, were persons of African descent and
race and persons of color and not white citizens."[10]

While Beckwith fervently wanted convictions for murder (and a sentence
of death by hanging), he realized the unlikelihood of a white jury convict-
ing white men of killing black people. Nevertheless, because the jury had so
many different ways to arrive at a conviction, Beckwith approached the trial
with cautious optimism.

In June 1873, a grand jury returned an indictment of all defendants on all
counts, and the manhunt began. The US attorney general promised Beckwith federal assistance in making arrests, but as summer turned to fall, the

attorney general began fearing the unsavory spectacle of putting one hundred white men on trial in a federal court in Louisiana. As a result, his support for the Colfax case—financial and otherwise—began to fade. With a small budget and even fewer men, Beckwith began scouring the Louisiana woods in search of the indicted defendants, many of whom were willingly harbored by local white people. While the federal manhunt was in progress, a Louisiana state prosecutor, J. Ernest Breda, courageously convened a grand jury in Colfax and secured indictments against 140 men. Before the trial began, Breda was confronted by a mob of sixty men wielding knives and guns—some of whom were actually defendants in the federal case. Breda fled Colfax with his life, and the trial never took place, making it clear "that the state was helpless to enforce its own laws."[11] The only hope was a federal prosecution.

By November 11, with no federal assistance, Beckwith's posse had made only seven arrests. Among the seven prisoners were Bill Cruikshank, Johnnie Hadnot (nephew of slain Jim Hadnot), and Bill Irwin. The wily Christopher Nash narrowly escaped capture by crossing the Red River on horseback with the posse in pursuit. Ninety other defendants were still on the loose. As the trial approached, intimidation and even slayings of witnesses became common. Black witnesses who wanted to testify thought better of it, and white folks, some with plenty of incriminating evidence, never considered cooperating.

The trial opened on February 23, 1874, in the massive granite Customs House on New Orleans's Canal Street, with Republican federal judge William Woods presiding. It took three days to seat a jury of nine white men, four of them Democrats, and three black men. The eloquent New Orleans attorney Robert Marr led the defense team and looked at the trial as an opportunity to boost white supremacy and eradicate carpetbaggers. Beckwith called sixty black witnesses but had virtually no credible white witnesses to buttress his case. A severe blow to the prosecution's case came when Dan Shaw, the white Republican sheriff, who was in the Colfax courthouse just prior to the massacre, testified for the defense—the beneficiary of bribes. Nevertheless, Beckwith was able to expertly expose the largely perjured testimony of many white witnesses. By March 11, when Robert Marr rose to give closing arguments for the defense, the steamy climate of the massive Customs House courtroom had taken its toll on everyone. A day later, Beckwith gave a nearly four-hour closing statement, reminding the jury that "someone is responsible for this crime, and someone must be punished, or justice is dead."[12]

The jury deliberated for less than a week, and on the evening of March 16, it announced its verdict. The jury was deadlocked on all but one defendant, who was acquitted. As a result, the only option was to declare a mistrial, which Judge Woods approved on the spot.

The second trial, in the case now called *United States v. Cruikshank et al.*, began on May 14, 1874, with a jury selected by May 20. In many respects, the second trial was a replay of the first trial, complete with witness intimidation, thickets of prevarication, and searing oratory. However, there was one fateful twist. In the 1870s, America did not have a system of appeals courts. That function was served by the Supreme Court justices, who traveled through their "circuit" in the summer, giving judicial advice and listening to cases on appeal. It so happened that Supreme Court associate justice Joseph Bradley was "riding circuit" in May 1874 and chose to occupy the bench with Judge Woods during the retrial of the Colfax case. Bradley was a New Jersey attorney who worked his way up through the Democratic Party until he was appointed to the Supreme Court by President Grant in 1870. "For all his erudition, Bradley seems never to have been troubled by slavery."[13] For him, the Civil War was fought for the preservation of the Union and not for civil rights; he claimed that, "I do not . . . hate Southern people. . . . I do not care a straw about their institutions."[14]

On June 9, the jury announced its verdict in the retrial: Cruikshank, Hadnot, and Irwin were found guilty on sixteen federal counts of conspiring to violate the civil rights of black citizens; the remaining defendants were found not guilty. As in the first trial, there were no murder convictions. Beckwith was outraged that the jury did not give him more convictions. Quite predictably, the defense entered a motion for arrest of judgment.

It was now up to Judge Woods and Justice Bradley to weigh in on the verdicts. Justice Bradley was in Washington when the verdicts were announced. Suspense centered on how Bradley would rule in the case and whether he would deliver his opinion by mail or in person. Despite the sweltering heat of the southern summer, Bradley decided to make the two-day train ride to New Orleans. He arrived late on the evening of June 26, apparently with few people aware of his return.

The next morning, Judge Woods convened the court and gave his opinion. There were no surprises. Woods observed that the trial had been fair and announced he would uphold the jury's verdicts. Then Woods announced, to the surprise of many, that when the court reconvened after lunch, Justice Bradley would give his opinion—in person.

In his long analytical opinion, Bradley dissected the three Reconstruction amendments (thirteenth, fourteenth, and fifteenth) and their relationships to the federal Civil Rights Act and the Enforcement Acts. He then focused on the *Cruikshank* case and eventually arrived at his decision that the defense motion for an arrest of judgment was valid and the guilty verdicts should be overturned. His path to that momentous decision and the claim that the Enforcement Acts are unconstitutional is worth investigating.

The first of several themes that appeared in Bradley's decision is that the Fourteenth Amendment protects citizens against actions by the state but not against actions by individuals or organizations. In his words:

> The main ground of objection [to the *Cruikshank* decision] is that
> the [federal Enforcement Act] is municipal in its character, operating
> directly on the conduct of individuals, and taking the place of ordinary
> state legislation; and that there is no constitutional authority for such an
> act, inasmuch as the state laws furnish adequate remedy for the alleged
> wrongs committed.[15]

In other words, the Enforcement Act provides federal protection against violations of civil rights committed by individuals. However, the Fourteenth Amendment guarantees federal protection only against violations committed by the state—not by individuals. Therefore, according to Bradley, Congress did not have the constitutional power to enact the Enforcement Acts, making them unconstitutional. Protection against violations of civil rights committed by individuals is the job of the states. Fortunately, Justice Bradley gave an example:

> When [the Fourteenth Amendment] declares that no state shall deprive
> any person of life, liberty, or property without due process of law, this
> declaration is not intended as a guaranty against the commission of
> murder, false imprisonment, robbery, or any other crime committed by

individual malefactors. . . . It is a constitutional security against arbitrary and unjust legislation [by the state] by which a man may be [prosecuted] in a summary manner and arbitrarily arrested and condemned. . . . It is a guaranty of protection against the acts of the state government itself.[16]

As Bradley saw it, the charges in the *Cruikshank* indictment, particularly the murder charges, involved the acts of individuals rather than state governments; therefore, these acts are beyond the reach of federal laws. As a result, Bradley rejected all the charges in the indictment.

Another thread that ran through Bradley's analysis is the astounding assertion that the prosecution failed to demonstrate that the Colfax crimes were racially motivated—as if the slaying of over one hundred black people in the heat of Reconstruction could have another explanation. Bradley's expectation was that "an indictment, under the Enforcement Act or Civil Rights bill, for violating civil rights, should state that the offense charged was committed against the person injured by reason of his race, color or previous condition of servitude."[17] Unless a crime is shown to be racially motivated, the prosecution of that crime is the responsibility of the state. Again from Bradley's opinion:

The duty of congress in the creation and punishment of offenses is limited to those offenses which aim at the deprivation of the colored citizen's enjoyment and exercise of his rights of citizenship and of equal protection of the laws because of his race, color, or previous condition of servitude.[18]

In Beckwith's argument of the case, Bradley was somehow unable to see a shred of racial motivation for the crimes. Regarding several counts that the defendants had violated various civil rights of the plaintiffs, Bradley reiterated:

The count does not contain any allegation that the defendants committed the acts complained of with a design to deprive the injured persons of their rights on account of their race, color or previous condition of servitude.[19]

But was not that motive obvious? No, said Bradley, "It ought not to have been left to inference; it should have been alleged. On this ground, therefore, I think this count is defective and cannot be sustained."[20] In several counts, prosecutor Beckwith explicitly cited racial motivations for the alleged crimes. Bradley claimed that those counts "were also defective on account of the vagueness and generality of the charge. . . . It is not merely informal, it is insufficient."[21]

And so it went. Beckwith listened as Justice Bradley ravaged and dismantled his case count by count. Beckwith was astounded. "He had just heard a Supreme Court justice declare that three men who had been found guilty of one of the greatest crimes [he] had ever known should go free because of drafting errors in the indictment."[22] The two judges were split as diametrically as possible. As the trial concluded, Judge Woods remarked:

> I regard the opinion of Justice Bradley with appropriate deference. But my opinion on the validity of the indictment has been carefully formed and is of long standing. I regret to disagree with my learned brother.[23]

The judges' differences led to a certificate of division, ensuring that the United States Supreme Court would hear the case.

White Louisiana erupted in celebration over Bradley's opinion. And the celebrations quickly turned bloody as the decision gave white people an open season on black folks with no threat of arrest or prosecution. A whiskey-fueled party in Colfax honoring the Colfax defendants—who could now roam freely— resulted in the brutal sporting murders of two local black residents. The wave of terror and murders continued throughout the summer, and although local authorities knew the perpetrators, they were helpless to make arrests.

By midsummer, a new white supremacist organization, the White League, was in full power, sponsoring terror throughout the South. Organized by defense attorney Robert Marr, the League's charter claimed that "there will be no security, no peace, and no prosperity for Louisiana until . . . the superiority of the Caucasian over the African . . . is acknowledged and established."[24] The work of the White League's fourteen thousand armed vigilantes culminated in the Coushatta Massacre, where for the first time even white folks—if they were Republicans or potential trial witnesses—were killed. Governor Kellogg observed that Bradley's opinion established "the principle that hereafter no white man could be punished for killing a negro."[25]

In the fall of 1874, Beckwith received a cable from the US attorney general advising him not to prosecute white supremacist crimes until the Supreme Court ruled on the *Cruikshank* case. The Democrats had claimed widespread victories in the recent state elections, largely because of low black voter turnout. The White League had taken control of the Louisiana state legislature, although a compromise brokered by President Grant left the embattled Republican governor in office. In a letter to the US attorney general, Governor Kellogg speculated portentously:

> If Louisiana goes, Mississippi will follow, and that end attained, all the results of the war so far as the colored people are concerned will be neutralized, all the reconstruction acts of Congress will be of no more value than so much waste paper and the colored people, though free in name, will practically be remitted back to servitude.

If the Supreme Court did not rule favorably, it would mean the end of Reconstruction.

Supreme Court Decision

On March 31, 1875, the Supreme Court convened to hear oral arguments in *United States v. Cruikshank*. Chief Justice Morrison Remick Waite, once described as being "at the front rank of second-rate lawyers," presided over a court with seven Republicans—including himself and Justice Joseph Bradley—and two Democrats.[26] Attorney General George Williams and Solicitor General Samuel Phillips argued the case for the government. By all accounts, they gave indolent and unpersuasive performances. The defense had an all-star eight-man team that included the passionate Robert Marr and David Dudley Field, elder brother of sitting Justice David Field. The legendary seventy-eight-year-old Reverdy Johnson provided expert legal analysis for the defense, as well as his share of hysteria, claiming that a decision in favor of the government would "elevate the black man above the white man."[27] Both sides rested after two days of testimony, and then the court disbanded for another summer of riding circuits.

Without a Supreme Court decision, and with Justice Bradley's federal court decision still binding, another summer of unfettered violence was inevitable. The federal courts in the South stopped prosecuting Enforcement Acts cases, realizing the futility of getting convictions. The worst violence occurred in Mississippi, where White League packs murdered three hundred black people before President Grant intervened with federal troops.

It was not until November 6, 1875, that the Supreme Court gave its unanimous decision: The acquittals rendered by Justice Bradley in the New Orleans courtroom would stand. Chief Justice Waite wrote a majority opinion that echoed the lower court opinion written by his close friend Justice Bradley. Again the justices ludicrously claimed "it is nowhere alleged in these counts that the wrong contemplated against the rights of these citizens was on account of their race or color."[28] And again, they observed, "the Fourteenth Amendment prohibits a State from depriving any person of life, liberty, or property without due process of law; but this adds nothing to the rights of one citizen as against another."[29] For such protection, citizens must look to the states.

With respect to Second Amendment rights, the opinion declared:

The right . . . of "bearing arms for a lawful purpose" . . . is not a right granted by the Constitution. Neither is it in any manner dependent upon that instrument for its existence. The second amendment declares that it shall not be infringed; but this . . . means no more than that it shall not be infringed by Congress. This is one of the amendments that has no other effect than to restrict the powers of the national government, leaving the people to look for their protection . . . to merely municipal legislation . . . or what was, perhaps, more properly called internal police."[30]

In other words, the justices argued, several of the rights in the indictment, including the right to bear arms, do not originate with the US Constitution. They have always been "one of the attributes of citizenship under a free government." They were not rights "granted to the people by the Constitution."[31] All the Constitution does is protect these rights against infringement by the federal government. Protection from actions by the states or by individuals must come from state and local laws. Finally, the arguments in the *Cruikshank* decision imply rather clearly that, as of 1875, the Second Amendment was not incorporated by virtue of the Fourteenth Amendment.

Aftermath of *Cruikshank*

The *Cruikshank* decision astounds many legal experts today as they look back with 150 years of hindsight. A simple nonlegal explanation of the decision is often offered—the country was dealing with bank failures in the Panic of 1873. Americans, particularly in the North and specifically those on the Supreme Court, were in a state of Reconstruction fatigue. The *Cruikshank* decision was simply an expedient way to dispense with the headaches of Reconstruction. If that were true and if Americans really wished to be done with Reconstruction, that wish was granted. Throughout the remainder of the 1870s, the southern states, one by one, brought Reconstruction to an end—through violence and terror virtually condoned by the Supreme Court decision; through rigged elections and voter intimidation; and through political corruption. By 1880, every southern state had been "redeemed," and they would remain that way for decades.

In 1880, the federal government dropped all charges against those indicted in the Colfax cases. Christopher Columbus Nash married into wealth, was elected mayor of Colfax, and thrived for many years. Democrats in Washington saw to it that Louisiana no longer needed Beckwith as a US attorney. As a result, he was relieved of his duties in 1877 and continued to practice law in New Orleans, where he died in "genteel poverty" in 1912. William Ward and William Phillips, two once-zealous Republicans—one black and one white— eventually tired of their battles, became Democrats, and promoted the white version of the Colfax Massacre story.

The Colfax trials also had significant fallout on the presidential election of 1876. The election is remembered today because, for the first time, one candidate—Democrat Samuel Tilden of New York—received the most popular votes, while the other candidate—Republican Rutherford Hayes of Ohio—won the electoral vote (by a margin of 185–184). That outcome should have given Hayes the presidency. The Democrats contested the electoral vote in South Carolina, Florida, and Louisiana. A commission of congressmen, senators, and Supreme Court justices (including Justice Joseph Bradley) was deadlocked. A deal was reached: the election of Hayes as president would stand if federal troops, who were maintaining the peace in Southern states, were withdrawn and Democrats were installed in state offices. The Republicans won the presidency and the Democrats, with no intent to protect black citizens, won the states.

Because of the *Slaughterhouse* and *Cruikshank* decisions, the Fourteenth Amendment was drained as an authority for limiting state abuses of basic constitutional rights. As a result, the slow process of incorporating the various rights enumerated in the Bill of Rights would not begin until the twentieth century. And the incorporation of the Second Amendment would not happen until the twenty-first century.

11 | ENFORCEMENT!

> The United States is the only modern industrial urban nation that persists in
> maintaining a gun culture. . . . And yet it remains, and is apparently determined to
> remain, the most passive of all the major countries in the matter of gun control.
>
> —RICHARD HOFSTADTER, "America as a Gun Culture"

MASS KILLINGS AND serial shootings each produce their own kind of horror. Mass killings are committed within minutes or hours with an unexpected
suddenness. Serial or spree shootings are prolonged and unpredictable, and
they last until the assailants are caught. People living in the greater Washington, DC, area during a three-week spell in October 2002 experienced directly
and unforgettably the second kind of horror. During that period, two expert
snipers prowled the Beltway suburbs killing ten people and wounding four
in random shootings, all of which had the same signature: the victims were
felled with a single shot from long range in a public place such as a gas station
or shopping center—and the getaway was invisible.

The Montgomery County Police Department, assisted by the FBI, the
Bureau of Alcohol, Tobacco, Firearms, and Explosives (ATF), and the US Secret
Service, finally apprehended the killers at an interstate rest area on October 24,
2002. The break in the case was a link to earlier shootings in Alabama, Louisiana, and Washington state by the same men; those crimes resulted in an additional seven deaths and seven injuries. The arrest of the killers led to several
startling discoveries.

First, the getaway vehicle in the Beltway shootings was a blue Chevrolet
Caprice with a back seat outfitted as a rear-facing "sniper's nest."[1] The killers
used a Bushmaster XM-15 .223-caliber semiautomatic rifle with a range of
over five hundred yards, equipped with a holographic sight. The weapon was
fired through a small hole cut in the trunk of the car. The stealth provided
by this lethal rig concealed the getaways and made the killings even more

unnerving. It also sent law enforcement officials on a false hunt for the wrong vehicle that likely extended the killers' spree by several days.

Apart from their inexplicable motives, the killers were a peculiar pair: a forty-one-year-old Gulf War veteran named John Allen Muhammad (formerly Williams) with a history of failed marriages and restraining orders, and seventeen-year-old Lee Boyd Malvo, a Jamaican-born undocumented immigrant with a turbulent and nomadic life. The relationship between the two men—apparently based on unfulfilled father-son needs, bodybuilding sessions, and misplaced trust—is another story in itself.[2] Muhammad and Malvo stood trial in Virginia in the fall of 2003 and were found guilty of murder and weapons charges. The men were also convicted in trials in Maryland. Muhammad was executed by lethal injection on November 10, 2009. After a Supreme Court ruling prohibiting execution of minors,[3] Malvo was sentenced to life in prison without parole.

More relevant to this chapter is the source of the gun. The investigation of the DC sniper case revealed that Muhammad had used the firing range at Bull's Eye Shooter Supply in Tacoma, Washington, to "hone his marksmanship."[4] Furthermore, when a trace was put on the Bushmaster rifle used in the murders, it led to the same store as the point of sale: the manufacturer sold the gun to Bull's Eye in July 2002. And when ATF agents sought records of the gun sale, the store owner came up empty. Malvo later told investigators that he stole the gun from the allegedly secure store. That gun turned out to be one of 238 guns that were unaccounted for over a three-year period in the inventory of the store.[5]

Then the real story began to unravel. ATF records showed that Bull's Eye was investigated as early as 1994 and was a habitual violator of numerous laws governing licensed dealers: among them guns stolen from the inventory, missing records, sale of crime weapons, and selling more than ten guns at a time to a single buyer. A *Seattle Times* investigation obtained ATF records showing that guns sold by Bull's Eye between 1997 and 2001 were used in fifty-two crimes. Only in 2003, with the link to the Beltway murders established, did the ATF belatedly revoke Bull's Eye's license.[6] In 2004, eight families of victims of the shootings reached a $2.5 million settlement with Bushmaster and Bull's Eye—said to be the first case in which a gunmaker settled for negligence leading to a crime.[7]

The ATF and Gun Trafficking

> We've got to enforce the gun laws that are on the books.
>
> —THEN-SENATOR BARACK OBAMA,
> NAACP Presidential Primary Forum, July 12, 2007

> We need to enforce the thousands of laws that are currently on the books. . . .
> Proposing more gun laws, while failing to enforce the thousands we already have,
> is not a serious solution to reducing crime.
>
> —WAYNE LAPIERRE, NRA executive director testimony
> before the Senate Judiciary Committee, January 30, 2013

> You can have all the gun control laws in the country,
> but if you don't enforce them, people are going to find a way to protect themselves.
>
> —MICHAEL STEELE, "Steele on Gun Control,"
> *Washington Post* interview, October 16, 2006

If that does not sound like bipartisan consensus, then nothing in the gun debate ever will. Enhanced enforcement and stiffer penalties are recommendations that come from all sides of the debate and from all wavelengths of the political spectrum. Why are these remedies so easy to propose and so difficult to implement?

Much of the responsibility for enforcing federal firearm laws falls on the ATF—a federal agency that works with federal, state, and local law-enforcement authorities. The fact that the bureau is known as ATF, not BATFE, reflects its serpentine history. Here is a drastically condensed version of that story.

Threatened by a new butter substitute made cheaply from animal fat, the butter industry convinced Congress in 1886 to pass the Oleomargarine Act authorizing a two-cent-per-pound tax on the new product. The earliest ancestor of the ATF was the Revenue Laboratory, established in the Treasury Department to collect the oleomargarine tax (the tax lasted until 1950). The ATF lineage then passed through the Bureau of Prohibition, created by the Treasury Department in 1920 to enforce prohibition laws. The

Prohibition Reorganization Act of 1930 moved the Bureau of Prohibition to the Justice Department, at which time Special Agent in Charge (SAC) Eliot Ness pursued the Chicago crime maestro Al Capone (as somewhat glorified in the television series *The Untouchables*). The repeal of prohibition by the Twenty-First Amendment in 1933 transferred the Bureau of Prohibition back to the Treasury Department as the Alcohol Tax Unit (ATU), charged with shutting down illegal distilleries and taxing legal alcohol—a campaign that also involved Eliot Ness in Ohio, Kentucky, and Tennessee until 1935. In 1941, the ATU became the enforcement agency for the recently passed National Firearms Act and Federal Firearms Act; for the first time, firearms were part of the ATU portfolio.

The Gun Control Act of 1968 and the Organized Crime Control Act of 1970 resulted in more renaming of the ATU and made it a division of the IRS. Then in 1972, the new Bureau of Alcohol, Tobacco, and Firearms (ATF) emerged as a separate agency within the Treasury Department. This period marked the second coming of the NRA, emerging as the leading gun rights advocacy group, fueled by new members and millions of dollars. It was not long before the ATF and the NRA locked horns. The NRA appeared to have the upper hand to the extent that Ronald Reagan, just elected in 1981, announced plans to extinguish the ATF altogether. Law-enforcement agencies spoke up and Reagan reversed course. He decided to keep the ATF but proposed moving it to the Secret Service—a move that gun rights groups saw as even more threatening than keeping the old ATF. Now it was the NRA that reversed course, as it pushed to keep the ATF alive in the Treasury Department.[8]

Finally, with the passage of the Homeland Security Act of 2002, the ATF moved to the Justice Department, where it resides today—renamed yet again as the Bureau of Alcohol, Tobacco, Firearms, and Explosives but with the same call letters ATF. Today's ATF faces daunting challenges enforcing federal firearms laws—and firearms make up only part of its mission (there is also A, T, and E). It currently operates twenty-five domestic field divisions and twelve international offices in six countries on a budget of (some would claim, "only") $1.2 billion.

Unlike narcotics or bootleg liquor, nearly all crime guns are legally made, with a manufacturer's serial number and a record of sale. Gun trafficking is the profit-driven diversion of legal guns into illegal arenas. Nearly half of the cases investigated in an ATF report involved a straw purchase, a sale in which a legal buyer knowingly purchases a gun for another person who is either a prohibited buyer or does not want to be associated with the sale.[9] The ATF's Form 4473, which gun buyers must complete for all purchases at a federally licensed dealer, ideally prevents straw purchases. The form has the question:

> Are you the actual transferee/buyer of the firearm(s) listed on this form? **Warning: You are not the actual buyer if you are acquiring the firearm(s) on behalf of another person. If you are not the actual buyer, the dealer cannot transfer the firearm(s) to you.**[10]

If nothing else, a straw purchaser *at least* violates a federal law by falsifying the required paperwork. Straw purchases are widely condemned even by gun advocacy groups, as evidenced by the "Don't Lie for the Other Guy" campaign of the National Shooting Sports Foundation. At the same time, the NRA recently lobbied to weaken a federal bill that would have increased penalties on straw purchases.[11]

In addition to straw purchases, an estimated 14 percent of gun-trafficking cases handled by the ATF involve the theft of weapons from licensed dealers.[12] By one estimate, between 2004 and 2011, about 175,000 firearms were listed as missing from dealer inventories. And that estimate is certainly low because in any single year, only about 20 percent of dealers undergo ATF inspections. An additional 10 percent of trafficking cases are thefts from private owners and carriers. The remaining trafficking cases involve transfers by corrupt dealers, unlicensed dealers, and fences (people who buy stolen guns and resell them).[13]

The ATF's most potent tool in fighting gun trafficking is a sophisticated, web-based data collection and analysis system for tracking crime guns. The system resides at ATF's National Tracing Center (NTC), located on a high-security, ten-acre campus in Martinsburg, West Virginia, about ninety miles from Washington, DC. The trace process begins when a gun is recovered at a crime scene and a law-enforcement agency (federal, state, local, tribal, or foreign) submits a request to NTC for a trace. The NTC system is fueled by millions of data records from multiple sources: data on sales at licensed dealers (buyer's name and address and the gun's make and serial number); data on previous gun transfers; reports of stolen firearms (which must be filed by licensed dealers); records of single sales of large quantities of guns; records from licensed dealers who have gone out of business (who are required to keep sales records); and data from all previously completed gun traces. Data began populating the NTC system in 1988, and in the years since then, the ATF has processed over five million trace requests (360,000 in 2014 alone).[14]

Using these immense data vaults, plus old-fashioned sleuthing and phone investigations, the NTC computers and staff attempt to reconstruct the lifetime of a crime gun—through its various owners, dealers, and transfers—back to the original buyer. The ATF estimates that 70 percent of all trace requests lead to the original owner of the gun, generally within three days.[15] A successful trace, often linked with other traces, can provide case-cracking leads in a crime investigation. Some traces fail because of lost or missing records (for example, because of guns stolen from licensed dealers), errors in data entry, and incomplete or obliterated serial numbers. Because of sparse data, guns manufactured before 1968 or by a foreign company tend to defeat the tracing system.

Despite its crime-solving potential, such an elaborate data-collection enterprise gives many people headaches, if not outright panic attacks. The NRA argues, "Firearm trace data may be biased. . . . The tracing system [was] . . . designed to help law enforcement agencies, . . . not to collect statistics."[16] The NRA also notes that traced guns are not always crime guns, as trace requests can be submitted for non-gun-related crimes such as traffic offenses. The haunting fear of gun rights groups is that trace data may find its way outside the strict boundaries of law-enforcement agencies and be used in civil court cases, by researchers, and, worst of all, by gun control groups. In response, the ATF claims it releases only coarse-grained summaries of trace data: number, type, caliber of crime guns; interstate pathways; top recovery cities; and time to recovery of all traced firearms.

By contrast, gun control advocates, such as Mayors Against Illegal Guns, see the gun-tracing system as a miracle—an indispensable instrument in eradicating gun trafficking. They heartily call for increased funding and technological improvements in the system. One such improvement is an enhancement called eTrace, launched in January 2005. The paperless system allows law-enforcement agencies to share trace data among themselves more easily than in the past. Over six thousand law-enforcement agencies and forty-three foreign countries use eTrace, processing roughly 373,000 trace requests in 2015.[17] The argument over gun tracing is another act in the American drama of public security versus personal privacy.

Despite the central role that the ATF plays in the nation's law-enforcement mission, the agency has its vocal detractors. They point to its history as one source of problems. Its many name changes and its expanding mission have left the bureau with an identity crisis and an uncertain place in the nation's law-enforcement picture. Critics combine that history with the ATF's performance during its lifetime and conclude that the ATF is a lost and dysfunctional agency. One critic and member of the National Association of Federal Agents inveighed, "They are always crying poverty, but ATF doesn't lack resources. They lack the ability to prioritize the use of resources effectively. And they have a horrible management culture in DC, which has rewarded the rogues and the abusers."[18]

Since the 1980s, the bureau has been excoriated for its overzealous enforcement practices. In 1982, a Senate subcommittee criticized both the ATF and the Gun Control Act, reporting that "based upon these hearings it is apparent that ATF enforcement tactics made possible by current federal firearms laws are constitutionally, legally, and practically reprehensible." It claimed that "agents anxious to generate an impressive arrest and gun confiscation quota" feathered their resumes by apprehending private gun collectors making legal sales.[19] The report is a litany of deficiencies of both the ATF and gun laws at that time. It was partially responsible for the Firearm Owners' Protection Act of 1986 that revised much of the Gun Control Act.

The ATF was centrally involved in the sieges at Ruby Ridge, Idaho, in 1992 and Waco, Texas, in 1993. Those immensely controversial and tragic events further damaged ATF's image in the eyes of many Americans. Adverse publicity continued in the mid-2000s with ATF's handling of eight gun shows in Richmond, Virginia. At a Congressional subcommittee hearing called to investigate the gun show raids, a ranking member opened with the proviso that the hearing "is not an indictment of the ATF, and we support the ATF's efforts to keep illegal guns off the streets and out of the hands of criminals." But then came the incriminating *however*:

> There are serious allegations about abusive practices, including racial
> profiling, coercive interrogations tactics, actions tantamount to arrest
> without probable cause, failure to apprise rights against self-incrimina-
> tion, and more.[20]

These incidents only burnished the ATF's reputation for heavy-handedness.

A more recent stain on the ATF image occurred in the so-called gun-
walking operations intended to strangle the flow of illegal guns into Mexico.
These sting operations, organized by ATF's Arizona Field Office between
2006 and 2011, pumped guns into the illegal market (letting guns *walk*)
in the hopes of tracing them to big-time gun traffickers and drug kings.
The last such project, "Fast and Furious," has become synonymous with
botched government operations. The estimated fourteen hundred guns that
were put into circulation during that operation were later found on both
sides of the border and implicated in the deaths of one US Border Patrol
agent and hundreds of Mexicans. In 2011, the operation became the focus
of a congressional investigation, during which then-Attorney General Eric
Holder admitted, "This operation was flawed in concept, as well as in execution."[21] In July 2012, a congressional committee released a 2,300-page report
on the "failed operation," noting, "From the outset, the case was marred
by missteps, poor judgments, and an inherently reckless strategy."[22] In the
next two years, the acting director of the ATF and several high-level ATF
officials resigned. In late 2014, after three years of foot-dragging, the Justice
Department released over sixty-five thousand pages of documents related
to "Fast and Furious." And the investigations continue.[23]

Some attribute ATF's mottled history to a chronically undernour-
ished budget. Between 2001 and 2012, the ATF appropriation by Congress increased 50 percent compared to a 144 percent increase for the FBI
over the same period.[24] Compounding budget matters, the ATF has lived
with an annoying pebble in its shoe since 2003, when the annual federal
appropriation to the ATF first carried a rider known as the Tiahrt Amendment, named after former Congressman Todd Tiahrt (R-KS). The rider,
a product of the gun rights lobby, places explicit restrictions on how the
ATF spends money. The early Tiahrt amendments required destruction of
NICS background-check information within twenty-four hours of a sale;
they prevented the ATF from requiring licensed firearm dealers to conduct

annual inventories to check for stolen guns; they limited unannounced inspections of licensed dealers to at most one a year; and they sharply limited access to ATF trace data—all of which compromised law enforcement. More recent versions of the amendment have been relaxed to allow access to trace data by state and local authorities for criminal investigations. The 2014 ATF appropriation includes $58 million in grants to strengthen state background checks, but it also extends ten riders that restrict how the ATF manages data, oversees licensed dealers, and regulates firearms. According to the Center for American Progress, the ATF works "blindfolded, and one hand tied behind its back."[25]

Finally, the ATF has not prospered with staffing, having fewer agents today than it did forty years ago. Since 2006, the position of director of the ATF has required Senate confirmation. Yet, between 2006 and 2013, the agency existed without a permanent (Senate-confirmed) director. The glacial progress in filling the top position is again attributable largely to intense NRA lobbying. Only in August 2013, after seven years of provisional leadership, was a permanent ATF director sworn in: B. Todd Jones, a former marine and US attorney, a trial lawyer, and one of the several acting ATF directors. Then, in March 2015, Jones announced his resignation despite his widely acknowledged effective leadership (to join the National Football League as chief disciplinary officer). The ATF is once again under an interim director.

Background Checks and the Famous Loophole

Visit the website armslist.com and you will appreciate the enormous challenge in regulating firearm transfers. The site is just one of several serpentine, nationwide bazaars that links those who want guns with those who have guns. One of the founders of the site described it saying, "Imagine a gun show that never ends."[26] On one particular day, the site listed about ninety-two thousand firearms for sale or trade—and armslist.com is just one of several such arms markets on the Internet.

To access armslist.com the first time, the visitor must agree to several conditions, including:

- I understand that ARMLIST DOES NOT become involved in transactions between parties and does not certify, investigate, or in any way guarantee the legal capacity of any party to transact; and

- If I am at all unsure about firearm sales or transfers, I will contact the Bureau of Alcohol, Tobacco, Firearms, and Explosives.

The site provides the seller's contact information, and the details of the transaction are worked out with the interested buyer. For example, meet in the courthouse parking lot Sunday at four p.m. and bring $350 in cash. Because they involve private parties, transactions on armslist.com and similar sites are unregulated by most state or federal laws. In most states, such gun sales are as unnoticed as selling a trampoline to a neighbor. Two people know the transaction occurred and there is no record. It is not surprising that gun control advocates see private firearm sales as a colossal loophole that must be plugged.

Recall that the original system of background checks appeared in the Brady Handgun Violence Prevention Act in 1993. Five years later, the online version went live under the banner of the National Instant Criminal Background Check System (NICS). Since its inception in 1998, NICS has been strengthened and streamlined in many ways, if only because of vast improvements in data management and communication technology.

It starts with dealers who apply to be federal firearm licensees (FFLs); this designation means they are registered with the ATF and must abide by ATF procedures. At the moment, there are 140,000 FFLs in various categories: about 54,000 retail dealers, 64,000 collectors (curios and relics, as the ATF calls them), 9,200 manufacturers, 7,800 pawnbrokers, plus a few smaller groups.[27] Anyone buying a gun from an FFL must complete the three-page Form 4473, on which the buyer confirms that he or she meets the federal requirements for purchasing a firearm: at least eighteen years of age; not a felon or under felony indictment; not an unlawful user of marijuana, depressants, stimulants, or narcotics; not subject to a restraining order; not an illegal immigrant; and not "adjudicated mentally defective."[28]

The purchaser data are swallowed electronically by the NICS system, where they are checked with databases of prohibited buyers. Some states rely on the FBI to do background checks using the NICS database; other "point-of-contact" states do the checks themselves using both NICS and state databases. Typically, 70 percent of applications are not matched with a prohibited buyer and the purchase from the FFL proceeds. The remaining applications are routed to a special group called the NICS Section (which has access to "protected information") for a second check. Roughly 75 percent of those cases result in an immediate determination (either approve or deny) while the FFL is still on the line. This means that over 90 percent of applications result in a fast decision that inconveniences neither the buyer nor the FFL.

How fast? From 2009 through late 2012 (years for which data are available), the average wait for an immediate determination was roughly nine seconds. For the last month of 2012—coinciding with President Obama's re-election and the Sandy Hook shootings—the average wait jumped to four minutes because of "unprecedented call volume." In fact, five of the ten busiest days in NICS's history were in the last six weeks of 2012.[29]

In its first full year of use (1999), NICS carried out 9.1 million background checks. The number of annual checks has increased steadily since then, reaching twenty-three million in 2015—roughly a 4 percent increase per year. Since 1999, over 233 million background checks have been done. In 2013, the leading state in background checks was Kentucky, with almost 1.6 million checks. To avoid the temptation of confusing background checks with gun sales, the NICS data tables carry a caveat:

> These statistics represent the number of firearm background checks initiated through NICS. They do not represent firearms sold. Based on varying state laws and purchase scenarios, a one-to-one correlation cannot be made between a firearm background check and a firearm sale.[30]

The fewer than 10 percent of applications that are not immediately resolved undergo additional review; some are approved and some are denied. During its lifetime, NICS has issued about 1.3 million denials—or about half of one percent of all checks performed. Over one-half of those denials (57 percent) were applicants who were "convicted of a crime punishable by more than one year or a misdemeanor punishable by more than two years."[31] A distant second in denials were applicants who were found to be fugitives from justice (10 percent). It is always possible that a denial will ultimately result in a sale either through an appeal or a reapplication.

Among gun rights proponents, one of the deep concerns about background checks is record keeping and the possibility that NICS data might become a national gun registry. Federal law requires FFLs to keep a record of firearm sales (purchaser and gun information) essentially until they go out of business. However, these records remain with the FFLs and are not comingled with federal records and databases. Only by a court order or in the course of a criminal investigation may FFL sales records be accessed.

While NICS continues to fortify its databases and make efficiency improvements, it is bombarded with opprobrium from all sides. It turns out that supporters of background checks are also critics. First, they generally believe the system is too weak and ineffectual. Federal law, which requires background checks on purchases only from FFLs, leaves open a floodgate of transfers that are unregulated in most states. Anywhere from 10 to 40 percent of gun sales take place without FFLs, through "loopholes" such as gun shows, Internet sales, and private transactions.[32] So one of the mantras of gun control is *close the loopholes*—either at the federal level or state by state.

Indeed, some states have strengthened the federal law. Nine states (including the District of Columbia) require a background check at the point of transfer for all sales (handguns only in two of those states); that is, dealers at gun shows must conduct background checks and private sales must take place at a licensed dealer. Two more states require background checks at gun shows only. And eight states regulate all sales by requiring buyers to obtain a purchase permit after passing a background check. Appealing to a rarely seen side of human nature, two states (Nevada and Oregon) allow private buyers to undergo a voluntary background check.

The holy grail of gun control is universal background checks—one sweeping federal law that requires background checks for licensed, gun show, and Internet sales, as well as private transfers (perhaps with exceptions for intra-family transfers). Universal background checks have a commonsense appeal. Why not apply the same rules—whatever they might be—to all gun sales? Recent polls show that 74 percent of people in NRA households, 79 percent of gun owners, and 85 percent of non-gun-owners endorse universal background checks.[33] In a recent survey of 113 sheriffs and police chiefs, 95 percent supported background checks on all gun sales.[34] And in another survey, 55 percent of licensed gun dealers supported universal background checks (with 35 percent expressing strong support).[35] And yet opposition remains fierce, as shown by the defeat of a background-check bill in Congress in 2013 (see chapter 17).

The system of background checks is only as good as the underlying databases. The federal databases currently consist of criminal, mental-health, drug-abuse, and domestic-violence records. Obtaining and maintaining those records is understandably difficult; it requires the cooperation and coordination of many state and local law-enforcement agencies. Supporters of background checks point to notorious gaps in the system and seek ways to make it less porous. Mental-health records have proven to be particularly unreliable. Mass murderers Seung-Hui Cho (Virginia Tech),[36] Jared Loughner (Tucson),[37] and James Holmes (Aurora)[38] had histories of mental illness and yet were able to pass background checks and obtain their weapons.

NICS critics also point to two other subtle provisions in the federal law. One is the law's "default-proceed" provision, which allows some purchasers to consummate a sale even after they have been denied by the system. This pathway is taken when a background check is delayed and the licensed dealer has not received a decision in three business days. In this case, the sale may proceed (by default). Department of Justice data show that in 2012, over 3,500 prohibited purchasers bought guns because of the default-proceed clause. The other leak in the system arises because some states allow buyers who already have state-issued licenses or permits (for example, a concealed-carry permit) to bypass a background check. These permits may certify that the buyer was once eligible for a purchase, but they do not identify a person who has since become ineligible to buy, perhaps because of a restraining order or a felony charge.

Background checks provide a battleground for dueling statistics. In 2001, the Bureau of Justice Statistics (BJS) released a report based on a survey of 203,000 prisoners serving time in state or federal prisons for crimes involving firearms.[39] The report is ingenious and revealing (and somewhat dated as well). Among the many insights provided by convicted gun criminals, we learn that 40 percent of the inmates obtained the gun used in their most recent offense from a family member or friend. Another 40 percent of the inmates obtained their gun illegally (theft or black market). Only 14 percent of the inmates obtained their gun from a retail outlet: 8.3 percent from a retail store, 3.8 percent from a pawn shop, 1.0 percent from a flea market, and 0.7 percent from a gun show.

Both sides have a heyday with these data. Gun rights groups point to the

1.7 percent of sales at gun shows and flea markets and claim that the gun show loophole is microscopic. They argue that extending background checks to gun shows is pointless. Gun control advocates point to the majority (about 70 percent) of sales from sources other than retail dealers and claim that extending background checks beyond FFLs is essential. The study also revealed that 84 percent of the convicts surveyed were prohibited purchasers at the time of their crime. A few of those prohibited buyers may have tried to lie-and-buy (purchase with falsified paperwork) at a licensed dealer. But the vast majority sought unregulated sources.

A study done at the same time by the ATF seems to contradict the BJS report. Tracking over eighty-four thousand illegal guns over two years, the ATF study concluded that 30 percent of the guns had passed through a gun show in their lifetime.[40] And yet, according to the BJS study, convicted gun users said they rarely obtained guns at gun shows. A likely explanation for the apparent inconsistency is that gun shows are not the primary source of guns for criminals. Rather, guns are purchased at gun shows by legal buyers and then transferred illegally through straw purchases. The same ATF study estimated that 46 percent of the illegal guns traced in that study involved a straw purchase.[41]

What about the objections raised by outright opponents of background checks? Once the frivolous objections, such as inconvenience, are removed, opponents of background checks denounce the system for at least two reasons. The first reason is that the federal government cannot be trusted to follow the law. The Brady Act has a provision, entitled "Prohibition relating to establishment of registration systems with respect to firearms," that forbids recording or transferring "any record or portion thereof generated by the system" to a federal or state facility. The law also prohibits using NICS "to establish any system for the registration of firearms, firearms owners, or firearm transactions or dispositions."[42] In the early days of NICS, the FBI kept records of FFL transactions for ninety days. Since 2004, according to the FBI, such records have been routinely destroyed within twenty-four hours. As mentioned earlier, the 1986 Firearms Owners' Protection Act (FOPA) backs up the assurances of the Brady Act by prohibiting the creation of a firearm registry. Nevertheless, the system of background checks is fertile ground for fears and conspiracy theories. The NRA claims the federal government has two good reasons to keep track of gun owners and their guns: "to take them and to tax them." [43]

Opponents to background checks also recite familiar refrains about many gun laws: they insult law-abiding gun owners and do nothing to stop criminals. With or without NICS—so the argument goes—criminals will always find a way to obtain firearms. The vast majority of those who subject themselves to background checks are law abiders. However, NICS has recently been producing over two hundred thousand denials per year—at least a few of which must have been genuinely prohibited buyers.

Looking back over eighty years of federal gun legislation, several things stand out. First, Congress has passed few truly significant gun laws—about one major act per decade. Second, federal gun laws are susceptible to expiration (the Assault Weapons Ban) or modification by later legislation (the Gun Control Act). Third, for many reasons—lack of funding, lack of leadership, insurmountable challenges—enforcement of federal gun laws has a history of occasional successes combined with off-setting impotency and debacles. For these reasons and undoubtedly more, most of the action in gun legislation takes place at the state level. The challenges may be different for the states, but they are certainly just as daunting, as we see shortly.

12 | A CENTURY PASSES

The failure to deal with ambiguity is one of the great disorders of the age.
It's a flight from reality.

—DAVID BROOKS, "The Tragic Situation," *New York Times*

IN THE DECADE following the convulsions of Reconstruction, labor disputes gradually overshadowed racial conflict as America's epochal upheaval. The epicenter for much of the turbulence was Chicago, where thousands of workers, many of them European immigrants, filled new jobs in the expanding furniture, garment, machinery, and meatpacking industries. Eventually, the simmering unrest erupted in the Haymarket Riot of 1886. But along the way, some pivotal events occurred that played a part in the American firearm story.

The global recession of the 1870s (originally called the Great Depression, later renamed the Long Depression) was an economic uppercut that put the country on its heels. High unemployment, collapsing banks, and failing businesses led to strikes, most notably the Great Railway Strike of 1877. Workers across the country organized and fought for better working conditions, higher wages, and an eight-hour workday. In Illinois, the state responded to these demonstrations by creating the First Regiment of the Illinois National Guard in 1874. Privately funded by wealthy industrialists, the guard was a select militia, with the thinly disguised purpose of assisting the police in suppressing labor protests.

Within a year, German immigrants reacted to the new antilabor force by forming Lehr und Wehr Verein (Education and Defense Association).[1] Incorporated under Illinois law, the organization was chartered to improve "the mental and bodily condition of its members so as to qualify them for the duties of citizens of a republic," a description that was also a bit of a disguise.[2] A sympathetic publication, *Vorbote*, acknowledged more accurately that the organization was "the workers' reaction against the formation of additional militia units designed to be used against them"[3] and then added, "When the workingmen are on their guard, their just demands will not be answered with bullets."[4]

The organization was active on several fronts: it stockpiled weapons and armed its members, demonstrated for the needs of workers, identified itself with socialist ideals, and organized rallies and parades that were often just excuses for beer drinking. However, the fact remains that the organization was never involved in armed conflicts with authorities.

Lehr und Wehr Verein and other worker self-defense groups quickly attracted members and their public events grew in size. Just as quickly, they were vilified in the Chicago press. In 1879, the *Chicago Tribune* let out a xenophobic scream, exclaiming:

> Communism has selected Chicago as its base of operations in the West. The large element of Poles, and Bohemians, and Germans in the city, reinforced by a very considerable sprinkling of Scandinavians, French, and Italians, and not a few of that class of Irishmen who care nothing for the teachings of their Church but hate the restraint of the laws, have given it a strong foundation upon which to build.[5]

The state legislature inflamed the situation further in May 1879 when it passed a law with two purposes: First it replaced the (privately funded) First Regiment of the Illinois National Guard with a state-supported militia officially called the Illinois National Guard. The law also made it illegal for any group, other than the National Guard or federal troops, to organize as a militia or to "drill or parade with arms" in any city of the state without a permit. The law drew immediate opposition from labor groups, as it empowered the governor to disarm workers and suppress their demonstrations. (Private companies such as Pinkerton's National Detective Agency were also hired by business owners to infiltrate the unions and crush demonstrations.)

The *Chicago Daily Times Herald* endorsed the militia law, making a curious comparison:

> The purpose of this statute was to compel the disbandment and prevent any organization hereafter of the extra-legal, and now illegal, military associations of the communist enemies of society, which in many northern cities are the counterpart of the lawless "Ku Klux Klans."[6]

With a modern perspective, historian Stephen Halbrook notes:

> Just as the Southern select militias of 1866 disarmed black laborers on behalf of the wealthier interests, the Illinois select militia of 1879 functioned to disarm immigrant laborers on behalf of the wealthier interests.[7]

The rising tension was a trip wire ready to be sprung. And it happened in September 1879 when Herman Presser, mounted on horseback carrying a cavalry sword, led a parade of four hundred Lehr und Wehr Verein members through the streets of Chicago. The marchers carried unloaded rifles and the parade was peaceable. However, to make a test case of the new militia law, Presser chose not to get a state-issued permit for the event. He was arrested for violating the new militia law, convicted in the Criminal Court of Cook County, and fined ten dollars. When the Illinois Supreme Court upheld the conviction, Presser appealed the case.

As labor unrest intensified in Chicago, the Presser case slowly meandered toward the US Supreme Court, where it was heard in November 1885. Presser claimed that the Illinois militia law under which he was convicted was invalid: "Its enactment was the exercise of a power by the [Illinois] Legislature forbidden to the states by the [US] Constitution."[8] He specifically claimed that the state militia law violated his Second Amendment rights.

Four of the Supreme Court justices who had heard the *Cruikshank* case ten years earlier were still on the court. In addition, Judge William Woods, who had ruled courageously for the conviction of white supremacists in the federal trials leading up to *Cruikshank*, had been elevated to the Supreme Court. In a strange twist of history, Justice Woods wrote the majority opinion in *Presser v. Illinois*—this time with a much different perspective.

The court ruled that the part of Illinois militia law prohibiting drilling and parading with arms was constitutional. By regulating activities such as armed marches, the state did not violate Presser's Second Amendment rights. As such, Presser's conviction was upheld. The real impact of the Supreme Court's opinion was not the injustice of a ten-dollar fine but rather its interpretation of the Fourteenth Amendment. Writing for the majority, Justice Woods opened his opinion by stating that the Second Amendment is "a limitation only on the power of the Congress and the national government, and not of the states."[9] In fact, the *Presser* opinion recited the language of *United States v. Cruikshank* with respect to the right to keep and bear arms:

> [It] is not a right granted by the Constitution. Neither is it in any manner dependent upon that instrument for its existence. The Second Amendment declares that it shall not be infringed, but this, as has been seen, means no more than that it shall not be infringed by Congress. This is one of the amendments that has no other effect than to restrict the powers of the national government, leaving the people to look [elsewhere] for their protection against any violation by their fellow citizens of the rights it recognizes.[10]

This validation of the *Cruikshank* opinion was certainly at odds with Woods's thinking ten years earlier. The opinion granted that the Second Amendment protected the state-supported Illinois National Guard; its members had a right to keep and bear arms. However, an unauthorized, self-formed militia, such as Presser's, did not have that right. According to the justices, a state law could legally violate that right.

Taken together, the *Presser* and *Cruikshank* decisions gave consistent narrow interpretations of the Fourteenth Amendment. More accurately, the Supreme Court in these cases appeared to be oblivious to the Fourteenth Amendment, denying that state governments were obliged to respect the various enumerated rights. The impact of these two opinions would last over a hundred years. It took that long for modern legal scholars to agree that, "*Presser* belongs to a bygone era of the nineteenth century when the Supreme Court rejected the application of the Bill of Rights to the states without considering whether the Fourteenth Amendment . . . made the Bill of Rights so applicable."[11]

A New Century

In the 1920s, mob violence replaced labor unrest in the streets of several large cities. In response to gang wars, specifically Chicago's St. Valentine's Day Massacre in 1929, Congress passed the National Firearms Act (NFA) in 1934. The law imposed a (then-prohibitive) $200 registration fee on so-called gangster guns: machine guns as well as shotguns and rifles with barrels less than eighteen inches in length. Congress rejected both a proposal to include handguns in the law and an outright ban on firearms.

A few years after passage of the NFA, the law had its first test when federal agents arrested two drifters, Jack Miller and Frank Layton, for transporting an unregistered sawed-off shotgun across the Oklahoma-Arkansas state line. In federal court, the defendants claimed that the operative sections of the NFA violated their Second Amendment rights. A federal judge ruled in their favor, the case was dismissed, and Miller and Layton were free. Unsatisfied by the decision, the federal government appealed the case and it went to the Supreme Court. The unanimous decision in *United States v. Miller*, announced in May 1939, focused on the militia preamble of the Second Amendment. In the majority opinion, Justice James McReynolds wrote:

> In the absence of any evidence tending to show that possession or use of a "shotgun having a barrel of less than eighteen inches in length" at this time has some reasonable relationship to the preservation or efficiency of a well regulated militia, we cannot say that the Second Amendment guarantees the right to keep and bear such an instrument.[12]

In other words, the justices knew of no military uses of a sawed-off shotgun, so Miller's Second Amendment rights could not have been violated. It is not surprising that the Supreme Court cited "an absence of evidence" in the *Miller* case. Miller and Layton neither appeared nor had attorneys representing them at the Supreme Court. Had there been a defense, it could have argued that sawed-off shotguns were, in fact, used during World War I and had a military purpose. In a final bizarre turn, before the case could be reheard in a lower court, Miller was found shot dead and Layton pled guilty as charged.

Modern scholarship suggests that the *Miller* case was "teed up" by the federal judge to serve as a test of the NFA's constitutionality.[13] If that was the purpose, then it succeeded; the NFA was ruled constitutional. Ever since the decision, the case has been thoroughly debated and used as a favorable precedent by both gun rights and gun control advocates. In focusing on the military uses of firearms, it affirmed that the right to keep and bear arms has limits and that reasonable restrictions are permissible—a victory for gun control. The *Miller* decision would be used as a precedent in several lower court cases to uphold firearm restrictions. However, viewed from another angle, the case is a gun rights triumph, as it upholds the right to bear at least those arms suitable to military use.

For seventy years after the *Miller* case, the Supreme Court did not rule on any case that dealt head-on with the Second Amendment.[14] And yet, throughout the twentieth century, the court was shifting the foundations of constitutional law in ways that would eventually bear on the Second Amendment. To recap, there is widespread agreement that the Bill of Rights originally restricted the powers of Congress but did not impose similar restrictions on the states. Ratified in 1868, the Fourteenth Amendment seemed to change that understanding by declaring that the states must respect the "privileges and immunities" of the citizens; exercise "due process" in matters of life, liberty, and property; and guarantee all people equal protection of the law. With the eloquence and vagueness of much of the Constitution, the Fourteenth Amendment left some important questions unanswered. Exactly what rights must be respected by the states? Is it just the rights spelled out in the Bill of Rights? Or does it include other unenumerated or implied rights, such as the right to self-defense and certain privacy rights?

The Supreme Court spent much of the twentieth century answering these questions through selective incorporation—the process by which the court proclaims that a particular right is protected under the Fourteenth Amendment from state laws that attempt to violate that right. For example, six different Supreme Court decisions between 1925 and 1996 incorporated the provisions of the First Amendment, anointing it with protection from state action.[15] And the unreasonable search and seizure provision of the Fourth Amendment was incorporated in 1949.[16] By the end of the twentieth century, the high court had incorporated most of the provisions of the Bill of Rights; the conspicuous exception was the Second Amendment.[17] The complex tale of the eventual incorporation of the Second Amendment is worth telling.

Origins of the Gun rights Movement

In its simplest terms, the debate over guns comes down to whether the Second Amendment guarantees an individual right or a collective, militia-related right to keep and bear arms. Gun rights advocates vehemently support the individual-rights view, while gun control advocates generally support at most a collective view. For much of the twentieth century, the country appeared to be at ease with moderate gun control—in part because the Supreme Court had not made an incorporation decision on the Second Amendment; in part because the few existing gun control laws (such as bans on machine guns) were reasonable and uncontroversial; and, in part, because of the somewhat equivocal precedent of the *Miller* case. Several factors led to the erosion of that gun control ambiance.

First, beginning in about 1960, crime in the United States became a frightening reality in the minds of many citizens. Between 1960 and 1990, the violent-crime rate increased nearly five-fold, while the homicide rate nearly doubled over the same period.[18] The fear of crime escalated with the shocking murders of John F. Kennedy, Martin Luther King Jr., Robert Kennedy, Malcolm X, and Sharon Tate—all covered with a media intensity never before seen (but still tame by today's standards). Congress responded to the crime surge with the Gun Control Act of 1968, which regulated interstate commerce of firearms, established a registration system for manufacturers and sellers of firearms, and restricted the sale of firearms to high-risk groups of people.

The Gun Control Act posed few onerous restrictions for private gun owners. In fact, several firearm manufacturers and the NRA supported the legislation. According to historian Jill Lepore, the NRA executive vice president at the time, Franklin Orth, testified before Congress that "we do not think that any sane American . . . can object to placing into this bill the instrument which killed the President of the United States" (a 6.5mm Carcano rifle).[19] Also at this time (as unearthed by journalist Craig Whitney), Charlton Heston was one of five celebrities who issued a statement that said in part, "Our gun control laws are so lax that anyone can buy a weapon. . . . Sixty-five hundred people are murdered every year with firearms in the United States. . . . The carnage will not stop until there is effective control over the sale of rifles and shotguns."[20]

Further movement on gun control occurred at this time when, once again, one hundred years later, guns became entwined with race. The civil-rights movement, usually associated with nonviolence, had a violent side that gained momentum when its peaceful tactics appeared to be failing. The teachings of Malcolm X inspired the Black Power movement, and Bobby Seale and Huey P. Newton gave it political muscle in the Black Panther

Party. Malcolm X proclaimed, "Article number two of the constitutional amendments provides you and me the right to own a rifle or a shotgun."[21] And indeed, after repeated confrontations with police in the San Francisco area, the Black Panthers realized that by carrying guns, they could level the playing field with police and have their voices heard. As Huey P. Newton said, with "weapons in our hands, we are no longer their subjects but their equals."[22] (At that time, California had a ban on carrying concealed weapons but allowed open carry.) The strategy of armed demonstrations culminated with a siege on the California state house on May 2, 1967. Although the Black Panthers were heavily armed, the incursion ultimately resulted in a nonviolent standoff. However, it became a historic event and a potent statement about the influence of a small, armed group.[23]

The Black Panther state house invasion led to the passage of one of the strictest gun control laws in the country, signed into law by then-Governor Ronald Reagan. The California law was followed by a wave of similar gun control laws in other states. In the next decade, the backlash created by these strict laws, combined with fears about the Gun Control Act and the ascent of the ATF, kick-started the gun rights movement. Perhaps ironically, some gun rights advocates point to the Black Panthers as one source of their own cause.

Gun rights issues also entered presidential politics in the 1970s. As president, Gerald Ford supported gun control legislation, having survived two assassination attempts seventeen days apart. However, in his campaign against Ronald Reagan for the Republican nomination in 1976, the two candidates put daylight between themselves on gun issues. Writing in the September 1975 issue of *Guns & Ammo*, Reagan deviated from the Republican party line observing, "The Second Amendment is clear, or ought to be. It appears to leave little, if any, leeway for the gun control advocate." He noted that Ford's attorney general, Edward Levi, wanted to ban handguns in high-crime areas. Then, foretelling arguments that would be familiar thirty years later, Reagan wrote, "Mr. Levi is confused. He thinks somehow that banning guns keeps them out of the hands of criminals. . . . Mightn't it be better in those areas of high crime to arm the homeowner and shopkeeper?"[24] Reagan lost the nomination in 1976. However, in the process, he staked out the gun rights position that would be adopted by the Republican Party when he became president four years later.[25]

Rising crime rates, Black Power, and the Republican shift on guns may have seemed unrelated at the time and remotely linked to the rise of gun rights. However, another event at this time had clear and immediate repercussions. Founded in 1871 by two (Union) Civil War veterans, the NRA was chartered "to promote rifle practice and for this purpose to provide . . . suitable ranges in the vicinity of New York."[26] For much of its existence, the NRA was dedicated to gun safety, gun education, and the interests of hunters and target shooters. In its early days, the organization supported gun control legislation.

By the 1970s, the NRA was gorging on new members, who were also buying guns for self-defense. With that surge in membership, the organization began its now-trademark functions of fund-raising and lobbying. And yet, the old-guard leadership was unaware of the changes just over the horizon. On the eve of its 1977 annual meeting in Cincinnati, the NRA was transformed.

At the time of the meeting, the NRA's chief lobbyist was a world-class marksman named Harlon Carter. At the age of seventeen, Carter shot and killed a fifteen-year-old boy in Laredo, Texas. Although he claimed self-defense, he was convicted of murder without malice aforethought. After serving two years of a prison sentence, the conviction was overturned (on the grounds that the jury had been given incorrect instructions about self-defense) and Carter began double careers in both the federal government and the NRA.[27] He served as chief of the US Border Patrol and as a commissioner in the Immigration and Naturalization Service. At the same time, he rose through the ranks at the NRA, holding the positions of executive vice president, president, and director of the then-new (and still thriving) NRA Institute for Legislative Action. The man had charisma; he was once described as "Moses, George Washington, and John Wayne rolled into one."[28] When Carter died in 1991, he had served both the federal government and the NRA for thirty-four years.

Carter arrived in Cincinnati in 1977 ready to change the soul of the NRA. He led the hardline wing of the organization in an overnight coup d'état that toppled the existing leadership. The NRA went into its annual meeting still connected to its roots; it emerged a new and redirected force ready to become the juggernaut that it is today. After a few years of Carter's leadership, membership and fund-raising went off the charts, and the organization's opposition to gun control became a crusade.

About this same time, a new enterprise entered the scene; today, we might call it a conservative think tank. Alan Gottlieb is a former nuclear engineer, a whirling dervish of an activist and entrepreneur, self-described as the "premiere anti-communist, free-enterprise, laissez-faire capitalist." [29] In 1974, he planted the seeds of the Second Amendment Foundation in Bellevue, Washington, fed them with his enormous energy, and then watched them grow. Gottlieb was a master at amassing mailing lists and he refined direct-mail marketing—strategies that he used to publish magazines, recruit members, hold conferences, and serve as all-around choreographer for gun rights causes. The timing was perfect: the young Second Amendment Foundation quickly found a vital role in the gun rights movement, and together they prospered. The Second Amendment Foundation flourishes today under Gottlieb's command, with over six hundred thousand members. It publishes journals and magazines (notably the iconic *The Gun Mag*), has an active book-publishing arm, maintains a visible media interface, and participates in as many as two dozen court cases at any time.

At the same time that the gun rights movement took flight, the gun control movement also got its start, although the takeoff was somewhat slower. In 1973, the University of Chicago was not one of the safer campuses in the country, as discovered by Mark Borinsky, who was a PhD student in psychology at the time. Walking home one night, he and a friend were robbed at gunpoint and nearly killed. The experience so scarred Borinsky that once he arrived in Washington, DC, for a new job, he vowed to support a group devoted to eliminating gun violence. To his surprise, he could not find such a group, so he founded one. Working out of a rented office with an operating budget he kept in his wallet, Borinsky quickly realized he needed some help. His $1.36 newspaper ad for someone with organizational abilities attracted Ed Welles. A World War II veteran and former CIA officer who served in Greece, Ethiopia, Nigeria, and Morocco, Welles was the multitalented personal assistant Borinsky needed. The two men became the National Council to Control Handguns (NCCH), the first organized group of the modern gun control movement.

It was April 1974 and the San Francisco killing spree known as the Zebra murders had already claimed thirteen victims. Twenty-three-year-old Nick Shields was loading his car in a residential neighborhood when a gunman killed him—randomly, execution style—with a .32-caliber handgun. [30] Pete

Shields was a wealthy marketing executive at DuPont at the time of his son's death. Soon after the tragedy, he resigned from his twenty-five-year career at DuPont and became the executive director at NCCH. By all accounts, Shields was the critical ingredient in the potion that grew NCCH from a roomful of inspired volunteers to a multimillion-dollar organization with hundreds of thousands of members.

In 1980, NCCH became Handgun Control, Inc. (HCI), which spawned an educational arm called the Center to Prevent Handgun Violence in 1983. In 1989, Sarah Brady, wife of Ronald Reagan's wounded press secretary, became chair of HCI. And in 2001, HCI became the Brady Campaign to Prevent Gun Violence and the Center to Prevent Handgun Violence became the Brady Center to Prevent Gun Violence. Both of the Brady organizations continue to thrive and are synonymous with gun control in America today.

Created in the same year as NCCH, the National Coalition to Ban Handguns (NCBH) was an invention of the United Methodist General Board of Church and Society. From the outset, NCBH was designed as a coalition of religious and other concerned organizations devoted to ending gun violence. In 1989, NCBH became the Coalition to Stop Gun Violence (CSGV), which is another pillar of today's gun control community. Over the years, CSGV enlarged its mission; it now lobbies for expanded background checks and an assault-weapons ban; it promotes microstamping as a high-tech method to trace guns; and it works to dilute the "insurrectionist message" of gun rights groups. Its forty-eight coalition members include a broad spectrum of religious, educational, and health organizations.

The 1970s also coincided with the entry of a new force in the gun debate: the academy. This unexpected power, hitherto on the sidelines, proved to be extremely influential, particularly in court cases. Motivated in part by NRA funding for an organization called Academics for the Second Amendment, scholarship on the Second Amendment became acceptable, then popular, and then plentiful. And that scholarship has been written almost exclusively in the same key. By one estimate, only three of eleven articles on the Second Amendment published in law journals in the 1960s supported the individual-rights interpretation of the Second Amendment. Between 1980 and 2000, the majority of the 125 articles published on the Second Amendment supported the individual-rights interpretation.[31]

In 1982, a Yale-trained attorney named Don Kates published the first gun rights paper in a top-ranked law journal. In a thorough and scholarly analysis of the origins of the Second Amendment and firearm jurisprudence, Kates built a formidable case leading to the conclusion that "unmistakably the Founders intended the second amendment to guarantee an individual right to possess certain kinds of weapons in the home in certain kinds of circumstances."[32] Despite his conclusion, Kates's article was measured and nonideological; he hoped it would be possible "to move forward to analyzing how rational, effectual gun control strategies can be reconciled with the constitutional scheme."[33]

The gun debate received a spirited boost from a 1989 article called "The Embarrassing Second Amendment," written by the eminent legal scholar Sanford Levinson. Noting the lack of attention given to the Second Amendment to date, he claimed that "members of the legal academy have treated the Amendment as the equivalent of an embarrassing relative, whose mention brings a quick change of subject. . . . That will no longer do."[34] He offered a guide to analyzing the Second Amendment and urged scholars to consider it on practical as well as constitutional grounds. He also acknowledged that gun control advocates, such as himself, might have to make concessions. At about this time, the individual-rights interpretation of the Second Amendment was anointed the "standard model," a term borrowed from physicists implying a widely accepted theory.[35]

With legal scholars on board, and a kindred Ronald Reagan in the White House on his way to replacing three Supreme Court justices and half of the federal judges, things looked promising for the gun rights movement. But not everyone was jumping on the train as it left the station. Former Chief Justice Warren Burger appeared on *The MacNeil/Lehrer NewsHour* in 1991 and famously begged to differ, saying that the individual-rights interpretation of the Second Amendment was "one of the greatest pieces of fraud, I repeat the word 'fraud,' on the American public by special interest groups I have ever seen in my lifetime."[36]

Burger was not alone in his interpretation of the Second Amendment at this time. Ten years earlier, in an opinion concerning the gun rights of felons, Justice Harry Blackmun observed matter-of-factly in a footnote that the Second Amendment guarantees no right to keep and bear a firearm that does not have "some reasonable relationship to the preservation or efficiency of a well regulated militia."[37]

Many years later, Justice John Paul Stevens recalled that Blackmun's "uncontroversial statement remained an accurate characterization of the Court's long-settled and correct understanding of the meaning of the Second Amendment."[38]

Nearing the High Court

While the lobbying efforts of the NRA and the gun rights publication mill were running at full strength, there was no comparable opposition. All that changed in an unpredictable instant with the assassination attempt on President Ronald Reagan on March 30, 1981. That awakening was the inspiration and namesake for the Brady Handgun Violence Prevention Act, eventually passed and signed in 1993.

One consequence of the Brady Act was a lawsuit, initiated by Jay Printz and Richard Mack ("Sheriff Mack") of Arizona, claiming that certain interim provisions of the Brady Act were unconstitutional. The case worked its way through the courts with mixed decisions and landed in the Supreme Court in 1997. In *Printz v. United States*, the court ruled that the provisions in question were, in fact, unconstitutional. The decision did not change the overall impact of the Brady Act; however, it did have an unexpected outcome.

Writing a separate concurring opinion in *Printz v. United States*, Justice Clarence Thomas veered into Second Amendment territory and speculated:

> [If] the Second Amendment is read to confer a *personal* right to "keep and bear arms," a colorable [legalese for *justifiable*] argument exists that the Federal Government's regulatory scheme, at least as it pertains to the purely intrastate sale or possession of firearms, runs afoul of that Amendment's protections.[39]

Thomas continued:

> Marshaling an impressive array of historical evidence, a growing body of scholarly commentary indicates that the "right to keep and bear arms" is, as the Amendment's text suggests, a personal right. . . . Other scholars,

however, argue that the Second Amendment does not secure a personal right to keep or to bear arms.[40]

Here was the recognition in a modern Supreme Court decision—at least a tangential suggestion—of an individual-rights interpretation of the Second Amendment.

There was also action on the state and local levels. Several Illinois cities and towns (Chicago, Morton Grove, Oak Park, Evanston, and Wilmette) enacted handgun bans in the early 1980s. The 1981 Morton Grove ban survived a federal court challenge, but the appeal to the Supreme Court was not granted.[41] However, the most troublesome of all gun control laws at the time was the oldest and strictest handgun ban in the country: the Washington, DC, ban had been in force since 1976—right in the NRA's backyard. This law banned possession of handguns, even in the home, and required that long guns be safely stored unassembled. Furthermore, crime rates in the district had been rising ever since the ban was passed. To gun owners, the ban was not only an insult but a useless and impotent law.

As the century turned, two conflicting lower-court decisions brought gun rights closer to the Supreme Court. Timothy Emerson was a Texas man going through a messy divorce and living under a temporary restraining order that forbade him from possessing a firearm. When he was arrested and indicted for carrying his Beretta pistol, he appealed the verdict as a violation of his Second Amendment rights. In 2001, the Fifth Circuit Court of Appeals clearly affirmed the right of law-abiding individuals to bear arms but ruled that in Emerson's case it did not apply because of the restraining order.[42] The Supreme Court denied an appeal of the case.

A year later, another federal case resulted in a decision that seemed to oppose the *Emerson* decision. *Silveira v. Lockyer*, argued in the Ninth Circuit Court of Appeals, involved a challenge to California's assault-weapon law. In this case, the court ruled that the Second Amendment grants a collective, but not an individual, right to bear arms.[43] The Supreme Court again chose not to hear an appeal. With these two federal cases reaching the threshold of the Supreme Court, it was only a matter of time before a Second Amendment case would finally be heard at the highest level.

The twentieth century ended with a palpable sense that the precarious equilibrium of America's gun debate was ready to topple—one way or the other. For the past thirty years, both sides had seen incremental gains and losses in the courts and state legislatures. However, deep tectonic rumblings seemed to threaten the fragile standoff. If nothing else, eight years of Democratic rule came to an end with the contested election of George W. Bush in 2000. Bush would appoint two new conservative Supreme Court justices during his two terms—both likely supporters of expanded Second Amendment rights. Furthermore, Bush's new cabinet included Attorney General John Ashcroft, an NRA member, and former Missouri senator and governor with pro-life and tough anti-crime positions. Four months after his confirmation as attorney general, Ashcroft wrote a succinct two-page letter to James Jay Baker, executive director of the NRA (in response to an earlier letter from the NRA inquiring about his views on the Second Amendment). Ashcroft got right to the point:

> While some have argued that the Second Amendment guarantees only a "collective" right of the States to maintain militias, I believe the Amendment's plain meaning and original intent prove otherwise.

After citing several court cases and legal publications, Ashcroft concluded:

> In light of this vast body of evidence, I believe it is clear that the Constitution protects private ownership of firearms for lawful purposes.[44]

Ashcroft's letter was reassuring to gun rights activists, but it was not a time for complacency. They still saw too many strict gun laws on the books and feared the passage of tougher new laws. They understood that the only way to reverse the encroaching tide of gun regulations and remove the menace of new laws was to secure a sympathetic ruling at the highest level. A favorable Supreme Court decision would finally resolve the question of incorporation and solidify an individual-rights interpretation of the Second Amendment. The wait for that day proved shorter than expected, and when it arrived, it brought a historic decision.

13 | CARRY, STAND, AND DEFEND

The powers not delegated to the United States by the Constitution, nor prohibited by it to the States, are reserved to the States respectively, or to the people.

—Tenth Amendment, US Constitution

TO HER CLASSMATES in a contracts course at the University of Colorado Law School, Katherine Whitney is a spirited, twenty-seven-year-old, third-year student, studying sixty hours per week for her law degree. Nothing suggests that she carries a loaded .38-caliber handgun, which she does lawfully under Colorado's concealed-carry law. Despite the state law, the university had long prohibited firearms on campus, arguing it has charter authority to set such policies. In 2012, the state supreme court settled the matter, ruling that the university must comply with state law. Ignoring wails of protest, many from faculty members, the university board of regents agreed to suspend the campus policy, enabling concealed-carry permit holders to have guns on campus.

Katherine first came to my attention when she attended a lively campus forum about the change in university gun policy. In a room crowded with vociferous folks who wanted guns nowhere in the same zip code, she took the floor, coolly identified herself as a gun owner, and with great conviction, explained why she carries a gun. When I met her a few weeks later, I expected an oral argument from an aspiring trial attorney. Instead, I was happily surprised by a hearty conversation with an unlikely advocate for gun rights.

Raised on a Kansas farm, Katherine was eight years old when her father taught her to shoot a BB gun. Target shooting and hunting became as ordinary as jump rope and dodgeball, and she moved comfortably to rifles, shotguns, and handguns. Every step of the way, she was indoctrinated with gun safety: "This is a weapon; if it's not treated properly, there can be some tragic consequences. It's unacceptable not to follow the basic rules of firearm safety."[1] Today, she attributes her willingness to carry a handgun to her familiarity with guns. "In fifteen seconds or less, I can take [my gun] apart and see that it is two pieces of metal, a spring, and some plastic. It's not going to kill someone. That gun is not dangerous until we add *me* to the equation or some other person. And then it transforms these two pieces of metal and some plastic into something that can kill someone." She knows that most people do not have that sort of comfort with guns. For those people, she has two messages: do not carry a gun without training, and try to learn more about guns.

Now living far from her Kansas home, Katherine has persuasive reasons for carrying a gun. "When I balance having guns in the classroom with being left defenseless the rest of the day, . . . I err on the side of preserving the right" of self-defense. "My life is no less valuable on-campus than it is off-campus." Like many gun rights advocates, she believes campus gun bans are dangerous. They broadcast to criminals that law-abiding people on campus are disarmed and vulnerable.

Katherine aims to correct widespread misunderstandings about guns. "I have met folks on campus who think that *concealed carry* means it is legal to bring an assault rifle into a classroom!" As long as that sort of misconception persists, any sort of agreement about guns is impossible. She is particularly alarmed that some faculty members are reluctant to talk to her about guns; she finds great irony in such a closed-minded and emotional reaction on a university campus—of all places. "It's been fascinating for me to see that the faculty . . . who claim to value diversity of ideas are so unwilling to even hear the other side."

One of her professors, who *was* willing to talk about guns in the classroom, was uneasy about Katherine bringing a gun to class. According to Katherine, the professor was concerned that "a gun in her classroom could undermine her authority and, if concealed carry becomes too common, the majority of students could be armed, shifting the balance of teacher-student dynamics." After they talked for twenty minutes over coffee, Katherine agreed not to carry her gun to that class. She says, "I can be respectful of her wishes." She believes that sort of accommodation is needed on both sides.

The fear that the campus might become awash in guns is likely exaggerated. The twenty-one-year-old age limit on concealed-carry permits prevents most students from carrying a gun on campus legally. Katherine speculates that more people carry guns on campus illegally than legally. And that is a familiar criticism of gun control laws: Careful gun owners tend to obey laws. However, those laws do not stop would-be criminals from possessing guns.

Katherine returned to the importance of understanding and tolerance. "It's normal . . . to be afraid of things you don't know or understand. I'm not afraid of my gun because I know it. . . . The emotionally passionate professors who oppose firearms on campus do not know firearms the same way I do. I'm afraid of all sorts of things I don't understand."

Miles apart in their perspectives on guns, Katherine and her professor represent two cultures that coexist in America today: Without stereotyping excessively, one culture believes in self-reliance; honors personal liberties, not the least of which is assured by an individualized Second Amendment; and finds gun control laws intrusive and anathema to its idea of a free society. The other culture venerates collective values such as social responsibility and public security; believes that guns on the streets, in the media, or hidden under coats are abhorrent; and, like many non-Americans, thinks America could be more civilized. There are many ways to view these conflicting cultures, one of which is to look at the diversity, inconsistency, and complexity of state gun laws.

We all visit other states and generally abide by the local laws. For example, speed limits, sales-tax rates, and gambling restrictions vary from state to state, and these differences present few difficulties for informed travelers. However, when it comes to state gun laws, it is a tangled web two hundred years in the making. Within each state, the legislature and courts have developed a set of laws reflecting the state's unique history and culture. Those laws cover the sale, purchase, transfer, manufacture, possession, and use of various types of firearms. To complicate matters, states regularly enact, amend, and repeal gun laws. By one analysis, 1,500 state gun bills were introduced in 2013 and 109 became law.[2] (Of those 109 laws, 39 tightened existing laws and 70 relaxed them.) When you put it all together, the result is a changing fifty-dimensional labyrinth.

Are Guns Like Cars?

According to recent data, about 220 million licensed drivers use about 250 million registered passenger automobiles in America.[3] These figures are fairly accurate because every state requires registration of vehicles, licensing of drivers, and insuring of automobiles. Beyond registration and licensing laws, each state has laws on seat belts and speed limits. Some states also require safety and emission inspections. Not incidentally, states collect millions of dollars each year in vehicle-ownership taxes. And both state and federal governments collect taxes on gasoline—without which vehicles would be useless.

While some Americans may find this system of laws and taxation intrusive, most believe that it amounts to effective, commonsense regulation that ensures public safety—well worth a little inconvenience. It raises money for state budgets, it pays for highways and bridges, and it has made driving safer. (Automobile fatalities have decreased by 40 percent since 1972, while the population has increased by 47 percent.)

So it is not surprising that many gun control advocates look to automobile regulations as a model for guns. Of course, automobiles are not mentioned in the Bill of Rights. Nevertheless, why not register all firearms and license firearm users? Why not levy special taxes on firearms? How about a tax on ammunition, without which firearms would be useless? What about accident or liability insurance? And if safety regulations can stanch the epidemic of automobile deaths, why not try analogous laws to reduce the toll of gun violence? It may all sound like a reasonable plan, but for better or for worse—depending on your point of view—it has not happened. There are three different sorts of regulations, some of which may be found in some states: rules about purchasing firearms, about licensing owners, and about registering firearms.

First, thirteen states (including the District of Columbia) require permits, eligibility certificates, or firearm owner IDs just to purchase handguns. Only six states require similar permits for long-gun purchases. In the remaining states, anyone meeting minimum federal requirements may purchase a gun.

Purchase permits restrict who buys a firearm, but they do nothing to restrict who ultimately possesses and uses the firearm. For this reason, five states, Illinois (all guns), Hawaii (all guns), the District of Columbia (all guns), New York (handguns), and Massachusetts (more complex) require that gun owners and users be licensed.[4] As with automobiles, firearm owners and users in these states must pass a proficiency test to get a license, and they must renew it periodically.

Permits and licenses certify individuals to own or use guns, but in most cases they do not link an individual to a specific gun. So the next step toward an ideal gun control world is firearm registration. In a fully inflated firearm registration system, gun owners would report their purchase of a weapon to a designated authority. The report would include a description of the owner and the weapon (including serial number). Furthermore, transfers of a weapon between individuals, as well as the theft or destruction of a weapon, would also be reported.

Supporters of firearm registration claim that it reduces the number of illegal owners and sales. It also enables fast tracing of firearms used in crimes. In a 2013 poll, two-thirds of respondents favored a federal government database to track all gun sales.[5] However, that level of support is not reflected in state legislatures. Only eight states (including the District of Columbia) require registration of handguns and only two states require registration of long guns.

Those who oppose comprehensive gun registration give at least four reasons: it is too late, it is too expensive, it is arguably illegal, and it is dangerous. It is too late because some three hundred million mostly unregistered guns are already in circulation. Opponents argue that it is unrealistic to start registering guns now. Also, the challenge of designing and implementing a functional registration system is expensive and impractical. (Critics can point to the software struggles of the Affordable Care Act as Exhibit A.) Then there is the legality of such a system. A 2007 federal law that beefed up the National Instant Criminal Background Check System specifically prohibits using NICS as a federal registry for firearms.[6] That law does not prohibit a federal registry independent of NICS and it does not prevent a state from creating its own registration system. However, combining these challenges, opponents claim that creating a gun registration system is a good definition of impossible.

Finally, there is the claim that gun registration is one short step away from gun confiscation, and for that reason, gun registration is dangerous. A recent alert on a gun rights website claims—with some exaggeration:

In the wake of New York's latest gun control law, the New York Police Department is now sending out notices to registered gun owners demanding that they give up their firearms, clear proof that gun registration leads to outright confiscations.[7]

The NYPD notice actually applies only to weapons covered by New York's 2013 SAFE Act, passed shortly after the Sandy Hook tragedy.

Holocaust survivor Kitty Werthmann recalls the imposed registration of firearms in Nazi-occupied Austria. Now over eighty years old, she appears at Tea Party conferences, urging Americans to "keep your guns, and buy more guns, and buy ammunition."[8] Those claims may sound like alarmist hysteria. But at least one serious scholar has advanced the same argument, noting that the Nazi regime used a gun registration system to seize the weapons of Jews.[9]

Gun control advocates and many Americans may see comprehensive gun registration as an ultimate end. However, it is hard to see a practical route leading from here to there.

Where and How to Carry

State and federal laws generally allow firearms in the home, in safe storage locations, or in one's car. So the remaining persistent questions deal with carrying firearms in public. The so-called carry laws illustrate perfectly the jungle that ensnares anyone trying to navigate firearm laws. Simplifying matters slightly, no federal law prohibits a private citizen from carrying firearms on public (non-federal) property. Instead, all such legislation is left to the states; and over the years, the states have fashioned a bewildering variety of laws on the subject.

In the early nineteenth century, carrying a concealed weapon was considered a sinister act—a sure sign of criminal tendencies. For that reason, many states passed laws prohibiting carrying a concealed weapon (starting with Kentucky and Louisiana in 1813 and followed by Indiana, Tennessee, and Virginia). By the end of the nineteenth century, most states had laws prohibiting the carrying of concealed weapons—some of the earliest gun control laws in America.[10] Looking back, it is ironic that most of the states had bans on concealed weapons, while the legal and socially accepted way to carry firearms was openly.

Matters began changing in the twentieth century. Without attracting much attention, New Hampshire (1923), Washington (1961), and Connecticut (1969) passed laws allowing a local authority, such as a sheriff or magistrate, to issue concealed-carry permits.[11] It was Florida's permissive concealed-carry law that attracted attention in 1987, and in the next twenty-five years, the remaining states joined the chorus. In 2013, Illinois became the last state (including the District of Columbia) to grant concealed-carry permits. The variously attributed theory behind concealed carry is that when the wolves cannot tell the lambs from the lions, the whole flock is safer.[12]

At one end of the spectrum, eight states allow concealed carry with no permit for residents.[13] (*Constitutional carry* is the euphemism for unrestricted concealed carry.) Thirty-three states have "shall issue" concealed-carry laws that require a local authority to issue a concealed-carry permit to an applicant, barring certain disqualifying conditions, such as a felony record or a history of mental illness; training may be required. More stringently, nine states have "may issue" laws whereby a local authority may selectively issue concealed-carry permits. The requirements for a concealed-carry permit vary in "may issue" states, but they generally involve rather porous conditions such as having a good character or being a reputable individual. Some states require training, a gun safety course, or firing live rounds to qualify for a permit. "May issue" laws, seen by some as too restrictive, are currently under legal challenge in several states.

That quick summary conceals the devilish details in state carry laws. Most states have clauses that prohibit concealed carry in certain public places, such as schools, college campuses, jails, courthouses, government buildings, bars, places of worship, sports arenas, hospitals, casinos, or mental-health facilities. Most states have two- to ten-year expirations on concealed-carry permits. Some states allow making names and personal information of permit holders a public record; other states prohibit collecting such data. Legal filigree abounds when it comes to weapons in vehicles, whether the weapon is a long gun (rifle or shotgun) or a handgun, and whether it is loaded or unloaded.

But we have not seen the real maze of concealed-carry laws until we get to reciprocity. Imagine fifty-one people (one from each state and the District of Columbia) in a room shaking hands with one another. If every person shakes the hand of every other person, a total of 1,275 different handshakes will occur. If each handshake means that one state recognizes the concealed-carry permit of the other state, then there are 1,275 different reciprocity agreements among the states. However, it is more complex than that for two reasons. First, some reciprocity agreements are not mutual. For example, California permits are honored in twenty other states, but California does not honor the permits of any other state. Second, some states issue two kinds of permits, one for residents and one for nonresidents. For example, South Carolina and Florida have reciprocity: they both honor resident permits issued in the other state. However, neither state recognizes a nonresident permit issued in the other state.

Here is the sort of (entirely licit) maneuver that can occur. A Colorado resident cannot carry a concealed weapon in Washington because the two states do not have a reciprocity agreement. However, Colorado does have an agreement with Utah, a state that issues nonresident permits, and Utah also has a reciprocity agreement with Washington. So a Colorado resident may get a nonresident permit from Utah, which will be honored in Washington, allowing the Colorado resident to conceal carry in Washington—despite the absence of an agreement between the two states.

Gun owners are responsible for navigating these reciprocity agreements and avoiding unintentional violations.[14] Seeking a simpler system, the House of Representatives passed a universal reciprocity bill in 2011, requiring every state to honor the permits issued in every other state. While this bill would have had the salutary effect of untangling the web of concealed-carry laws, it also would have subjected all states to the least restrictive laws. The companion bill died in a Senate committee, and national reciprocity never became law. Another attempt in 2013 also failed.

While lawmakers were busy passing concealed-carry laws, they paid little attention to the issue of open carry (carrying a gun in plain sight), which had been legal in most states for decades. No federal law outlaws open carry. At the state level, it is another swirl of laws and conditions. Forty-seven states have always allowed some form of open carry—simply because laws were never passed to forbid it. California, Florida, Illinois, and the District of Columbia ban open carry of both handguns and long guns. In some states, a permit is required for open carry or municipal laws may outlaw open carry in the absence of a state ban. In other states, the right to carry openly applies only to unloaded weapons or only to handguns. And then there are anomalies. North Dakota allows open carry of handguns only during the day but long guns at any time. In open-carry Mississippi, "exhibiting the weapon in a rude, angry, or threatening manner in the presence of three or more persons" can result in a $500 fine.[15]

To many people, the sight of a law-abiding citizen toting an unconcealed gun down a grocery-store aisle can be unsettling. And most gun owners seem to respect that sensibility. Alan Gottlieb, founder of the Second Amendment Foundation and a formidable gun rights pit bull admitted, "I'm all for open carry laws. But I don't think flaunting it is very productive for our cause. It just scares people."[16] Until recently, open carry did not agitate lawmakers or the public because so few people practiced it. But that is changing.

A new campaign to promote the open carry of guns blossomed in several states under the national banner of OpenCarry.org. With the motto "A Right Unexercised Is a Right Lost," the movement gained visibility with demonstrations across the country. In 2008, two Utah residents posed for a photograph at the Salt Lake City airport brandishing their Glock handguns in front of a "No Weapons" sign. In fact, open carry at that particular place in the airport was legal and the signs were eventually removed. In 2009, ten people showed up outside an Obama event in Phoenix legally and openly carrying firearms—one a semiautomatic rifle. A similar crowd greeted Obama in New Hampshire, where one sign read, "It is time to water the tree of liberty."[17] At a rally in San Antonio in October 2013, several hundred men, women, and children gathered with unloaded long guns to remember the 190 people who died at the Alamo in 1836; it was all legal.

While many businesses were banning weapons on their premises, Starbucks grabbed a unique marketing opportunity and welcomed legal gun carriers. Gun rights groups launched a Starbucks Appreciation Day, while their opponents asked for "Brew Not Bullets." In September 2013, Starbuck's CEO Howard Schultz, caught in the crossfire, published an open letter announcing a delicate change of policy. Saying that "Starbucks is not a policy maker and as a company we are not pro- or anti-gun," Schultz asked customers to leave their guns outside with the understanding that Starbucks staff would not confront gun-carrying customers or ask them to leave their stores.[18]

Defend Your Castle and Make My Day

Some of the most controversial gun laws in America today concern the old moral and legal conundrum of self-defense. In the Anglo-American tradition, the first testament on the right to self-defense is William Blackstone's *Commentaries on the Laws of England*, published in 1769. In his interpretation of English common law, Blackstone explained that if a person or "husband and wife, parent and child, master and servant" is "forcibly attacked in his person or property, it is lawful for him to repel force by force; and the breach of the peace, which happens, is chargeable upon him only who began the affray. For the law, in this case, respects the passions of the human mind; and . . . makes it lawful in him to do himself that immediate justice, to which he is prompted by nature, and which no prudential motives are strong enough to restrain."[19] He continues:

> Self-defense, therefore, as it is justly called the primary law of nature, [cannot be] taken away by the law of society.[20]

In other words, it is lawful to exercise the primordial instinct to defend one's person and property. Blackstone also realized it's not quite so simple. He warns:

> Care must be taken, that the resistance does not exceed the bounds of mere defense and prevention; for then the defender would himself become an aggressor.[21]

And Blackstone's fragile line between the role of defender and aggressor has bedeviled lawmakers, judges, and law-enforcement agents ever since.

The right of self-defense as interpreted by Blackstone, together with the English maxim that "a man's house is his castle," seeped into colonial laws and court decisions.[22] In 1895, a dispute over a cow in Arkansas led to a revealing US Supreme Court decision that grappled with a fundamental question about self-defense. To shorten a long tale, three angry brothers confronted a Mr. Beard on his Arkansas property. One of the brothers, Will Jones, pulled a pistol from his coat and brandished it. When Beard ordered the brothers to leave his property, Jones approached Beard, and Beard grabbed a nearby shotgun. Rather than firing, Beard struck Jones over the head with his gun. Beard later testified "my gun was loaded, having ten cartridges in the magazine. I could have shot him, but did not want to kill him, believing that I could knock him down with the gun and disarm him, and protect myself without shooting him." Jones later died of his injuries in what the court called a "fatal difficulty." [23] A lower court ruled that Beard was guilty of manslaughter.

The case raises the question of whether a person must first retreat to avoid a confrontation in order to claim self-defense. The lower court in the Beard case instructed the jury that even if Beard was on his premises "in lawful pursuit of his business" and Jones "was doing an act of apparent or real deadly violence," then Beard should have avoided the confrontation "by getting out of the way of that danger." The lower court further instructed the jury that the only place in which the defendant was not obliged to retreat is "in his dwelling house." [24]

The case made its way to the Supreme Court. Kentucky attorney and justice John Harlan was eighteen years into a thirty-three-year term on the Supreme Court when he wrote the opinion in the *Beard* case. A majority of the justices took issue with the instructions given to the jury in the lower court. Citing earlier court cases that dealt with the doctrine of "retreating to the wall," Harlan concluded:

A man assailed on his own grounds, without provocation, by a person armed with a deadly weapon and apparently seeking his life is not obliged to retreat, but may stand his ground and defend himself with such means as are within his control. [25]

Twenty-six years later, the US Supreme Court reaffirmed the *Beard* decision; and again, it is helpful to understand the thinking behind this 1921 decision. Bad blood had festered between two Texans, Brown and Hermis, for a long time. When Hermis twice threatened Brown with a knife and claimed "one of them would go off in a black box," Brown began carrying a pistol. [26] Soon after that incident, Hermis showed up at Brown's work site and approached him with a knife. Brown retreated to get his pistol, and when Hermis struck him, Brown shot and killed Hermis. Brown was convicted of second-degree murder in a district court.

Once again, a question about instructions to the lower court jury took the case to the US Supreme Court. The lower court judge had instructed the jury:

It is necessary to remember, in considering the question of self-defense, that the party assaulted is always under the obligation to retreat so long as retreat is open to him, provided that he can do so without subjecting himself to the danger of death or great bodily harm.[27]

Bostonian and Civil War veteran Oliver Wendell Holmes wrote the majority opinion, objecting to the jury instructions and claiming:

If a man reasonably believes that he is in immediate danger of death or grievous bodily harm from his assailant he may stand his ground and that if he kills him he has not succeeded the bounds of lawful self-defense.[28]

Holmes added "detached reflection cannot be demanded in the presence of an uplifted knife."[29]

Court precedents were used in self-defense cases for many decades until the states began codifying their own laws. In 1985, Colorado passed the country's first castle law. Officially called the Homeowners Protection Act, it was quickly anointed the "make my day" law.[30] It states in part:

Any occupant of a dwelling is justified in using any degree of physical force, including deadly physical force, against another person when that other person has made an unlawful entry into the dwelling, and when the occupant has a reasonable belief that such other person has committed a crime in the dwelling in addition to the uninvited entry, or is committing or intends to commit a crime against a person or property in addition to the uninvited entry, and when the occupant reasonably believes that such other person might use any physical force, no matter how slight, against any occupant.[31]

The law does not justify the wholesale use of deadly force under any circumstances. First, the intruder must make an unlawful entry. However, mere trespassing is not enough. In addition to the uninvited entry, the occupant must have a reasonable belief that an additional crime has or will be committed. And finally, the occupant must believe that the intruder will use physical force. Importantly, this law stops at the front door and does not justify the use of force on the premises, in a vehicle, or in public places.

Most states now have "make my day" laws in versions both weaker and stronger than Colorado's law. Some state laws specifically require the occupant to retreat or use less than deadly force whenever possible, while other laws are clear that no retreat is required. A critical progression occurred when castle laws were extended to vehicles and businesses. And once that slippery process began, it was a short step to the issue of self-defense in public.

Stand Your Ground

Anyone could understand her terror. She had worked late and was heading to her car in a deserted Tallahassee parking garage when a pair of headlight beams washed over her. A car loaded with six young men slowly approached, and it did not look good. She could tell by the taunts and obscenities that the men were drunk or on drugs. "They made it clear what they intended to do," she recalled. "I felt sure I was going to die, or be left in a condition where I would have wished I had died."[32]

She flashed for an instant on her three daughters expecting her home at any time. Then, without a thought of retreat or surrender, she reached into her handbag and pulled out a loaded .38-caliber revolver. It shone brightly in the headlights, and the would-be assailants quickly decided they were stalking the wrong victim. The car reversed, accelerated, and disappeared into the night.

The parking garage showdown occurred in 1986, and it was not the only incident that forged Marion Hammer's titanium convictions about gun rights. Growing up fatherless in rural South Carolina, she started target shooting at the age of six. She recalls firing at tin cans on a fence, thinking, "hit that big red tomato on that can dead center."[33] She was soon helping her grandfather bring home squirrels and rabbits for the dinner table. With that kind of head start, it is not surprising that she became an award-winning markswoman and certified firearms instructor.

However, Marion Hammer's calling was not marksmanship; it was activism. The passage of the 1968 federal Gun Control Act inflamed her. The law changed her life because it "imposed restrictions on law-abiding people who had done absolutely nothing. . . . The Congress stampeded into taking that action because of the heinous acts of criminals and assassins. . . . I got angry that I was being punished and I hadn't done anything wrong."[34]

Her fury turned to action in 1975 when she founded Unified Sportsmen of Florida as an affiliate of the NRA. USF was needed because "Florida was seeing . . . a burst of gun control measures being filed by northerners who had moved to South Florida and had brought the stuff that they had moved away from with them."[35] USF was the first step into a lifetime of advocacy for gun rights that took Marion Hammer to the highest levels of leadership in the gun rights movement.

The USF gave Hammer a platform from which to launch her career, lobbying for both the USF and the NRA. She was elected to the NRA board in 1982 and about the same time she began one of her signature campaigns—the fight for a concealed-carry law in Florida. Both her supporters and enemies credit Hammer with providing the muscle, the brains, and the tenacity needed to pass the "shall issue" concealed-carry law that caught the nation's attention. The fact that every state now has some version of a concealed-carry law can be listed on Hammer's résumé.

The work on Florida's concealed-carry law sharpened Hammer's lobbying skills and announced that she was a force of nature. The new law magnified her stature (she stands four feet eleven) and stretched her powerful reach. She climbed through the ranks at the NRA and in 1995 was elected its first female president—joining the likes of Ulysses S. Grant (who preceded her) and soon to be joined by Charlton Heston (who followed her). She assured everyone that a woman would not let up on the gun rights throttle. Under her reign, the NRA saw a surge in membership, in part because of minorities and admiring women. While President Clinton's 1994 federal assault-weapons ban was a defeat for the NRA, the NRA under Hammer's leadership contributed to the widespread defeat of Democrats in Congress in 1994 and 1996. At this time, she told the *New York Times* that the best way to end the gun control debate in the United States would be to "get rid of all Liberals."[36]

After three years at the top of the NRA, Hammer returned to Florida to devote herself to lobbying. Anything with the scent of state gun control became the target of her prodigious energy. She pushed legislation relieving shooting ranges of liability for environmental cleanups. She lobbied successfully for a law to keep names of concealed-carry permit holders off the public record. Her work helped defeat bills that would ban firearms in hospitals, nursing homes, college campuses, and cemeteries. She overcame business opposition to ensure passage of a guns-at-work law, allowing employees to keep guns locked in their cars at work. And she launched Eddie Eagle, the NRA's gun safety program for children.

Hammer did not stop with gun issues. In 1999, over ten thousand Florida schoolchildren voted to change the state bird from the mockingbird to the scrub jay. Hammer opposed the scrub jay because their habit of eating out of a person's hand looked like begging, laziness, and a "welfare mentality."[37] She preferred mockingbirds and their willingness to fight larger birds and protect their nests. The mockingbird is still the Florida state bird.

However, Hammer's crowning act was Florida's stand-your-ground law. By all accounts, she wrote and nurtured the bill and watched it become law on October 1, 2005.[38] Signed by then-governor Jeb Bush, the law's operative language says:

> A person who is not engaged in an unlawful activity and who is attacked in any other place where he or she has a right to be has no duty to retreat and has the right to stand his or her ground and meet force with force, including deadly force if he or she reasonably believes it is necessary to do so to prevent death or great bodily harm to himself or herself or another or to prevent the commission of a forcible felony.[39]

Furthermore, a person who uses the law as an affirmative defense and prevails "is immune from criminal prosecution and civil action for the use of such force, unless the person against whom force was used is a law enforcement officer."[40] The law is explicit about "no duty to retreat." However, the alarm for many critics was the "reasonably believes" clause. Particularly in crimes in which there is no witness other than the perpetrator, how is a judge or jury to decide reasonable belief?

The new law was celebrated and censured. Critics called it the "shoot first" or "right to commit murder" law. Law-enforcement officials excoriated it. Attorney General Eric Holder weighed in saying, "It's time to question laws that senselessly expand the concept of self-defense and sow dangerous conflict in our neighborhoods."[41] The Brady Campaign to Prevent Gun Violence branded Hammer and the NRA as "masterminds of a dangerous paranoid mentality," responsible for making Florida an "armed utopia."[42]

The law's sponsor, Dennis Baxley, justified the law as a way to protect tourists. The NRA publication *American Hunter* gave the law an ovation:

> Thanks in no small part to the tireless efforts of our own former President Marion P. Hammer, law-abiding Floridians may now stand their ground and defend themselves against attack by violent criminals without fear of criminal prosecution or civil lawsuit.[43]

Hammer explained her mighty support for the bill saying, "what I like to call bleeding heart criminal coddlers want to give a criminal an even break, so that when you're attacked, you're supposed to turn around and run, rather than standing your ground and protecting yourself and your family and your property."[44]

Justifiable homicides in Florida increased from 33 in 2006 (prior to enforcement of the law) to 102 in 2007 (the first year of enforcement); the rates have remained at the 2007 level ever since. The *Tampa Bay Times* is conducting an ongoing study of Florida stand-your-ground cases since the law was enacted. The study currently catalogs nearly 250 cases, of which 134 cases were fatal. As of October 2014, in forty-five of those fatal cases, the accused was convicted of a crime; in seventy-five cases, the perpetrator was granted immunity under the law or the case was dismissed; and fourteen cases were pending.[45] Reading the details of these cases, it is clear that the law has enabled some private citizens to protect themselves and avoid injury or death. However, the law has also been used (unsuccessfully) as a defense in road-rage incidents, neighborhood disputes, and popcorn assaults in movie theaters.[46] More precisely, according to political scientist Robert Spitzer, in almost 80 percent of the fatal cases in which a stand-your-ground defense "succeeded," the person standing ground could have avoided a confrontation by retreating, and in nearly 70 percent of the fatal cases, the victim was unarmed.[47]

A task force commissioned by Governor Rick Scott studied the Florida law and released a report in February 2013. Of over ten thousand public comments received by the task force, about 75 percent expressed opposition to the law. While individual members of the task force suggested significant changes to the law, the report concludes:

All persons who are conducting themselves in a lawful manner have a fundamental right to stand their ground and defend themselves from attack with proportionate force in every place they have a lawful right to be.[48]

Critics of Florida's law claim it is enforced inconsistently. Here are two cases that are hard to square consistently. The first case was the center of a media maelstrom and hardly needs recounting. It is the February 26, 2012, slaying of seventeen-year-old Trayvon Martin by George Zimmerman, a twenty-eight-year-old insurance adjuster, part-time criminal-justice student, and neighborhood-watch coordinator.

After the shooting, Zimmerman was taken into custody, claimed that Martin attacked him, and explained the shooting as an act of self-defense. Citing Florida's stand-your-ground law, police released Zimmerman after a five-hour interrogation. After six weeks of public outcry over police inaction, special prosecutor Angela Corey charged Zimmerman with second-degree murder and manslaughter. The case went to trial on June 24, 2013, and an all-female jury began deliberating on July 12, returning a not-guilty verdict on all charges the next day. Many observers (including law sponsor Baxley) doubted that Zimmerman's actions fit the conditions for a stand-your-ground defense. Zimmerman's attorneys must have agreed; they did not use the stand-your-ground law to seek immunity. Rather, they won the case with a self-defense argument.

The slaying of Trayvon Martin in February 2012 brought worldwide attention to Florida's stand-your-ground law; but it was not the first test of the law in the state. A much different case was going to trial the day Trayvon Martin was killed. Marissa Alexander and Rico Gray both had previous charges of domestic violence in the course of their brief, turbulent marriage. On August 1, 2010, a week after the birth of their baby, a dispute erupted and Gray, who outweighed Alexander by one hundred pounds, allegedly battered and threatened her. Alexander fled to the garage but was unable to escape through a locked door. She returned to the house with a gun and fired a warning shot over Gray's head. Gray fled and called police, who charged Alexander with three counts of aggravated assault.

The path to a verdict was long and contentious. Simplifying matters considerably, a judge in a preliminary hearing ruled that Alexander could not use a stand-your-ground defense because she could have avoided the confrontation by finding another way to escape the situation. Shortly later, Alexander refused a plea offer and took the case to trial. In prosecuting the case, the same Angela Corey who later handled the George Zimmerman case argued that Alexander acted out of anger, not fear, and she also ruled out a stand-your-ground defense. A jury of three men and three women took twelve minutes to return a guilty verdict on all three counts. A few days later, Alexander's attorney filed a motion for a retrial, which was denied. On May 11, 2012, Alexander was sentenced to twenty years in prison under Florida's mandatory sentencing laws.

During the following year, condemnation of the Alexander verdict rained down from all sides. Alexander's defense team appealed and finally prevailed. On September 26, 2013, a state appeals court panel granted Alexander a new trial. The panel reached its decision not by stand-your-ground considerations but by way of a procedural technicality. In Alexander's new trial in November 2014, prosecutors sought a sentence of sixty years in prison.[49] Instead, Alexander accepted a plea bargain for an additional sixty-five days in prison (in addition to the 1,030 days she had already served). She was released in February 2015, was under house arrest for two years, and now has a felony record for life.

How similar are the cases of Marissa Alexander and George Zimmerman? Alexander's case involved a history of simmering domestic violence; Zimmerman's case sprung from a fatal twenty-minute encounter between two strangers. The state ruled that its stand-your-ground law did not apply to Alexander, who used a legal gun in her home for apparent self-defense and caused no injuries in the process. The stand-your-ground law delayed Zimmerman's arrest for six weeks, although in the end, the case was presented as one of self-defense. The situation is summed up well by a judge in the *Alexander* case, who rejected a motion for a retrial in that case. He admitted that "maybe I would be agreeing to a new stand-your-ground motion, which highlights some of the difficulties we are struggling with procedurally implementing this new law."[50]

Florida's stand-your-ground law did not stay in Florida. Soon after the Florida bill passed, Marion Hammer and the NRA worked with a conservative amanuensis for state legislatures known as the American Legislative Exchange Council (ALEC). Together they produced a model stand-your-ground law and sent it to other states for adoption. With or without the help of ALEC, twenty-seven states now have stand-your-ground laws. The laws in some states do not allow a delay in making an arrest, as happened in the *Zimmerman* case. And some state laws do not provide defendants with full immunity as the Florida law does.

The future of stand-your-ground laws across the country is uncertain. Some states are passing new stand-your-ground laws, while in other states, opponents are attempting to dismantle existing laws. Law professor and objective firearm author Adam Winkler sums up the situation:

> Non-gun owners are questioning stand-your-ground laws. . . . But the gun lobby is too strong to allow such laws to be repealed. For better or worse, stand your ground laws are here to stay.[51]

What May Be Next

Federal firearm laws have proved difficult to pass. However, state gun laws have proliferated as fifty different states carry out their individual gun-law experiments based on history, culture, and demographics. An open-carry law may be acceptable in a ranching town in Wyoming but may not make much sense in San Francisco. A law requiring owner-identification cards may reduce crime in Chicago but would be seen as a government invasion by every resident of Elko, Nevada.

Looking ahead, adding to the churning that occurs within each state, another current may bring a different sort of gun legislation. In 2010, Montana passed its Firearms Freedom Act, which protects firearms made and kept in the state from federal laws. Since then, seven states have passed laws that either proscribe the enforcement of federal firearm laws in the state or prohibit state agencies from assisting with federal law enforcement. Another twenty-five states are headed down similar paths.[52] These laws are the beginning of a new "nullification movement" that challenges the powers of Congress under the Tenth Amendment.[53] The Montana law reached the Supreme Court in 2014 but was denied a hearing. Issues such as this will only protract the battle between state authority and federal power that has been waged for the last two centuries.

14 | THE COURT SPEAKS

For all that the framers quarreled over the wording of the Constitution, they never indicated that they understood their intentions should bind future generations. All that mattered, they thought, was the Constitution itself.

—JEFFREY TOOBIN, *The Oath*

IT WAS JULY 20, 2012, scarcely twelve hours after the Aurora, Colorado, theater shootings in which a lone gunman killed twelve people and injured another seventy. Piers Morgan was taping his CNN talk show to be aired later that night. Given the events of the day, it made sense, at least to Morgan and CNN, to choose gun control as the subject of the show. However, Morgan's guest that night differed on that choice. We pick it up after Morgan welcomed his guest.

> GUEST: Honestly, Piers, I think this is the wrong night to be doing this and I wish you'd waited to have this segment until after the funerals. This is a time in Colorado and nationally when it would have been better to have more of the segments you did before with the families, when people could be unified in helping the victims.
>
> MORGAN: If I could jump in there! Let me just challenge you on that! If I may, let me just challenge you on that! A lot of people who do not want strengthening gun control have said, this is not the day to debate it. I'll tell you the day to debate it. It would have been yesterday to prevent it from happening. When you have a young man like this able to legally get 6,000 rounds of ammunition off the Internet and to buy four weapons including an assault rifle and for all of this to be perfectly legal in modern America, allowing him to carry out the biggest shooting in the history of the United States, that I'm afraid means it's too late for this debate, for people that lost their lives. So don't

patronize me about when we should be talking about the gun control debate. You tell me a good reason why we should not strengthen the laws now to stop another young man like him going into the store tomorrow buying four more weapons and 6,000 rounds of ammunition on the Internet, and killing and shooting another 70 people in America!

GUEST: Because we don't even know the full facts of this situation yet, it's another reason why it would have been prudent for you to wait a few days until we know more about this. . . . You've said many times on the air, America has too many guns. You want to drastically reduce the number of guns. So if your whole point is there's too many guns, we've got to get rid of lots of them, drastically constrict things, and you somehow think that's going to make it better. Well, there's no real evidence that it will. If you want to talk about specific reforms that involve this specific guy, and prevent future people like him, that's fine. But let's wait until we find the information instead of rushing the nation into this pro/con thing that sells a lot of commercials on TV. But it's inappropriately divisive right now. . . . Can you give the people a little bit of breathing room?

MORGAN: OK, you've made your point. . . . I'm not interested in having a debate about whether we can debate gun control. Let's move on to . . .[1]

Morgan's bludgeoning of a guest was nothing new or unexpected—particularly a gun rights guest. What was notable was the guest's imperturbable civility in the face of Morgan's assault. The guest looked unflappably into the camera and tried to call for a time-out. Morgan was not about to be derailed and chose to escalate the interview. In turn, the guest tried a courteous summary of his position: Let's first get the facts. There's no real evidence that reducing the number of guns will make things better. Then Morgan released the ejector seat. Case dismissed. Winner: the sensitive gun rights advocate. Loser: the bombastic TV personality.

Morgan's guest that night was one of the media's go-to guys for the gun rights perspective—an articulate and dispassionate commentator who can discuss the Second Amendment without sounding irrational or fanatic. And when challenged on a legal or constitutional technicality, he quickly and respectfully vaporizes most opponents. He is David Kopel, research director at the libertarian Independence Institute in Denver, associate policy analyst at the Cato Institute, an adjunct professor at the University of Denver Sturm College of Law, and a former assistant attorney general of Colorado. That is enough to fill every waking hour. But it does not. He somehow finds time to be one of today's most visible scholars on gun issues.

To claim that Kopel is prolific is like saying Bill Gates is well off. A visit to Kopel's website testifies to his remarkable output.[2] There one sees scholarly papers in top-flight law journals, popular articles in magazines, newspaper op-eds and columns, and numerous briefs in federal and Supreme Court cases. And that is just Second Amendment issues. His output is far greater when one includes his work on the environment, health, the First Amendment, history, and religion. Kopel has a YouTube channel, appears frequently on radio and television talk shows, and writes regularly for a constitutional law blog.[3] He was on the legal team that prevailed in the 2008 *Heller* case before the US Supreme Court (more on this case later in this chapter). He has an NRA-qualified expert rating for handguns and also speaks French, Spanish, and Italian.

Kopel agreed to meet with me, although I knew that a couple of hours of conversation would do little to expose the depth of his thinking and the breadth of his scholarship. We gathered around a massive mahogany table in a spacious conference room next to his office at the Independence Institute. A framed copy of the Bill of Rights hung on one wall. Across from it was a quarter-acre of bookshelves filled with a set of Colorado Revised Statutes plus leather-bound books on the history of guns and all legal matters. Kopel looked vaguely rabbinical, although he wore jeans and a University of Michigan (JD magna cum laude, 1985) rugby jersey over a purple T-shirt—probably not his usual court attire.

Despite his libertarian leanings and his vocal endorsement of gun rights politics, Kopel is a registered Democrat. His father was originally a Dewey Republican who became a Humphrey Democrat and eventually a distinguished twenty-two-year Colorado legislator. His mother was a devoted Democrat who had some influence in her husband's conversion. Kopel remembers growing up eating pretzels at Democratic fundraisers. As a high-school student, he was drawn to the civil-rights policies of Scoop Jackson.

Like Humphrey and Kennedy, he supported "an affirmative strong federal government that's going to help people and help lead the nation. . . . We want strong national defense and we are very, very anti-Communist because we are liberals, we believe in liberty, and global Communism and the Soviet Union are the antithesis of that. Now, that group of the Democratic party no longer exists."[4] He sees no mismatch between his political affiliation and his stand on many social issues. "I've remained fairly consistent in my views, but the party has changed." He looks forward to "the day when the party moves back to its traditional Andrew Jackson-Thomas Jefferson roots and gets better on national security." As a general rule, "everybody should be always changing and evaluating and refining their positions."

Given Kopel's voracious curiosity and intellect, I wondered why he chose to focus on Second Amendment issues. He likes First Amendment issues as much, but he "can't be omnicompetent at everything at the expert level." With Second Amendment commentary, he saw "an opportunity to make a contribution by adding expertise on a topic where serious expertise and public debate were lacking." Kopel was waiting at the door in the mid-1980s when scholarship on the Second Amendment began to flourish. It was a "place where it was easier to get published at a higher level and to make contributions that were getting cited by Congress and used in the public debate." He quickly rushed in and filled the literature with his historical and policy analyses of gun rights. Then he wryly added, "Certainly my wife would have found it more respectable for me to become a First Amendment specialist."

One of the purposes for my visits was to get Kopel's practical policy recommendations on reducing gun violence in America. He had plenty of ideas, but surprisingly, none of his top three suggestions involved changing firearm laws.

> We've been doing the gun-control debate in this country since the 1960s. And in the back and forth have actually come up with an overall reasonably good and balanced policy in most states. So is there room for further improvement? Yes, but are there any improvements out there that you would say would lead to dramatic reduction in criminal violence? The answer is probably not. And the far greater possibilities for reducing gun crime are those that involve just reducing violent crime in general.

His remedies are all on the sociological and cultural side. First, we have a desperate need to reduce the number of broken and fatherless families and we must improve parenting: "The core reason for crime is the criminal's lack of self-control." Next, we must make improvements in public education, which "means running the schools for the benefit of the students and the families rather than for the benefit of the National Education Association." And third on his list is reducing the waste in law enforcement and prisons.

> A large amount of law-enforcement resources in this country—that includes prisons, but also the working time of the law-enforcement officer on the beat—is misused, I think, in morals enforcement, particularly drug control. If you took the amount of law-enforcement time and money that has been put into marijuana enforcement over the last forty years, and you said, "we're going to put that into violent-crime enforcement" . . . that would have also significantly reduced violent crime.

I asked about regulating guns more strictly with respect to mental illness (see chapter 15). Kopel cited a study finding 18 percent of homicide prisoners in state prisons with serious mental illness. He agreed that "a much improved mental-health system to help those people before they commit the crime for which they then get incarcerated for twenty years would be tremendously valuable." Moreover:

> The treatment you do with an involuntary commitment of somebody for four months could save you the incarceration costs of somebody for twenty-five years—not to mention the treatment could help the individual become a tax payer instead of a tax consumer as a prisoner. And of course would also save the life of whoever got killed.

He is skeptical about new laws on reporting mental illness for the purposes of background checks. Such laws are tricky because they may breach patient confidentiality. Furthermore, they are usually disastrous because they "are written by people who don't understand mental health, are essentially gunphobes and bigots, and are just doing stuff off the top of their head."

I knew Kopel's time was limited because he was sixty days away from a high-stakes federal court case in Denver, and he needed to work nonstop on the case. In 2013, the Colorado legislature passed new gun laws: one banning the sale, possession, or transfer of large-capacity magazines and one expanding mandatory background checks. State and local gun lobbies on both sides of the battle fought the bills fiercely and spent record amounts of money. In the end, the bills became laws.

Kopel was the attorney of record on a suit against the state (actually the governor) to repeal the laws. The plaintiffs were fifty-five Colorado sheriffs and thirty interested or affected parties. In the days remaining before the trial, Kopel had to submit pretrial orders, attend pretrial conferences, and orchestrate his team of attorneys and plaintiffs. All of that work had to be distilled into thirty hours—on a chess clock—of testimony and arguments. "Believe me, I think about that every day, about how we're going to be efficient."

Two months after our meeting, Kopel and his team presented their case, which claimed that the new gun laws violated the Second Amendment, the Fourteenth Amendment, and the Americans with Disabilities Act. Two months later, Chief US District Court Judge Marcia Krieger announced her verdict in the bench trial: it was a judgment in favor of the defendant on all claims. After the trial, Kopel was philosophical, saying, "We believe [the judge] got it wrong as a matter of law. We think we have a very strong case in the court of appeals."[5] And within a few days, Kopel announced that he planned to appeal the ruling in the Tenth Circuit Court. If that appeal does not succeed, Kopel vows the next step is the US Supreme Court—where he has had some success in the past.

|

According to local lore, the gun case that ultimately reached the Supreme Court originated with a few happy-hour drinks consumed by a pair of young Washington, DC, attorneys in June 2002.[6] Clark Neily and Steve Simpson worked at the Institute for Justice, a libertarian law office that specializes in civil-liberties cases and, more specifically, in minimizing the reach of government into the lives of individuals. Neither man had a fanatic stake in gun laws, and gun rights was not in the institute's portfolio; however, it was a singular civil-liberties issue that was unresolved at the time. They speculated about whether the new Bush administration's and Attorney General John Ashcroft's sympathetic stances on gun rights might augur well for a favorable decision from the Supreme Court. They also understood the crushing time and labor required to prepare a case, as well as the small chance that it would even be heard by the high court: it hears fewer than one hundred cases per year (down from 150 cases a few decades ago) and those cases amount to about 1 percent of all cases that the court receives for consideration. Nevertheless, the high-stakes idea seemed worth pursuing.

At the age of forty-five, Robert Levy had made millions in a financial-services software company that he founded. In order to start a second career, he enrolled in law school at George Mason University just outside of Washington, DC. By the time Levy received his law degree (first in his class), he was thoroughly connected with the Capitol's legal community and found work at the Cato Institute, which suited his libertarian proclivities. As a member of the board of the Institute for Justice, Levy caught wind of the Neily-Simpson plan for a gun rights case. Levy was interested in the Second Amendment for constitutional (but not personal) reasons and was soon part of the team.

Along the way, they recruited an ambitious, thirty-one-year-old litigator named Alan Gura, who had a fledgling private-law practice in the area. After graduating from Cornell Law School, Gura worked his way through a federal clerkship and the California attorney general's office before moving to DC to serve as counsel for the Senate Committee on the Judiciary. Gura had at least two critical qualifications for the prospective gun case. Although he had never argued a case before the Supreme Court, he was supremely self-confident and had no reservations about testing his skills on the brightest stage. Furthermore, he was opportunistic. An appearance—let alone a victory—in such a case would write his name in large legal print for all to see.

As the attorneys schemed, they realized how the pieces might fit together. Specifically, Washington, DC—a federal enclave with the strictest of gun bans—presented an ideal opportunity for a case that could settle the Second Amendment incorporation question. Next, the attorneys knew that the challenge of the DC gun ban relied critically on finding the right plaintiffs. A clean police record and good standing in the community were desirable; evidence that the gun ban had adversely affected the plaintiff was essential. After the Levy team screened dozens of candidates, six plaintiffs emerged—three women, three men, four white and two black—who had the age, economic, racial, and gender diversity required. Finally, the high cost of taking a case all the way to the Supreme Court was quickly settled: Levy was willing to underwrite the entire project.

Word of the challenge to the DC gun ban soon reached the NRA, which wasted no time putting a stick in the spokes of the young attorneys' plans. From the NRA's perspective, nothing good could come of a pick-up team of inexperienced attorneys launching a high-profile Second Amendment case. In fact, the risk of an unfavorable decision was so great that the NRA mobilized a stable of attorneys, headed by four-time Supreme Court victor Stephen Halbrook, to scuttle the plans of the Levy team.

In February 2003, the Levy team filed its challenge of the DC gun ban in a federal district court, naming the District of Columbia as a defendant. Two months later, the NRA filed a different challenge to the gun ban, naming Attorney General John Ashcroft as defendant. A year later, a federal district court judge dismissed both cases.

The two teams immediately began round two by appealing their cases. A three-judge panel for the Court of Appeals for the District of Columbia Circuit heard the NRA case first. It ruled that the plaintiffs had not attempted to register a gun in Washington, DC, and therefore had not been denied or injured by the gun ban; in legal terms, the NRA plaintiffs lacked "standing." The coast was now clear for the Levy team.

It was not until March 9, 2007, (four years after the initial suit) that the three-judge panel announced its decision. Only one of the six plaintiffs was deemed to have standing. The plaintiff that saved the case was Dick Heller, a licensed security guard at a federal building, where he carried a handgun for his job. Critically important, he had already applied for a permit to keep a gun in his home for private use, and his application was denied. So he could claim that he had been adversely affected by the gun ban, which gave him the all-important standing. By a 2–1 vote, the panel overturned the gun ban, affirming Heller's Second Amendment right to possess a handgun.

Now it was the turn of the District of Columbia to appeal. The administration of Mayor Adrian Fenty filed an appeal to the Supreme Court, with small likelihood that the high court would even touch the case. However, on November 20, 2007, the justices granted a precious petition for a *writ of certiorari*, meaning the case would appear on the docket later in the term. Both sides prepared their merits briefs and responses, gathering a remarkable sixty-seven *amicus* (friends-of-the-court) briefs. Among the forty-seven briefs supporting Heller were those from 55 senators, 250 representatives, and Vice President Dick Cheney; attorneys general of 31 states; the Association of American Physicians and Surgeons (opposing a brief filed by the American Academy of Pediatrics); Jews for the Preservation of Firearms Ownership; the NRA; Pink Pistols; and Gays and Lesbians for Individual Liberty. Among the twenty briefs for the district were those from the American Bar Association, eighteen prominent district attorneys, eighteen members of the House of Representatives, and the American Jewish Committee.

The Supreme Court heard oral arguments in *District of Columbia v. Heller* on March 18, 2008. Spectators began lining up outside the Supreme Court building two days before the doors opened at ten o'clock. Representing the District of Columbia was the venerable former Acting Solicitor General Walter Dellinger, a veteran of many Supreme Court appearances and congressional hearings. Offering the views of the federal government was then-Solicitor General Paul Clement. At the age of forty-three, he had argued over fifty cases before the Supreme Court. A familiar figure at the court, he was a renowned master of oral argument. Arguing for Heller and making his first appearance before the Supreme Court was the still very young Alan Gura.

Dellinger stood and faced the justices first. He began a well-rehearsed account of the collective, militia-based interpretation of the Second Amendment in defense of the gun ban. Not long into his argument—as often happens in oral arguments—he was interrupted by Justice Anthony Kennedy with a question suggesting that individual ownership of firearms, not the militia, was the key purpose of the Second Amendment. Both sides had cast Kennedy as the wild-card vote in an otherwise evenly divided court. Perennial Supreme Court journalist Marcia Coyle, who witnessed the exchange, reported that "Kennedy tipped his hand. . . . Dellinger knew at that moment that he was going to lose."[7]

Alan Gura was understandably hyper-charged as he began his argument. Two sentences into it, Justice Antonin Scalia interrupted, "Talk a little slower; I'm not following you." Gura adjusted his throttle and then began what amounted to an extended conversation with most of the justices, discussing the relative weight of the militia clause and the rights clause of the Second Amendment, whether the right to "keep and bear arms" was one or two rights, and debating the types of weapons that might not be protected under the amendment. Despite frequent interruptions, Gura pressed the point that an individual-rights interpretation of the Second Amendment required over-turning the DC gun ban.

After years of preparation, decades of waiting, and centuries of uncer-tainty, the furious, pressure-filled oral arguments were over in ninety min-utes. Then, more waiting began, while the justices deliberated, chose sides, and wrote opinions. Three months later, on the last day of the court's term, the justices announced their decision. This was the third year of Chief Justice Robert's court, and 5–4 decisions between the majority conservative wing and the minority liberal wing had become familiar. The *Heller* case was no exception. Chief Justice Roberts and Justices Kennedy, Scalia, Thomas, and Alito upheld the lower-court ruling overturning the district gun ban. In the dissent were Justices Stevens, Breyer, Ginsburg, and Souter.

Justice Scalia's majority opinion and one of the dissenting opinions written by Justice Stevens were familiar recitations of historical evidence and dueling interpretations of the framers' intents. After an agonizing word-by-word anal-ysis, the majority opinion recognized that the amendment was created to pre-serve the militia. But that was not the only purpose; "it surely elevates above all other interests the right of law-abiding, responsible citizens to use arms in defense of hearth and home."[8] The dissenting opinion fired back saying, "The majority's exegesis has utterly failed to establish that [claim] as a matter of text or history." Contrary to the majority's "strained and unpersuasive reading" of the text, "there is no indication that the Framers of the Amendment intended to enshrine the common-law right of self-defense in the Constitution." Rather, it protects only "the right to use and possess arms in conjunction with service in a well-regulated militia"; it does not ensure "the right to possess and use guns for non-military purposes like hunting and personal self-defense."[9] Like two immoveable beasts butting heads, the two sides shed no new or clarifying light on the meaning of the Second Amendment.

Gun control advocates took some solace in the restrictions that the major-ity opinion left intact. The ruling applied only to handguns, and, furthermore, the opinion carried restrictions:

Nothing in our opinion should be taken to cast doubt on longstanding prohibitions on the possession of firearms by felons and the mentally ill, or laws forbidding the carrying of firearms in sensitive places such as schools and government buildings.[10]

A dissent written by Justice Breyer struck a more practical tone that recognized modern realities. Citing Washington, DC, crime statistics, he opined that the Supreme Court should not "second-guess the [City] Council in respect to the number of gun crimes, injuries, and deaths, or the role of handguns."[11] Such decisions, he suggested, should be left to homegrown lawmakers who know local problems better than the high court.

The *Heller* decision was grabbed by the media, spun by pundits, and interpreted by scholars, inviting diverse speculation about what it really meant. Gura's performance was heroic, at least for the gun rights side. And Gura felt vindicated: "I don't believe that anyone could have done a better job. . . . Other lawyers could have done a good job, they wouldn't have done *as* good a job, and certainly no one else was lining up to do this work five years ago."[12] Heller exulted in the decision, quoting author Robert Heinlein: "An armed society is a polite society."[13] Robert Levy, one of the originators of the case, said the decision was "a major victory for the Constitution. It's not everything we could have hoped for, but it lays a solid foundation for a step-by-step dismantlement of unconstitutional gun control regimes in a handful of U.S. jurisdictions."[14] The NRA's Wayne LaPierre called the decision "a great moment in American history. It vindicates individual Americans all over the country who have always known that this is their freedom worth protecting."[15]

Violence Policy Center director Kristen Rand condemned the decision saying, "It turns legal logic and common sense on its head" because it "ignored our nation's history of mass shootings, assassinations, and unparalleled gun violence."[16] Paul Helmke of the Brady Center to Prevent Gun Violence found some consolation:

Our fight to enact sensible gun laws will be undiminished by the . . . decision in the *Heller* case. While we disagree with the ruling, . . . the decision clearly suggests that other gun laws are entirely consistent with the Constitution.[17]

Justice Scalia was a devout champion of originalism, which he essentially defined in his opinion:

> Constitutional rights are enshrined with the scope they were understood to have when the people adopted them, whether or not future legislatures or (yes) even future judges think that scope too broad.[18]

In other words, jurists should look to the text of a legal document and the original public meaning rather than interpreting the document in a modern context. Originalism has been resurgent on the Roberts court, which has provoked a scornful backlash. Writing several years before the *Heller* decision, Pulitzer Prize–winning, Stanford historian Jack Rakove wrote an authoritative, entertaining, and credible castigation of originalism that rises above the trench warfare of the gun debate. His argument boils down to the claim that one cannot practice originalism without knowing the history. Originalist arguments are "often mounted by campaigners not intimately familiar with the terrain. These are raiders who know what they are looking for, and having found it, they care little about collateral damage to the surrounding countryside that historians better know as context."[19] Noting that individual-rights proponents often rely on originalist thinking, Rakove calls the Second Amendment "the highest stage of originalism."[20] While originalism might work in some cases, he claims that gun rights is the least appropriate target of originalism:

> It is reasonable to conclude that the most compelling arguments for [gun] regulation stem from the perception that this is one realm of human behavior where the concerns of the present have every right to supersede obsolescent understanding of generations long past.[21]

And if that were not enough:

> It is far from self-evident truth that originalism is the sole authoritative mode of constitutional interpretation, nor do many who dabble in the originalist analyses always reflect on the logic of what they are doing.[22]

Some legal scholars marveled at the ways in which Scalia's majority opinion departed from strict originalism and often relied on the opposing living-constitution interpretation. Yale scholar Reva Siegel surgically dismantled the opinion shortly after it was handed down, saying that the originalist "constitutional interpretation is in considerable tension with the reasoning of *Heller* itself." The *Heller* opinion, she continued, "discounts evidence drawn from the amendment's drafting history, appearing to favor evidence remote in time."[23] One of several corners into which Siegel paints the *Heller* majority is its willingness to protect weapons that were not in existence in 1800, while excluding from protection the kinds of weapons necessary to resist tyranny in 1800.

Legal analyst Jeffrey Toobin was more laconic in assessing Scalia's originalist thinking: "Scalia translated a right to military weapons in the eighteenth century to a right to handguns in the twenty-first."[24] Outspoken Seventh Circuit judge Richard Posner claimed prophetically, "The only certain effect of the *Heller* decision . . . will be to increase litigation over gun ownership."[25]

The *Heller* decision was path-breaking. It established the individual right to keep and bear arms within vaguely specified bounds. However, it was inconclusive in at least one important respect. Because the case originated in the federally administered District of Columbia, the ruling had no bearing on the states and specifically did not touch the question of incorporation of the Second Amendment. Nobody doubted that should the plaintiffs prevail, the case would serve merely as a preamble for the ultimate showdown: Could a *Heller*-type decision be found to hold in all the states? It would take another landmark decision two years later to settle that question.

15 | GUNS AND THE MIND

> People endorse whichever position reinforces their connection
> to others with whom they share important commitments.
>
> —DAN KAHAN, "Fixing the Communications Failure"

HERB MULLIN HAD a normal childhood growing up around Santa Cruz, California, in the 1960s.[1] The son of a World War II veteran, he was bright, sociable, good-natured, athletic, and voted most likely to succeed by his high-school classmates. His descent over the edge may have begun shortly after graduation when a good friend died in a car accident. The tragedy was full of portent for Mullin: he built shrines to his lost friend in his bedroom, he easily found his way to marijuana and LSD, and his friends and family watched the onset of bizarre and threatening behavior. In 1969, he voluntarily sought treatment in a mental hospital for the first time and was diagnosed with paranoid schizophrenia; but neither his hospital stay nor his treatment helped. Instead, a tangled odyssey began.

Mullin went from yoga to boxing to Bible study groups to extreme diets, migrating without purpose from the Bay Area to Hawaii and back. He lived in cheap hotels, in jails, on the streets, and at home with his parents. He attempted, but failed, to join the coast guard and the marines. He heard voices, mutilated himself, communicated telepathically, and began responding to "cosmic emanations." He was in and out of psychiatric hospitals, staying long enough to get treatment and show improvement. Then, once released, he lapsed in his medications, and the cycle repeated.

In September 1971, while living in Santa Cruz with his parents, Mullin heard a prophecy that a cataclysmic earthquake would soon destroy California. Voices in his mind convinced him to make human sacrifices in order to prevent the earthquake. For once, he had a mission and he began his brutal campaign to save the world. His first victim was a homeless Good Samaritan whom he battered with a baseball bat. A few days later, he mercilessly knifed and vivisected a female hitchhiker. On All Souls' Day, voices drew him into a Catholic church, where he stabbed a beloved priest in a confessional booth. Deciding his work would be cleaner with guns, he next shot and killed five acquaintances, including two children, in a single day. Then came four campers who telepathically gave Mullin permission to shoot them, he said. The last of thirteen victims fell on February 13, when Mullin randomly shot a former prizefighter. Witnesses of the final murder led police to Mullin, who surrendered quietly. Six months later, he was sentenced to life in prison on several counts of first- and second-degree murder.

Herb Mullin's story is one of the most hideous in the annals of American crime. It raises the question: Given his erratic behavior and diagnoses of severe mental illness, why was Mullin not committed to a mental hospital, or "institutionalized," in the years leading up to his murder spree? Despite reports that he was "a danger to himself and gravely disabled," Mullin was never hospitalized involuntarily for more than seventeen days at a time. The answer to that question is complex and has divided the mental-health community for decades. And we deal with the same issues today when mental illness and guns get entangled.

Mental-Health Care in America

The National Institute of Mental Health estimates that 18 percent of the US population is diagnosable in any given year with one of the three hundred recognized mental-health disorders. Roughly 9.8 million adults, or about 4.2 percent of the adult population, have a severe, debilitating mental illness (such as schizophrenia, bipolar disorder, or major depression).[2] It is estimated that 60 percent of adults with any mental illness receive no treatment.[3]

The relationship between mental illness and violent behavior is poorly understood. Experts differ on the strength of the link and some insist that it does not exist at all. One report cites research showing a slightly elevated risk for violent behavior among people with schizophrenia and bipolar disorder compared to matched controls. However, when those conditions are accompanied by substance abuse, the risk of violent behavior increases significantly.[4] Overall, people with severe mental illness commit an estimated 5 to 10 percent of all homicides, and they are often untreated or deal with substance abuse.[5]

Delbert Elliott is the director of the Center for the Study and Prevention of Violence at University of Colorado–Boulder and science editor of the surgeon general's report on youth violence.[6] When asked about the link between mental illness and violent behavior, he said, "The research on that is fairly consistent. There is a small connection and it's exacerbated by drugs. . . . Mental [illness] is one risk factor that is relatively weak until you start combining it with other risk conditions like drug use and high levels of exposure to violence." Speaking about violence in films, television, and video games, he cited the surgeon general's report: "A lot of people think this is a huge factor in violence. We looked at that and indeed it is a risk condition, but it was one of the very weak risk conditions."[7]

Unfortunately, when mass shootings occur, mentally ill people are often snatched from obscurity and turned into headlines, creating a false association between gun violence and mental illness. It is true that of sixty-two mass shootings (involving four or more fatalities) in the last thirty years, about 60 percent involved a person who showed "signs of possible mental health problems" prior to the killings.[8] However, mass and spree shootings are rare events. Of the over one hundred thousand people killed or injured by guns each year, only a small fraction (perhaps 0.05 percent in a typical year) involve mass or spree killings. The others are victims of gang shootings, domestic violence, accidents, and crime. On the day of the Aurora or Sandy Hook shootings, it is likely that eighty to ninety other Americans died of gun violence. Those deaths occur every day and most of them do not involve mental illness. The far graver association is between mental illness and suicide: over 90 percent of people who commit suicide were diagnosed with mental illness, and in a majority of those deaths, a gun is used.[9]

The problem of guns, violence, and mental illness is part of a greater crisis: the disintegration of the mental health–care system in a movement known as deinstitutionalization. In 1955, when the US population was 164 million, the patient population in mental hospitals was 558,000, or about 1 patient for every 300 citizens. In 2006, when the US population was 300 million, the patient population was 40,000, or about 1 patient for every 7,500 citizens—a level last seen in the nineteenth century. There is no disputing the numbers associated with deinstitutionalization. The debate concerns why it happened and whether it was justified.[10]

As told by mental health–care advocate E. Fuller Torrey, the collapse of the mental health–care system originated in California in the 1960s through a perhaps unintended collaboration among politicians, attorneys, and some mental-health specialists. The political side of the demise started with the passage of the Lanterman-Petris-Short (LPS) Act in 1969. This Republican-sponsored, budget-saving law (signed by then-governor Ronald Reagan) limited involuntary psychiatric hospitalizations to seventeen days unless a patient was demonstrably "imminently dangerous." And according to the bill's sponsors, *demonstrably* meant "physical evidence of danger must be displayed in a court of law."[11]

The LPS Act also meshed perfectly with the new Medicaid and Medicare programs, which provided benefits for mentally-ill patients provided they were not hospitalized and they lived in the community. Emptying state mental hospitals became an obvious way for states to shift health costs to the federal government. The LPS Act quickly took its toll. By 1973, California had closed all but two of its state psychiatric hospitals and discharged 63 percent of its psychiatric inpatients. The number of patients dropped from 37,000 prior to passage of the LPS Act to 7,000 in 1973, and to 4,200 in 2003.[12]

But it was not just a matter of politicians trying to cut spending. Ken Kesey's novel and the resulting film *One Flew Over the Cuckoo's Nest* famously vilified conditions in mental hospitals. The dehumanizing conditions in many institutions, as well as the dependency and helplessness that they instilled in patients led many practitioners to create new alternatives. One new option, introduced in Britain, was known as community mental-health services. The idea was to provide an array of distributed public and private treatment options (such as day facilities, outpatient treatment, halfway houses) that would replace traditional psychiatric hospitals. The emergence of new drugs also gave hope that mental patients could be successfully treated outside of a hospital setting.

At this time, there was also widespread cynicism about mental illness itself—a belief among some that if a disorder cannot be localized, like a broken leg, then it does not exist. Psychiatrist and outspoken defender of deinstitutionalization Thomas Szasz denied the very existence of mental illness, claiming that there are no objective ways to detect mental illness. He excoriated mental institutions in his influential book *The Myth of Mental Illness*, supporting the belief that, "Either we are all mad or none of us is mad."[13] Furthermore, the mental-health profession was the target of skepticism as critics associated practitioners with Communism, drug use, and countercultural values. The final piece of the mosaic came from libertarians (which included Thomas Szasz), who asserted that involuntary commitment to institutions is unreasonable government intrusion. These advocates, who on principle favored personal rights above government interference, hailed the LPS Act because it gave patients freedom to decide whether or not to be hospitalized.

Pharmacological miracles that could treat mental disorders proved elusive as patients often denied their illness (a condition called anosognosia) or refused to stay on medications. Similarly, the promise of community-based alternatives to psychiatric hospitals never quite materialized as expected. Instead, the evacuation of psychiatric hospitals had a predictable effect. Discharged patients found themselves on the streets, in halfway houses, in jails and prisons, and easy targets of victimization. In the early 1970s, a Los Angeles County sheriff estimated that half of his inmates were "in need of urgent psychiatric care."[14] About the same time, a psychiatrist studying the situation in San Mateo County reported that "as a result of LPS, mentally disordered persons are being increasingly subject to arrest and criminal prosecution." As a result, the jails were "drowning in patients."[15]

While these changes were occurring in California, a dismantling of the mental-health system occurred in Wisconsin by a different route. Alberta Lessard was twenty-five years into a teaching career in rural Wisconsin when bouts of aberrant behavior got her involuntarily committed to a mental-health center in 1971. She was diagnosed with paranoid schizophrenia and advised to seek treatment. Rather than seeking treatment, she sought legal counsel. Two young attorneys, swept up by the mental illness–denial movement in California, took the Lessard case to a federal district court. A three-judge panel ruled that Wisconsin's relatively lenient law on involuntary commitment of mental patients was unconstitutional.[16] Whereas the current law required "clear and convincing" evidence of danger to others for involuntary commitment, the panel claimed that stronger "beyond a reasonable doubt" evidence is required. Within three years, the Wisconsin legislature responded with just such a law that raised the bar for involuntary commitment. According to one analyst, the effect of the law, if strictly enforced, was to "put a virtual end to involuntary commitment" of psychiatric patients.[17] (In the face of fierce opposition, the Wisconsin legislature later reversed its 1975 law and returned to more lenient conditions for involuntary commitment.)

This swirling crosscurrent of politics, medicine, and social change engulfed Herb Mullin. In all of his commitments to mental institutions, the "imminently dangerous" clause of California's LPS Act could never be satisfied. As a result, Mullin was never involuntarily committed for more than the legal limit of seventeen days, and he became one of the untethered refugees of the floundering mental-health system. It is telling that when Mullin was sentenced for his crimes, the jury refused to accept an insanity plea, knowing that it could result in his release back into the mental-health system and then back to the streets.

After the California and Wisconsin experiments, the deinstitutionalization wave swept over most states during the next thirty years. With budget shortfalls and realigned priorities in many states, the wave still surges ahead today. Between 2009 and 2012 over half of the states cut mental health–care budgets—some by as much as 35 percent. In some states, mental-health funds have been shifted into Medicaid services, in order to secure federal matching funds, leaving mental patients with even less support. Guns and mental illness is a serious problem, as discussed below. And yet, it is important to remember that it is just part of a far larger and unresolved crisis in this country today.

Guns and Mental Illness

Guns don't kill! People kill! That is the rally cry of gun rights advocates, urging us to focus on the perpetrators and not on the weapons. For this reason, some of the most frequently cited remedies for gun violence are *keep guns away from people with mental illness* and *fix the mental-health system*. Polls show that these solutions are widely supported, and indeed they are easy to support without violating basic gun rights. At the same time, they prove to be extremely complex, laden with challenges that stretch beyond gun control.

Where are we today and how do today's laws address guns and mental illness? At the moment, the mechanism for keeping guns away from people with mental illness is the NICS background check system and its many linked-in state systems. That framework is based on the amended Gun Control Act of 1968, whose nine "prohibitor" categories include persons who have "been adjudicated as a mental defective" or have "been committed to any mental institution."[18]

The language of the act is both offensive and nebulous.[19] Fortunately, a follow-up federal regulation provides some help in understanding the meaning of the term "mental defective":

(a) A determination by a court, board, commission, or other lawful authority that a person, as a result of marked subnormal intelligence, or mental illness, incompetency, condition, or disease (1) is a danger to himself or to others; or (2) lacks the capacity to manage his own affairs.

(b) The term shall include (1) a finding of insanity by a court in a criminal case, and (2) those persons found incompetent to stand trial or found not guilty by lack of mental responsibility.[20]

The same regulation tells us that "commitment to a mental institution" means:

a formal commitment of a person to a mental institution by a court, board, commission, or other lawful authority. The term includes a commitment to a mental institution involuntarily . . . for mental defectiveness or mental illness, . . . [or] for other reasons, such as drug use. *The term does not include a person in a mental institution for observation or a voluntary admission to a mental institution.*[21]

That is a sparse foundation on which to build a federal law. Working through it logically, the regulation implies that involuntary commitment to a mental institution disqualifies a person from purchasing or possessing a firearm, as does a determination of mental illness by a court, board, commission, or other lawful authority. It also implies that, at least in some cases, voluntary commitment to a mental institution does not necessarily disqualify a person. From there, it is up to the states, the courts, law-enforcement agencies, and the mental-health community to assemble a system that respects the rights and privacy of people with mental illness, while ensuring some measure of public safety.

The gateway to a firearm purchase is the NICS system, which is only as good as its databases. And mental-health records in the NICS system are incomplete and porous. It is worth looking at the difficulties that arise. First, the courts have been divided on the interpretation of the Gun Control Act language "commitment to a mental institution involuntarily." Does it refer only to inpatient treatment? Or does it include outpatient treatment and short-term emergency treatment? After the *Heller* and *McDonald* Supreme Court decisions, at least one federal court has been reluctant to rule outpatient and emergency treatment as grounds for depriving patients of their Second Amendment rights.[22] One interpretation is that patients undergoing anything less than full involuntary inpatient treatment should be allowed to buy and possess firearms. As we will see shortly, this policy has had dreadful consequences.

Second, the federal regulation language "a determination by a court, board, commission, or other lawful authority" is problematic. Mental-health determinations and commitment decisions are generally made in the courts. However, physicians and other health-care providers also make mental-health determinations, particularly in emergency and outpatient situations. Depending on state laws, a health-care provider may or may not be recognized as a "lawful authority" for the purpose of prohibiting possession of a firearm under the Gun Control Act. In other words, the opinion of a mental-health expert may not be recognized as legally admissible.

Matters get more complicated when we turn to the states, their laws on privacy, and their policies on reporting to NICS. Not surprisingly, "a variety of technological, coordination, and legal (i.e., privacy) challenges limit the states' ability to report mental health records" to the NICS system.[23] And the states have responded to the challenges in different ways.

Several factors explain the great variation in state reporting practices. One difficulty is fairly mechanical: across the states, mental-health records are kept in different places. Unlike criminal records that are reported by law-enforcement agencies, mental-health records may originate in courts, psychiatric institutions, nursing homes, or local mental-health departments, often with no central clearinghouse. A recent Government Accounting Office study found that in 2010, about 114,000 mental-health records originated in Illinois in various departments and institutions. Only five thousand of those records were reported to NICS, not thorough any willful neglect but for lack of coordination.[24]

A much more delicate challenge for states in reporting mental-health records arises with state laws on privacy and commitment of mental patients.[25] The federal Health Insurance Portability and Accountability Act (HIPAA) provides patients with basic privacy rights for their health records (specifically, who can see health records with and without the consent of the patient). HIPAA provides minimum standards that the states may sharpen or make more protective. Suffice it to say that state privacy laws vary literally all over the map. Overall, twenty-three states have laws that require courts or possibly mental-health institutions to report mental-health records either to NICS or to a state agency that reports to NICS. Seven states allow but do not require reporting mental-health records to NICS. Eight states collect mental-health records, but their laws do not mention reporting to NICS. The remaining twelve states have no laws that require collection of mental-health records. The twenty-seven states that do not have a requirement to report to NICS "appear to lack the authority under the HIPAA privacy rule to report" disqualifying mental-health records to NICS, although this question is unsettled as of now.[26]

Despite the convolutions of privacy laws, there are some positive trends. The number of mental-health records submitted by the states to NICS has increased, from about 129,000 to 1.2 million between 2004 and 2011. The increase is largely due to the contributions of twelve states, which have laws that allow or require reporting mental-health records to NICS.[27] During most of the lifetime of the NICS system (1998–2012), nearly one million denials have been issued. Of those denials, just over 1 percent were on mental-health grounds. (As with all NICS denials, appeals may result in a reversal of the original judgment.)

Hopefully, this quick survey reveals the abyss of legal, health, and privacy technicalities that make reporting mental-health records so difficult. The laws and regulations can seem less informative than a roadmap without words. Nevertheless, those laws and regulations must be applied every day in countless background checks and mental-health decisions. Several cases illustrate the challenges in coordinating background checks and mental-health records.

Seung-Hui Cho was diagnosed with anxiety and major depressive disorders when he was in middle school. An early harbinger of his tendencies was his fascination with the Columbine High School shootings. As a student at Virginia Tech, he was reclusive, he continued to display aberrant behavior, and he wrote violent poetry. Sixteen months before Cho killed thirty-two people and wounded seventeen more on April 16, 2007, he had a hearing to determine whether his mental condition warranted involuntary commitment to a mental hospital. The conclusion of the hearing was that he "presents an imminent danger to himself as a result of mental illness."[28] He received a court order for involuntary outpatient treatment. And here the case entered a murky space between the law and psychiatry.

Neither federal law nor Virginia state law was clear on whether outpatient treatment—as opposed to involuntary commitment—disqualifies a person for firearm purchase or possession. In the absence of a clear policy, Cho was not reported to the NICS database as a prohibited purchaser. In February and March of 2007, he purchased two handguns, successfully passing two background checks with the required thirty-day waiting period between purchases. He had no difficulty purchasing ten-round magazines on eBay. At this point, Cho was fully armed and ready to carry out the deadly Virginia Tech shootings. Two weeks after the shootings, Virginia's governor issued an executive order requiring that patients, such as Cho, with involuntary outpatient treatment be reported to NICS. The executive order became law a year later—a year too late.[29]

Most would agree that the Virginia Tech shootings resulted, in part, because of a failure to report critical mental-health records to the NICS database. A more subtle lapse occurred in the September 2013 Washington Navy Yard rampage. The shooter, Aaron Alexis, had a history of gun-related arrests, none of which produced a criminal record. He was honorably discharged from the navy reserve after a "pattern of misconduct."[30] Earlier in the summer, he sought help at two different veterans' hospitals, with complaints of hearing voices and being controlled by electromagnetic waves. During those visits, Alexis received medication for insomnia, without a judgment on his mental health. When Alexis visited a gun store and shooting range near Washington, DC, he completed a background check, tested an AR-15 in the firing range, and purchased a Remington 870 shotgun and ammunition. (As a Virginia nonresident, he was prohibited from buying a handgun.) At the time of the shootings, Alexis had a security clearance that gave him access to the Navy Yard. He had no criminal records or mental-health history that made him a prohibited buyer. In hindsight, it is easy to criticize the background-check system. But in the lead-up to the shootings, it was not clear to anyone that Alexis's behavior warranted abrogating his rights to possess a firearm.

Apart from background checks, law-enforcement agencies face difficult decisions when it comes to searching for, seizing, and returning weapons taken during a mental illness–related incident. Suppose a person with legally acquired guns is reported with threatening or pathological behavior. Should those guns be confiscated, and for how long and who decides? Those decisions often require balancing public safety with personal rights, and they may not represent the best interests of law enforcement.

The *New York Times* documents several representative cases. Paul Colflesh had stopped taking medication for depression when his wife called 911 saying that he was drinking, had a loaded gun, and was threatening suicide—not for the first time. Police arrived, found Colflesh incoherently drunk, and seized his handgun. A few days later, Colflesh gave the police a statement from his physician stating that he had resumed his medication and was no longer suicidal or dangerous to others. Two months later, Colflesh had his gun again, in respect of his Second Amendment rights.[31]

Another incident involves a Connecticut man with a history of paranoid schizophrenia. Fifty-five-year-old Mark Russo was off his medication, ranting about the recent Newtown shootings, and in a delusional state. He threatened to kill his mother if police tried to take the eighteen shotguns and rifles that he kept at her house. Under Connecticut law, police are authorized to seize weapons in such a situation and hold them for up to a year. Accordingly, the police took Russo's weapons and seven high-capacity magazines, despite his defiant claims that his rights had been violated. Unless Russo has additional run-ins with the law, he is entitled to take possession of "all my guns and ammo and knives" a year after the incident. The police lamented, "if a year has gone by and nothing new has happened, there's nothing we can do. . . . It's unfortunate, and it's something that has to be addressed." Presumably, Russo currently appears on a list of prohibited buyers, so if he attempts to buy a gun, his background check would result in a denial. But because he acquired his guns when laws were less strict, he cannot be legally disarmed.[32]

In December 2013, a thoroughbred panel of mental-health and gun violence experts called the Consortium for Risk-Based Firearm Policy released a comprehensive set of recommendations on mental illness and gun violence.[33] The underlying axiom of that report is that the best predictor of future violence is not a determination of mental illness but rather a history of past violence. Therefore, decisions on gun ownership should be based on records and measures of past violence.

The consortium's three-legged proposal is grounded in practical experience and is politically ambivalent. The first leg is to clarify the language of the Gun Control Act by making short-term emergency hospitalization grounds for firearm disqualification. However, the prohibition would be temporary—five years is recommended—and after a one-year waiting period, patients could appeal to a specific restoration process to regain gun-ownership rights. The restoration depends on a finding by a certified health-care provider that the patient is unlikely to be a danger to self or others.

The second leg is to use new violence-predicting indicators to determine gun disqualification. Under the recommendations, an individual would be disqualified from firearm purchases and possession if he were convicted of a violent misdemeanor (ten-year prohibition), were subject to a temporary domestic-violence restraining order (for the duration of the order), were convicted of two or more DUI charges in five years (five-year prohibition), or were convicted of two or more drug-related misdemeanors in five years (five-year prohibition).

The third leg would strengthen and clarify the authority of law-enforcement officers to remove weapons from people who endanger themselves or others. In emergency situations of immediate threat, the removal of firearms would be warrantless and temporary. In cases of credible threat (for example, by petition from family members), a new gun violence restraining order would allow the removal. A process of appeal and restoration would be available to return confiscated guns. Models for such a process exist in several states (Connecticut, Texas, and Indiana). They are based on violence predictors, not on mental-health determinations, and they give law-enforcement officers much clearer guidance than current laws.

The challenge of reducing gun violence, particularly when it is related to mental illness, is daunting. However, the evidence-based, apolitical report of the consortium is a place to begin; it offers the consensus of experts who have spent their careers confronting that challenge. Whether legislators in the states have the political will to prioritize the crisis of gun violence and implement the recommendations of the consortium—or any policies that make mental illness a realistic filter for gun ownership—remains to be seen.

Social Psychologists Weigh In

Somewhere in the mysterious landscape of the American mind is an uncharted divide—a jagged boundary between watersheds—that separates people for whom a world with guns is desirable from people who would be much happier in a world without guns. Beyond the immediate purposes for owning guns, what mindsets enable some people to embrace guns while some have no intention of ever touching one? What is it that arouses their fears? Are there any convincing explanations for the psychological differences between these two groups of people?

Further understanding of the psychological differences between gun enthusiasts and gun detractors—if, indeed, these differences exist—might be found in recent theories in social psychology. A useful framework is provided by the research of Jonathan Haidt, who teaches at New York University and has become something of a celebrity after writing two successful books. One of them, *The Righteous Mind*, presents a theory to explain why "good people are divided by politics and religion."[34] Haidt's work offers a useful perspective on divisive issues in the world around us—and perhaps on guns as well.

Haidt begins with several premises and does a good job of justifying them. The first premise is that when people form opinions and make decisions, they first use their intuition and then follow with reasoning. The eighteenth-century Scottish philosopher David Hume advanced this idea, expressing it succinctly as "reason is, and ought only to be the slave of the passions"[35] (where Hume's idea of *passion* lines up well with Haidt's use of *intuition*). We form opinions first by *seeing that*, which is the quick work of the intuition, followed by *reasoning why*. Haidt likens a person to a large elephant carrying a small rider. In any given situation, the elephant reacts first and sets the course. Only later does the rider react and attempt to exert control over the elephant or explain its action. The rider-elephant idea explains the well-known pitfall of confirmation bias— our tendency to grab evidence that confirms a decision we have already made and to overlook evidence that might steer us in a different direction.

Haidt's second premise outlines two different ways of viewing the world. In one perspective, the world consists of many individuals, decisions are best made analytically, and questions of morality are resolved using principles of fairness and doing no harm. In the second view, the world consists of collections of individuals and the relationships among them, decisions are made holistically, and questions of morality may involve values in addition to fairness and avoiding harm. Haidt did not just invent these perspectives; he observed them. The individualistic perspective is typical of Western societies and is held by a small minority of "WEIRD" people—Western, Educated, Industrialized, Rich, and Democratic. Haidt discovered through his research of other cultures and through ethnological studies that the collective perspective is much more common worldwide. In these collective cultures, decisions and opinions, particularly in the moral realm, involve do-no-harm and fairness but are based on other principles as well.

The final step in Haidt's program is to identify the moral foundations that people use in making decisions and forming opinions. Just as we have taste receptors for sweet, sour, salty, bitter, and savory, Haidt thinks of moral foundations as moral receptors. The search for moral foundations is based on considerable empirical research, which leads to six foundations, or sets of values, that occur in pairs of opposites:

Care/harm
Liberty/oppression
Fairness/cheating
Loyalty/betrayal
Authority/subversion
Sanctity/degradation

Haidt explains the six foundations in detail by way of practical examples. Importantly, he also presents evidence for both genetic and cultural origins of the foundations. We inherit these foundations in our genes in a "first draft" and then modify them as we grow and adapt to our surroundings. Each foundation is a scale: individuals fall on one end of the scale if they resonate with the first value in a pair and on the other end of the scale if they align with the second value in the pair. Briefly, here are the foundations.

- The Care/harm foundation honors the principle of *do no harm*. It might be triggered by cruel treatment of people or animals, and it responds with acts of protection or sympathy.
- The Liberty/oppression foundation rests on principles of freedom. Individuals aligned with the foundation strongly oppose tyranny, oppression, threats to individual liberty, or by a system that exploits disadvantaged people.
- The Fairness/cheating foundation is based on the belief that some people should not benefit disproportionately at the expense of others. It relies on the tenet that rewards should be based on work done.
- The Loyalty/betrayal foundation valorizes allegiance to a group or a system of beliefs; it is triggered adversely by acts of infidelity.
- On the favorable side, the Authority/subversion foundation is based on respect for authority, particularly when it preserves order and justice. It opposes acts of disobedience, disrespect, and resistance.
- Finally, the Sanctity/degradation foundation takes different forms. Its positive side is associated with purity (of body and mind), cleanliness (avoidance of germs and disease), possibly chastity, the sanctity of certain objects or practices, and an abhorrence of waste and contamination.

Having established his foundations, Haidt aims to match them with the political spectrum. Using online surveys with large, cross-cultural samples, he asked respondents to self-identify as liberals or conservatives. Then he asked many carefully designed questions to gauge respondents' alignment with the six foundations. Haidt reports the following strong correlations:

Liberal politics = Care/harm and Fairness/cheating
Conservative politics = Liberty/oppression, Loyalty/betrayal, Authority/subversion, Sanctity/degradation

The correlations, which were observed across many countries and demographic categories, are striking. The responses of self-described political liberals align strongly with the Care/harm and Fairness/cheating foundations. And the responses of self-described political conservatives align with the

Liberty/oppression, Loyalty/betrayal, Authority/subversion, and Sanctity/degradation foundations.

Haidt does not apply his theory to guns. However, it is plausible to associate certain moral foundations with the gun rights and gun control points of view. Without making unwarranted stereotypes, the goal is to identify certain attitudes that are shared by many in the gun rights and gun control communities and then try to match them with the foundations.

The most common concern of gun control advocates is the human toll of gun ownership: guns inflict more than one hundred thousand deaths and injuries each year. This concern is well aligned with the Care/harm foundation. Furthermore, the opinions of some gun control supporters are formed by an aversion to guns—a sense that using devices that can wreak death so effortlessly violates a deep humanistic principle. This feeling is an expression of the Sanctity/degradation foundation.

The gun rights position is more diverse. It argues for a fundamental individual right to own guns, which is an expression of the Liberty/oppression foundation. The desire of some gun enthusiasts to venerate American history, to espouse patriotism, or to defend home and honor are also manifestations of the Liberty/oppression foundation. The self-defense rationale, particularly when it comes to a confrontation with an armed criminal, is a desire to level the playing field and to equalize power in a standoff. This need is consistent with the Fairness/cheating foundation. The allegiance to the cause of gun rights, shown in membership in clubs and financial support of gun rights organizations, lines up well with the Loyalty/betrayal foundation. The Authority/subversion foundation may enter the picture in the indignation expressed by some gun owners with a perceived intrusion of gun laws. The mapping of gun attitudes to foundations looks like this:

Gun Control = Care/harm and Sanctity/degradation
Gun Rights = Liberty/oppression, Fairness/cheating, Loyalty/betrayal,
    and Authority/subversion

This apolitical analysis of gun attitudes reveals patterns similar to those found by Haidt. Two moral foundations appear to animate gun control advocates and four foundations motivate gun enthusiasts. Keeping score is not the point; however, there are two practical implications of this analysis—to the extent that it is valid. First, the goal of any public-relations campaign is changing the minds of opponents or undecided people. According to Haidt's analysis, the gun rights side—or the conservative side more generally—has four different levers of persuasion to pull. In contrast, the gun control side— or the liberal side more generally—has only two handles of moral persuasion to grab. With respect to political campaigns, cognitive scientist George Lakoff has noted the advantage that conservatives have in the battle to change minds.[36] Perhaps gun rights advocates have a similar edge.

Second, Haidt's work suggests a strategy for changing minds. His elephant-rider model of human decision- and opinion-making says that the way to change the mind of an individual is not through reasoning (trying to get the rider to look in a different direction). Rather, it requires appealing to an individual's intuition and shifting the balance of his or her moral foundations (changing the direction of the elephant). When trying to recruit an opponent to a cause, a politician (or clergyman or advertising consultant or salesperson) should attempt to awaken in the opponent the moral foundations that underlie that cause.

Cultural Theory of Risk

Another arena of social science called the cultural theory of risk has much to say about how we form opinions on divisive social and political issues—and that includes gun control. The work is compelling because it supports the belief that the path to understanding and resolving the gun debate lies in neither more data collection and statistical analyses nor in possibly misdirected policies and laws. Rather, it passes through the softer, more ductile realms of psychology and culture.

The cultural-risk theory can be traced back at least thirty years, and during those years it has provided a framework for explaining how individuals use social norms to assess risk, form opinions, and make decisions.[37] The theory is a departure from theories of rational choice traditionally used by economists, which assume that consumers apply analysis, logic, and data to arrive at decisions. According to cultural-risk theory, when individuals (particularly nonexperts) assess the risk associated with controversial issues such as nuclear power plants, vaccinations, genetically modified foods, or continued use of fossil fuels, they ultimately rely on moral norms and cultural orientations and not on empirically based analytical thinking. Experiments have shown that a diverse group of individuals, all given the same objective, neutral facts about a contentious issue, fragments into subgroups. And those subgroups are formed by different assessments of risk based on different sets of cultural values.[38]

For example, imagine two women, given the same facts about crime rates and gun laws, forming an opinion about gun control. One woman sees that strong gun control prohibits her from carrying a gun for self-defense. The other woman sees that weak gun control enables more people to carry guns, making her more vulnerable to an assault or accident. How do these women make a decision on gun control in the face of these opposing risks? Cultural-risk theory asserts that it is not done by analyzing crime data and gun laws. Rather, it is done by identifying with a particular cultural orientation and assessing the risks involved—possibly unconsciously. The first woman attributes a greater risk to being unable to defend herself and opposes stronger gun control. The second woman attributes more risk to an encounter with an armed assailant and supports stronger gun control.

It generally takes a team of social psychologists, scientists, legal scholars, and political theorists to explain how we arrive at opinions about contentious social, scientific, and political issues. That potent training comes together in the one person of Dan Kahan: He is trained in social psychology, equipped with a Harvard law degree, and is now on the faculty of the Yale Law School. He has applied cultural-risk theory prolifically to a wide range of issues, including gun control. At the peril of vastly oversimplifying a well-formulated theory, Kahan and his colleagues proposed a scale of cultural orientations that runs from hierarchical/individualistic to egalitarian/solidaristic.

The hierarchical/individualistic person typically values independent initiative and autonomy; respects authority but rejects unnecessary regulation; and dislikes deviance from traditional values. The egalitarian/solidaristic person typically opposes unjust disparity; supports regulation and intervention to minimize various forms of inequality; and values collective and community initiatives.[39]

This scale of orientations has been refined over the years and researchers have discovered that it is well correlated with opposing opinions on issues such as race, sexual orientation, and capital punishment. For example, a hierarchical/

individualistic person would tend to oppose gay rights (viewed as a form of deviance), support a large military (a statement of authority), reject spending on social programs (a collective initiative), and approve of capital punishment (a penalty for deviance). An egalitarian/solidaristic person would typically have opposing opinions on these issues.[40]

Kahan and colleagues have applied cultural orientations to the question of gun control. Using survey responses to several gun control questions, the researchers determined how much various factors, such as gender, race, geography, urban/rural location, religion, political party, and fear of crime contribute to opinions on gun control. Among the many factors tested was the cultural-orientation scale. The results of this analysis (called multivariable regression) provided some sharp results. As Kahan describes it, "the more egalitarian and solidaristic an individual's worldview, the more likely that person was to support gun control; likewise, the more hierarchical and individualistic the respondent's worldview, the more likely she was to oppose gun control."[41] Furthermore, cultural orientation had a far greater effect on gun control attitudes than any other factor—four times the effect of either political views or party affiliation.

Armed with the cultural theory of risk, Kahan is able to make some keen observations about how we form and change opinions. First, as observed earlier, bombarding listeners or constituents with stacks of data and sophisticated statistical analyses is a lost cause. It is like selling breakfast cereal by showing consumers the molecular structure of the ingredients. If this approach worked, we might expect to see attitudes about gun control track changes in violent-crime rates—and they do not. Furthermore, if people used only facts and logic to make decisions, we would not see seemingly illogical survey results; for example, respondents claiming to support stricter gun laws to reduce violent crime, while admitting that stricter laws would not reduce crime. (And it works the other way also when respondents oppose gun control, while believing that gun control does not prevent them from carrying guns for self-defense.)

When people are undecided about an issue and unmoved by fact- or data-driven arguments, they turn to their cultural orientations. According to Kahan's research, when debating divisive issues, people are not "really arguing about what empirical data to trust; they are attempting to push certain risks (for example, risks associated with lax or strict gun laws) to the center of the perceptual stage . . . because risk regulation is pregnant with visions of a good society."[42]

> Those involved in the gun control debate aren't really arguing about whose perception of risk is more grounded in empirical reality; they are arguing about what it would *say* about our shared values to credit one or the other side's fears through law. For the individualist and hierarchical opponents of gun control, it would be a cowardly and dishonorable concession to our own physical weaknesses for us to disarm all private citizens in the interest of public safety. For the [egalitarian and solidaristic] proponent of gun control, it would send an unacceptable message of mutual distrust in each other's intentions, of collective indifference to each other's welfare . . . to arm herself as a means of keeping the civil peace.[43]

In other words, an individual forms opinions and evaluates risks by deciding whether or not those decisions enhance our society and its values. And an individual's idea of what improves society is determined by cultural orientations.

One last question should be asked: Where do cultural orientations come from? How does a person become an individualist and hierarchical adult? I asked Kahan this question. Surprisingly, he said he was not sure, but his best answer is that "we are socialized into them by the accident of who our parents are and where we live."[44] Once those seeds are planted, we tend to associate with people who hold similar cultural values (a form of availability bias). This insularity only reinforces our beliefs and values. Equally important, when making decisions, we often rely on authorities; and we have an inexhaustible supply of authorities (and charlatans) to help us make decisions. We assign the most credibility to those who hold similar cultural values, and in the process, both our opinions and our cultural beliefs are reinforced.

Kahan thinks the formation of cultural orientations is not such an interesting question. The more important question is how we start as "autonomous, reasoning agents in a free society," presumably able to sort through facts objectively, and somehow end up so vastly divided in opinion (what he calls self-reinforcing dissensus). This question leads to one of Kahan's current campaigns: solving the "science communication problem."[45] But that is another story.

16 | THE COURT SPEAKS AGAIN

The Framers did not write the Second Amendment in order to protect
a private right of armed self-defense. . . . There has been, and is,
no consensus that the right is, or was, "fundamental."

—JUSTICE STEPHEN BREYER, minority opinion, *McDonald v. Chicago*

We repeat those assurances here. Despite the municipal respondents' doomsday
proclamations, incorporation does not imperil every law regulating firearms.

—JUSTICE SAMUEL ALITO, majority opinion, *McDonald v. Chicago*

"WHAT IS EMINENTLY plain is that both sets of lawyers . . . came loaded
for bear, on the assumption that the Supreme Court majority would rule
as it did."[1] Federal judge Milton Shadur of the Northern District of Illinois
was referring to three lawsuits that began landing in his court the day of the
Supreme Court's *Heller* decision in June 2008. When *Heller* produced a gun
rights victory, the suits—already prepared and poised for launch—sprung
to life.

The NRA filed two suits challenging the handgun bans of Chicago and
neighboring Oak Park.[2] The third suit, *McDonald v. City of Chicago*, also
challenged the Chicago gun ordinance and took its name from one of four
individual plaintiffs, Otis McDonald, Adam Orlov, and David and Colleen
Lawson.[3] McDonald was a black, seventy-six-year-old building manager at
the University of Chicago who rose to the head of his local union. He and
his family had lived in suburban Morgan Park for forty years. As he watched
gangs and drug dealers invade his once-peaceful neighborhood, McDonald
wanted a handgun in his house to protect himself and his family. Unfortunately, Chicago's handgun ordinance—in place for almost thirty years—was
a virtual ban: it criminalized possession of unregistered handguns, while

making registration of handguns by ordinary citizens impossible. Like the other plaintiffs, McDonald had attempted to register a handgun and was denied.

Journalist Brian Doherty recalled an interview with McDonald in October 2010:

> McDonald started attending gun rights rallies down in Springfield. "I learned a lot about this Washington, D.C., case [Heller]," he says, "and that's what made me know the Lord was guiding me. I just felt so sure they were going to win the case." A friend McDonald met at a gun rally told [Alan] Gura about him. When Gura needed clients, the two met and took to each other instantly. . . . McDonald recalls telling Gura: "Are you willing to go all the way? Then I'm your man, with the name and all. Furthermore, we are going to win."[4]

In December 2008, Judge Shadur ruled in the two NRA cases. Respecting the hierarchy of the court system, he deferred to a 1982 decision in the Seventh Circuit Court of Appeals, which "occupies a higher position in the judicial firmament" than his court. That decision (*Quilici v. Morton Grove*) upheld a handgun ban in nearby Morton Grove, citing precedents going back to the *Cruikshank* case of 1873.[5] Shadur concluded his brief opinion:

> This court—duty bound as it is to adhere to the holding in *Quilici*, rather than accepting the plaintiff's invitation to "overrule" it (!)—declines to rule that the Second Amendment is . . . applicable to the Chicago and Oak Park ordinances.[6]

In this one sentence, Shadur summarized the core question that would be debated in the higher courts. At issue was the question of whether an individual right to keep and bear arms is protected against infringement by state and local laws. The *Heller* case settled this matter for the District of Columbia but not for the fifty states. The litigants in Shadur's court were essentially asking him to rule that the *Heller* decision also applied to the states. Shadur's responded, Not so fast; that is a decision for judges above myself.

The cases met a similar fate when they were consolidated and heard in the Seventh Circuit Court in June 2009. The three-judge panel, headed by esteemed Circuit Judge Frank Easterbrook, cited precedents that it was unwilling to overrule and it upheld the local ordinances—but not before suggesting how it *might* rule if it had the authority.

> The Constitution establishes a federal republic where local differences are to be cherished as elements of liberty rather than extirpated in order to produce a single, nationally applicable rule. . . . Federalism is an older and more deeply rooted tradition than is a right to carry any particular kind of weapon. How arguments of this kind will affect proposals to "incorporate" the second amendment are for the Justices rather than a court of appeals.[7]

The plaintiffs showed their determination to bring their cases to a judgment day. One day after the Seventh Circuit Court handed down its decision, the NRA submitted a petition for a *writ of certiorari*—the formal request for the Supreme Court to hear a case. One week later, the McDonald team filed its petition. Given the recent *Heller* decision and the urgent question about its applicability to the states, the Supreme Court granted the petition for the *McDonald* case on September 30, 2009. The case would be heard by the high court in less than six months.

The granting of *certiorari* was like a cannon fired at the start of a six-month race. Armadas of attorneys set sail and began preparing the required merits briefs for the petitioners (the McDonald side) and the respondents (the City of Chicago). Although the court did not grant the NRA's petition for *certiorari*, it allowed the NRA to submit a brief on behalf of the petitioners and allowed NRA attorneys to share the time allotted to the petitioners for oral arguments.

A technical detour is needed to appreciate the intricacies of the *McDonald* case. There are two possible paths that might be used to protect gun rights against state and local laws—the process called incorporation. Both paths pass through the Fourteenth Amendment. In principle, an argument for incorporation may appeal either to the Fourteenth Amendment's privileges or immunities clause or to its due process clause.[8] At the top of every brief submitted to the Supreme Court in the *McDonald* case, the same "Question

Presented" was posed: whether the Second Amendment right to keep and bear arms is incorporated as against the states by the Fourteenth Amendment's privileges or immunities or due-process clauses.

A question of a fundamental right, such as the right to possess firearms, would seem to be a clear case of privileges or immunities: roughly speaking, one would argue that the privilege to possess a gun is immune from violation. However, the *Slaughterhouse* and *Cruikshank* cases of the 1870s effectively nullified the privileges or immunities approach, and that path to incorporation has not been used for any rights for over a century. The only successful path to incorporation of fundamental rights has relied on the due-process clause.

Therefore, it appeared to be a strategic gamble when the *McDonald* merits brief, written by *Heller* hero Alan Gura and Chicago attorney David Sigale, chose to take the path of privileges or immunities. Claiming that "*Slaughter-House*'s illegitimacy has long been all-but-universally understood,"[9] Gura and Sigale proposed to use the *McDonald* case as "a rare opportunity to correct a serious error" in constitutional law.[10] They planned to resurrect the privileges or immunities argument as a skirmish in the larger war of protecting Second Amendment rights. Their nearly one-hundred-page brief explained the virtues of the privileges or immunities clause and how it should be used to incorporate the Second Amendment. Only in the final pages did they outline a possible argument based on the due-process clause.

By contrast, the merits brief submitted by the NRA took the more traditional approach. Written by a team headed by NRA counsel and constitutional historian Stephen Halbrook, the brief observed that the Chicago handgun ban is no different than the District of Columbia ban that was struck down in the *Heller* case. It asserted that the right to keep and bear arms "preexists the Constitution" and is "fundamental . . . to liberty and our free society." It then methodically bolstered the claim that the Fourteenth Amendment "was intended and understood to protect the right to keep and bear arms." Specifically:

> Incorporation into the Due Process Clause would be fully consistent with the common understanding of the Fourteenth Amendment. . . . Indeed, *not* incorporating the Second Amendment would be a jarring and unjustifiable departure from . . . history and precedent.[11]

Because briefs are circulated before the Supreme Court hears the case, each side has a preview of the arguments that it must refute. Running over one hundred pages, the respondents' (City of Chicago) brief carried out hand-to-hand combat with the petitioners' arguments:

> The Second Amendment does not bind state and local governments. Neither the Court's selective incorporation doctrine under the Due Process Clause nor the Privileges or Immunities Clause provides a basis for imposing the Second Amendment on the States and establishing a national rule limiting arms regulation.[12]

The respondents' brief argued that "firearms are designed to injure or kill; conditions of their use and abuse vary widely around the country." For these reasons, the right to keep and bear arms is not "implicit in the concept of ordered liberty"—a concept that is often used as a test of a fundamental right.[13] And because the right to keep and bear arms is not fundamental, it is not eligible for incorporation and need not be protected by state and local laws. To the contrary, the regulation of firearms preserves, not intrudes on, ordered liberty.

Anticipating an attack along the privileges or immunities front, the respondents' brief also argued that "history shows no general public understanding or congressional intent that the Privileges or Immunities Clause was meant to impose the Bill of Rights on the States."[14] The brief urged the court to respect its own precedents and adhere to the principle of *stare decisis*—stand with the decision.

Both sides recruited interested parties to submit amicus briefs, a task that involved the work of literally thousands of (mostly) attorneys. Among the thirty-two parties that submitted briefs in support of the McDonald/NRA side were attorneys general of thirty-eight states; fifty-eight senators and 251 members of the House; several conservative or libertarian think tanks; and a coalition of law-enforcement and training organizations. Jews for the Preservation of Firearms Ownership filed a supporting brief, noting that "the 70 million innocent civilians murdered in the 20th Century's eight major genocides were direct victims of 'gun control' laws and policies that disarmed them."[15] "Dedicated to the Godly principles of law on which this country was founded," the Foundation for Moral Law also joined the parade of plaintiffs' friends.[16]

Collecting half as many amicus briefs as the opposition, the respondents found support from fifty-five members of the House; the United States Conference of Mayors; a coalition of educational, health, religious, and gun control organizations; and the Association of Prosecuting Attorneys and District Attorneys. Citing its "long history of investigating, monitoring, exposing, and combating Extremists," the Anti-Defamation League also submitted a supporting brief.[17]

In a familiar standoff of dueling statistics, a brief submitted by several law-enforcement organizations claimed that the Chicago gun ban was a failure, citing the sharp rise in Chicago's violent-crime rate relative to other large cities immediately after the year the handgun ban was imposed. The brief declared that "Chicago after the handgun ban is much more dangerous, relative to other large American cities, than was Chicago before the ban."[18]

In sharp opposition, a pair of criminal-justice professors submitted a brief summarizing their sophisticated "multilevel" study of Chicago handgun homicide data. After analyzing data from other large cities and controlling for key variables, the study concluded that the handgun ban "has helped reduce handgun homicides involving family members and intimate partners. It has also favorably impacted Chicago's overall handgun homicide rate relative to other cities once economic and demographic factors are considered. The Chicago handgun ban has saved hundreds of lives."[19] To reconcile the conclusions of these two briefs, it is worth noting that they report on different variables: overall crime rate and handgun homicide rate. It is possible that overall crime rate increased and handgun homicide rate decreased as a result of the gun ban.

By March 2010, the legions on both sides of the case had marshaled thousands of pages of historical, legal, and criminological fodder for the justices and their staffs. Each side led the justices through its own version of Second Amendment history and jurisprudence. Each side pressed on the justices its own preferred definition of critical ideas, such as fundamental rights and ordered liberty. Each side attempted to make convincing its own analysis of complex crime data. And each side predicted the ominous consequences of an adverse decision. The cold scholarly language of the many briefs barely concealed the roiling passions and high stakes just beneath the words. All that remained was for the thousands of pages of written testimony to be condensed into two half-hour oral arguments before the high court.

A Day in Court

"Mr. Chief Justice, and may it please the Court." It was ten a.m. on Tuesday, March 2, 2010, and Alan Gura made the traditional overture that precedes every oral argument before the US Supreme Court. And then Gura launched into the opening statement of *McDonald v. City of Chicago*.

> Although Chicago's ordinances cannot survive the faithful application of due process doctrines, there is an even simpler, more essential reason for reversing the lower court's judgment. The Constitution's plain text, as understood by the people that ratified it, mandates this result.[20]

He wasted no time getting into intricacies of constitutional law that seemed far removed from the question of whether a seventy-six-year-old Chicagoan could carry a handgun for self-defense. Gura claimed that the traditional due-process argument would suffice to overturn the Chicago handgun ban. However, he would present a simpler argument to reverse the lower court decision (upholding the ban). Referring to the Fourteenth Amendment, he continued:

> In 1868, our nation made a promise to the McDonald family; they and their descendants would henceforth be American citizens, and with American citizenship came the guarantee enshrined in our Constitution that no State could make or enforce any law, which shall abridge the privileges or immunities of American citizenship.

With his privileges and immunities strategy declared, Gura continued, "the rights secured by the Fourteenth Amendment were understood to include the fundamental rights honored by any free government and the personal guarantees of the . . ."

Less than a minute into the oral argument, Chief Justice John Roberts interrupted Gura's monologue. "Of course, this argument is contrary to the *Slaughter-House Cases*, which have been the law for 140 years. It might be simpler, but . . . it's a heavy burden for you to carry to suggest that we ought to overrule that decision."

The art of oral argument requires staying afloat under the justices' verbal shelling, giving quick, credible answers to serpentine questions, and being able to find the way back to the original script. Coming so soon in Gura's oral argument, Justice Roberts's suggestion that Gura was headed down the wrong path was ominous.

Without losing his bearings, Gura responded quickly and boldly. Referring to the *Slaughterhouse Cases*, he asserted that, "the Court has always found that when a case is extremely wrong, when there is a great consensus that it was simply not decided correctly, especially in a constitutional matter, it has less force."

Justice Roberts may have wanted to respond to Gura, but Justice Sonia Sotomayor jumped in first. "What injustice has been caused by it that we have to remedy? . . . In which ways has ordered liberty been badly affected?" she asked. Her point was that we have survived for a long time without relying on the privileges or immunities argument. Why introduce it now? According to Sotomayor, "ordered liberty" has not been sacrificed.

Gura responded respectfully but rather obliquely. "Justice Sotomayor, States may have grown accustomed to violating the rights of American citizens, but that does not bootstrap those violations into something that is constitutional." Without enough time for anyone to understand exactly what Gura meant, Justice Ruth Bader Ginsburg interjected. Her quivering voice compelled everyone to listen even more intently, as she chased a more recondite point concerning exactly which rights would be covered by a privileges or immunities argument. "If you could clarify your conception of privileges and immunities. Am I right in thinking that to keep and bear arms would be included even if we had no Second Amendment, as you envision privileges and immunities?"

"Justice Ginsburg, that is correct. The framers and the public understood the term . . ."

"Just tell us the dimensions of what it is. I mean, we have the eight amendments, so I know you say that's included. Keep and bear arms would be included even absent the Second Amendment. What unenumerated rights would we be declaring privileges and immunities under your conception of it?"

Oral arguments often become a well-mannered tag-team match—except that one side has only one lonely protagonist. Before Gura could complete his response, Justice Antonin Scalia, the most verbal of the justices, intervened.

"Mr. Gura, do you think it's at all easier to bring the Second Amendment under the privileges and immunities clause than it is to bring it under our established law of substantive due process?"

"It's . . ."

Without waiting for an answer, Justice Scalia repeated the question. "Is it easier to do it under privileges and immunities than it is under substantive due process?"

Gura searched and stammered for the first time. "It's easier in terms, perhaps, of . . . of the text and history, the original public understanding of . . ." Sensing where he was going with that response, Scalia rescued Gura with another question.

"No, no. I'm not talking about whether *The Slaughter-House Cases* were right or wrong. I'm saying, assuming we give, you know, the privileges and immunities clause your definition, does that make it any easier to get the Second Amendment adopted with respect to the States?"

"Justice Scalia, I suppose the answer to that would be no, because . . ."

With his patented sarcasm, Scalia interrupted. "And if the answer is no, why are you asking us to overrule 150, 140 years of prior law, when you can reach your result under substantive due. . . . I mean, you know, unless you're bucking for a place on some law school faculty."

The laughter in the courtroom gave Gura a few moments to get oriented; and then the onslaught resumed. Justice John Paul Stevens soon spoke up, returning to Justice Ginsberg's hypothetical question about, "what if we had no Second Amendment." Justices Roberts and Kennedy probed about whether incorporation protected just the core of the right or "all the refinements and sophistication with which we interpret them for the federal government."

The exchange between the justices and Gura remained abstract until Justice Stephen Breyer finally brought the discussion back to the reality of gun control. In his gravelly and emphatic baritone voice, he began, "Okay. How does that work? . . . Is this right different from others?"

"Well . . . ," Gura attempted.

And then Breyer gave the most pragmatic and passionate soliloquy of the entire hearing.

All you have to do is look at the briefs. Look at the statistics. You know, one side says a million people killed by guns. Chicago says that their gun law has saved hundreds, including—and they have statistics—including lots of women in domestic cases. And the other side disputes it.

This is a highly statistical matter. Without incorporation, it's decided by State legislatures; with [incorporation], it's decided by Federal judges. Now, think of this, too: That when you have the First Amendment, . . . there's always a big area where it's free speech versus a whole lot of things, but not often free speech versus life. When it's free speech versus life, we very often decide in favor of life.

Here every case will be on one side guns, on the other side human life. Statistics, balancing life versus guns. How are federal judges in your opinion, rather than legislatures in the States in a federal system—how are federal judges supposed to carry this out? I want to see where we're going.

In making his point, Breyer confirmed which side would get his vote. Gura waded into this new line of inquiry. "Federal judges should carry this out in the same way that was announced in this Court's decision in *Heller*." Breyer could not help interrupting with some retribution and humor. "*Heller*, I didn't think, . . . explained it with total clarity, but that's a dissenter's view."

After laughter in the courtroom subsided, Breyer returned to his question. "Suppose Chicago says . . . by banning handguns, not in the hills, not hunting, nothing like that, nothing outside the city—in the city we save several hundred human lives every year. And the other side says, we don't think it is several hundred, and, moreover, that doesn't matter. How do you decide the case?"

At last, Gura managed to get in a fairly concise answer. "We decide that by looking, not to which side has the better statistics, but rather to what the framers said in the Constitution, because that policy choice was made for us in the Constitution. . . . The City cannot ban guns that are within the common use as protected by the right to arms."

In terms of pressure, heat, and reputations at stake, it is hard to imagine a more demanding arena than the small lectern before the bench of the US Supreme Court. In Gura's twenty-minute oral argument, his prepared remarks met a detour early in the ordeal. He spent his remaining time fielding questions, conjuring responses with lightning speed, and speaking no more than five consecutive sentences without interruption. The justices rarely moved beyond technical questions of constitutional law and Gura left much of his original script unaired. Suddenly he was finished. By all accounts, his performance was masterful.

Gura used twenty of the thirty minutes of oral argument allotted to the plaintiffs. By prior agreement, the NRA had ten minutes to argue for the plaintiffs; and representing the NRA was the formidable Paul Clement, who had appeared in the *Heller* oral arguments. In his opening, Clement announced confidently that he would follow the more traditional due-process path for incorporation of the Second Amendment.

> Mr. Chief Justice, and may it please the Court: Under this court's existing jurisprudence, the case for incorporating the Second Amendment through the due process clause is remarkably straightforward. The Second Amendment, like the First and the Fourth, protects a fundamental preexisting right that is guaranteed to the people . . .

But with his second sentence still hanging, Justice Stevens pounced. "Mr. Clement, would you comment on Justice Kennedy's question about whether that necessarily incorporates every jot and tittle of the federal right? . . . Why does this incorporation have to be every bit as broad as the Second Amendment itself?"

Although Clement spent most of his allotted time in reaction mode, he salvaged nearly three minutes of uninterrupted oration, in which he made the case for "incorporating not just the right [to keep and bear arms] but the jurisprudence that came with that right." According to Clement, the Supreme Court should not only protect the core right but also require that federal precedents associated with that right are also binding. Justice Stevens countered that the court has a history of protecting the core right only and letting lower courts establish their own case law. Stevens bolstered that argument by appealing to a heroic advocate of the due-process clause—Justice John Marshall Harlan II, who served from 1955 to 1971. "We have followed Justice Harlan, rather than the majority in a number of cases in recent years. . . . He is very much against you, and he is a very important member of our history."

Clement responded adroitly saying it might be more useful to go back to Justice Harlan's grandfather, also Justice John Marshall Harlan, who served from 1877 to 1911. This maneuver on Clement's part effectively diverted the discussion to another question, and so it went. Accustomed to arguing for a full thirty minutes, Clement's weaving and parrying for only ten minutes scarcely raised a sweat. And he likely changed no opinions on the bench.

Then it was time for the respondents. Washington, DC, "solo attorney," Justice Department attorney, and Penn Law School professor James Feldman handled the entire oral argument. A survivor of nearly fifty Supreme Court appearances and a party to over one hundred briefs, Feldman could breathe the rarified air of the high court. He lost no time getting to the point.

> Mr. Chief Justice, and may it please the Court: The Second Amendment should not be incorporated and applied to the States because the right it protects is not implicit in the concept of ordered liberty. States and local governments have been the primary locus of firearms regulation in this country for the last 220 years.

Reminding the justices of the arguments laid out in the merits brief, Feldman asserted that, "Firearms, unlike anything else that is the subject of a provision of the Bill of Rights, are designed to injure and kill. And the very same features that make firearms valuable for self-defense as the Court noted in Heller also . . ."

Justice Scalia had heard enough. "When is the last time an opinion of ours made that test implicit in the concept of ordered liberty? It sounds very nice. But when was the last time we used it? I think it was 1937."

"I don't believe it was, Your Honor. The . . ." Feldman managed to cite two cases to make his point before Justice Kennedy stepped into the breach and helped Feldman finish an answer to Scalia's question. With that skirmish behind him, Feldman forged ahead, arguing that the right to keep and bear arms was not sufficiently fundamental to warrant incorporation. Gun laws should be debated and passed locally where they could be designed to meet local needs.

> What I'm saying is that the right that is embodied in the wide variety

of different State constitutions . . . what the States have determined as a result of their own processes and in light of their own conditions is that you can't ban all kinds of firearms, but you can ban some kinds of firearms.

Chief Justice Roberts offered a compromise position. "All the arguments you make against incorporation, it seems to me, are arguments you should make in favor of regulation under the Second Amendment." Feldman was not willing to accept this option. "As far as the right to self-defense goes, that's something that has always been effectively regulated through the political process and especially at the State and local level."

It was a spirited debate in which Feldman spent more time responding to questions than giving a recital of his argument. It circled several times on the question of whether the Second Amendment is fundamental to the American system of ordered liberty. Chief Justice Roberts asked, "Why wouldn't you think, for all the reasons given in *Heller*, that the Second Amendment right is essential to our system?" Feldman reminded the Justices of what they had decided in the *Heller* case: "The question that the Court was addressing in *Heller* was not how important the Second Amendment right was, or how implicit it is in our system. . . . It was . . . what restrictions did the framers of the Second Amendment impose on the Federal Government."

Justice Kennedy piled on. "If it's not fundamental, then *Heller* is wrong, it seems to me."

"No, I don't think that's right." Feldman countered. "The question is . . . what did they impose . . . as restrictions upon the government when the Second Amendment was ratified."

Then back to Chief Justice Roberts. "I don't see how you can read *Heller* and not take away from it the notion that the Second Amendment . . . was extremely important to the framers in their view of what liberty meant." Feldman rephrased his position.

It was important, but actually what *Heller* said is this: The right that's in the Second Amendment preexisted its inclusion in the Bill of Rights. . . . The reason it was put into the Bill of Rights was because the framers were concerned about the Federal Government disarming the militia. The

right of self-defense, which has been previously recognized and valued
. . . according to *Heller*, quote, "had little to do with its codification."

Then Scalia convolved the discussion further with a tautological conversation
stopper. "That may be the reason it was put there. But it was put there. And
that's the crucial fact. It is either there or it is not there."

Feldman was attempting to make a crucial argument for his case, but he
was talking into a strong headwind from the conservative justices. His aim
was to point out what he viewed as a constitutional bait-and-switch: The Second Amendment was ratified for one purpose—as a safeguard against government tyranny. And yet today, its incorporation was justified for another
purpose—as a means of self-defense. That shift in purpose made the Second
Amendment right different than other fundamental rights, thereby disqualifying the Second Amendment for incorporation. This argument had been
rejected in the *Heller* case and would be rejected again by the majority in the
McDonald case.

Given the unlikeliness of the Court reconsidering its *Heller* decision, it was
an uphill trudge for Feldman. After thirty minutes of give and take, but little
apparent movement, he closed his argument. Even some in the opposition felt
that Feldman had done as good a job as anyone could have done.

Waiting for a major Supreme Court decision is like waiting for the first
hurricane of the season: you know it is coming, but not exactly when or how
significant it will be. Decisions in landmark cases, such as *McDonald*, are
often the last to appear. On June 28, 2010, the last day of the term, there was
no doubt that the *McDonald* decision would be announced. In less than a half
hour, Justice Alito, author of the majority opinion, and Justice Breyer, author
of one of the dissenting opinions, gave oral summaries of their opinions.

The outcome was significant but hardly unexpected, especially given the
flow of the oral arguments. The majority opinion reaffirmed the court's ruling
in the *Heller* case.

Self-defense is a basic right, recognized by many legal systems from
ancient times to the present, and the *Heller* Court held that individual
self-defense is "the central component" of the Second Amendment
right.[21]

In his opinion, Justice Alito called the arguments of the respondents "implausible," "stunning," and "nothing less than a plea to disregard 50 years of incorporation precedent." The majority recited its version of Second Amendment history, made the case for incorporation of the Second Amendment under the due-process clause, and dismantled the arguments of the dissenting justices. The oasis of hope for the gun-regulation side was the majority's caution, quoted from *Heller*, that the right to keep and bear arms is not "a right to keep and carry any weapon whatsoever in any manner whatsoever and for what ever purpose." It then added faint reassurance that in spite of Chicago's "doomsday proclamations, incorporation does not imperil every law regulating firearms."[22]

The case brought an unusual pageant of opinions. Justices Roberts, Scalia, and Kennedy joined Alito in the majority opinion, with Scalia writing his own personal opinion. Justice Thomas concurred with the majority decision but wrote a fifty-five-page opinion laying out a "more straightforward path" to the same conclusion, via the privileges or immunities clause. Justice Stevens wrote his own sixty-page dissenting opinion, saying that "firearms have a fundamentally ambivalent relationship to liberty" and that "liberty encompasses neither the common-law right of self-defense or a right to bear arms." He reiterated his belief that gun laws are better left to state and local legislatures familiar with the needs and desires of their citizens. And he predicted presciently that the *McDonald* decision "invites an avalanche of litigation that could mire the federal courts in fine-grained determinations."[23]

And finally, Justice Breyer wrote a dissenting opinion joined by Justices Ginsburg and Sotomayor. Arguing against incorporation, Breyer, in great historical and legal detail, explained why the majority had failed to show that the Second Amendment right is fundamental to the American scheme of liberty. Like Stevens, he also feared the heavy burden that the decision would place on the judicial system. He recited a litany of now-famous questions that would confront judges trying to interpret the thousands of local gun regulations:

Does the right to possess weapons for self-defense extend outside the home? To the car? To work? What sort of guns are necessary for self-defense? Handguns? Rifles? Semiautomatic weapons? When is a gun semiautomatic? Where are different kinds of weapons likely needed?

Does time-of-day matter? Does the presence of a child in the house matter? Does the presence of a convicted felon in the house matter? . . . When do registration requirements become severe to the point that they amount to a constitutional ban? Who can possess guns and what kinds? Immigrants? Prior drug offenders? Prior alcohol abusers?[24]

According to Breyer, "judges do not know the answers to the kinds of empirically based questions that will often determine the need for particular forms of gun regulation. . . . There is no institutional need to send judges off on this 'mission-almost-impossible.'" He concluded his practical and technical opinion:

The Framers did not write the Second Amendment in order to protect a private right of armed self-defense. . . . There has been, and is, no consensus that the right is, or was, "fundamental." . . . With respect, I dissent.[25]

The decision exposed a deeply cleaved court, whose two distant shores had barely shifted since the *Heller* case. Of interest to scholars, the decision did resolve an annoying legal loose end, which was the incorporation of the Second Amendment. At last, the Second Amendment could be added to the list of other rights that enjoyed some protection from state and local laws. However, for those with a more pragmatic interest in the case, the decision was "infuriatingly abstract."[26] The opinions on both sides used more ink arguing about legal theories than spelling out specific guidelines on admissible restrictions on gun use. Ironically, the decision did not settle the fate of the Chicago gun ban. The case was returned to the Seventh Circuit, where federal judges decided—with little guidance from the Supreme Court—how Chicago would need to modify its gun laws. In June 2014, Chicago's handgun ban was ruled unconstitutional. The Chicago City Council replaced it with an ordinance placing strict controls on sales of handguns. The ordinance allows sales only in certain parts of the city and outlaws sales at gun shows.

Many Court analysts forecasted the impact of the *McDonald* decision on the lower courts: "The dueling of lobbyists will now be replicated by dueling attorneys."[27] "The real action will be in the lower courts, to which fall the grubby tasks of applying the constitutional principles the Supreme Court pronounces."[28] "The Court has put the federal judiciary to the never-ending task of quasi-legislating a gun code."[29] The decision "increases the number of possible constitutional claims, and it also increases the opportunities for litigation."[30] And the decision "is destined to be a virtual full employment act for gun rights lawyers."[31]

For gun rights advocates, the decision was exalting. The NRA's Wayne LaPierre praised it as "a great moment in American history . . . a vindication for the great majority of American citizens who have always believed the Second Amendment was an individual right and freedom worth defending." He continued on a realistic note:

> We are practical guys. . . . The NRA will work to ensure this constitutional victory is not transformed into a practical defeat by activist judges. . . . The NRA will not rest until every law-abiding American citizen is able to exercise the individual right to buy and own a firearm for self-defense or any other lawful purpose.[32]

Nearly a year after the *McDonald* decision, the NRA won another legal battle when it recovered over $1.3 million in attorneys' fees for its work on the Chicago gun cases.[33]

Supporters of gun regulation were getting accustomed to finding scant consolation in defeat. Paul Helmke, then-president of the Brady Center and Brady Campaign to Prevent Gun Violence, was pleased with the *McDonald* decision:

> [It] reaffirmed . . . that the Second Amendment individual right to possess guns in the home for self-defense does not prevent our elected representatives from enacting common-sense gun laws to protect our communities from gun violence. We are reassured that the Court has rejected, once again, the gun lobby argument that its "any gun, for anybody, anywhere" agenda is protected by the Constitution.[34]

He noted that after the 2008 *Heller* decision, at least 240 legal challenges were brought to existing gun laws—nearly all of which were unsuccessful. His hopes for similar fallout from the *McDonald* case were realized. According to a count by the Law Center to Prevent Gun Violence, as of early 2015, there were over nine hundred challenges to gun laws in state and federal courts since the *Heller* decision. Ninety-six percent of those challenges failed to overturn the existing laws.[35]

We tend to think of Supreme Court decisions as great keystones that suddenly lock the pieces of a complicated issue together with finality. That may happen with a few unanimous decisions, but it certainly does not describe the net effect of the *Heller* and *McDonald* cases. Gun rights people got the confirmation of individual rights that they had sought for decades. Gun-regulation people took comfort that neither decision ruled out unspecified restrictions to unfettered gun rights. In their eloquent inconclusiveness, the justices gave both sides something to celebrate and they gave both sides even more to argue about.

Three years after the *McDonald* decision, dissenting Justice John Paul Stevens looked back on these two gun cases. He had no second thoughts:

> I dissented in both of those cases and remain convinced that both decisions misinterpreted the law and were profoundly unwise. Public policies concerning gun control should be decided by the voters' elected representatives, not by federal judges.[36]

Stevens then offered his fantasy solution to the gun debate—at once simple and impossible. He suggested adding five words to the Second Amendment:

> A well regulated Militia, being necessary to the security of a free State, the right of the people to keep and bear Arms *when serving in the Militia* shall not be infringed.[37]

17 | A YEAR PASSES

> It's not true that life is one damn thing after another;
> it is one damn thing over and over.
>
> —EDNA ST. VINCENT MILLAY[1]

IT WAS THE morning of December 14, 2012, when an isolated twenty-year-old man, living with his single mother in Newtown, Connecticut, stormed into Sandy Hook Elementary School. Armed with his mother's legally purchased Bushmaster AR-15 and several magazines, the gunman needed only ten merciless minutes to kill twenty first-graders and six staff people. He had already slain his sleeping mother at their home, and he finished the ghastly deed with himself. The details of the country's second-worst school shooting (to date) are so unforgettably etched in our memories that they hardly bear recounting.

Within hours of the shootings, the depth of the carnage was known and in the midst of a holiday season, sorrow, outrage, and disbelief washed over the nation. The public reaction was swift. President Obama, only a month before he would be inaugurated for his second term, suddenly had an unthinkable crisis on his hands. He addressed the nation, saying, "We're going to have to come together and take meaningful action to prevent more tragedies like this, regardless of the politics."[2] The president traveled to Newtown two days later and led a community vigil, where his remarks turned to gun control. Feeling the leverage granted by a second term, he pledged to use "whatever power this office holds" to halt the relentless march of gun violence.[3]

Newtown was an unknown, bucolic, relatively crime-free community that left people thinking, "If it can happen here, it can happen anywhere." At the time of the shootings, Connecticut was known as a gun control state; it had an assault-weapons ban and a handgun-licensing system. Newtown was home of law-abiding hunters and it had two licensed shooting ranges (which the Newtown killer and his mother visited). But in the two years before the school shootings, residents had lodged hundreds of complaints about gunfire at unauthorized ranges in the woods near town. When town leaders attempted to corral the illicit shooting, a civic battle erupted, which was in progress when the school shootings took place. And then a further irony: Newtown is the home of the National Shooting Sports Foundation, the trade organization for the firearm industry.

As calls for tighter gun restrictions echoed across the country, representatives of gun rights groups were silent—for a while. In a radio interview, six days after the shooting, Larry Pratt of Gun Owners of America expressed hard-headed sympathy over the Sandy Hook tragedy. "This was one more tragedy that occurred in a gun-free zone. . . . You cannot protect yourself in a school. My heart breaks all the more knowing that we set up this situation."[4] A day later, the NRA's Wayne LaPierre picked up the theme at a nationally televised press conference. Speaking of the "incomprehensible loss as a result of this unspeakable crime," he stressed the need to banish gun-free zones. Toward that end, he offered NRA resources to establish a National School Shield Emergency Response Program that would provide an armed guard for every school. He quotably reminded viewers "the only thing that stops a bad guy with a gun is a good guy with a gun."[5] Amid all the emotion, gun scholar David Kopel was pragmatic:

> The only item on the agenda of today's antigun advocates that realistically could have prevented a psychopath from stealing his mother's legally registered guns would be banning and confiscating the more than 300 million firearms in the United States.[6]

President Obama quickly appointed a stakeholder task force chaired by Vice President Joe Biden; the committee had less than a month to submit its recommendations. Biden went into a sleepless "time warp," holding twenty-two meetings with 229 law-enforcement agencies and organizations on all sides of the firearm debate.[7] He declared, "I have never seen the nation's conscience so shaken by what happened at Sandy Hook. The world has changed and is demanding action."[8]

Biden's committee delivered its report on time with top priority given to banning assault weapons and large capacity magazines, ending illegal gun trafficking, fortifying the background-check system, and strengthening federal mental-health programs. The next day, Obama ignited the campaign by issuing twenty-three executive orders to tighten existing laws, promising to "put everything I've got into this and so will Joe."[9] Fueled by a re-election mandate, widespread public support, and millions of new dollars from groups such as Michael Bloomberg's Mayors Against Illegal Guns, the White House went into high gear.

A Year in Congress

Across town, the first session of the 113th Congress convened in the first week of January. Three weeks of media frenzy had hardly softened the memory of the Sandy Hook tragedy. Public support for gun control spiked (as did gun sales) and many legislators returned to Washington with an invincible zeal to pass new, tighter gun laws. Within days, new firearm bills were piling up. Among the first bills out of the mill was Senator Dianne Feinstein's (D-CA) new federal assault-weapons ban, designed as an improved incarnation of the 1994 Assault Weapons Ban. Representative Carolyn McCarthy (D-NY) introduced a House version of the bill—one of five firearm bills she introduced in 2013.

Like its predecessor, Senator Feinstein's bill listed features of weapons that would be banned by the bill. It also outlawed magazines with more than a ten-round capacity. However, to give the bill a chance of passage, it made a significant concession: all assault weapons purchased before the law's enactment were exempt from the ban. For gun rights supporters, the bill was just the latest infuriating and senseless attack on the rights of gun owners. For gun safety advocates, the bill gave hope for desperately needed reform that might help stanch the tide of gun violence. Both sides escalated fund-raising and unleashed their lobbyists. The first stop for the bill was the Senate Judiciary Committee, where the members had some high-stakes, low-civility exchanges. Perhaps the most memorable skirmish was between Senator Ted Cruz (R-TX) and Senator Feinstein:

CRUZ: Would she [Senator Feinstein] consider it constitutional for
Congress to specify that the First Amendment shall apply only to the

following books and shall not apply to the books that Congress has
deemed outside of the protection of the Bill of Rights?

FEINSTEIN: I'm not a sixth grader. Senator, I've been on this committee
for twenty years. I was a mayor for nine years. I walked in, I saw people shot. I've looked at bodies that have been shot by these weapons.
. . . In Sandy Hook, youngsters were dismembered. Look, there are
other weapons. . . . After twenty years, I've been up close and personal
to the Constitution. I have great respect for it. . . . It's fine you want
to lecture me on the Constitution. I appreciate it. Just know I've been
here a long time.[10]

The bill squeezed through the Senate Judiciary Committee on party lines and
a month later it went to the full Senate. Supporters of the 1994 Assault Weapons Ban had paid a price in extinguished political careers, and the lesson had
not been forgotten. This latest attempt at an assault-weapon ban was still a
poison pill for legislators; it was defeated by a 60–40 vote.

The best hope for meaningful gun control legislation settled on a bill that
would strengthen the system of federal background checks. One poll at the
time tallied 85 percent of respondents supporting background checks on private and gun show sales.[11] In a poll of gun owners, half of whom were NRA
members, 82 percent of respondents favored background checks on anyone
purchasing a gun.[12] With public support at that level and with elected officials
listening to their constituents, how could such a bill possibly fail? Here is how
it happened.

Crafting a broadly supported bill on stronger background checks would
require someone who was both passionate about fighting gun violence and
capable of working with gun rights forces. The best person in the Senate with
those cross-cutting qualifications was Senator Joe Manchin (D-WV), a former governor, a long-time NRA member, and someone deeply transformed
by the Sandy Hook tragedy. Manchin worked tirelessly with NRA lobbyists
and legal experts to design a bill that extended background checks to gun
shows and Internet sales, while still being digestible by gun owners. Along
the way, Manchin found an ally in Senator Pat Toomey (R-PA), who was
A-rated by the NRA and willing to engage in a bipartisan effort. The resulting
bill, called the Safe Communities, Safe Schools Act, was introduced in early

April. It fortified the existing system of background checks and it also carried NRA-required safeguards to prohibit the creation of a federal gun registry.

According to a well-excavated inside account, Manchin expected NRA neutrality on the bill—meaning at worst, no opposition.[13] However, plans unraveled after the bill was introduced. Washington, DC, is a breezy place and the no-compromise Gun Owners of America and the National Association for Gun Rights caught wind of the bill. Both organizations, proudly more fanatic about gun rights than the NRA, accused the NRA of conspiring with the opposition and selling out the interests of gun owners. The NRA was faced with an arguably life-changing choice, and it made a tactical decision. The NRA's expected neutrality suddenly turned to a frontal assault against the bill, accompanied by a seismic mobilization of its members. The earthquake reached Congress, and senators analyzed the costs of the potentially career-ending bill. On April 17 (two days after the Boston Marathon bombing), the first major gun bill in twenty years reached the floor of the Senate. What looked like a historic victory for gun control a few weeks earlier fell short of passage by six votes.

Gun violence victim and former Arizona representative Gabrielle Giffords was at the Capitol during the final vote; her presence did not change the outcome. She later wrote, "A minority of senators gave in to fear and blocked common-sense legislation. . . . I'm furious. I will not rest until we have righted the wrong these senators have done."[14] A spokesman for the Gun Owners of America declared, "We feel confident this will spell the end of gun control for the 113th Congress. The gun registry defined the battle over universal background checks."[15] Referring to universal background checks, Senate Majority Leader Harry Reid responded, "There are very few things that 90 percent of Americans agree on. This is just the beginning. It is not the end."[16]

In all, 282 crime and law-enforcement bills were introduced in Congress in 2013, the majority of them dealing with firearms: the Stop Online Ammunition Sales Act, the Large Capacity Ammunition Feeding Device Act, the Gun Show Loophole Closing Act, the Handgun Licensing and Registration Act, the NRA Members' Gun Safety Act (weakening background checks), the Crackdown on Deadbeat Gun Dealers Act, and the list goes on. It is difficult to recap a year of trench warfare in Congress, multimillion-dollar lobbying, contentious committee meetings, impassioned testimony by grieving parents, and a perpetual media bath. However, the tangible outcome of all that tur-moil was negligible: no significant firearm legislation was passed—save the renewal of a twenty-year-old law on undetectable firearms. A bill favorable to gun owners, mandating reciprocity among all states for concealed-carry permits, was also defeated.

Perhaps it is not surprising that Congress clear-cut the forest of gun con-trol bills. According to one report, 205 members of the House (47 percent) and 42 members of the Senate (42 percent) received contributions from the NRA during the 2012 election campaign. Over half of the House members and exactly half of the Senate members in 2013 had received contributions from the NRA sometime in the past.[17] In the 2012 election campaign, the NRA spent an estimated $18.6 million to elect their A-rated national can-didates. The big spender in the 2012 election on the gun control side was Mayor Michael Bloomberg's PAC, which reported $3.3 million in indepen-dent expenses.[18] The Brady Campaign to Prevent Gun Violence spent an invisible $5,800.[19]

A Year in the States

In the states, the story of 2013 gun laws fills a book with fifty uncoordinated chapters. By one analysis, 1,500 state gun bills were introduced in 2013 and 109 became law. Of those laws, thirty-nine tightened existing laws and sev-enty relaxed existing laws.[20] By another tally, twenty-seven states introduced one thousand gun bills in 2013. Of the 136 bills that became laws, 43 tightened existing laws, while 93 relaxed existing laws.[21] Eleven states attempted to pass nullification laws permitting states to ignore federal firearm laws or not coop-erate in their enforcement; four states succeeded. Regardless of how you do the bookkeeping, the result is a roughly two-to-one easing of gun laws in the states.

To varying degrees, many forces influenced the course of gun legislation in the states in 2013: public pressure, media exposure, the fate of political careers, closed-door horse-trading, and, perhaps most significantly, money. According to one analysis, gun rights organizations poured in roughly $15.2 million in 2013 for lobbying to repeal or weaken existing state gun laws.[22] By contrast, gun control organizations spent $2.2 million during the same period to fight for stronger state laws.[23] Interestingly, both sides, collectively, cut their gun-law lobbying budgets the following year.

Apart from the gyrations of lawmakers, what else happened during 2013? By several measures, despite the emotional response to Sandy Hook, not much changed in its aftermath. The number of gun-related deaths held steady at about 33,500, with two-thirds of those deaths due to suicides. The number of children killed by guns inched upward, reaching 194 victims under age twelve for the year (103 homicides, 84 accidents, 127 in the home).[24] And continuing a twenty-year trend, the national violent-crime rate continued to drop.

During the year, there were twenty-five school shootings after Sandy Hook, resulting in eighteen deaths and twenty-five injuries.[25] One school rampage occurred in Colorado on the eve of the one-year Sandy Hook anniversary. A total of twenty-six mass killings (four or more victims, excluding the shooter) took the lives of 116 people.[26] The worst of these incidents occurred on September 16 at the Washington Navy Yard and resulted in twelve deaths.

Advocacy groups for the eradication of gun violence appeared like saplings watered by the tears of citizens who never before thought of themselves as activists. Parents and spouses of Sandy Hook victims created Sandy Hook Promise. After a year, nearly three hundred thousand people had made the promise to "support sensible solutions to prevent gun violence" and helped raise $3.5 million.[27] Modeled on Mothers Against Drunk Driving, Indianapolis mother Sharon Watts launched Moms Demand Action for Gun Sense in America as her response to Sandy Hook. A year later, the organization had 130,000 members with chapters in every state. The group channels its resources to sensible gun reform through social networking.[28] The Sandy Hook tragedy also launched Americans for Responsible Solutions, led by former Arizona congresswoman Gabrielle Giffords and her husband Mark Kelly.[29] As gun owners who barely survived a mass shooting, they were sadly, but perfectly, positioned to create a lobbying force to steer Congress to reasonable gun control policies.

Mayors Against Illegal Guns (MAIG), founded and funded by former New York mayor Michael Bloomberg, saw a surge in visibility and membership during 2013. The group now claims one thousand member mayors, from nearly every state. Its robust budget provided a cavalcade of print and television ads that were a soundtrack for the 2013 congressional firearm debates. MAIG then teamed up with Moms Demand Action for Gun Sense in America to form a new coalition called Everytown for Gun Safety. And in April 2014, Bloomberg upped the ante, pledging $50 million of his personal wealth to challenge the treasuries of gun rights groups.

Gun rights groups saw an increase in membership after Sandy Hook—a common consequence of a mass shooting or a threat of tighter gun laws. The NRA reported 100,000 new paying members in the eighteen days following Sandy Hook, bringing its total membership to an estimated 4.2 million.[30] As a nonprofit organization, the NRA reported revenues of $256 million in 2012 (and another $43 million in revenue for the NRA Foundation). Founded in 2001, the National Association for Gun Rights (NAGR) claims to be the fastest-growing gun rights group in America. By some measure, the claims may be accurate. NAGR's revenue increased from $3.8 million in 2011 to $16.4 million in 2013.[31]

Gun sales and NICS firearm background checks are not perfectly correlated. Nevertheless, it is significant that five of the ten busiest days in NICS's history were in the last six weeks of 2012—the weeks following President Obama's re-election and the Sandy Hook tragedy.[32] Two publicly traded firearm companies had exceptional years. For the fiscal year ending April 30, 2013, Smith & Wesson reported a 43 percent increase in sales that reached a record $587 million.[33] Sturm Ruger saw a 45 percent increase in sales for the third quarter of 2013.[34] And the NRA reached best-seller status with the one-millionth sale of its self-published *Basics of Pistol Shooting*—after only four years in print.

A Year in the Courts

The minority justices in the *McDonald* case may have lost the battle, but they won a victory in prophecy. The *McDonald* decision, they accurately foretold, "invites an avalanche of litigation that could mire the federal courts."[35] Following the 2010 *McDonald* decision, federal and state court rooms resounded with the cacophony of attorneys arguing for and against the repeal of existing gun laws. Here is a small sample of significant decisions.

After the *Heller* ruling, the District of Columbia responded with its Firearms Regulation Amendment Act—the strictest possible gun law it could pass and still comply with the Supreme Court decision. The new law required re-registration of existing guns (long guns and handguns), imposed a strict registration process for new guns, and banned assault weapons and high-capacity magazines; it went into effect in March 2009. Within days, attorneys for Dick Heller, the plaintiff in the *Heller* case, filed suit in federal court, claiming that the new law saddled gun owners with onerous burdens that violated the *Heller* decision. The sequel case—called *Heller II*—found its way to the Court of Appeals for the District of Columbia, where on October 4, 2011, a three-judge panel ruled 2–1 in favor of the district: the new gun law could stand.[36] However, in July 2014, the US District Court for the District of Columbia ruled in the case *Palmer v. District of Columbia* that the district's virtual prohibition on carrying a handgun outside the home was unconstitutional—another victory for Alan Gura. As a result, the district now allows a qualified person to carry a handgun, provided it has been registered with the district police.[37]

Within a month of the Sandy Hook tragedy, the New York legislature passed the Secure Ammunition and Firearms Enforcement (SAFE) Act, which included an assault-weapon ban and a seven-round limit on magazines.[38] The speed at which the law was written and enacted boded well for gun control across the country. However, a group of New York firearm businesses and advocacy groups quickly challenged the law. On the last day of 2013, a federal judge rendered a decision, striking down the magazine provision but upholding the assault-weapon ban.[39] A US Court of Appeals upheld that decision in 2015. Connecticut also enacted a ban on assault weapons and high-capacity magazines soon after the Sandy Hook shootings. That law saw an immediate challenge, but the law was upheld a year later in federal district court in January 2014.[40] Similar challenges and appeals occurred in other states. In Illinois, the Seventh Circuit overturned the state's ban on carrying concealed weapons as well as Chicago's prohibition of firing ranges in the city.[41]

With a Democratic state house and a sympathetic governor, Colorado succeeded in passing more restrictive laws in 2013: one banning large-capacity magazines and another strengthening background checks. However, legislators who championed those laws paid the price: the president of the state senate and another senator were unceremoniously yanked from office by special recall votes and a third senator resigned in the face of an expensive recall vote. A coalition of fifty-four Colorado sheriffs opposed the new laws and filed suit against the state in federal court. A federal judge upheld the laws, triggering appeals to the Second Circuit Appeals Court.

In March 2014, the Georgia legislature left no doubt—by two-to-one margins in both houses—about where it stands on gun control. The Safe Carry Protection Act of 2014 allows the permitted carrying of guns in churches, bars, schools zones, most areas of airports, and restaurants. Critics called it the most "extreme gun bill in America" and the "guns everywhere bill." Supporters complained that the original bill had been diluted but still hailed it as "the most comprehensive pro-gun" law in a long time.[42] A month later, Governor Nathan Deal earned his NRA A-rating and signed the bill into law. A proposed provision allowing guns on college campuses did not become law. A week after the law passed (arguably unrelated to the law, which went into effect on July 1), a gunman wounded six people and killed himself at a FedEx facility in Kennesaw, Georgia. Three weeks after the law passed, Paine College in Augusta, Georgia, saw two separate shooting incidents in two days.

The pattern in these cases is probably clear. In each case, plaintiffs generally target new or existing gun laws and claim they violate the gun rights enshrined by the *McDonald* case. The opposition (often state and local governments) points to the restrictions and the "long-standing prohibitions" allowed by *McDonald* and claims that those laws are sensible and defensible. In the end, judges and juries must weigh the burden a law imposes on gun owners against the gains in public safety conferred by the same law. The balancing is never objective, consistent, or easy.

Over seventy cases since *Heller* have percolated up through the courts and arrived on the doorstep of the Supreme Court, where the justices have chosen not to hear them. In early 2014, the Supreme Court received a petition for arguably the most significant firearms case since *McDonald*. *Drake v. Jerejian*, which originated in New Jersey, asked the high court to extend the *Heller* and *McDonald* decisions to possession outside the home. If successful, this case would have essentially vitiated may-issue permits, declaring that "justifiable need" cannot be a condition for issuing a concealed-carry permit: authorities would have to issue concealed-carry permits to anyone who met minimal requirements, such as training and background checks. On May 5, 2014, the justices denied the petition, and state laws on public carry were left intact—at least for a while.

Finally, one curious case did reach the Supreme Court in 2014. Its outcome is significant because it calls into question the procedures for purchasing fire-arms and, specifically, the meaning of a straw purchase. Bruce Abramski, a former Virginia police officer, purchased a handgun in 2009 from a licensed dealer. On his 4473 form, Abramski answered *Yes*, he was the actual buyer of the gun. Soon thereafter, he sold the gun, through a licensed dealer using a background check, to his uncle for $400. Subsequently, Abramski was arrested on unrelated charges, and that arrest led to his conviction for falsify-ing the federal 4473 paperwork. An appeals court upheld the conviction and the case reached the Supreme Court in January 2014.

Abramski claimed that because he and his uncle were legally eligible to own guns, the sale was legal. In oral arguments, the justices debated Con-gress's intent in enacting the Gun Control Act of 1967, which governs fire-arm purchases. Does it prohibit all sales of a firearm after the original sale? Surely not; otherwise there could be no used gun sales. If not, then what restrictions, if any, does the law impose on subsequent transfers? For exam-ple, must the original buyer wait, say, one year before selling a gun? Does the law apply only to the initial buyer prohibiting him from making a straw purchase? Does it allow Al Capone (as one justice asked) to be the recipient of a straw purchase? In June 2014, a 5–4 majority upheld the conviction, citing the critical importance of background check information in curb-ing gun trafficking. Justice Elena Kagan wrote for the majority, saying that accurate information about the gun buyer "is fundamental to the lawfulness of a gun sale."[43]

The Supreme Court's dance on a knife-edge will undoubtedly continue as it declines to hear some gun cases and rules narrowly in the few cases it chooses to hear. In December 2015, a ban on the sale and ownership of assault weapons and high-capacity magazines in Highland Park, Illinois, reached the doorstep of the high court. With only four votes needed for the court to hear the case, it was denied 7–2. The minority, Justices Scalia and Thomas, claimed the lower court's upholding of the ban "flouted" the *Heller* and *McDonald* decisions.[44] Their colleagues apparently had a different opinion, prompting constitutional-law scholar Adam Winkler to wonder whether "the Supreme Court is having second thoughts about the Second Amendment."[45]

And so ended a year in America's gun life. A school shooting—more hor-rendous than all others—wrenched the nation from a complacent stupor, kicked legions of pro- and anti-gun advocates into high gear, propelled Congress and state legislatures into a flame-throwing year of legislation, tied court dockets in knots, and caused an unprecedented outpouring of money. Both sides could claim victories and both sides saw defeats. In the end, the fine grain of the gun policy landscape may have shifted, but on average, it looked much as it did at the beginning of the year.

18 | REDUCING GUN VIOLENCE

Progress is impossible without change,
and those who cannot change their minds cannot change anything.

—GEORGE BERNARD SHAW

THE PRECEDING CHAPTERS of this book are intended to provide the foundation needed to bridge the breach in today's gun debate: an understanding of the history of the Second Amendment, the laws and court cases it has bred, and a familiarity with America's complex gun culture. Without that bridge a meaningful dialogue—whether it is between advocacy groups, neighbors, or legislators—is impossible.

The daily toll of gun violence and the relentless recurrence of public shootings have focused our attention on a national crisis. But despite the magnitude of that crisis, we seem incapable of change. What did we learn from an event like Sandy Hook? And what action did we take to counter gun violence after Sandy Hook? And if we do not learn and act after Sandy Hook—or Columbine, Aurora, Tucson, or many others—what will it take to lead us to a cure for gun violence?

One answer is that nothing needs to be done, except to stay the course and avoid backsliding into stricter gun control. After all, Chicago's 900 gun homicides in 1994 dropped to 390 in 2014. Crime rates across the country saw a similar decline over the same period. Nonfatal firearm victims are one-third of what they were in the mid-1990s.[1] Such trends are proof—so this particular argument goes—that armed citizens and permissive gun laws deter crime and reduce gun violence. The gun laws already on the books are adequate; we just need to enforce those laws. The occasional mass killings that briefly gain national attention represent a small fraction of all gun deaths; they are the price we pay to exercise our rights. America is unique because of the abundant personal liberties its citizens enjoy today. Let us keep it that way.

However, many Americans believe the status quo is not acceptable. Many compare US gun violence rates to those in other countries and are puzzled or embarrassed. Many think that the death of one child by gunfire is one too many. A society in which armed guards protect schools or in which vulnerable people must carry guns to feel safe is not the America they envision. Cherished liberties must be balanced with law and order.

If there is a road between these two polar positions, it will surely be paved with compromises. And to have any impact, those compromises must be politically realistic (enactable as laws), enforceable (leading to arrests and prosecutions), and effective (resulting in reduction of gun violence). For example, the proposed 2013 federal assault-weapon bill was not politically realistic. It had great symbolic meaning as legislators attempted to respond to the Sandy Hook tragedy, but it did not take a political clairvoyant to see that it had little chance of becoming law. Existing laws mandating safe storage and childproofing of firearms have undoubtedly reduced tragic accidents, but they are difficult to enforce—until it is too late.

What follows is a list of several proposals for reducing gun violence that are realistic, enforceable, and effective. They are realistic in the sense that they could become laws without significant concessions by reasonable people who are serious about reducing gun violence. And, if enacted and enforced, these measures would effectively reduce gun violence.

Common Sense and Compromise

John Dingell is a former Democratic congressman from Michigan, the longest-serving member of Congress (continuously from 1955 to 2015), a longtime NRA member with an A+ rating, and a proponent of lenient gun laws. James Baker is a distinguished Republican from Texas and a former secretary of state and treasury. Despite their political differences, Baker and Dingell have a "strong love of guns." They are lifelong hunters and devout supporters of robust individual Second Amendment rights. After the Sandy Hook tragedy, they offered some thoughts on gun violence in a joint letter to the *New York Times*. The letter was a plea for legislators and citizens alike to adjust their perspectives and summon a new tolerance for differing viewpoints. They write:

Common sense should prevail. We must get away from a mind-set that has owners of firearms worried that "they are going to take our guns away." The Second Amendment guarantees that won't happen.[2]

In other words, gun rights advocates who fear losing their guns to ATF marauders need a reality adjustment. In addition to the Second Amendment, they have recent Supreme Court decisions to protect their rights. In all the future Americas one might imagine, government-enforced mass disarmament is not a part of any of them. At the same time, gun control advocates who dream of a gun-free America must confront their own illusions. As much as some would like to live in country cleansed of its three hundred million guns, it is unrealistic. Congress and state legislatures will ban baseball as a national pastime before it passes universal gun confiscation laws.

For the foreseeable future, Americans will be divided on gun ownership, on their need for guns, and on their opinions of gun laws. Combine those countermanding public pressures with the glacial churning of the legislative process and the mired turning of judicial wheels, and neither a gun-free society—at one extreme—nor a lawless country flooded with guns—at the other extreme—is likely. The system has enough inertia to ensure that we are far more likely to regress to the mean than to find the extremes.

Adam Winkler, an objective gun author and constitutional-law scholar, calls for "ratcheting down emotions" plus a dose of realism. It is time "to move beyond disarmament and to recognize the permanence of guns in America. . . . The guns are here to stay."[3] Taming passions is also emphasized by gun control advocate Robert Walker, who observes that "When it comes to guns, our individual choices, as well as public policy, should be guided by the evidence, not by our emotions."[4]

The media must be part of the solution as well. As legal scholar David Kopel observes, "A fairer and less biased media would help . . . reduce the emotional temperature." When the media "claim that semiautomatic rifles are only good for mass murder, and when they maximize coverage of atrocious gun crimes (relegating self-defense stories to, at most, local papers), the people who only know guns via media become very angry that anyone could oppose gun control. At the same time, media demonization has the demonstrated effect of driving ever-increasing numbers of gun owners into membership in the National Rifle Association."[5]

Progress will be made only when we bring the sidelines of the playing field back within sight of each other and work on realistic and effective measures. There is no place for either fantasies (a world without guns) or conspiracy theories (Sandy Hook was a government plot). Progress will be made only when all sides embrace compromise and when legislators listen to their constituents and resist the venal temptations of lobbyists. Progress will be made only when emotions are supervised by reason, when careless statistics are treated with caution, when we abandon false and deeply rooted stereotypes, and when we all make genuine attempts to understand opposing points of view.

Categories of Gun Violence

Gun violence is usually associated with highly publicized mass shootings. However, these tragic events account for a negligible number of firearm deaths and injuries. To focus our efforts properly, it is helpful to recall how the toll of gun violence actually occurs. Here is a general breakdown of annual firearm deaths, representative of several recent years:

- Of the approximately thirty-three thousand annual firearm deaths, 63 percent are due to suicide. Fifty-one percent of all suicides are committed with guns and 85 percent of gun suicide attempts are successful.[6]
- Accidents account for about 3 percent of firearm deaths.[7]
- Setting aside a small number of justifiable homicides, the remaining roughly one-third of firearm deaths are homicides.
- Of the firearm homicides, about 15 percent were committed in the course of a felony, 47 percent were non-felony-related, and 38 percent were of unknown cause.[8]
- About 55 percent of the non-felony-related homicides are due to arguments.[9]
- The FBI attributes only 673 homicides per year to gang activity—a figure far below many estimates. A significant percentage of the homicides in the "unknown" category also have gang- and drug-related causes.[10]

Of these figures, the one that first rivets the attention is the suicide rate. A reduction in gun suicides, through enhanced prevention, intervention, and mental-illness and gun safety programs would have a significant impact on gun violence.

Gang violence is a heavy contributor to overall gun violence. And gun trafficking is the pathway that feeds guns to gangs. More effective enforcement of gun-trafficking laws and the strengthening of proven gang-intervention initiatives (such as the programs of the Office of Juvenile Justice and Delinquency Prevention and the National Crime Prevention Council) are essential components of a comprehensive gun violence reduction campaign.[11]

Perhaps the most elusive source of gun violence is non-felony-related "social" violence, some of which takes place between family members and acquaintances. The homicides in this category have systemic social roots that are manifested in violent behavior. And when guns are nearby, violent behavior can turn deadly. Gun researchers Philip Cook and Kristin Goss point out how obvious the problem is and how extensive the solutions must be:

> Without a doubt, then, one strategy for reducing gun violence is to reduce criminal violence generally. If we would take steps to reduce alcohol and drug abuse, offer better treatment for mental illness, reduce school dropout rates, and deploy police resources more strategically, crime rates would fall further and guns would be of correspondingly less concern.[12]

Guns are not the sole cause of gun violence. Clearly, there are deeper, endemic causes that can be addressed only through comprehensive social, economic, and educational strategies.

Gun Safety

Gun rights activists acknowledge that rights come with responsibilities and many pro-gun groups foster a greater awareness of best practices in gun safety. Chris Stone of Gun Owners of America believes that "promoting a culture of responsible and safe gun ownership" is one of the top three remedies for gun violence.[13] He notes that the NRA and National Association for Gun Rights have similar goals. The NRA launched its Eddie Eagle GunSafe Program in 1988 to teach under-eight-year-olds the steps to take when finding a gun. It has reached some twenty-five million children through curriculum materials and DVDs. With a network of nearly one hundred thousand certified instructors, the NRA also offers gun safety courses to gun owners. Cynics may claim that youth programs serve only to recruit lifelong followers, but to the extent that they instill gun safety, they should be encouraged.

Robert Spitzer, an objective scholar of gun issues, and hardly a firebrand, cited "launching a campaign to advocate gun safety—safety in storage, use, and training—emphasizing that guns are dangerous and need to be treated with care by owners" as one of his top three gun violence remedies.[14] With a slightly different emphasis, gun rights attorney and scholar Stephen Halbrook lists in his top three remedies "promotion of community-based, voluntary training programs for safe and appropriate use of firearms for self defense."[15]

Ardent gun control adepts may find gun safety programs a gratuitous solution—and one that would be unnecessary in a country without guns. But it is not a gun-free world, so gun safety programs should be supported, strengthened, and promoted. Opposing them is like protesting guardrails on mountain highways.

Violence in the Media

Is there something in the American way of life—perhaps inherited from past generations or perhaps a byproduct of technological growth—that explains an affinity for firearms? One often-cited theory is the impact of violence in the media: video games, films, television, and social media. Opinions on guns, violence, and the media abound, and many come straight from the gut. Ralph Nader called the creators of violent video games "electronic child molesters."[16] Talking about video games, gun rights activist Tony Fabian observes that "we fostered a culture where . . . unnatural death is OK. . . . The decision to end human life is becoming an easy decision to make because there are no real perceived consequences."[17]

Targeting video games may seem like a diversion that takes the glare off guns and gun owners. Experts agree that the link between video games and violence is weak, if not missing altogether. The real question concerns video games and aggressive criminal behavior. A 2015 task force of the American Psychological Association found that, particularly among young adults, "The research demonstrates a consistent relation between violent video game use and increases in aggressive behavior, aggressive cognitions and aggressive affect," although the link between violent video games and criminal violence has yet to be established.[18] However, an open letter to the task force from over two hundred academics pointed out that, "during the video game epoch, youth violence in the United States and elsewhere has plummeted to 40-year lows."[19]

Without wading too deeply into the video game argument, here are two expert opinions that are miles apart. Brad Bushman, a social psychologist at Ohio State University, is a major contributor to the theory of a positive link between media and aggression. He sums it up as follows:

> On average, the research shows that exposure to violent video games increases aggressive thoughts, it increases angry feelings, it increases physiological arousal such as heart rate and blood pressure, which may explain why it also increases aggressive behavior. . . . It decreases helping behavior and it decreases feelings of empathy for others and the effects occur for males and females regardless of their age and regardless of where they live in the world.[20]

On a distant shore, psychologist Chris Ferguson at Stetson University claims:

> I think anybody who tells you that there's any kind of consistency to the aggression research is lying to you. There's no consistency in the aggression literature, and my impression is that at this point it is not strong enough to draw any kind of causal, or even really correlational links between video game violence and aggression, no matter how weakly we may define aggression.[21]

Ferguson added that the debate "has been very acrimonious and controversial, . . . particularly given the role of some moral crusading that creeps into it and rather distorts the science."[22]

And then there are the data. US sales of video games have soared in the last two decades, while violent-crime rates have declined steadily. And countries that have higher per capita spending on video games than America (Japan, South Korea, and the Netherlands) also have orders of magnitude lower rates of gun violence.[23] The most we can conclude is that more research is needed to deepen our understanding of the links—if any—between violence in the media and aggressive behavior. Without solid research to gain that understanding, passing new laws seems premature.

Expanding Background Checks

Choose your analogy. In airport security lines, it is not the case that one-third of travelers are allowed to bypass screening. At highway tollbooths, one-third of motorists are not given a free pass. Liquor stores do not allow one-third of underage patrons to purchase alcohol without showing an ID. The analogies may not be perfect, but they indicate the illogic and fundamental inequity of the current system of firearm background checks in which roughly (estimates vary) one-third of gun sales are not accompanied by a background check.

Those who oppose extending background checks, or favor eliminating them altogether, resort to familiar arguments: criminals do not obey the law, criminals find guns through nonregulated sources, and background checks only inconvenience legal buyers. Opponents also point to the impracticality of universal background checks, claiming that regulating Internet and private sales is impossible.

Those who support extending background checks—and it is a significant majority according to polls—point to NICS background-check data. The system has resulted in roughly eighty thousand annual denials. Many of those denials resulted in a terminated sale to a prohibited buyer. Extending background checks to gun show, Internet, and private sales can only increase the number of denials. And every sale denied to a dangerous owner is a potential disaster averted.

Lack of compliance is a monstrous problem with background checks in private transfers. Both parties must be willing to visit a licensed dealer and submit the required paperwork. However, laws are never passed with the expectation of complete compliance. Speed limits are routinely exceeded, people jaywalk, and petty thefts plague plenty of business owners. Total obedience is never the outcome of making laws. Rather, laws are directed at both abiders and non-abiders. Through enforcement, they ensnare non-abiders and levy penalties for threatening public safety. Equally important, laws set expectations for conduct that law-abiders respect.

Libertarian attorney Robert Levy was an architect of the *Heller* Supreme Court case that reversed the Washington, DC, handgun ban. He had an unexpected reaction to the failed 2013 federal background check (Manchin-Toomey) bill. He wrote, "Stonewalling the [bill] was a mistake, both politically and substantively." With reasonable modifications, he felt the bill was viable.

> Gun-rights supporters should not stand in the way of reasonable reform. The Manchin-Toomey proposal, with the changes I've suggested, would offer substantial benefits while imposing tolerable restrictions, none of which intrude on our core Second Amendment liberties. Gun-rights advocates should get behind it and push for its passage.[24]

By contrast, John Lott, an influential analyst of crime and firearm data and a supporter of more lenient gun laws, had a different opinion of background checks. He opposes extending the current system and would rather see the current system fixed. Because "there is a crime-reducing benefit to background checks, it . . . should be paid for out of general revenue." Furthermore, Lott's dissection of recent data shows that anywhere between 94 and 99 percent of the denials issued by the current system are false positives.[25] These erroneous denials combined with delays in processing background checks lead to inconvenience for gun buyers.

Other gun rights experts criticize background checks as an infringement on personal rights and an irreversible step in the wrong direction. Despite explicit language in state and federal laws that prohibits the creation of databases, some gun rights groups fearfully insist that background checks will lead to a federal registry. Chris Stone of Gun Owners of America believes that the first step in reducing gun violence is getting rid of "unconstitutional gun control measures that . . . prevent people who are law-abiding citizens from free access to firearms."[26] Similarly, the NRA, which once supported background checks at gun shows, now opposes any extension of background checks until the current system is fixed.

> The NRA opposes criminalizing private firearms transfers between law-abiding individuals, and therefore opposes an expansion of the background check system. . . . The NRA supports meaningful efforts to address the problems of violent crime and mass violence in America, through swift and certain prosecution of violent criminals; securing our schools; and fixing our broken mental health system.[27]

Clearly, we are far from consensus on background checks. However, more encompassing laws and better enforcement on background checks make sense and are fundamentally fair. By filtering even a small percentage of prohibited buyers, stronger laws can have an impact on gun violence. However, given the experience of 2013, a federal law for universal background checks is unlikely in the near future. Fortunately, the states have invented various ways to tighten the current federal law on background checks. Eleven states now require background checks at gun shows. With variations, nine states require that background checks for all gun transactions be done through a licensed dealer. Eight states require purchasers to have a permit before completing any transfer. If the states continue to pass laws regulating gun show, private, and Internet sales, then federally mandated universal background checks—a measure supported by a large majority of gun owners and non-owners alike—may not be necessary.

Finally, a new and astounding loophole came to light in 2015 when it was discovered that the federal terrorist watch lists are not linked to the background check system for guns; that is, a suspected terrorist might not necessarily show up as a prohibited buyer in a background check. Congressional Republicans defeated bills that would close the terror list loophole in December 2015. Governor Dannel Malloy of Connecticut announced that he would sign an executive order banning such sales in his state.[28] Could there be a more persuasive appeal to common sense?

When it comes to airport security lines, renewing a driver's license, and slowing down in school zones, most people understand that safety and social order take priority. These practices may be momentarily inconvenient, but they do not represent a meaningful loss of personal freedom. It is time that legislators listen to their constituents and apply the same attitude to background checks, mandatory gun safety classes, and other fleeting "annoyances" that would reduce gun violence.

Mental Illness

Chapter 15 describes the challenges of reconciling mental illness with the availability of firearms. Given these realities, what policies or laws might keep potentially dangerous people with mental illness away from guns? For many experts on both sides of the debate, improving the reporting of mental-illness records to the NICS database is near the top of their list of remedies for gun violence. Furthermore, there is no dearth of ideas about how to do it.

David Kopel observed that the number of mass shootings has not changed in the past thirty years. However, the number of *random* mass shootings has increased, and he attributes the increase to media glorification of mass killers and the deinstitutionalization of people with mental illness. Like many gun rights advocates, he scorns new laws that restrict access to guns by law-abiding (and presumably mentally sound) gun owners.

> People who are serious about preventing the next Newtown should embrace much greater funding for mental health and strong laws for the civil commitment of the violently mentally ill.[29]

Gun rights groups steadfastly oppose record-keeping of gun purchases. But when it comes to mental illness, the NRA makes an exception, calling for "an active national database of the mentally ill," provided it is up-to-date and accurate.[30] It should not deprive recovered patients or people with outdated mental-illness diagnoses of their gun rights. And by all means, it must not overreach and ensnare mentally sound gun owners.

Another voice arises from mental health-care professionals, who emphasize the rights and dignity of people with mental illness. Mental-health gun policies carry the risk of unfairly targeting people with a history of mental illness, and the resulting stigma may deter them from seeking treatment. The National Alliance on Mental Illness (NAMI) notes that "gun violence is overwhelmingly committed by people without mental illness." The organization's recommendation on gun violence calls for "reasonable, effective, consistently and fairly applied firearms regulation and safety as well as widespread availability of mental health crisis intervention, assistance and appropriate treatment."[31] Said more concisely, guns should not be easier to obtain than mental-health care. Combining that sweeping goal with the condition that "in the absence of demonstrated risk, people should not be treated differently with respect to firearms regulation because of their lived experience with mental illness"[32] is a challenging agenda.

Despite legislative setbacks in 2013, the Obama administration pressed ahead with executive orders that could bring NAMI's ideal world nearer. Under these orders, the Department of Justice was authorized to award $27 million to forty-two states to help them improve reporting to the NICS system. Obama also issued executive orders to clarify language in the Gun Control Act so that "committed to a mental institution" includes outpatient treatment and to relax HIPAA rules to allow states more complete reporting of mental-health records.

Gun violence committed by people with severe mental illness has focused attention on a much larger public-health crisis. As a result, there is broad support for programs that address the deficiencies of mental-health care in this country. If increased funding for these programs becomes an imperative at the federal and state levels, we can hope for a double victory: overall improvement in the care of people with mental illness and a strike against gun violence.

Research on Gun Violence

Many of the reasons for America's greatness originate with its formidable and unmatched ethos of research, innovation, and technological development. Scientists and engineers, working in universities, government institutions, and private laboratories transform basic research into manufactured solutions that improve everyday life around the world. Because of this vast enterprise, we have new drugs that relieve pain and eradicate diseases, more efficient and safer automobiles and airliners, and generation-jumping electronic devices and computer networks that have changed everyday life. America has a world-dominating tradition of discovery and innovation that answers questions and solves problems. The care and feeding of this scientific-health-engineering complex consumes about $400 billion per year, or nearly 3 percent of the gross domestic product. Of this total, $140 billion comes from federally funded programs[33] and the rest from the private and business sectors.[34]

Despite America's remarkable tradition of research and development, a startling vacuum exists when it comes to federally funded research on firearm violence. For decades, gun rights organizations have questioned the uses of research related to firearms, partly in the belief that it might lead to stiffer gun control policies. By contrast, for criminology, psychology, public-policy, and public-health researchers, who typically work in colleges, universities, and other think tanks, such investigations are both legitimate and desperately needed. Greater understanding of gun violence requires communication among these disciplines, which federal funding could facilitate.

The starvation of public funding for research on gun violence began in 1996, after the House-cleaning of congressional Democrats. The newly elected wave of conservative lawmakers in the House of Representative managed to cut the budget for firearm-related research in the National Center for Injury Prevention and Control (within the Centers for Disease Control and Prevention) by $2.6 million—exactly the amount that had been spent on such research the previous year. The defunding legislation carried the warning that "none of the funds made available for injury prevention and control at the Centers for Disease Control and Prevention may be used to advocate or promote gun control."[35] Arthur Kellerman, who received federal funds for research on gun violence prior to 1996, noted that "no federal employee was willing to risk his or her career and the agency's funding to find out" the meaning of that warning. He added that deaths from automobile accidents, fires, and drowning have been reduced over the last twenty years "without banning automobiles, swimming pools, or matches. Instead it came from translating research into effective interventions."[36]

CDC funding for such research currently stands at $100,000 out of a total budget of $6 billion. The guidelines for CDC-funded research state specifically:

> In addition to the restrictions in the Anti-Lobbying Act, CDC interprets the language in the CDC's Appropriations Act to mean that CDC's funds may not be spent on political action or other activities designed to affect the passage of specific Federal, State, or local legislation intended to restrict or control the purchase or use of firearms.[37]

Similar budget cuts and admonitions have been levied in other agencies that sponsor gun-related research. In recent years, the National Institutes of Health (NIH) has allocated about $1 million annually for firearms-related research out of a $31 billion budget.

The NRA has been accused of orchestrating the precipitous declines in funding.[38] The organization responded that it was only trying to separate politics and scientific research. Chief NRA lobbyist Chris Cox explained, "our concern is not with legitimate medical science. Our concern is they were promoting the idea that gun ownership was a disease that needed to be eradicated."[39]

Representative Jay Dickey of Arkansas was the "NRA's point person in Congress" and introduced the 1996 appropriations amendment that cut funding for gun violence research. Mark Rosenberg was director of the National Center for Injury Prevention and Control at that time. Once "on opposite sides of a heated battle," this odd couple wrote a powerful *Washington Post* editorial in 2012 recommending an increase in federal funding for firearm-related research. Their title says it all: "We Won't Know the Cause of Gun Violence until We Look for It." Noting that the $240 million spent on traffic-safety research since 1996 has saved hundreds of thousands of lives, they lament that there has been virtually "no publicly funded research on firearm injuries." They agree that "ways to prevent firearm deaths can be found without encroaching on the rights of legitimate gun owners."[40]

More recently, there have been signs of a thaw in the funding freeze. One of President Obama's January 2013 executive orders called for increased funding for firearms-related research. By the end of that summer, the National Institutes of Health announced it was "opening funding opportunities" for research on "violence with a particular focus on firearm violence."[41] The level of funding was unspecified.

Also in response to Obama's executive orders, the CDC, the Institute of Medicine, and the National Research Council—a high-wattage collection of research institutions—convened a panel of experts to identify research priorities related to gun violence, gun safety, risks and interventions, and the influence of video games and the media. Within months, the committee released its report spelling out key research questions. The report accurately claims that the current state of knowledge on gun violence is inconclusive and plagued by bad data. In summarizing past research, the report observes:

> Studies that directly assessed the effect of actual defensive uses of guns
> have found consistently lower injury rates among gun-using crime
> victims compared with victims who used other self-protective strategies.
> Effectiveness of defensive tactics, however, is likely to vary across types

of victims, types of offenders, and circumstances of the crime, so further research is needed both to explore these contingencies and to confirm or discount earlier findings.[42]

Such observations give the report a balanced tone that should belie claims that the committee is a gun control whitewash.

If Dickey and Rosenberg can find agreement on funding for firearm violence research, there is hope that rival political groups can also find common ground. We need to understand the connections (or lack of) between violence, on one hand, and mental illness, media, and music, on the other. We need to find better predictors of violent behavior, with and without guns. A mountain of policy analysis needs to be done to assess the usefulness of existing laws, to repeal those that are ineffective, and to implement laws that have a better chance of reducing gun violence. We need to understand the circulation of illegal guns and find better ways to enforce trafficking laws. And we should strive for technological advances that improve gun safety. Federally funded, peer-reviewed, politically agnostic research can shed light on these and other critical questions. The nation has the tools needed to answer such questions and it is entirely within its tradition to do so.

Enforce Existing Laws

Both sides of the gun debate agree that enhanced law enforcement and stiffer penalties for gun crimes are needed. But as we have seen, implementing these consensus recommendations is difficult. Perhaps the biggest target for more aggressive law enforcement is gun trafficking: the diversion of legal guns into illegal arenas. It is often said that no federal law explicitly addresses gun trafficking. However, there are federal laws whose violation certainly implies trafficking. For example, a straw purchase generally requires falsifying a federal 4473 form during a background check, which is a federal crime (statutory maximum sentence of ten years). Knowingly selling or transferring guns to a felon, fugitive from justice, drug abuser, undocumented immigrant, juvenile, or someone convicted of domestic violence is a federal offense (statutory maximum sentence of ten years). In most situations, it is illegal for an unlicensed person to sell a gun to someone from another state or for an unlicensed resident of one state to buy a gun in another state. Obliterating or altering serial numbers on guns, stealing guns, and knowingly selling a stolen gun are federal crimes that point to trafficking. So federal laws exist, which, when enforced, will reduce gun trafficking.

The following snapshot illustrates the track record of the ATF and the justice system in enforcing federal gun laws. According to the Department of Justice, approximately seventy-six thousand firearm sales were rejected through the NICS system in 2010; nearly half were because of a prior felony indictment or conviction. Of those rejections, a mere 62 cases were referred for prosecution (down from 273 in 2006). Of the 62 referred cases, 44 cases were actually prosecuted (down from 174 in 2006), and 13 of those 44 cases resulted in a guilty plea or verdict (down from 73 in 2006).[43] Even counting the federal cases that were referred to the states for prosecution, the number of cases that ultimately led to a conviction was stunningly small compared to the number of denials. Critics claim that there is room for improvement in bringing law-breakers from arrest to conviction. They seem to have good evidence.

Existing federal laws are often difficult to enforce because of loopholes or vague language. For example, the sharp end of the federal firearms code opens with the statement, "It shall be unlawful for any person except a licensed importer, licensed manufacturer, or licensed dealer, to engage in the business of importing, manufacturing, or dealing in firearms."[44] No court has adequately defined *in the business of*. How many gun sales does it take to be *in the business of*? The same firearm code uses the language "knows or has a reasonable cause to believe" five times in describing prohibited buyers and illegal transactions. It has been difficult for prosecutors to argue that a dealer had *a reasonable cause to believe* that he was breaking the law.

Because of the ambiguity and opacity in current laws, there is renewed support for federal laws that specifically and clearly address gun trafficking. A survey by the Police Executive Research Forum found that 96 percent of law-enforcement officers polled favored establishing a federal crime for gun trafficking and straw purchases.[45] In the past two years, federal lawmakers have introduced bills and advocates have proposed bills that clarify and tighten the meaning of a straw purchase; that increase the maximum penalty for a straw purchase; that strengthen penalties for private sales to prohibited buyers; that increase penalties for illegal sales of two or more guns (gun running) and for selling guns into a known chain of illegal gun transfers; and that ban exporting of guns. To date, no federal legislation has resulted from these attempts.[46]

Independent of whether new laws are passed or old laws are amended, there is an urgent need to fortify federal law–enforcement resources. Groups that call for more potent enforcement of gun laws must also work for policies and appropriations that enable that enforcement. The ATF is a cornerstone of federal law enforcement in this country. With its spotted past, the bureau may need to be reconfigured, reinvented, merged, or renamed. It is time to give the law-enforcement enterprise the tools, staff, and budget needed to do the job well.

Two Futures

In the last two centuries, events have occurred, which, at the time, seemed like watersheds in America's history of guns. For example, the ratification of the Fourteenth Amendment, the first federal firearms laws in the 1930s, the Gun Control and Brady Acts, and the *Heller* and *McDonald* Supreme Court decisions appeared to be turning points—events that could finally settle the disputes over firearm policies and lead to closure. In retrospect, we see them more accurately not as conclusions but as chapter breaks in a longer story. It is worth speculating about where that longer story might end.

America has two possible and different futures with respect to guns. The first future is more likely, while the second is more desirable. The first future continues our history of dealing with symptoms. The second confronts the causes of gun violence and seeks cures.

The first future should feel familiar because it is more of the same reality we have come to know. In this future, some people will continue living fearfully in a society they find somewhat uncivilized and they will continue campaigning to restrict guns on the streets, in the media, and hidden under coats. In this first future, there will also be some people raised on a strong diet of self-reliance and personal liberty, who find restrictive gun laws intrusive, unconstitutional, and anathema to their idea of a free society. They will continue to contribute money and write lawmakers to repeal unwanted laws.

In this future, the inexorable tension between these two views will continue twisting the fibers of our society, as it has done for several decades.

282 | CHAPTER 18

There will be occasional tempests but no major changes in climate. We can expect an occasional jolt from a public tragedy or school shooting that will re-energize the opposing forces in the gun debate. Those forces will clash in courtrooms, in the media, in state houses, and in town halls. There will be minor gains and losses on both sides, and plenty of compromise, but the tense equilibrium that exists today will continue. In this future, guns will continue to define America's character as a nation.

To explain the second future, we must recall that the most frequently cited single reason for gun ownership in America is self-defense (48 percent of respondents in a 2013 poll, up from 26 percent in 1999).[47] And then we must imagine a society in which that gut-felt need to be armed for protection no longer exists—a society in which the many contributors to gun violence have been overcome. This society would be one in which

- no person—because of gender, sexual orientation, age, or poverty—feels threatened by violence or exploitation;
- fear does not prevent ordinary people from pursuing socially acceptable activities, such as living and walking alone in the neighborhood of their choice;
- individuals balance personal gain and private liberties with a broader commitment to community and common well-being;
- we have closed the chasms of inequality in education, wealth, and opportunity;
- we understand that being an American citizen is not a right without obligations; rather, it is a stroke of fortune and a privilege that carries fundamental responsibilities;
- elections are not sold to the highest bidder but are determined by a truly one-person-one-vote system;
- the federal government respects the boundaries beyond which unwarranted intrusion into the lives of private citizens is forbidden; and
- political, religious, and business leaders share the vision of such a society and work with civility and forbearance to achieve it.

This second future is not gun free. Hunters, trapshooters, cowboy action enthusiasts, competitive marksmen, ranchers, and collectors would still own firearms and register them, use them in safe surroundings, and carry and store them securely. But it is also a society in which Americans who own guns primarily for self-defense would no longer feel the need to do so. This disarmament of self-defenders would occur voluntarily because of fundamental changes in shared values.

Americans have made equally bedrock transformations before. In its lifetime, this country has seen fundamental social and political change with respect to women's suffrage, civil rights, and same-sex marriage. It will take an equally profound transformation to take us to the second future and agree on effective solutions to gun violence.

Protagonists as well as citizens in the gun debate might find guidance from the recent transpartisan movement, which is devoted to getting beyond the acrid and divisive politics that currently debilitates American public discourse. In a few words, the movement's principles involve at least temporarily suspending one's personal entrenched positions; listening to adversaries and learning about opposing positions; supporting leaders who are open-minded critical thinkers, not beholden to special interests and money; and valuing compromise solutions over absolute victories.[48] These attitudes are enormously relevant to the gun debate.

In a recent opinion piece, Arthur Brooks, president of the conservative American Enterprise Institute, laments the worsening, polarized state of political discourse in this country. In observations relevant to the gun divide, he notes that opposing sides no longer view each other with mere anger but rather with contempt: a "rejection and social exclusion in both the short and long term" that leads to "permanent enmity." Brooks sought advice from the Dalai Lama, "one of the world's experts in bringing people together." His Holiness makes two points. First, do not look to political parties or institutions to initiate change. Change begins with individuals. And second, individuals instigate change by renouncing bitterness and "aspiring to what the Dalai Lama calls 'warmheartedness' toward those with whom we disagree." In His Holiness's words, "I defeat my enemies when I make them my friends." Brooks claims this outlook is not flimsy new-age pabulum but "actually tough and practical advice. . . . Our duty is to be respectful, fair, and friendly to all, even those with whom we have great differences."[49]

It is impossible to predict which of the two gun futures will prevail, say, twenty years from now. What might make the second future possible, rather than the first future inevitable? Scientists talk of phase transitions; others call them tipping points. Could there be an event that might suddenly carry the gun debate into utterly different territory that offers a clear path to the second future? Or will our collective intransigence and attachment to unquestioned beliefs ensure that the first future—with its violence, fear, fact-free polemics, and broken dialogue—persists for years to come?

Regardless of which of these two futures emerges, we should keep sight of the unifying end, on which most of us *do* agree: the eradication of gun violence on our streets and in our homes. Reaching that goal requires a better understanding of guns and the different cultures that make up American society. And with that understanding must come a new spirit of compromise and tolerance. Hopefully, this book is a step in that direction.

Notes

Chapter 1

1. Piers Morgan, Twitter post, July 20, 2012, 4:45 a.m., https://twitter.com/piersmorgan.
2. Associated Press, "Gun Sale Background Checks Spike after Aurora," CBS News, September 19, 2012, http://www.cbsnews.com/news/gun-sale-background-checks-spike-after-aurora/.
3. Erich Pratt, "Colorado Shooting Shows the Failure of Gun Control Laws," US News & World Report, July 26, 2012, http://www.usnews.com/debate-club/does-the-colorado-shooting-prove-the-need-for-more-gun control-laws/colorado-shooting-shows-the-failure-of-gun control-laws.
4. *Piers Morgan Tonight*, CNN, July 23, 2012.
5. Michael Bender, "NRA Solicits Funds after Colorado Slayings," *Seattle Times*, August 7, 2012.
6. Barack Obama, Remarks by the President at the National Urban League Convention, New Orleans, LA, July 25, 2012, https://www.whitehouse.gov/the-press-office/2012/07/25/remarks-president-national-urban-league-convention.
7. Stacy Washington, interview by Cam Edwards, *Cam & Co*, NRA News, July 25, 2012, https://www.nranews.com/series/cam-and-company.
8. Bill Moyers, "Video Essay: Living Under the Gun," Moyers and Company, July 20, 2012, http://billmoyers.com/segment/bill-moyers-essay-living-under-the-gun/.
9. Dave Workman, "Cracking Down on Law-Abiding Gun Owners Won't Prevent Crime," US News & World Report, July 26, 2012, http://www.usnews.com/debate-club/does-the-colorado-shooting-prove-the-need-for-more-gun control-laws/cracking-down-on-law-abiding-gun-owners-wont-prevent-crimes.
10. Frank Lautenberg, news conference at City Hall, Manhattan, quoted in Laurie Ure, "Democrats Propose Limits on Online Ammo Sales," CNN Politics, July 20, 2012, http://www.cnn.com/2012/07/30/politics/democrats-ammo-sales/.
11. Antonin Scalia, Fox News interview with Chris Wallace, July 29, 2012, citing the majority opinion in District of Columbia v. Heller, 554 U.S. 570 (2008).
12. Centers for Disease Control and Prevention, Fatal Injury Reports, National and Regional, 1999–2014, http://www.cdc.gov/injury/wisqars/fatal_injury_reports.html.

13.   Ibid.

14.   Centers for Disease Control and Prevention, *Nonfatal Injury Reports, 2001–2014*, http://webappa.cdc.gov/sasweb/ncipc/nfirates2001.html.

15.   Philip J. Cook and Jens Ludwig, *Gun Violence: The Real Costs* (Oxford: Oxford University Press, 2000), quoted in Cook and Goss, *The Gun Debate*, 54.

16.   Estimates of defensive gun uses (DGUs) are discussed in chapter 5.

17.   Justin McCarthy, "More Than Six in 10 Americans Say Guns Make Homes Safer," Gallup Poll, November 7, 2014, http://www.gallup.com/poll/179213/six-americans-say-guns-homes-safer.aspx. Several other polls, including the General Social Survey (GSS), find similar figures and trends.

18.   "Overwhelming Support for No-Fly, No-Buy Gun Law, Quinnipiac University National Poll Finds; Support for Background Checks Tops 90 Percent Again," Quinnipiac University, https://www.qu.edu/news-and-events/quinnipiac-university-poll/national/release-detail?ReleaseID=2364. Other polls show similar results with support for stricter laws near 50 percent for the last decade. Polls prior to 2005 show higher levels of support (55–65 percent) for stricter gun laws.

19.   "Historical Trends: Guns," Gallup polls, October 12–15, 2014, and April 26–27, 1999, http://www.gallup.com/poll/1645/guns.aspx.

20.   "Historical Trends: Guns," Gallup polls, October 12–15, 2014, and August 29–September 5, 2000, http://www.gallup.com/poll/1645/guns.aspx.

21.   For a collection of polling results, see Polling Report's data at http://www.pollingreport.com/guns2.htm.

22.   Aaron Smith, "Obama's Re-election Drives Gun Sales," CNN Money, November 9, 2012, http://money.cnn.com/2012/11/09/news/economy/gun control-obama/. More recently, see Gregor Aisch and Josh Keller, "What Happens after Calls for New Gun Restrictions? Sales Go Up," *New York Times*, June 13, 2016, http://www.nytimes.com/interactive/2015/12/10/us/gun-sales-terrorism-obama-restrictions.html.

23.   Federal Bureau of Investigation, National Instant Criminal Background Check System, https://www.fbi.gov/services/cjis/nics.

24.   "Historical Trends: Guns," Gallup poll, December 19–22, 2012, http://www.gallup.com/poll/1645/guns.aspx.

25.   "Why Own a Gun? Protection Is Now Top Reason," Pew Research Center poll, March 12, 2013, http://www.people-press.org/2013/03/12/why-own-a-gun-protection-is-now-top-reason/.

26.   "Personal Safety Top Reason Americans Own Guns Today," Gallup poll, October 28, 2013, http://www.gallup.com/poll/165605/personal-safety-top-reason-americans-own-guns-today.aspx.

27.   "Beliefs about Sandy Hook Cover-Up, Coming Revolution Underlie Divide on Gun Control," Fairleigh-Dickinson University Public Mind poll, May 1, 2013, http://publicmind.fdu.edu/2013/guncontrol/.

28.   *Small Arms Survey 2007: Guns and the City*, Graduate Institute of International Studies in Geneva, Switzerland (Cambridge: Cambridge University Press, 2007), gives

the low end of this range. Dan Griffin claims the estimate of 310 million is low. Dan Griffin, "Gun Ownership by the Numbers," The Daily Caller, November 4, 2014, http://dailycaller.com/2014/11/04/gun-ownership-by-the-numbers/.

29. Lois Beckett, "Gun Inequality: US Study Charts Rise of Hardcore Super Owners," *Guardian*, September 16, 2016, https://www.theguardian.com/us-news/2016/sep/19/us-gun-ownership-survey.

30. International comparisons of gun and crime data are always tenuous. However, the conclusion with respect to gun ownership is clear. See comparative international data in *Small Arms Survey 2007: Guns and the City*, Graduate Institute of International Studies in Geneva, Switzerland (Cambridge: Cambridge University Press, 2007).

31. "The Demographics and Politics of Gun-Owning Households," Rich Morin, Pew Research Center, July 15, 2014.

32. Charlton Heston, "The Second Amendment: America's First Freedom," in Dizard, Muth, and Andrews, *Guns in America*, 199–206.

33. Roger McGrath, "A Tradition of Arms: Americans' Love Affair with Guns," *New American*, June 3, 2013, 34.

34. Winkler, *Gunfight*, 13.

35. Robert Dykstra, *The Cattle Towns* (New York: Alfred A. Knopf, 1968), quoted in Winkler, *Gunfight*, 165.

36. Larson, *Lethal Passage*, 39, 41.

37. Roth, *American Homicide*, 10.

38. U.S. Const. amend II.

39. Cornell, *A Well-Regulated Militia*.

40. In 2014, several psychiatric evaluations deemed Holmes competent to stand trial. On January 20, 2015, jury selection began with the goal of winnowing a pool of nine thousand to twelve jurors and twelve alternates. Three months later, the trial began: Holmes pled not guilty by reason of insanity and the prosecution announced it would seek the death penalty. In July, 2015, the jury rejected Holmes's insanity defense and found him guilty on all counts. Six weeks later, he received twelve life sentences plus 3,318 years in prison without parole. In May 2016, several survivors and victims' families filed a civil suit against the Cinemark theater company.

Chapter 2

1. The engraving is in the collection of the Gilder Lehrman Institute of American History in New York.

2. *Boston Gazette and Country Journal*, March 12, 1770. Reproduced in "Boston Massacre as Reported in the Boston Gazette," Boston Massacre Historical Society, http://www.bostonmassacre.net/gazette/.

3. The Quartering Act of 1765 was passed by the British Parliament to require colonial governments to provide quarters for British troops in barracks or, if necessary, public houses, inns, and livery stables. The Quartering Act of 1774 went further by allowing British troops to stay in private homes if necessary.

4.   *Boston Gazette*, March 12, 1770.

5.   Partial transcripts and depositions for the Boston Massacre trials have survived to this day and make fascinating reading. See "John Adams and the Boston Massacre Trial of 1770," Library of Congress Law Library, https://www.loc.gov/law/help/rare-books/john_adams.php, or "Boston Massacre Trials," University of Missouri Kansas City Law School, http://law2.umkc.edu/faculty/projects/ftrials/bostonmassacre/bostonmassacre.html.

6.   "Boston Massacre Trials," University of Missouri Kansas City Law School, http://law2.umkc.edu/faculty/projects/ftrials/bostonmassacre/bostonmassacre.html.

7.   "Summary of the Boston Massacre Trial," Boston Massacre Historical Society, http://www.bostonmassacre.net/trial/trial-summary4.htm.

8.   Adams, *Diary of John Adams, March 5, 1773*.

9.   Ibid.

10.   Ammerman, *In the Common Cause*.

11.   Samuel Adams, *Boston Gazette*, February 27, 1769. See "Right of Revolution," The Founders' Constitution, vol. 1, ch. 3, doc. 4, University of Chicago Press, http://press-pubs.uchicago.edu/founders/documents/v1ch3s4.html. Blackstone's analysis appears in his *Commentaries on the Laws of England*, first published in 1766.

12.   "Declaration and Resolves of the First Continental Congress, no. 7," October 14, 1774. See the Avalon Project, Yale Law School, http://avalon.law.yale.edu/18th_century/resolves.asp.

13.   "Edmund Burke, Speech on Conciliation with the Colonies," The Founders' Constitution, vol. 1, ch. 1, doc. 2, University of Chicago Press, http://press-pubs.uchicago.edu/founders/documents/v1ch1s2.html.

14.   Ralph Waldo Emerson, "Concord Hymn" (1836).

15.   In addition to seizing arms in Concord, the British were equally interested in capturing Samuel Adams and John Hancock, who were staying in Lexington. Revere rode from Boston to Lexington with William Dawes, recruiting as many as forty other riders along the way. On the ride from Lexington to Concord, the British captured Revere. Only Dawes reached Concord.

16.   Halbrook, *The Founders' Second Amendment*, 129.

17.   Ibid., 157.

18.   Quincy, *Observations on the Act of Parliament*, 39.

19.   Daniel Dulany, *Considerations on the Measures Carrying on with Respect to the British Colonies in North America* (London: R. Baldwin, 1774), 57, quoted in Halbrook, *The Founders' Second Amendment*, 50.

20.   Cornell, *A Well-Regulated Militia*, 13.

21.   Ibid., 12.

22.   Ibid., 2.

23.   George Washington to John Jay, 15 August 1786, National Archives, Founders Online, http://founders.archives.gov/GEWN-04-04-02-0199.

Chapter 3

1. Kahan and Braman, "More Statistics, Less Persuasion," 1294.
2. "Crime in the United States 2013," Federal Bureau of Investigation, Uniform Crime Reports, https://ucr.fbi.gov/crime-in-the-u.s/2013/crime-in-the-u.s.-2013/tables/1tabledatadecoverviewpdf/table_1_crime_in_the_united_states_by_volume_and_rate_per_100000_inhabitants_1994-2013.xls.
3. "Criminal Victimization 2012," Bureau of Justice Statistics, National Crime Victimization Survey, October 2013, http://www.bjs.gov/content/pub/pdf/cv12.pdf.
4. "National Vital Statistics Reports: Deaths: Final Data for 2013," Centers for Disease Control and Prevention, http://www.cdc.gov/nchs/data/nvsr/nvsr64/nvsr64_02.pdf.
5. "Crime in the United States 2013," Federal Bureau of Investigation, Uniform Crime Reports, https://ucr.fbi.gov/crime-in-the-u.s/2013/crime-in-the-u.s.-2013/tables/table-12/table_12_crime_trends_by_population_group_2012-2013.xls.
6. Small Arms Survey, *Small Arms Survey 2007: Guns and the City*, Graduate Institute of International Studies in Geneva, Switzerland (Cambridge: Cambridge University Press, 2007).
7. Dan Griffin, "Gun Ownership by the Numbers," The Daily Caller, November 4, 2014, http://dailycaller.com/2014/11/04/gun-ownership-by-the-numbers/.
8. Kleck and Gertz, "Armed Resistance to Crime."
9. Hemenway, "Survey Research and Self Defense Gun Use."
10. David Kopel, "The Fallacy of 43 to 1," Originally appeared in National Review Online, January 31, 2001. Now see Dave Kopel, http://davekopel.org/NRO/2001/The-Fallacy-of-43-to-1.htm.
11. Kellerman and Reay, "Protection or Peril?"
12. "Protect Children Not Guns Factsheet: 2014 Child Gun Deaths," Children's Defense Fund, December 2015, http://www.childrensdefense.org/library/data/2015-protectchildrennotgunsfactsheet.pdf, citing data from "About Underlying Cause of Death, 1999–2014," CDC WONDER Online Database, http://wonder.cdc.gov/ucd-icd10.html.
13. The child gun death toll cited in the first claim includes all teenagers. Some of those deaths are the result of gang wars or bad drug deals. Deaths for children under fourteen years of age are about 350 per year.
14. Mitt Romney, speaking at the second presidential debate at Hofstra University on October 16, 2012, was in error.
15. Except in about ten states that ban them, it is legal to purchase and own automatic weapons (such as machine guns). Buyers must pass a background check, which includes fingerprints and a photograph, and pay a one-time $200 transfer tax.
16. In addition to the UCR system and the NCVS, the FBI introduced the National Incident-Based Reporting System (NIBRS) in the mid-1980s. It collects detailed information about individual crimes from law enforcement agencies. Only 25 percent of agencies, mostly in small cities, file reports with NIBRS.

17. http://gss.norc.org.

18. Associated Press, "Grandma, 72, Shoots at Home Intruder in California, Defends Actions," Fox News, June 12, 2013, http://www.foxnews.com/us/2013/06/12/grandma-72-shoots-at-intruder-misses-in-calif/.

19. "Heroic College Student Uses Gun to Save Lives of Other Students," John Lott's Website, May 5, 2009, http://johnrlott.blogspot.com/2009/05/heroic-college-student-uses-gun-to-save.html. Originally reported in "College Student Shoots, Kills Home Invader," WSB-TV, Atlanta.

20. Dick Perrefort, "Prosecutor: Father-Son Shooting 'Justified,'" Newstimes, March 14, 2014, http://www.newstimes.com/news/article/Prosecutor-Father-son-shooting-justified-5317947.php.

21. Jack Healy, "Unarmed and Gunned Down by Homeowner in His 'Castle,'" New York Times, October 23, 2012, http://www.nytimes.com/2012/10/24/us/castle-law-at-issue-after-fatal-montana-shooting.html?_r=0.

22. Thomas Hayes, "Gunman Kills 22 and Himself in Texas Cafeteria," New York Times, October 17, 1991.

23. Kleck and Gertz, "Armed Resistance to Crime."

24. The estimate of 1.5 million was reported in Philip Cook and Jens Ludwig's Guns in America using the DGU criteria used by Kleck. The estimate of 108,000 was from the NCVS of 1993.

25. Lott, More Guns, Less Crime, and Lott and Mustard, "Crime, Deterrence, and Right-to-Carry Concealed Handguns."

26. Quoted in Winkler, Gunfight, 76.

27. Webster and Ludwig, "Myths about Defensive Gun Use and Permissive Gun Carry Laws."

28. Lott, More Guns, Less Crime, 59.

29. Ibid., 80.

30. Ayres and Donohue, "Shooting Down the 'More Guns Less Crime' Hypothesis."

31. Ibid., 1197.

32. Ibid., 1202.

33. Ibid., 1285.

34. Ibid., 1286.

35. Abhay Aneja, John Donohue, and Alexandria Zhang, "The Impact of Right to Carry Laws and the NRC Report: The Latest Lesson for the Empirical Evaluation of Law and Policy," Stanford Law and Economics Olin Working Paper No. 461, September 4, 2014.

36. Clifton Parker, "Right-to-Carry Gun Laws Linked to Increase in Violent Crimes, Stanford Research Shows," Stanford News interview of John Donohue, November 14, 2014.

37. Cramer and Burnett, Tough Targets.

38. "Victims Let Down by Poor Crime-Reporting," Her Majesty's Inspectorate of

Constabulary, November 18, 2014, http://www.justiceinspectorates.gov.uk/hmic/news/news-feed/victims-let-down-by-poor-crime-recording/.

39. Cook and Goss, *The Gun Debate*, 118.

40. http://www.gunviolencearchive.org.

41. Wellford, Pepper, and Petrie, *Firearms and Violence*.

42. Ibid.

Chapter 4

1. Thomas McGraw, "Mr. Hamilton's Growth Strategy," *New York Times*, November 11, 2010. The debt-to-income ratio for the federal government in 1790 is said to have been 46 to 1, compared to about 6 to 1 in 2012. Treasury Secretary Alexander Hamilton is credited with engineering a recovery and reducing the ratio to 8 to 1 by 1800.

2. Zinn, *A People's History of the United States*, 91–92.

3. The Riot Act received support from unexpected quarters. Patriot Sam Adams, believing that the British instigated the rebellions, helped draw up the Riot Act and proposed suspending the right of habeas corpus. He claimed that unlike in a monarchy, rebellion in a republic should be punishable by hanging.

4. The Springfield Armory served as the nation's center for manufacturing military firearms from 1777 through 1968, when it was closed and made a national historic site.

5. Richards, *Shays' Rebellion*.

6. James Madison invited Patrick Henry to attend the Constitutional Convention. Some time later, according to many sources, Henry was asked in a public debate why he decided not to attend and he gave his famous response. See Encyclopedia Virginia, http://www.encyclopediavirginia.org/Henry_Patrick_1736-1799#start_entry.

7. The canonical source for documents and commentary related to the Constitutional Convention is Elliot's *Debates*, or more completely, *The Debates in the Several State Conventions on the Adoption of the Federal Constitution*. Madison's notes can also be found in *Notes of the Debates in the Federal Convention of 1787*. Madison's notes are compiled at the Avalon Project, http://avalon.law.yale.edu/subject_menus/debcont.asp, and Teaching American History, http://www.teachingamericanhistory.org.

8. Adrienne Koch, introduction to Madison, *Notes of the Debates*, xiii.

9. Robert Waln, "Biographies of the Signers to the Declaration of Independence," in *The Portfolio*, vol. 17, July–December 1824, ed. John Hall (Philadelphia: Harrison Hall, 1824), 450.

10. Halbrook, *The Founders' Second Amendment*, 176.

11. John Kaminski, Gaspare Saladino, Richard Leffler, Charles Schoenleber, and Margaret Hogan, eds., *The Documentary History of the Ratification of the Constitution* (Madison: State Historical Society of Wisconsin, 1988), 8:43, quoted in Halbrook, *The Founders' Second Amendment*, 177. The first source has a digital edition (University of Virginia Press) at http://rotunda.upress.virginia.edu/founders/RNCN.html.

12. By September 1787, some of the delegates had left Philadelphia. The three

delegates who did not sign the Constitution were Edmund Randolph and George Mason of Virginia and Elbridge Gerry of Massachusetts.

13.   "Madison Debates, September 17," Avalon Project, http://avalon.law.yale.edu/18th_century/debates_917.asp.

14.   Cornell, *A Well-Regulated Militia*, 43.

15.   U.S. Const. art. I, § 8.

16.   Noah Webster, *An Examination into the Leading Principles of the Federal Constitution* (Philadelphia, PA: Richard and Hall, 1787), quoted in Halbrook, *The Founders' Second Amendment*, 177.

17.   Hamilton is credited with writing fifty-one of the articles, Madison with twenty-six articles, and Jay with five articles. The remaining articles were collaborations.

18.   The author of the *Federal Farmer* is unknown. For many years, it was thought to be Richard Henry Lee, a Virginia delegate to the Continental Congress. More recently, some scholars have attributed the work to Melancton Smith of New York.

19.   *Federal Farmer* XVI, http://www.constitution.org/afp/fedfar00.htm.

20.   *Federal Farmer* XVIII, http://www.constitution.org/afp/fedfar00.htm.

21.   *The Federalist* no. 45, http://thomas.loc.gov/home/histdox/fedpapers.html.

22.   *The Federalist* no. 46, http://thomas.loc.gov/home/histdox/fedpapers.html.

23.   A detailed summary of the ratification process in each state is given in Halbrook, *The Founders' Second Amendment*, 191–215.

24.   Elliot, *Debates*, 3:46.

25.   Elliot, *Debates*, 3:379, quoted in Halbrook, *The Founders' Second Amendment*, 223.

26.   Elliot, *Debates*, 3:386, quoted in Halbrook, *The Founders' Second Amendment*, 225.

27.   Bogus, "The Hidden History of the Second Amendment," 321.

28.   Elliot, *Debates*, vol. 3.

29.   Halbrook, *The Founders' Second Amendment*, 231.

30.   Only twenty senators attended the opening session of the Senate. New York had not yet held elections, and North Carolina and Rhode Island had not yet ratified the Constitution.

31.   Charlene Bangs Bickford, ed., *The Documentary History of the First Federal Congress of the United States of America* (Baltimore, MD: Johns Hopkins University Press, 1986), 4:10, quoted in Halbrook, *The Founders' Second Amendment*, 253.

32.   *Federal Gazette*, June 18, 1789, quoted in Halbrook, *The Founders' Second Amendment*, 257.

33.   Waldman, *The Second Amendment*, 53.

34.   Halbrook, *The Founders' Second Amendment*, 257.

35.   Bickford, *The Documentary History of the First Federal Congress*, 4:28, quoted in Halbrook, *The Founders' Second Amendment*, 262.

36.   James C. Hutson, "The Bill of Rights," *This Constitution*, no. 18, 36 (Spring/Summer 1988), quoted in Halbrook, *The Founders' Second Amendment*, 264.

37.   *Journal of the First Session of the Senate of the United States of America* (Washington, DC: Gales and Seaton, 1988), 71, quoted in Halbrook, *The Founders' Second Amendment*, 275.

38.   U.S. Const. amend. II.

39.   In symbolic gestures on its 150th anniversary, Massachusetts, Connecticut, and Georgia ratified the Bill of Rights in 1939.

Chapter 5

1.   Jordan Teicher, "Why Do You Own a Gun?," *Slate*, January 21, 2016, http://www.slate.com/blogs/behold/2016/01/21/kyle_cassidy_asked_americans_why_they_own_guns_photos.html.

2.   Background on trapshooting can be found at the Amateur Trapshooting Association, http://www.shootata.com, and the Trapshooting Hall of Fame, http://www.traphof.org.

3.   "A Dead Shot with a Rifle," *New York Times*, July 6, 1878.

4.   "The Carver-Bogardus Match," *New York Times*, February 21, 1883.

5.   Trapshooting, skeet shooting, and sporting clays are the three competitive shotgun target shooting sports. In skeet shooting competitors shoot from eight different positions around a semicircle. Targets are launched from both high and low traps, often with random release times. Sporting clays involves a course laid out over natural terrain with ten to fifteen different stations, each equipped with a trap that launches targets. The three sports have distinct histories and are governed by independent organizations.

6.   Ibid., 1.

7.   Ibid., 93.

8.   Mauser, *Walking in Daniel's Shoes*, 126.

9.   All quotes from author interview in Denver, Colorado, on January 7, 2016.

10.   Jonathan Rauch, "Pink Pistols," Salon.com, March 14, 2000, http://www.salon.com/2000/03/14/pistol/.

11.   Ibid.

12.   Gwendolyn S. Patton, "The Pink Pistols Utility Manual," Pink Pistols, updated October 2013, http://pinkpistols.org/PPUtilityManual.pdf.

13.   All quotes from Gwen Patton from author telephone interview, March 18, 2014.

14.   Cane-Fu is a martial art with canes used for self-defense. See http://www.canemasters.com.

15.   Author notes, March 9, 2014.

16.   Kohn, *Shooters*, 39.

Chapter 6

1.   Ferling, *Adams vs. Jefferson*, 141.

2.   All quotes are taken from the complete transcript of the Selfridge trial: Lloyd and Caines, *Trial of Thomas Selfridge*.

3. Ibid., 84.
4. Ibid., 104.
5. Ibid., 85.
6. Ibid., 87.
7. Ibid., 87.
8. Ibid., 57.
9. Ibid., 31.
10. Ibid., 131.
11. Ibid., 8.
12. Ibid., 158.
13. Ibid., 101.
14. Ibid., 101.
15. "Mr. Selfridge," *Port Folio* 3 (1807), 259, quoted in Cornell, *A Well-Regulated Militia*, 115. The case centered on the right to self-defense, which is guaranteed in British common law, rather than the right to bear arms, which is guaranteed in the US Constitution.
16. Penn. Const. art. I, § 21.
17. Del. Const. art. I, § 20.
18. Ga. Const. art. I, § 1, para. 1.
19. Ohio Const. art. I, § 4.
20. Mass. Const. pt. 1, art. XVII.
21. Md. Const. art. XXVIII.
22. Tenn. Const. art. I, § 26.
23. Miss. Const. art. III, § 12.
24. St. George Tucker, ed., *William Blackstone Commentaries* (Clark, NJ: Lawbook Exchange, 1996 [1803]), quoted in Kopel, "The Second Amendment," 1377.
25. Kopel, "The Second Amendment," 1378.
26. Cornell, *A Well-Regulated Militia*, 130.
27. Kopel, "The Second Amendment," 1380.
28. Houston v. Moore, 18 US (1820), quoted in Cornell, *A Well-Regulated Militia*, 133.
29. Story's dissent included the first mention of the Second Amendment in a Supreme Court opinion, although he only asserted in passing that the amendment supported his position.
30. Story, *Commentaries on the Constitution of the United States*, 3:746.
31. Front-loading, single-shot handguns had been in use for several centuries, and the design of a revolving multiple-shot handgun had recently been patented in England. Colt's contribution was designing revolvers with interchangeable parts.
32. Roth, *American Homicide*, 21, 180.
33. Cornell, *A Well-Regulated Militia*, 140.
34. Bliss v. Commonwealth, 12 Ky. (2 Litt.) 90 (1822).

35. Ibid.
36. Tennessee Act of 1837–1838, ch. 137, sec. 2.
37. Aymette v. State, 21 Tenn. (2 Hum.) 154 (1840).
38. Ibid.
39. State v. Buzzard, 4 Ark. (2 Pike) 18 (1842).
40. Kopel, "The Second Amendment," 1423.
41. Cornell, *A Well-Regulated Militia*, 160.
42. Spooner, *The Unconstitutionality of Slavery*.
43. Barron v. Baltimore, 32 US (7 Pet.) 243 (1833). Barron's case claimed a violation of the Fifth Amendment prohibition of government taking of private property without compensation.
44. Ibid.
45. For example, Nunn v. State, 1 Ga. (1 Kel.) 243 (1846) in Georgia and State v. Chandler, 5 La. Ann. 480 (1850) in Louisiana.

Chapter 7

1. The John Browning story is taken almost exclusively from the superb biography: Browning and Gentry, *John M. Browning*. The coauthor is John M. Browning's eldest son.
2. Ibid., 53.
3. Ibid., 43.
4. Ibid., 58–59.
5. After each shot of the early repeating rifles, the next round was loaded from a magazine by a manual action.
6. Philip B. Sharpe, *The Rifle in America* (New York: Funk and Wagnall, 1958), quoted in Browning and Gentry, *John M. Browning*, 103.
7. Browning and Gentry, *John M. Browning*, 108.
8. Harold Williamson, *Winchester: The Gun that Won the West* (Washington, DC: Combat Forces Press, 1952), quoted in Browning and Gentry, *John M. Browning*, 109.
9. Browning and Gentry, *John M. Browning*, 145.
10. These pistols were called automatic pistols and marketed as such. In fact, they were semiautomatic pistols.
11. Browning and Gentry, *John M. Browning*, 219.
12. Philip B. Sharpe, quoted in Browning and Gentry, *John M. Browning*, 218.
13. Gun historian Captain Paul A. Curtis, 1931, quoted in Browning and Gentry, *John M. Browning*, 218.
14. Buchanan, *Gunpowder, Explosives and the State*, 2.
15. Peterson and Elman, *The Great Guns*, 13.
16. Ibid., 27.
17. Ibid., 25.
18. Dillin, *The Kentucky Rifle*, xi.

19.   The origin of this adage is unknown. It appeared after the Civil War, so Samuel Colt likely did not invent it. A variation is "God created men and Sam Colt made them equal."

20.   Cameron Hopkins, "Why the Gun Business Defies Analysis," *American Rifleman*, November 12, 2010.

21.   Josh Horwitz, "The Truth about Gun Sales," *Huffington Post*, January 9, 2012, http://www.huffingtonpost.com/josh-horwitz/the-truth-about-gun-sales_b_1193498.html.

22.   "Fundamentals: Annual Income Statement," Smith & Wesson Holding Corp., http://ir.smith-wesson.com/phoenix.zhtml?c=90977&p=irol-fundIncomeA.

23.   "Ruger Is on a Roll," Business Wire, August 20, 2012, http://www.businesswire.com/news/home/20120820006298/en/Ruger-Roll#.VaFQhEtIeGg.

24.   Josh Beckerman, "Sturm Ruger's Profit Drops but Demand Improves," MarketWatch, May 4, 2015, http://www.marketwatch.com/story/sturm-rugers-profit-drops-but-demand-improves-2015–05–04–184851439.

25.   *Firearms Commerce in the United States: Annual Statistical Update 2016*, Bureau of Alcohol, Tobacco, Firearms, and Explosives, https://www.atf.gov/resource-center/docs/2016-firearms-commerce-united-states/download.

26.   Josh Horwitz, "When It Comes to Data on Firearm Sales, Gun Lobby Still Shooting Blanks," *Huffington Post*, February 6, 2012, http://www.huffingtonpost.com/josh-horwitz/when-it-comes-to-data-on_b_1256769.html.

27.   Cook and Goss, *The Gun Debate*, 79.

28.   "Weapons and Markets," Small Arms Survey, http://www.smallarmssurvey.org/weapons-and-markets.html.

Chapter 8

1.   Albion Tourgée (1838–1905) was a Union soldier and Republican writer, attorney, and judge who lived much of his life in the South. He served as attorney and judge in many Ku Klux Klan trials, represented black plaintiffs in the civil-rights case *Plessy v. Ferguson* before the US Supreme Court, and coined the term "color-blind." He founded the National Citizens' Rights Association, arguably the forerunner of the NAACP.

2.   Swanson, *Manhunt*, 6.

3.   Analysis of an audiotape combined with eyewitness reports have led to a theory that a second gun—perhaps friendly fire—was involved in Kennedy's assassination. The convicted assassin, Sirhan, is serving a life sentence in the Richard J. Donovan Correctional Facility in San Diego County, California, while attorneys seek his release.

4.   Sidney Andrews, "Three Months among the Reconstructionists," *Atlantic*, February 1866, http://www.theatlantic.com/magazine/archive/2012/02/three-months-among-the-reconstructionists/308809/.

5.   W. E. B. DuBois, "The Freedman's Bureau," *Atlantic*, March 1901, https://www.theatlantic.com/past/docs/issues/01mar/dubois.htm.

6.   According to US Senate records, Johnson was suffering from typhoid fever

and drank three shots of whiskey before entering the "overheated Senate chamber." The quote is by Republican Senator Zachariah Chandler in a letter to his wife, Letitia Grace, March 4, 1865. Senate Historical Office, http://www.senate.gov/artandhistory/history/common/generic/VP_Andrew_Johnson.htm.

7.   Trefousse, *Andrew Johnson*, 236.

8.   U.S. Const. amend. XIII, § 1.

9.   Texas Black Codes, 1866, ch. 127, § 1–2.

10.   Ibid.

11.   South Carolina Statutes at Large: An act preliminary to the legislation induced by the emancipation of slaves, 1865, https://archive.org/details/statutesatlargeo13repu.

12.   *Harper's Weekly*, January 1866, quoted in Cornell, *A Well-Regulated Militia*, 169.

13.   Quoted in Foner, *Reconstruction*, 243.

14.   1866 Civil Rights Act, 14 Stat. 27–30, April, 1866.

15.   Ibid.

16.   Foner, *Reconstruction*, 250.

17.   Quoted in ibid., 253.

18.   This line was part of a stirring speech given by Stevens on June 13, 1866, on the floor of the House of Representatives. The speech ended with "I now, sir, ask for the question." The ensuing roll call vote resulted in a 120–32 passage of the amendment.

19.   U.S. Const. amend. XIV, § 1.

20.   Ibid.

21.   Ibid.

22.   Ibid.

23.   Foner, *Reconstruction*, 257.

24.   The Comity Clause of the Constitution (art. IV, § 2) declares that, "The Citizens of each State shall be entitled to all Privileges and Immunities of Citizens in the several States."

25.   John Bingham, "The Constitutional Amendment," *Cincinnati Commercial*, August 1866, quoted in Cornell, *A Well-Regulated Militia*, 174.

26.   Cong. Globe, 39th Cong., 1st Sess. 1182 (1866), quoted in Cornell, *A Well-Regulated Militia*, 172.

27.   Quoted in Epps, *Democracy Reborn*, 244.

28.   Quoted in Epps, *Democracy Reborn*, 111.

29.   H.R. Doc. No. 265, at 740 (1870).

30.   Cited in Cornell, *A Well-Regulated Militia*, 19.

31.   The Enforcement Act of 1871 (17 Stat. 13) was also known as the Civil Rights Act of 1871, the Force Act of 1871, the Ku Klux Klan Act, or the Third Enforcement Act.

32.   California Democratic Senator Eugene Casserly, quoted in Foner, *Reconstruction*, 455.

33.   United States v. Hall, 26 F. Cas. 79, quoted in Lane, *The Day Freedom Died*, 115.

34.   Majority opinion, Slaughterhouse Cases, 83 U.S. 36 (1873), 60. The Supreme Court decision was the consolidation of three separate cases.

35.	Quoted in Lane, *The Day Freedom Died*, 119. Lane gives an excellent summary of the Slaughterhouse Cases.

36.	Slaughterhouse Cases, 83 U.S. 36 (1873), 74.

37.	Ibid., 77.

38.	Lane, *The Day Freedom Died*, 122.

39.	Slaughterhouse Cases, 83 U.S. 36 (1873), 96.

Chapter 9

1.	*The Federalist* no. 28.

2.	Jefferson, *The Works of Thomas Jefferson*, 1:122.

3.	The US Code is built in three steps. Laws and acts of Congress (often called *slip law*) are first listed roughly in the order in which they were passed. At the end of each two-year session, all legislation for that session is bound in a volume of the Statutes at Large (often called *session law*). Finally, new laws are integrated into the US Code not chronologically but according to over fifty titles. The makers of the US Code (the Office of the Law Revision Counsel) reconciles the new laws with existing laws by noting amendments, replacements, and deletions.

4.	26 U.S.C. § 5841.

5.	Hardy, "The Firearms Owners' Protection Act."

6.	Haynes v. United States, 390 U.S. 85 (1968).

7.	The revisions to the 1934 NFA are called Title II and appear in Title 26 (Internal Revenue Service) of the US Code. The provisions of the 1968 GCA are called Title I and appear in Title 18 (Crimes and Criminal Procedures) of the US Code. The Gun Control Act of 1968 also subsumed the relatively less important Federal Firearms Act of 1938.

8.	Pub. L. 90–618, 82 Stat. 1213–1214, 18 U.S.C. § 921.

9.	*The Right to Keep and Bear Arms: Report of the Subcommittee on the Constitution of the Committee on the Judiciary* (Washington, DC: US Government Printing Office, 1982).

10.	132 Cong. Rec. H1665, H1696, and H1751, quoted in Hardy, "The Firearms Owners' Protection Act," 586.

11.	James Brady died on August 24, 2014. His death was ruled a homicide.

12.	At the age of sixty-one, John Hinckley was released from St. Elizabeth's Hospital in Washington, DC, on September 10, 2016.

13.	"1992 Democratic Party Platform," American Presidency Project, http://www.presidency.ucsb.edu/ws/?pid=29610.

14.	The Public Safety and Recreational Firearms Use Protection Act, originally 18 U.S.C. § 922(v)(1), is the subsection of the Violent Crime Control and Law Enforcement Act of 1994 that contains the ban on assault weapons.

15.	"Violence Policy Center Issues Statement on Expiration of the Federal Assault Weapons Ban," September 2004, http://www.vpc.org/press/press-release-archive/violence-policy-center-issues-statement-on-expiration-of-federal-assault-weapons-ban/.

16.   Christopher S. Koper, *Updated Assessment of the Federal Assault Weapons Ban: Impacts on Gun Markets and Gun Violence, 1994–2003*, Report to the National Institute of Justice, US Department of Justice, June 2004.

17.   Robert Farley, "Did the 1994 Assault Weapons Ban Work?," FactCheck.org, February 1, 2013, http://www.factcheck.org/2013/02/did-the-1994-assault-weapons-ban-work/.

18.   18 U.S.C. § 922(q).

19.   United States v. Lopez, 514 U.S. 549 (1995).

20.   15 U.S.C. § 7901. The key text is that the law is designed to "prohibit causes of action against manufacturers, distributors, dealers, and importers of firearms or ammunition products, and their trade associations, for the harm solely caused by the criminal or unlawful misuse of firearm products or ammunition products by others when the product functioned as designed and intended."

21.   Quoting Wayne LaPierre, "President Bush Signs 'Protection of Lawful Commerce in Arms Act,' Landmark NRA Victory Now Law," NRA-ILA, October 26, 2005, https://www.nraila.org/articles/20051026/president-bush-signs-protection-of-br.

22.   18 U.S.C. § 922. In part, the law states that "it shall be unlawful for any licensed importer, licensed manufacturer, or licensed dealer to sell, deliver, or transfer any handgun to any person other than any person licensed under this chapter, unless the transferee is provided with a secure gun storage or safety device . . . for that handgun."

23.   15 U.S.C. § 1601.

24.   18 U.S.C. § 922. In part, the law states that "it shall be unlawful for any person to manufacture, import, sell, ship, deliver, possess, transfer, or receive any firearm (A) that, after removal of grips, stocks, and magazines, is not as detectable [as a test object] by walk-through metal detectors calibrated; or (B) any major component of which, when subjected to inspection by the types of x-ray machines commonly used at airports, does not generate an image that accurately depicts the shape of the component."

25.   Keith Wagstaff, "Despite Plastic Gun Ban, 3-D Printed Firearms Still Have a Future," NBC News, December 9, 2013, http://www.nbcnews.com/technology/despite-congressional-ban-3-d-printed-guns-still-have-future-2D11718212.

Chapter 10

1.   Schuyler Colfax was President Grant's first vice president.

2.   Lane, *The Day Freedom Died*, 25.

3.   The account of the Colfax Massacre is primarily from Lane, *The Day Freedom Died*, and secondarily from Keith, *The Colfax Massacre*. Unless otherwise indicated, all quotes are from Lane.

4.   Lane, *The Day Freedom Died*, 48.

5.   Ibid., 64.

6.   Ibid., 91.

7.   Ibid., 10.

8.   Ibid., 111.

9.   Quoted in ibid., 124.

10. Quoted in ibid., 125.

11. Ibid., 143.

12. Ibid., 183.

13. Ibid., 191.

14. Quoted in ibid., 192.

15. United States v. Cruikshank, 25 F. Cas. 707 (C.C.D. La. 1874).

16. Ibid.

17. Ibid.

18. Ibid.

19. Ibid.

20. Ibid.

21. Ibid.

22. Lane, *The Day Freedom Died*, 210.

23. Quoted in ibid., 211.

24. James K. Hogue, *Uncivil War: Five New Orleans Street Battles and the Rise and Fall of Radical Reconstruction* (Baton Rouge: Louisiana State University Press, 2006), 125, quoted in Lane, *The Day Freedom Died*, 217.

25. Quoted in Lane, *The Day Freedom Died*, 216.

26. *Nation*, January 22, 1874, quoted in Lane, *The Day Freedom Died*, 231.

27. *Baltimore Sun*, April 2, 1875, quoted in Lane, *The Day Freedom Died*, 237.

28. United States v. Cruikshank, 92 U.S. 542 (1876).

29. Ibid.

30. Ibid.

31. Ibid.

Chapter 11

1. "A Byte Out of History: The Beltway Snipers, Parts 1 and 2," FBI, October 22, 2007, https://www.fbi.gov/news/stories/2007/october/snipers_102207.

2. Dean Murphy, David Gonzales, and Jeffrey Gettleman, "Retracing a Trail: The Suspects; The Mentor and the Disciple: How Sniper Suspects Bonded," *New York Times*, November 3, 2002, http://www.nytimes.com/2002/10/29/us/retracing-a-trail-the-weapon-shop-slows-us-inquiry-into-rifle.html.

3. Roper v. Simmons, 543 U.S. 551 (2005).

4. Mike Carter, Steve Miletich, and Justing Mayo, "Errant Gun Dealer, Wary Agents Paved Way for Beltway Sniper Tragedy," *Seattle Times*, April 29, 2003, http://community.seattletimes.nwsource.com/archive/?date=20030429&slug=gundealer29.

5. Arkadi Gerney and Chelsea Parsons, "Lost and Stolen Guns from Gun Dealers," Center for American Progress, June 18, 2013, https://www.americanprogress.org/issues/guns-crime/report/2013/06/18/66693/lost-and-stolen-guns-from-gun-dealers/.

6. Jennifer Sullivan, "Judge Rules against Former Tacoma Gun-Shop Owner in D. C. Sniper Case," *Seattle Times*, September 28, 2009, http://www.seattletimes.com/seattle-news/judge-rules-against-former-tacoma-gun-shop-owner-in-dc-sniper-case/.

7. Jim McElhatton, "Families of Sniper Victims Reach Settlement," *Washington Times*, September 9, 2004, http://www.washingtontimes.com/news/2004/sep/9/20040909-095944-5026r/.

8. Larson, *Lethal Passage*, 121–43.

9. *Following the Gun: Enforcing Federal Laws against Firearms Traffickers*, Bureau of Alcohol, Tobacco, and Firearms (ATF), June 2000, 11.

10. ATF Firearms Transaction Record Part I – Over-the-Counter (Form 4473), https://www.atf.gov/file/61446/download.

11. Jordy Yager and Mike Lillis, "Key Provision of Gun Bill Could Be Stripped after NRA Opposition," The Hill, April 4, 2013, http://thehill.com/homenews/senate/291553-key-provision-of-gun-bill-could-be-stripped.

12. *Following the Gun*, 11.

13. Ibid.

14. *ATF Firearms Tracing Guide: Tracing Firearms to Reduce Violence*, US Department of Justice, Bureau of Alcohol, Tobacco, Firearms, and Explosives, November 2011.

15. "The Low-Tech Way Guns Get Traced," *All Things Considered*, National Public Radio, May 20, 2013.

16. "The Tiahrt Amendment on Firearms Traces: Protecting Gun Owners' Privacy and Law Enforcement Safety," NRA-ILA News and Issues, January 15, 2013, https://www.nraila.org/articles/20130115/the-tiahrt-amendment-on-firearms-traces-protecting-gun-owners-privacy-and-law-enforcement-safety.

17. Fact Sheet—eTrace: Internet-Based Firearms Tracing and Analysis, Bureau of Alcohol, Tobacco, Firearms, and Explosives, March 2016, https://www.atf.gov/resource-center/fact-sheet/fact-sheet-etrace-internet-based-firearms-tracing-and-analysis.

18. David Kopel, personal communication, January 29, 2014.

19. *The Right to Keep and Bear Arms: Report of the Subcommittee on the Constitution of the Committee of the Judiciary*, United States Senate, February 1982.

20. *BATFE Gun Show Enforcement*: Hearing Before the Subcomm. on Crime, Terrorism, and Homeland Security of the House of Representatives Comm. on the Judiciary, February 15 and 28, 2006.

21. Kerrigan, *Historic Documents of 2011*, 597.

22. *Fast and Furious: The Anatomy of a Failed Operation Part I of III*, Comm. on Oversight and Government Reform, July 31, 2012.

23. "Operations Fast and Furious Fast Facts," CNN, April 21, 2015, http://www.cnn.com/2013/08/27/world/americas/operation-fast-and-furious-fast-facts/.

24. *Commerce, Justice, Science, and Related Agencies: FY2014 Appropriations*, Congressional Research Service, November 4, 2013.

25. Winnie Stachelberg, Arkadi Gerney, and Chelsea Parsons, "Blindfolded, and One Hand Tied Behind Its Back," Center for American Progress, January 13, 2013, https://www.americanprogress.org/issues/civil-liberties/report/2013/03/19/56928/blindfolded-and-with-one-hand-tied-behind-the-back/.

26. Michael Luo, Mike McIntyre, and Griff Palmer, "Seeking Gun or Selling One,

Web Is a Land of Few Rules," *New York Times*, April 17, 2013, http://www.nytimes.com/2013/04/17/us/seeking-gun-or-selling-one-web-is-a-land-of-few-rules.html?pagewanted=all.

27.   *Firearms Commerce in the United States: Annual Statistical Update*, US Department of Justice, Bureau of Alcohol, Tobacco, Firearms, and Explosives, 2014.

28.   This is language of the Gun Control Act of 1968, 18 U.S.C. § 922(g)(4).

29.   As of mid-2016, the single busiest day for NICS background checks was November 27, 2015 (over 185,000 checks). The single busiest week was December 17–23, 2012 (over 953,000 checks). NICS data are regularly updated at "National Instant Criminal Background Check System (NICS): Reports and Statistics," https://www.fbi.gov/services/cjis/nics.

30.   National Instant Criminal Background Check System; see, for example, https://archives.fbi.gov/archives/about-us/cjis/nics/reports/2013-operations-report.

31.   "National Instant Criminal Background Check System (NICS) Operations 2014," FBI, https://www.fbi.gov/file-repository/2014-nics-ops-report-050115.pdf/view.

32.   The percentage of non-FFL transfers is one of the most contested numbers in the firearm debate. The often-cited 40 percent originates with Cook and Ludwig, *Guns in America* (based on data from a 1994 survey). In "The '40 Percent' Myth" (*National Review*, January 24, 2013, http://www.nationalreview.com/article/338735/40-percent-myth-john-lott), John Lott gives several reasons why that figure could be as low as 10 percent.

33.   "Why Own a Gun? Protection Is Now the Top Reason," Pew Research Center, March 12, 2013, http://www.people-press.org/2013/03/12/why-own-a-gun-protection-is-now-top-reason/.

34.   "Subject to Debate," Police Executive Research Forum Newsletter, Jan/Feb 2013, http://www.policeforum.org/assets/docs/Subject_to_Debate/Debate2013/debate_2013_janfeb.pdf.

35.   Wintemute, "Support for a Comprehensive Background Check."

36.   Neil Osterweil, "Virginia Tech Missed 'Clear Warnings' of Shooter's Mental Instability," MedPage Today, August 30, 2007, http://www.medpagetoday.com/psychiatry/anxietystress/6546.

37.   Peter Langman, "Jared Loughner: What Kind of Psychosis?," *Psychology Today*, January 16, 2011.

38.   Jack Healy, "Jury Rejects Mental Illness Argument for James Holmes in Aurora Theater Rampage," *New York Times*, August 3, 2015.

39.   "Firearm Use by Offenders," Bureau of Justice Statistics, November 2001, http://bjs.gov/content/pub/pdf/fuo.pdf.

40.   *Following the Gun: Enforcing Federal Laws against Firearms Traffickers*, Bureau of Alcohol, Tobacco, and Firearms (ATF), June 2000, quoted in Arkadi Gerney and Chelsea Parsons, "The Gun Debate 1 Year After Newtown: Assessing Six Key Claims About Gun Background Checks," Center for American Progress, December 13, 2013, https://www.americanprogress.org/issues/guns-crime/report/2013/12/13/80795/the-gun-debate-1-year-after-newtown/.

41.   Ibid.

42.   Brady Handgun Violence Prevention Act, Pub. L. No. 103–159, 107 Stat. 1542.

43.   Wayne LaPierre speech, Conservative Political Action Conference (CPAC), Washington, DC, March 15, 2013, https://www.theguardian.com/world/2013/mar/15/nra-wayne-la-pierre-guns-cpac.

Chapter 12

1.   Much of the account of Lehr und Wehr Verein is taken from Christine Heiss, "German Radicals in Industrial America: The Lehr und Wehr Verein in Gilded Age Chicago," in Hartmut Keil and John Jentz, eds., *German Workers in Industrial Chicago 1850–1920* (DeKalb: Northern Illinois University Press, 1983), quoted in Halbrook, "The Right of Workers to Assemble and to Bear Arms."

2.   Presser v. Illinois, 116 U.S. 252 (1886), 254–55.

3.   *Vorbote*, May 1, 1875, quoted in Heiss, "German Radicals in Industrial America," 211, quoted in Halbrook, "The Rights of Workers," 7–8.

4.   *Vorbote*, June 26, 1875, quoted in Nathan Fine, *Labor and Farmer Parties in the United States: 1828–1928* (New York: Rand School of Social Science, 1928), 106–7, quoted in Halbrook, "The Rights of Workers," 8.

5.   *Chicago Tribune*, March 24, 1879, quoted in Halbrook, "The Rights of Workers," 15.

6.   *Chicago Daily Times Herald*, September 1, 1879, quoted in Halbrook, "The Rights of Workers," 31.

7.   Halbrook, "The Rights of Workers," 31.

8.   Presser v. Illinois, 116 U.S. 252 (1886).

9.   Ibid.

10.   Ibid.

11.   Halbrook, "The Rights of Workers," 60.

12.   United States v. Miller, 307 U.S. 174 (1939).

13.   Frye, "The Peculiar Story of *United States v. Miller*," 63.

14.   In Kopel, Halbrook, and Korwin, *Supreme Court Gun Cases* and Korwin and Kopel, *The Heller Case*, the authors do a valuable service by exhaustively summarizing the ninety-six Supreme Court cases prior to 2008 that either cite the Second Amendment or use a gun-related word. Nearly all of these cases mention the Second Amendment tangentially and do little to advance its interpretation.

15.   For example, Gitlow v. New York, 268 U.S. 652 incorporated the right to free speech.

16.   Wolf v. Colorado, 338 U.S. 25.

17.   The Third and Seventh Amendments and certain provisions of the Fifth and Sixth Amendments are currently considered unincorporated by the Supreme Court.

18.   Uniform Crime Reporting Statistics, U.S. Department of Justice, http://www.ucrdatatool.gov/Search/Crime/State/RunCrimeStatebyState.cfm.

19.   Quoted in Jill Lepore, "Battleground America," *New Yorker*, April 23, 2012, 45.

20.   Craig Whitney, *Living with Guns: A Liberal's Case for the Second Amendment* (New York: Public Affairs, 2012), 6.

21.   Quoted in Lepore, "Battleground America," 45.

22.   Curtis Austin, *Up against the Wall: Violence in the Making and Unmaking of the Black Panther Party* (Fayetteville: University of Arkansas Press, 2008), 54, quoted in Winkler, *Gunfight*, 237.

23.   Winkler, *Gunfight*, 230–47.

24.   Ronald Reagan, *Guns & Ammo*, September 1975.

25.   The shift in the position of the Republican Party is described in Toobin, *The Oath*. Toobin suggests the Republican platform underwent a reversal with respect to gun control between 1972 and 1976. The 1972 platform states, "Safeguard the right of responsible citizens to collect, own and use firearms for legitimate purposes, including hunting, target shooting and self-defense." The 1976 platform states, "We support the right of citizens to keep and bear arms. We oppose federal registration of firearms."

26.   "A Brief History of the NRA," NRA, https://home.nra.org/about-the-nra/.

27.   Bruce Lambert, "Harlon B. Carter, Longtime Head of Rifle Association, Dies at 78," *New York Times*, November 22, 1991, http://www.nytimes.com/1991/11/22/us/harlon-b-carter-longtime-head-of-rifle-association-dies-at-78.html.

28.   Osha Gray Davidson, *Under Fire: The NRA and the Battle for Gun Control* (New York: Henry Holt, 1993), 30, quoted in Larson, *Lethal Passage*, 137.

29.   "Center for the Defense of Free Enterprise," Lobbywatch.org, http://www.lobbywatch.org/profile1.asp?PrId=248.

30.   The name Zebra came from the radio frequency used by a task force assigned to solve the killing spree. In July 1976, four African American men were convicted of the racially motivated murders.

31.   Winkler, *Gunfight*, 95.

32.   Kates, "Handgun Prohibition and the Original Meaning of the Second Amendment," 273.

33.   Ibid.

34.   Levinson, "The Embarrassing Second Amendment."

35.   Glenn Harlan Reynolds, "A Critical Guide to the Second Amendment," *Tennessee Law Review* 62 (1995): 461–511.

36.   Warren Burger interviewed by Charlayne Hunter-Gault, *The MacNeil/Lehrer NewsHour*, Public Broadcasting Service, December 16, 1991.

37.   Lewis v. United States, 385 U.S. 206, 87 S. Ct. 424.

38.   Stevens, *Five Chiefs*, 149.

39.   Printz v. United States, 521 U.S. 898 (1997).

40.   Ibid.

41.   Quilici v. Morton Grove, 695 F.2d 261.

42.   United States v. Emerson, 270 F.3d 203 (5th Cir. 2001).

43.   Silveira v. Lockyer, 312 F.3d 1052 (9th Cir. 2002).

44.   Letter from John Ashcroft to James Baker, May 17, 2001. See also Fox

Butterfield, "Broad View of Gun Rights Is Supported by Ashcroft," *New York Times,* May 24, 2001.

Chapter 13

1.   All quotes of Katherine Whitney are from author interview, November 19, 2012.

2.   "State Gun Laws Enacted in the Year Since Newtown," *New York Times,* December 10, 2013, http://www.nytimes.com/interactive/2013/12/10/us/state-gun-laws-enacted-in-the-year-since-newtown.html?_r=0.

3.   "Licensed Drivers, Vehicles Registrations, and Resident Population," Bureau of Transportation Statistics, US Department of Transportation, http://www.rita.dot.gov/bts/publications/passenger_travel_2016/tables/fig2_7.

4.   Massachusetts has a complicated system with four different licenses for purchasing and possession.

5.   "In Gun Control Debate, Several Options Draw Majority Support," Pew Research Center, January 9–13, 2013, http://www.people-press.org/2013/01/14/in-gun-control-debate-several-options-draw-majority-support/.

6.   28 C.F.R. § 25.9(b)(3). The relevant text says: "The NICS, including the NICS Audit Log, may not be used by any Department, agency, officer, or employee of the United States to establish any system for the registration of firearms, firearm owners, or firearm transactions or dispositions, except with respect to persons prohibited from receiving a firearm."

7.   Kit Daniels, "Proof: Gun Registration Leads to Confiscation," Infowars, November 27, 2013, http://www.infowars.com/proof-gun-registration-leads-to-confiscation/.

8.   Drew Zahn, "Hitler Survivor Tells Americans: 'Buy More Guns,'" WND, January 4, 2014, http://www.wnd.com/2014/01/hitler-survivor-tells-americans-buy-more-guns/.

9.   Halbrook, *Gun Control in the Third Reich.*

10.   Winkler, *Gunfight,* 166.

11.   New Hampshire and Washington were shall-issue states, and Connecticut was a may-issue state.

12.   The adage has been attributed at least to Charlton Heston and Wayne LaPierre. See Angie Drobnic Holan, "Fact-Checking the NRA on 'Right to Carry,'" Politifact, February 16, 2011, http://www.politifact.com/truth-o-meter/article/2011/feb/16/fact-checking-nra-right-carry/.

13.   Alaska, Arizona, Idaho, Kansas, Maine, Vermont, West Virginia, and Wyoming have constitutional carry.

14.   Among the valuable websites that summarize concealed-carry laws and reciprocity agreements are the Law Center to Prevent Gun Violence (http://smartgunlaws.org), Handgunlaw.us (http://www.handgunlaw.us), USA Carry (http://www.usacarry.com), Gun Laws by State (http://www.gunlawsbystate.com), and NRA-ILA (http://www.nraila.org/gun-laws.aspx), along with relevant websites for individual states.

15.   MS Code § 97–37–19 (2013).

16.   Ian Urbina, "Locked, Loaded, and Ready to Caffeinate," *New York Times*, March 7, 2010.

17.   Declan McCullagh, "Gun-Toting Man Draws Scrutiny Outside Obama Town Hall," CBS News, August 11, 2009, http://www.cbsnews.com/news/gun-toting-man-draws-scrutiny-outside-obama-town-hall/.

18.   Stephanie Strom, "Starbucks Seeks to Keep Guns Out of Its Coffee Shops," *New York Times*, September 18, 2013.

19.   Blackstone, *Commentaries on the Laws of England, Book III*.

20.   Ibid.

21.   Ibid.

22.   Coke, *The Institutes of the Laws of England*. The full statement is: "A man's house is his castle—and where shall a man be safe if it be not in his own house?" Also appearing in Coke is: "The house of every one is to him as his castle and fortress, as well for his defence against injury and violence as for his repose." Coke likely quoted earlier sources.

23.   Beard v. United States, 158 U.S. 550 (1895).

24.   Ibid.

25.   Ibid.

26.   Brown v. United States, 256 U.S. 335 (1921).

27.   Ibid.

28.   Ibid.

29.   Ibid.

30.   Named after a line in the Clint Eastwood film *Sudden Impact*.

31.   C.R.S. 18–1–704.5.

32.   Rick Bragg, "Leader as Hard as Nails Is Taking Reins at N.R.A.," *New York Times*, April 14, 1996.

33.   Ibid.

34.   Quoted in member profile of Marion Hammer, NRA on the Record, June 9, 2014, http://www.nraontherecord.org/marion-hammer/.

35.   Ibid.

36.   Bragg, "Leader as Hard as Nails."

37.   Michael Bender, "Marion Hammer, the NRA's Most Powerful Weapon," Bloomberg Business Week, May 17, 2012, http://www.bloomberg.com/news/articles/2012-05-17/marion-hammer-the-nras-most-powerful-weapon.

38.   With little commotion, Utah passed the nation's first stand-your-ground law in 1994.

39.   FL Stat. § 776.013(3) (2013).

40.   Ibid.

41.   Eric Holder, Address to NAACP, Orlando, FL, July 16, 2013, quoted in Perry Stein, "Holder: Time to Reexamine 'Stand Your Ground' Laws," Talking Points Memo, http://talkingpointsmemo.com/livewire/holder-time-to-reexamine-stand-your-ground-laws.

42. Quoted in Ann O'Neill, "NRA's Marion Hammer Stands Her Ground," CNN, April 15, 2012, http://www.cnn.com/2012/04/15/us/marion-hammer-profile/.

43. Quoted in Chris Brown, "Marion Hammer: The NRA Lobbyist behind Florida's Stand Your Ground Legislation," Media Matters, March 22, 2012, http://mediamatters.org/blog/2012/03/22/marion-hammer-the-nra-lobbyist-behind-floridas/184284.

44. Quoted in Paul Rosenberg, "Who Killed Trayvon Martin?," Al Jazeera, March 24, 2012, http://www.aljazeera.com/indepth/opinion/2012/03/2012324185050876362.html.

45. Darla Cameron and William M. Higgins, "Florida's Stand Your Ground Law," *Tampa Bay Times*, http://www.tampabay.com/stand-your-ground-law/fatal-cases.

46. An altercation in a Tampa theater over texting and thrown popcorn led an ex-police officer to fatally shoot another moviegoer. See Michael Daly, "Ex-Cop's Shooting of Texting Moviegoer Ends in Tragedy," The Daily Beast, January 15, 2014, http://www.thedailybeast.com/articles/2014/01/15/ex-cop-s-shooting-of-texting-moviegoer-end-in-tragedy.html.

47. Robert Spitzer, "Stand Your Ground Makes No Sense," *New York Times*, May 4, 2015.

48. Jennifer Carroll, *Task Force on Citizen Safety and Protection*, February 21, 2013, http://www.flgov.com/wp-content/uploads/2013/02/Citizen-Safety-and-Protection-Task-Force-Report-FINAL.pdf.

49. Marissa Alexander v. State of Florida, 1D12–2469.

50. Charles Broward, "Judge Denies Jacksonville Woman New Trial Despite 'Stand Your Ground' Claim," Jacksonville.com, *Florida Times-Union*, May 3, 2012, http://jacksonville.com/news/crime/2012-05-03/story/judge-denies-jacksonville-woman-new-trial-despite-stand-your-ground.

51. Patrick Jonsson, "Why Zimmerman Verdict Might Not Roll Back 'Stand Your Ground' Laws," *Christian Science Monitor*, July 17, 2013.

52. http://firearmsfreedomact.com.

53. The argument is that firearm laws do not fall within the taxing or commerce authority of Congress. Therefore, by the Tenth Amendment, firearm laws are entirely within the purview of the states.

Chapter 14

1. "Piers Morgan vs. David Kopel," YouTube video, 2:32, from an interview on CNN on July 20, 2012, https://www.youtube.com/watch?v=XumMF-_2kIg.

2. www.davekopel.com.

3. *The Volokh Conspiracy*, Washington Post, http://www.washingtonpost.com/news/volokh-conspiracy/wp/author/kopeld/.

4. All quotes of David Kopel are from an author interview at the Independence Institute, Denver, Colorado, January 29, 2014.

5. Eli Stokes, "Judge Upholds Colorado's Gun Laws, Tosses Lawsuit; Plaintiffs Will Appeal," Fox 31 Denver, June 26, 2014, http://kdvr.com/2014/06/26/judge-upholds-colorados-gun-laws-tosses-lawsuit/.

6. The story of the *Heller* case is told in detail in at least four books: Winkler, *Gunfight*; Doherty, *Gun Control on Trial*; (more briefly) Toobin, *The Oath*; and Coyle, *The Roberts Court*.

7. Coyle, *The Roberts Court*, 175, 176.

8. District of Columbia v. Heller, 554 U.S. 570 (2008).

9. Ibid.

10. Ibid.

11. Ibid.

12. Quoted in Doherty, *Gun Control on Trial*, 97.

13. Robert Heinlein, *Beyond This Horizon* (Riverdale, NY: Baen Publishing, 1942). The novel inspired the name of the Polite Society, an organization that provides training and organizes competitions for users of handguns.

14. Quoted in Korwin and Kopel, *The Heller Case*, 292.

15. Ibid., 325.

16. Ibid., 333.

17. Ibid., 331.

18. District of Columbia v. Heller, 554 U.S. 570 (2008).

19. Rakove, "The Second Amendment," 105.

20. Ibid., 107.

21. Ibid., 107.

22. Ibid., 108.

23. Siegel, "Dead or Alive," 196, 197.

24. Toobin, *The Oath*, 114.

25. Richard Posner, "In Defense of Looseness," *New Republic*, August 27, 2008, http://www.newrepublic.com/article/books/defense-looseness.

Chapter 15

1. The story of Herb Mullin is told in many sources, among them Torrey, *The Insanity Offense*.

2. Sarra L. Hedden, et. al., *Behavioral Health Trends in the United States: Results from the 2014 National Survey on Drug Use and Health*, Report of the Substance Abuse and Mental Health Services Administration (SAMHAS) of the US Department of Health and Human Services, September 2015, http://www.samhsa.gov/data/sites/default/files/NSDUH-FRR1-2014/NSDUH-FRR1-2014.htm; cited in "Any Mental Illness among U.S. Adults" and "Serious Mental Illness among U.S. Adults," National Institute of Mental Health, http://www.nimh.nih.gov/health/statistics/index.shtml.

3. "Mental Illness Facts and Numbers," National Alliance on Mental Illness (NAMI), March 2013, https://www2.nami.org/factsheets/mentalillness_factsheet.pdf.

4. "Mental Illness and Violence," Harvard Mental Health Letter, January 1, 2011, http://www.health.harvard.edu/newsletter_article/mental-illness-and-violence, and "Are People with Serious Mental Illness Who Are Not Being Treated Dangerous?," Treatment Advocacy Center Backgrounder, March 2014, http://www.treatmentadvocacycenter.org/storage/documents/violent-behavior-backgrounder.pdf.

5.   "Violent Behavior: One of the Consequences of Failing to Treat Individuals with Severe Mental Illnesses," Treatment Advocacy Center Briefing Paper, April 2011, http://www.treatmentadvocacycenter.org/resources/consequences-of-lack-of-treatment/violence/1381.

6.   *Youth Violence: A Report of the Surgeon General*, Office of the Surgeon General, Department of Health and Human Services, 2001.

7.   Author interview, May 6, 2014.

8.   Mark Follman, "Mass Shootings: Maybe What We Need Is a Better Mental-Health Policy," *Mother Jones*, November 9, 2012.

9.   "Risk of Suicide," National Alliance for Mental Illness, https://www.nami.org/Learn-More/Mental-Health-Conditions/Related-Conditions/Suicide.

10.   Torrey, *The Insanity Offense*, 2–3.

11.   Ibid., 28.

12.   Ibid., 42.

13.   Quoted in ibid., 30.

14.   Quoted in ibid., 45.

15.   M. F. Abramson, "The Criminalization of Mentally Disordered Behavior: Possible Side-Effect of a New Mental Health Law," *Hospital and Community Psychiatry* 23 (1972): 101–5, quoted in Torrey, *The Insanity Offense*, 47.

16.   Lessard v. Schmidt, 349 F. Supp. 1078.

17.   Alan Stone, *Mental Health and Law: A System in Transition* (New York: Jason Aronson, 1976), quoted in Torrey, *The Insanity Offense*, 79.

18.   18 U.S.C. § 922(d).

19.   In 2013, Senator Lindsey Graham (R-SC) introduced the NICS Reporting Improvement Act that, in part, would replace "mental defective" with "mentally incompetent" and "mental institution" by "psychiatric hospital." The bill was not enacted.

20.   27 C.F.R. 478.11.

21.   Ibid. Emphasis added.

22.   554 U.S. 570 (2008), quoted in Edward Liu, et. al., *Submission of Mental Health Records to NICS and the HIPAA Privacy Rule*, Congressional Research Service, April 15, 2013, 5.

23.   Ibid., 7.

24.   Ibid., 8.

25.   A summary of state policies on commitment is given in *State Standards for Assisted Treatment*, Treatment Advocacy Center, http://www.treatmentadvocacycenter.org.

26.   *Submission of Mental Health Records*, 12.

27.   "Fatal Gaps: How Missing Records in the Federal Background Check System Puts Guns in the Hand of Killers," Mayors Against Illegal Guns, November 2011, https://everytownresearch.org/reports/fatal-gaps/.

28.   Virginia Tech Review Panel, "Mass Shootings at Virginia Tech: April 16, 2007," August 2007, quoted in *Submission of Mental Health Records*, 4.

29. Ibid.

30. Kristina Wong, "Honorable Discharge for Navy Yard Shooter Who Had a 'Pattern of Misconduct,'" *Washington Times*, September 17, 2013, http://www.washingtontimes.com/news/2013/sep/17/honorable-discharge-navy-yard-shooter-who-had-patt/.

31. Michael Luo and Mike McIntyre, "When the Right to Bear Arms Includes the Mentally Ill," *New York Times*, December 21, 2013.

32. Ibid.

33. *Guns, Public Health and Mental Illness: An Evidence-Based Approach for State Policy*, Consortium for Risk-Based Firearm Policy, December 2, 2013, 3–4.

34. Haidt, *The Righteous Mind*.

35. Hume, *A Treatise of Human Nature*.

36. Lakoff, *The Political Mind*. Lakoff uses a different set of values than Haidt (such as empathy vs. authority) but arrives at similar conclusions.

37. Douglas and Wildavsky, *Risk and Culture*.

38. Kahan, "Fixing the Communications Failure."

39. Kahan and Braman, "More Statistics, Less Persuasion." Kahan actually works with two scales, hierarchical vs. egalitarian and individualistic vs. communitarian, which are more refined than the single scale described here.

40. The correlations between the scale and opinions on various political and social issues were established using forty years of data in the General Social Survey of the National Opinion Research Center at the University of Chicago.

41. Kahan and Braman, "More Statistics, Less Persuasion," 1306–7.

42. Ibid., 1317.

43. Ibid., 1317–18.

44. E-mail correspondence, June 16, 2015.

45. Kahan, Jenkins-Smith, and Braman, "Cultural Cognition of Scientific Consensus."

Chapter 16

1. Quoted in Lyle Denniston, "Second Amendment Drama: Act II," SCOTUS-blog, February 25, 2010, http://www.scotusblog.com/2010/02/second-amendment-drama-act-ii/.

2. NRA v. City of Chicago (08 C 3697) 617 F. Supp. 2d 752 (2008). NRA v. Village of Oak Park (08 C 3696) 617 F. Supp. 2d 752 (2008).

3. McDonald v. City of Chicago (08 C 3645).

4. Brian Doherty, "Otis McDonald, R.I.P.," Hit and Run blog, Reason.com, April 6, 2014, http://reason.com/blog/2014/04/06/otis-mcdonald-rip-the-man-who-got-the-se.

5. Quilici v. Village of Morton Grove, 695 F. 2d 261 (2008).

6. Quilici v. Village of Morton Grove, 617 F. Supp. 2d 752 (2008).

7. NRA v. City of Chicago, 567 F.3d 856 (7th Cir. 2009).

8. The Fourteenth Amendment says, in part, "No state shall make or enforce any law which shall abridge the privileges or immunities of the citizens of the United

States; nor shall any State deprive any person of life, liberty, or property, without due process of law."

9. McDonald v. Chicago, Petitioners' Brief, 8.

10. Even at the time of the *Slaughterhouse* decision, some justices believed it was a mistake. A dissenter in the case said the decision turned "what was meant for bread into a stone." *Slaughterhouse*, 83 U.S. at 129, J. Swayne dissenting.

11. McDonald v. Chicago, Brief for Respondents at the National Rifle Association of America, Inc. et. al, in Support of Petitioners, 8.

12. McDonald v. Chicago, Brief for Respondents City of Chicago and Village of Oak Park, 4.

13. Ibid., 4.

14. Ibid., 7.

15. McDonald v. Chicago, Brief of Amicus Curiae Jews for the Preservation of Firearms Ownership, in Support of the Petitioners, 1.

16. McDonald v. Chicago, Brief of Amicus Curiae Foundation for Moral Law, in Support of the Petitioners, 1.

17. McDonald v. Chicago, Brief of Amicus Curiae Anti-Defamation League in Support of Respondents, 1.

18. McDonald v. Chicago, Brief of Amicus Curiae International Law Enforcement Educators and Trainers Association (ILEETA), et. al., in Support of Petitioners.

19. McDonald v. Chicago, Brief and Appendix of Professors of Criminal Justice as Amici Curiae, in Support of Respondents.

20. All quotes from the oral arguments are from the transcript of the oral arguments, McDonald v. Chicago, 561 U.S. 3025 (2010).

21. McDonald et. al. v. City of Chicago et. al., 561 U.S. 3025 (2010).

22. Ibid.

23. Ibid.

24. Ibid.

25. Ibid.

26. Editorial, "The Court: Ignoring the Reality of Guns," *New York Times*, June 28, 2010.

27. Lyle Denniston, "Analysis: Gun Rights Go National," SCOTUSblog, June 28, 2010, http://www.scotusblog.com/2010/06/analysis-gun rights-go-national/.

28. Glenn Harlan Reynolds, "What Bolstering Gun Rights Will Mean," *New York Times* forum, June 28, 2010.

29. Donna Schuele, "What Bolstering Gun Rights Will Mean," *New York Times* forum, June 28, 2010.

30. Jack Balkin, "What Bolstering Gun Rights Will Mean," *New York Times* forum, June 28, 2010.

31. Saul Cornell, "What Bolstering Gun Rights Will Mean," *New York Times* forum, June 28, 2010.

32. Wayne LaPierre, "NRA statement Regarding U.S. Supreme Court Decision

McDonald v. City of Chicago," NRA-ILA, June 28, 2010, https://www.nraila.org/articles/20100628/statement-by-wayne-lapierre-executive-v.

33. "NRA Recovers 1.3 Million Dollars in Attorneys' Fees for Work on Supreme Court McDonald Case and Related Cases," CalGunLaws, November 2, 2012, http://www.calgunlaws.com/nra-recovers-1-3-million-dollars-in-attorneys-fees-for-work-on-supreme-court-mcdonald-case-and-related-cases/.

34. "Statement of Brady President Paul Helmke on Second Amendment Ruling by US Supreme Court," PR Newswire, June 28, 2010, http://www.prnewswire.com/news-releases/statement-of-brady-president-paul-helmke-on-second-amendment-ruling-by-us-supreme-court-97309384.html.

35. "Post-*Heller* Litigation Summary," Law Center to Prevent Gun Violence, March 31, 2015, http://smartgunlaws.org/wp-content/uploads/2014/11/Post-Heller-Litigation-Summary-March-2015-Final-Version.pdf. Some of these cases are not direct challenges to gun laws but criminal cases in which gun laws are used as an argument.

36. Stevens, *Six Amendments*, 128.

37. John Paul Stevens, "The Five Extra Words That Can Fix the Second Amendment," *Washington Post*, April 11, 2014, https://www.washingtonpost.com/opinions/the-five-extra-words-that-can-fix-the-second-amendment/2014/04/11/f8a19578-b8fa-11e3-96ae-f2c36d2b1245_story.html?utm_term=.c788447e9fc3.

Chapter 17

1. The poet and playwright Edna St. Vincent Millay (1892–1950) said *something like this*. The line has been paraphrased slightly differently by at least three biographers.

2. White House Press Conference, December 14, 2012.

3. Remarks by the president at Sandy Hook Interfaith Prayer Vigil, December 16, 2012, https://www.whitehouse.gov/the-press-office/2012/12/16/remarks-president-sandy-hook-interfaith-prayer-vigil.

4. *Jesse Lee Peterson Radio Show*, December 20, 2012.

5. NRA press conference, December 21, 2012.

6. David Kopel, "The N. R. A. Is Still Vital, Because the 2nd Amendment Is," *New York Times*, January 3, 2013.

7. Philip Rucker and Peter Wallsten, "Biden's Gun Task Force Met with All Sides, But Kept Its Eye on the Target," *Washington Post*, January 19, 2013.

8. "Full Transcript of Biden and Obama's Remarks on Gun Laws," *New York Times*, January 16, 2013.

9. Peter Baker and Michael D. Shear, "Obama to 'Put Everything I've Got' into Gun Control," *New York Times*, January 16, 2013, http://www.nytimes.com/2013/01/17/us/politics/obama-to-ask-congress-to-toughen-gun-laws.html?src=ISMR_AP_LO_MST_FB.

10. Amy Davidson, "Feinstein and Cruz Fight About Guns," *New Yorker*, March 14, 2013, http://www.newyorker.com/news/amy-davidson/feinstein-and-cruz-fight-about-guns.

11.   "In Gun Control Debate, Several Options Draw Majority Support," Pew Research Center, January 14, 2013.

12.   Frank Luntz, "Gun Owners Support Some Controls," *Washington Times*, August 9, 2012. Luntz did the polling in this study for Mayors Against Illegal Guns. However, he came from an "NRA family" and once polled for the NRA. The sample consisted of 945 gun owners, half of whom were NRA members.

13.   Robert Draper, "Inside the Power of the N.R.A," *New York Times Magazine*, December 15, 2013.

14.   Gabrielle Giffords, "A Senate in the Gun Lobby's Grip," *New York Times*, April 17, 2013.

15.   Jennifer Steinhauer, "Gun Control Effort Had No Real Chance, Despite Pleas," *New York Times*, April 17, 2013.

16.   Ibid.

17.   Lee Drutman, "NRA's Allegiances Reach Deep into Congress," Sunlight Foundation, December 18, 2012, http://sunlightfoundation.com/blog/2012/12/18/nra-and-congress/.

18.   Suevon Lee, "By the Numbers: Comparing Spending by Gun Rights and Gun Control Interest Groups," ProPublica, December 31, 2012, http://www.propublica.org/article/by-the-numbers-comparing-spending-by-gun rights-and-gun control-interest-gr.

19.   Lee Drutman, "Explaining the Power of the National Rifle Association in One Graph," Sunlight Foundation, December 17, 2012, https://sunlightfoundation.com/blog/2012/12/17/gun-spending/.

20.   Karen Yourish, Wilson Andrews, Larry Buchanan, and Alan McLean, "State Gun Laws Enacted in the Year Since Newtown," *New York Times*, December 10, 2013.

21.   Sarah Childress, "How the Gun rights Lobby Won after Newtown," *PBS Frontline*, December 10, 2013, http://www.pbs.org/wgbh/pages/frontline/social-issues/newtown-divided/how-the-gun rights-lobby-won-after-newtown/.

22.   Center for Responsive Politics, https://www.opensecrets.org/industries/lobbying.php?ind=Q13++.

23.   Center for Responsive Politics, https://www.opensecrets.org/industries/lobbying.php?ind=Q12++.

24.   Mark Follman, "At Least 194 Children Have Been Shot to Death since Newtown," *Mother Jones*, December 10, 2013.

25.   Brandy Zadrozny, "The School Shootings You Didn't Hear About—One Every Two Weeks since Newtown," Daily Beast, December 12, 2013, http://www.thedailybeast.com/articles/2013/12/12/the-school-shootings-you-didn-t-hear-about-one-every-two-weeks-since-newtown.html.

26.   Paul Overberg, Meghan Hoyer, Mark Hannan, Jodi Upton, Barbie Hansen, and Erin Durkin, "Explore the Data on U.S. Mass Killings Since 2006," *USA Today*, http://www.usatoday.com/story/news/nation/2013/09/16/mass-killings-data-map/2820423/.

27.   http://www.sandyhookpromise.org.

28.   http://momsdemandaction.org.

29.   http://americansforresponsiblesolutions.org.

30.   Katie Glueck, "NRA: 100,000 New Members after Sandy Hook Shooting," Politico, January 10, 2013, http://www.politico.com/story/2013/01/nra-100k-new-members-after-sandy-hook-86001.html.

31.   All revenue statements from IRS 990 forms. For 2011 and 2012, see http://990s.foundationcenter.org/990_pdf_archive/542/542015951/542015951_201212_990O.pdf?_ga=1.33910564.46480960.1474744707; for 2013 and 2014, see http://990s.foundationcenter.org/990_pdf_archive/542/542015951/542015951_201412_990O.pdf?_ga=1.62786729.46480960.1474744707.

32.   "NICS Firearm Checks: Top 10 Highest Days/Weeks," National Instant Criminal Background Check System, https://www.fbi.gov/file-repository/nics_firearm_checks_top_10_highest_days_weeks.pdf/view.

33.   Aaron Smith, "Record Sales for Smith & Wesson," CNN Money, September 6, 2013, http://money.cnn.com/2013/06/26/news/companies/smith-wesson-guns/.

34.   Matthew Rocco, "New Firearms Lift Sturm Ruger 3Q Sales to 45% Gain," Fox Business, November 6, 2013, http://www.foxbusiness.com/industries/2013/11/06/new-firearms-lift-sturm-ruger-3q-sales-to-45-gain/.

35.   McDonald et al. v. City of Chicago et al., 561 U.S. 3025 (2010).

36.   Heller v. District of Columbia, 670 F. 3d 1244 (2011).

37.   David Kopel, "Licensed Handgun Carry Law Now Legal in District of Columbia: Palmer v. DC," Washington Post, July 28, 2014.

38.   New York Secure Ammunition and Firearms Enforcement (SAFE) Act 2013.

39.   New York State Rifle and Pistol Association v. Cuomo, 990 F. Supp. 2d 3498 (W.D.N.Y. 2013).

40.   Shew, et al. v. Malloy, et al., No. 3:2013cv0079.

41.   Moore v. Madigan, 702 F. 3d 933, 942; Ezell v. Chicago, 651 F. 3d 684.

42.   Herbert Buschbaum, "Amid Wave of Pro-Gun Legislation, Georgia Proposes Sweeping Law," New York Times, March 24, 2014.

43.   Lyle Denniston, "Opinion Analysis: No Stand-In Gun Buyers Allowed," SCOTUSblog, June 16, 2014, http://www.scotusblog.com/2014/06/opinion-analysis-no-stand-in-gun-buyers-allowed/.

44.   Friedman et. al. v. City of Highland Park, Illinois, On petition for writ of certiorari; denied December 7, 2015.

45.   Adam Liptak, "Supreme Court Won't Hear Challenge to Assault Weapon Ban in Chicago Suburb," New York Times, December 7, 2015.

Chapter 18

1.   Michael Planty and Jennifer Truman, "Firearm Violence, 1993–2011," May 2013, Bureau of Justice Statistics, http://www.bjs.gov/content/pub/pdf/fv9311.pdf.

2.   James Baker and John Dingell, "Bipartisan Hunting Buddies," New York Times, January 29, 2013.

3.   Adam Winkler, "We Can Ratchet Down the Passions," *New York Times*, January 6, 2013.

4.   Robert Walker, "Passion Shouldn't Preclude Common Sense," *New York Times*, January 6, 2013.

5.   David Kopel, "A Divide in the Gun Debate Widened by Misunderstanding," *New York Times*, January 6, 2013.

6.   "National Vital Statistics Report: Deaths: Preliminary Data, Centers for Disease Control and Prevention," Centers for Disease Control and Prevention, October 2012, http://www.cdc.gov/nchs/data/nvsr/nvsr61/nvsr61_06.pdf.

7.   Ibid.

8.   "Table 12—Murder Circumstances, 2007–2011," *Crime in the United States 2011*, FBI, https://www.fbi.gov/about-us/cjis/ucr/crime-in-the-u.s/2011/crime-in-the-u.s.-2011/offenses-known-to-law-enforcement/expanded/expanded-homicide-data. The data given in the text are percentages, which have not changed significantly since 2011.

9.   Ibid.

10.   Ibid.

11.   OJJDP Strategic Planning Tool, https://www.nationalgangcenter.gov/SPT/ and "Strategy: Gang Prevention through Community Intervention with High-Risk Youth," National Crime Prevention Council, http://www.ncpc.org/topics/violent-crime-and-personal-safety/strategies/strategy-gang-prevention-through-community-intervention-with-high-risk-youth.

12.   Cook and Goss, *The Gun Debate*, 60.

13.   Chris Stone, author phone interview, January 13, 2014.

14.   Robert Spitzer, e-mail to author, December 18, 2013.

15.   Stephen Halbrook, e-mail to author, December 23, 2013.

16.   Quoted in Erik Kain, "The Truth about Video Games and Gun Violence," *Mother Jones*, June 11, 2013.

17.   Tony Fabian, author interview, January 15, 2014.

18.   American Psychological Association, "Technical Report on the Review of the Violent Video Game Literature," August 13, 2015, http://www.apa.org/news/press/releases/2015/08/technical-violent-games.pdf.

19.   "Scholars' Open Statement to the APA Task Force on Violent Media," September 26, 2013, signed by 230 scholars, https://www.scribd.com/doc/223284732/Scholar-s-Open-Letter-to-the-APA-Task-Force-On-Violent-Media-Opposing-APA-Policy-Statements-on-Violent-Media.

20.   Brad Bushman, e-mail to author, January 20, 2014, based on Anderson, et al., "Violent Video Game Effects on Aggression, Empathy, and Prosocial Behavior in Eastern and Western Countries."

21.   Craig Ferguson, e-mail to author, January 21, 2014, quoted in Jason Schreier, "From Halo to Hot Sauce: What 25 Years of Violent Video Game Research Looks Like," Kotaku, January 17, 2013, http://kotaku.com/5976733/do-video-games-make-you-violent-an-in+depth-look-at-everything-we-know-today.

22.   Craig Ferguson, e-mail to author, January 21, 2014.

23.   Max Fisher, "Ten-Country Comparison Suggests There's Little or No Link between Video Games and Gun Murders," *Washington Post*, December 17, 2012.

24.   Robert Levy, "A Libertarian Case for Expanding Background Checks," *New York Times*, April 26, 2013.

25.   John Lott, "The Problem with Brady Background Checks: Virtually All of Those Denied Purchasing a Gun Are False Positive," John Lott's Website, June 13, 2011, http://johnrlott.blogspot.com/2011/06/problem-with-brady-background-checks.html.

26.   Chris Stone, author phone interview, January 13, 2014.

27.   Chris Cox, "Statement from Chris Cox, NRA-ILA Executive Director, Regarding Inaccurate NBC Story Alleging that NRA Won't Oppose Background Check Bill," NRA-ILA, March 12, 2013, https://www.nraila.org/articles/20130312/statement-from-chris-w-cox-nra-ila-executive-director-regarding-inaccurate-nbc-story-alleging-that-nra-wont-oppose-background-check-bill.

28.   Elizabeth Harris and Eric Lichtblau, "Connecticut to Ban Sales to Those on Federal Terrorism List," *New York Times*, December 10, 2015.

29.   David Kopel, "Guns, Mental Illness, and Newtown," *Wall Street Journal*, December 18, 2012.

30.   Wayne LaPierre, NRA press conference, December 21, 2012, "Text of the N.R.A. Speech," *New York Times*, http://www.nytimes.com/interactive/2012/12/21/us/nra-news-conference-transcript.html.

31.   NAMI Public Policy Platform, Section 10: Criminal Justice and Forensic Issues, National Alliance on Mental Illness, http://www.nami.org/About-NAMI/Policy-Platform/10-Criminal-Justice-and-Forensic-Issues.

32.   Ibid.

33.   According to the Office of Management and Budget, the largest recipients of federal research and development money in the fiscal year 2013 appropriation are the Department of Defense (50 percent), the Department of Health and Human Services (which includes NIH) (22 percent), followed by the Department of Energy, NASA, National Science Foundation, and the Department of Commerce (which includes National Institute of Standards and Technology).

34.   Privately funded research, at an undetermined level, is done at a few universities and think tanks. A new research institute supported by private funds is the Avielle Foundation (http://www.aviellefoundation.org). Founded by the scientist-parents of a Sandy Hook victim, Avielle Rose Richmond, the organization investigates the neurological and medical origins of violence.

35.   Omnibus Consolidated Appropriations Bill, HR 3610, Pub L No. 104-208, http://www.gpo.gov/fdsys/pkg/PLAW-104publ208/pdf/PLAW-104publ208.pdf.

36.   Kellerman, "Silencing the Science on Gun Research."

37.   "CDC Funding and Grants Guidelines, Additional Requirement—13: Prohibition on Use of CDC Funds for Certain Gun Control Activities," http://www.cdc.gov/grants/additionalrequirements/ar-13.html.

38.   Michael Luo, "NRA Stymies Firearms Research, Scientists Say," *New York Times*, January 25, 2011.

39.   Ibid.

40.   Jay Dickey and Mark Rosenberg, "We Won't Know the Cure for Gun Violence until We Look for It," *Washington Post*, July 27, 2012.

41.   NIH News Release, "NIH Calls for Research Projects Examining Violence," September 27, 2013, http://www.nih.gov/news/health/sep2013/nih-27.htm.

42.   Alan Leshner, Bruce Altevogt, Arlene Lee, Margaret McCoy, and Patrick Kelley, eds., *Priorities for Research to Reduce the Threat of Firearm-Related Violence*, Institute of Medicine and National Research Council (Washington, DC: National Academies Press, 2013).

43.   Ronald Frandsen, "Enforcement of the Brady Act, 2010: Federal and State Investigations and Prosecutions of Firearms Applicant Denied by a NICS Check in 2010," Department of Justice Report, August 2012.

44.   18 U.S.C. 922(a)(1).

45.   "PERF Members Express Support for Key Elements of Obama Gun Violence Plan," *Subject to Debate: A Newsletter of the Police Executive Research Forum*, January/February 2013, http://www.policeforum.org/assets/docs/Subject_to_Debate/Debate2013/debate_2013_janfeb.pdf.

46.   H. R. 452 *Gun Trafficking Prevention Act of 2013* was introduced in February 2013 and referred to committee, where it died.

47.   "Why Own a Gun? Protection Is Now the Top Reason," Pew Research Center, February 2013, http://www.pewresearch.org/daily-number/why-own-a-gun-protection-is-now-top-reason/.

48.   Gerzon, *The Reunited States of America*.

49.   Arthur Brooks, "Bipartisanship Isn't for Wimps, After All," *New York Times*, April 10, 2016.

Bibliography

Adams, John. *Diary of John Adams, March 5, 1773*. Edited by L. H. Butterfield. Cambridge, MA: Belknap Press of Harvard University Press, 1962.

Ammerman, David. *In the Common Cause: American Response to the Coercive Acts of 1774*. New York: W. W. Norton, 1974.

Anderson, Craig, Nobuko Ihori, Brad Bushman, Hannah Rothstein, Akiko Shibuya, Edward Swing, Akira Sakamoto, and Muniba Saleem. "Violent Video Game Effects on Aggression, Empathy, and Prosocial Behavior in Eastern and Western Countries: A Meta-Analytic Review." *Psychological Bulletin* 136, no. 2 (2010): 151–73.

Ayres, Ian, and John Donohue. "Shooting Down the 'More Guns Less Crime' Hypothesis." *Stanford Law Review* 55 (2003): 1193–1312.

Blackstone, William. *Commentaries on the Laws of England, Book III*. Oxford: Clarendon Press, 1765–1769.

Bogus, Carl. "The Hidden History of the Second Amendment." *U.C. Davis Law Review* 31, no. 2 (1998): 309–408.

Browning, John, and Curt Gentry. *John M. Browning: American Gunmaker*. Morgan, UT: Browning Press, 1993.

Buchanan, Brenda, ed. *Gunpowder, Explosives and the State: A Technological History*. Aldershot, England: Ashgate Publishing, 2006.

Coke, Edward. *The Institutes of the Laws of England*. London: Societie of Stationers, 1628.

Cook, Philip, and Jens Ludwig. *Guns in America: Results of a Comprehensive National Survey on Firearms Ownership and Use*. Washington, DC: National Institute of Justice, 1997.

Cook, Philip J., and Kristin A. Goss, *The Gun Debate: What Everyone Needs to Know*. Oxford: Oxford University Press, 2014.

Cornell, Saul. *A Well-Regulated Militia: The Founding Fathers and the Origins of Gun Control in America*. Oxford: Oxford University Press, 2006.

Cramer, Clayton, and David Burnett. *Tough Targets: When Criminals Face Armed Resistance from Criminals*. Washington, DC: Cato Institute, 2012.

Dillin, John G. W. *The Kentucky Rifle*. York, PA: George Shumway, 1967.

Dizard, Jan, Robert Muth, and Stephen Andrews, eds. *Guns in America: A Historical Reader*. New York: New York University Press, 1999.

Doherty, Brian. *Gun Control on Trial: Inside the Supreme Court Battle over the Second Amendment*. Washington, DC: Cato Institute, 2008.

Douglas, Mary, and Aaron Wildavsky. *Risk and Culture*. Berkeley: University of California Press, 1983.

Elliot, Jonathan, ed. *The Debates in the Several State Conventions on the Adoption of the Federal Constitution*. 5 vols. Washington, DC: Published under the Sanction of Congress, 1836.

Epps, Garrett. *Democracy Reborn: The Fourteenth Amendment and the Fight for Equal Rights in Post-Civil War America*. New York: Henry Holt, 2006.

Ferling, John. *Adams vs. Jefferson: The Tumultuous Election of 1800*. Oxford: Oxford University Press, 2004.

Foner, Eric. *Reconstruction*. New York: Harper Collins, 1988.

Frye, Brian. "The Peculiar Story of *United States v. Miller.*" *NYU Journal of Law and Liberty* 3 (2008): 48–82.

Fuller, E. Torrey. *The Insanity Offense: How America's Failure to Treat the Seriously Mentally Ill Endangers Its Citizens*. New York: W. W. Norton, 2012.

Gerzon, Mark. *The Reunited States of America: How We Can Bridge the Partisan Divide*. Oakland, CA: Berrett-Koehler, 2016.

Haidt, Jonathan. *The Righteous Mind: Why Good People Are Divided by Politics and Religion*. New York: Pantheon Books, 2012.

Halbrook, Stephen P. *The Founders' Second Amendment: Origins of the Right to Bear Arms*. Chicago: Ivan R. Dee, 2008.

———. *Gun Control in the Third Reich: Disarming the Jews and "Enemies of the State."* Oakland, CA: Independent Institute, 2014.

———. "The Right of Workers to Assemble and to Bear Arms: *Presser v. Illinois*, One of the Last Holdouts against the Application of the Bill of Rights to the States." *University of Detroit Mercy Law Review* 76 (Summer 1999): 943–89.

Hardy, David T. "The Firearms Owners' Protection Act: A Historical and Legal Perspective." *Cumberland Law Review* 17 (1986).

Hemenway, David. "Survey Research and Self Defense Gun Use: An Explanation of Extreme Overestimates." *Journal of Criminal Law and Criminology* 87, no. 1430 (1997): 1430–45.

Hogue, James K. *Uncivil War: Five New Orleans Street Battles and the Rise and Fall of Radical Reconstruction*. Baton Rouge: Louisiana State University Press, 2006.

Hume, David. *A Treatise of Human Nature, Book 2: Of the Passions*. London: 1738.

Jefferson, Thomas. *The Works of Thomas Jefferson*. Edited by Paul Leicester Ford. New York: G. P. Putnam's Sons, 1904–1905.

Kahan, Dan. "Fixing the Communications Failure." *Nature* 463 (January 21, 2010): 296–97.

Kahan, Dan, and Donald Braman. "More Statistics, Less Persuasion: A Cultural Theory of Gun-Risk Perceptions." *University of Pennsylvania Law Review* 151, no. 4 (April 2003): 1291–1327.

Kahan, Dan, Hank Jenkins-Smith, and Donald Braman. "Cultural Cognition of Scientific Consensus." *Journal of Risk Research* 14, no. 2 (2011): 147–74.

Kates, Don, Jr. "Handgun Prohibition and the Original Meaning of the Second Amendment." *Michigan Law Review* 82 (1982): 204–73.

Keith, Leeanna. *The Colfax Massacre.* Oxford: Oxford University Press, 2008.

Kellerman, Arthur. "Silencing the Science on Gun Research." *Journal of the American Medical Association* 309, no. 6 (2013): 549–50.

Kellerman, Arthur L., and Donald T. Reay. "Protection or Peril? An Analysis of Firearm-Related Deaths in the Home." *New England Journal of Medicine* 314, no. 24 (1986): 1557–60.

Kerrigan, Heather, ed. *Historic Documents of 2011.* Los Angeles: SAGE Publications, 2013.

Kleck, Gary, and Marc Gertz. "Armed Resistance to Crime: The Prevalence and Nature of Self-Defense with a Gun." *Journal of Criminal Law and Criminology* 86, no. 1 (1995): 150–87.

Kohn, Abigail. *Shooters: Myths and Realities of America's Gun Culture.* Oxford: Oxford University Press, 2008.

Kopel, David. "The Second Amendment in the Nineteenth Century." *Brigham Young University Law Review* (1998): 1362–1544.

Kopel, David, Stephen Halbrook, and Alan Korwin. *Supreme Court Gun Cases.* Scottsdale, AZ: Bloomfield Press, 2003.

Korwin, Alan, and David Kopel. *The Heller Case: Gun Rights Affirmed.* Scottsdale, AZ: Bloomfield Press, 2008.

Lakoff, George. *The Political Mind.* New York: Penguin Books, 2009.

Lane, Charles. *The Day Freedom Died.* New York: Henry Holt, 2008.

Larson, Erik. *Lethal Passage: The Story of a Gun.* New York: Vintage Books, 1995.

Levinson, Sanford. "The Embarrassing Second Amendment." *Yale Law Journal* 99 (1989): 637–59.

Lloyd, T., and George Caines. *Trial of Thomas Selfridge, Attorney at Law, Before the Hon. Isaac Parker, Esq, for Killing Charles Austin, on the Public Exchange, in Boston, August 4, 1806.* Boston: Russell and Cutler, Belcher and Armstrong, and Oliver and Monroe, 1806.

Lott, John, and David Mustard. "Crime, Deterrence, and Right-to-Carry Concealed Handguns." *Journal of Legal Studies* 26 (1997): 1–68.

Lott, John R., Jr. *More Guns, Less Crime: Understanding Crime and Gun Control Laws.* Chicago: University of Chicago Press, 1998.

Madison, James. *Notes of the Debates in the Federal Convention of 1787, Reported by James Madison.* New York: W. W. Norton, 1966.

Mauser, Tom. *Walking in Daniel's Shoes.* Ocean Star Publishing, 2012.

Middlekauff, Robert. *The Glorious Cause: The American Revolution 1763–1789.* Oxford: Oxford University Press, 2005.

Peterson, Harold, and Robert Elman. *The Great Guns*. New York: Grosset and Dunlap, 1971.

Quincy, Josiah, Jr. *Observations on the Act of Parliament Commonly Called the Boston Port-Bill; With Thoughts on Civil Society and Standing Armies*. Boston: Boston N.E., 1774.

Rakove, Jack. "The Second Amendment: The Highest Stage of Originalism." *Chicago-Kent Law Review* 76, no. 1 (December 2000): 103–66.

Reynolds, Glenn Harlan. "A Critical Guide to the Second Amendment." *Tennessee Law Review* 62 (1995): 461–511.

Richards, Leonard. *Shays' Rebellion: The American Revolution's Final Battle*. Philadelphia: University of Pennsylvania Press, 2002.

Roth, Randolph. *American Homicide*. Cambridge, MA: Harvard University Press, 2009.

Siegal, Reva. "Dead or Alive: Originalism as Popular Constitutionalism in Heller." *Harvard Law Review* 191 (2008): 191–245.

Spooner, Lysander. *The Unconstitutionality of Slavery*. Boston: Bela Marsh, 1860.

Stevens, John Paul. *Five Chiefs: A Supreme Court Memoir*. New York: Little Brown, 2011.

———. *Six Amendments: How and Why We Should Change the Constitution*. New York: Little Brown, 2014.

Swanson, James. *Manhunt: The 12-Day Chase for Lincoln's Killer*. New York: Harper Collins, 2006.

Toobin, Jeffrey. *The Oath*. New York: Doubleday, 2012.

Trefousse, Hans. *Andrew Johnson: A Biography*. New York: W. W. Norton, 1989.

Waldman, Michael. *The Second Amendment: A Biography*. New York: Simon and Schuster, 2014.

Webster, Daniel, and Jens Ludwig. "Myths about Defensive Gun Use and Permissive Gun Carry Laws." *Berkeley Media Studies Group* (2000): 1–8.

Wellford, Charles, John Pepper, and Carol Petrie, eds. *Firearms and Violence: A Critical Review*. Washington, DC: National Academies Press, 2005.

Whitney, Craig. *Living with Guns: A Liberal's Case for the Second Amendment*. New York: Public Affairs, 2012.

Winkler, Adam. *Gunfight: The Battle over the Right to Bear Arms in America*. New York: W. W. Norton, 2011.

Wintemute, Garen. "Support for a Comprehensive Background Check and Expanding Denial Criteria for Firearm Transfers: Findings from the Firearms Licensee Survey." *Journal of Urban Health* 91, no. 2 (April 2014): 303–19.

Zinn, Howard. *A People's History of the United States*. New York: Harper Collins, 1995.

Index